AUTOCRACY AND INSURGENCY
IN ORGANIZED LABOR

New Politics Series:

Soviet Communism and the Socialist Vision
edited by Julius Jacobson

Autocracy and Insurgency in Organized Labor
edited by Burton Hall

Series Editor: Julius Jacobson

AUTOCRACY AND INSURGENCY IN ORGANIZED LABOR

Edited by

BURTON HALL

Transaction Books
New Brunswick, New Jersey
Distributed by E.P. Dutton & Company

The essays in this book were first published in *New Politics* magazine

Copyright © 1972
New Politics Publishing Company

Published by Transaction Books, New Brunswick, New Jersey 08903
Library of Congress Catalog Number: 73-164981
ISBN: 0-87855-004-6 (cloth); 0-87855-504-8 (paper)

Printed in the United States of America

To Sol Salzhandler

Contents

Introduction

This is a book about the labor movement viewed from inside the unions. Its authors are union members and other persons active, in one capacity or another, in union affairs. The concern of the essays collected here, however, is not merely with the mechanics of union operation or of union representation, but with unionism itself. The authors examine the problems of unionism; they report on union struggles in which they, themselves, are directly involved and they explore problems that affect the labor movement as a whole. Their purpose is not only to interpret the unions philosophically but to change them into what unions ought to be: workers' organizations run by workers to serve workers' interests.

The essays appeared originally in *New Politics* over the past ten years; with few exceptions, within the past five. To the student of politics and of labor affairs, the collection seeks to offer a full, or nearly full-length view of the unions: it may serve him both as informative eye-opener and as a useful text. But more important, this collection seeks to give the active trade unionist a broader understanding of the struggles in which he finds himself engaged by viewing them in terms of the similar struggles of other workers in other industries and unions.

If there is one theme running through the book as a whole, it is what Sylvia Kopald, writing nearly half a century ago, described with some astonishment as "this amazing separation that exists between union leaders and union rank and file."[1] What she was referring to was not merely the contrast between the material conditions of the leaders and of the rank and file. Primarily, she drew attention to the conflicts between leaders and ranks—and to the way in which such conflicts took on the aspect of actual class struggle, with even rival leaders uniting to fight off, with all the power and violence that entrenched machines can command, any challenge from the rank and file.

The same emphasis is still required. It is interesting but not enough to know that National Maritime Union chief Joseph Curran, for example, draws a salary of more than $100,000, or that he maintains estates in Dutchess County, New York and Boca Raton, Florida, or that he rides around in an NMU-supplied limousine driven by an NMU-salaried chauffeur—while NMU members, workers in a declining and low-paying industry, are barely able to support themselves and their families. Or to know that retired Ladies' Garment Workers' Union president David Dubinsky enjoys his golden years on a $25,000 per-year pension plus a union-supplied limousine while retired garment workers struggle to survive on pensions of $714 or $900 per year (depending upon whether they retired at age 62 or 65).

More to the point is the conflict between "leaders" and "led." The "separation" is revealed when one discovers that when NMU members complain to President Curran that their wages are too low, Curran replies that they earn too much; that when garment workers struggle for a better living they find themselves fighting not only their employers but the union itself, for the ILGWU actively combats on behalf of the employers all pressure to raise wages and pensions to decent levels. And when rank-and-file coal miners, workers in the nation's most dangerous non-military industry, demand protection for their safety and health on the job, they find the whole might and power of the union turned against them.

Or consider the legislative front. In March 1971 when an extension of the Economic Stabilization Act of 1970—a law ostensibly designed to permit regulation of prices, rents and virtually every other economic category but in reality used only to permit a presidential "freeze" on construction workers' wages—was proposed in Congress the AFL-CIO lined up *behind* the proposal: not one congressman linked with Labor voted against it.[2] And whenever legislation to protect the democratic rights of union members is proposed, the political might and fury of the entire Labor establishment is invariably mobilized in opposition.

These, one might say, are peaceful expressions of the "amazing separation." The murder of Jock Yablonski and the multiple skull fractures suffered by NMU dissident James Morrissey as the result of beating just outside the "Joseph Curran Building" may serve as reminders that there are more violent expressions. The interests of union officials in America, almost as a class, appear to be in conflict, sometimes rough and violent conflict, with the class interests of rank-and-file workers.

But why is this "amazing separation" so much more marked in the United States and, to a lesser extent, in Canada, than in other nontotalitarian countries? Is it because corruption is more endemic to American than, say, to European business life? Is a Fred Ferrara or a Martin Rarback simply a product of the bribery customary in American business or are they and others like them corrupted by the institutionalized system of labor relations that prevails in the United States and Canada?

One interpretation that has interested me would regard the legal and contractual pattern of American labor relations, so unlike anything that exists outside North America, as at least a significant part of the explanation. Both before and after the adoption of the Wagner Act, American labor law has placed employers in a position to dominate the nature and drift of union policy—not directly but through the dependency of union officials upon the employers' good will. Before 1935, the employer was free to set up a union of *his* own choosing and require his employees to join it; or he could select a union pleasing to him—one, let us say, that excluded "non-Caucasians" from membership and thus from employment and which abjured strikes—and enter into binding contracts with it. Since 1935, the practice has been more complicated. But it remains true that the leader in autocratic control of his union has more need for the employer's "goodwill" than he does for the support or respect of his union's membership. Once the union attains legal authority as the "exclusive bargaining representative" of the 26,000 workers in 200 New York City hotels, for example—who together comprise a single legal "bargaining unit"—it becomes reasonably clear that neither the union nor its leaders will ever be ousted by a rebellion of these dispersed rank-and-file workers. But they *could* be ousted by an organized expression of employer displeasure. So whose displeasure is most to be feared and most to be avoided?

At any rate, the basic features of the American "system" of labor relations have been looked upon by the system's more eminent defenders as guarantors of just that kind of "harmony" and "stability" that employers desire: i.e., the kind that gives employers the upper hand. Not long ago, Theodore Kheel, one of the better-known American labor arbitrators, visited Great Britain and delivered to the American and foreign press his wisdom on what the British should do. Britain, he said, should adopt the chief features of American labor contract. That way it would attain "productive stability." It should adopt five features in particular. British employers, he said, "should give exclusive recognition to the union with majority representation; should have contracts for fixed terms; should have no-strike clauses in the contracts; provide for binding arbitration of disputes under the contracts; and should mandate legal enforcement of the contracts."[3] If Britain were to adopt these features of American labor relations, he implied, then perhaps it would become "Americanized" in the sense of a much greater degree of labor peace. He did not bother to add that, for the same reasons, Britain might also enjoy as much corruption, racketeering and "sweetheart" dealing between employer and corrupt union leader as America now enjoys. And that British workers, struggling for better living and working conditions, might find their union leaders confronting them as enemies, as allies of their employers—just as American workers so often do.

To what extent does this situation represent the desires of those who control American business and government? Probably only so far as the betrayal of union members by union leaders does not involve the actual exchange of money. So long as the union leader is merely friendlier to the employer than he is to the union rank and file, and is not actually in the employer's pay, their relationship has the approval of official society. And that seems only natural. The policy of protecting the interests of workers set forth in the preamble of the Wagner Act has always been looked upon by those hardheaded realists who may be presumed to be privy to the views of our governing class as being distinctly subordinate to the other policy, also stated in the preamble, of minimizing industrial "strife."

The latter policy, obviously enough, aims at corroding the adversary relationship that is presumed to exist whenever two groups bargain with each other through designated representatives. And to corrode that adversary relationship is to pervert the meaning of bargaining. That things haven't gone quite so far in the bulk of American industry is obvious: there are still more union representatives (though far fewer than there were years ago) who fight, or intend to fight, for the workers they represent than there are those who consciously sell such workers out. But since the workers, as a rule, have had little or nothing to do with selecting their "exclusive bargaining representative" and have little or no chance of replacing it, there is every reason to suppose that the practice of collective bargaining in the United States will drift in precisely the direction suggested above; indeed, as we have been trying to suggest, that drift is already noticeable.

When the friendship between employers and union leaders goes beyond sentiment, however, and develops a pecuniary basis, then it would appear to exceed even the official government policy of avoiding industrial "strife." This, at least, is how the Senate investigating committees have appeared to look at the matter when evidence of widespread corruption in union-employer dealings has been presented to them. Congress's remedy, proposed as the "Kennedy-Ervin" bill and adopted as the "Landrum-Griffin" act, provides, among other things, for fair union elections. It sets forth a list of electoral rights and provides that whenever any of these rights has been violated, the Secretary of Labor shall have the power to bring suit (if he chooses to do so) and to have the election set aside. Such an act might portend a reform of substantial proportions if only the relationship between the Secretary of Labor and the officials of the major unions was such that it permitted effective regulation of the latter by the former.

However, nobody has ever imagined that the relationship between union leaders and the Secretary of Labor was an adversary one. One of the customary functions of Labor department officials and especially of those charged by law with the duty of protecting union members' rights to fair elections, is to make speeches at union conventions proclaiming their unfaltering friendship for the union's leaders. They are rarely if ever called upon to proclaim their interest in rank-and-file union members battling the leaders: if they actually did proclaim such interest, nobody would believe them. In the course of a losing oral argument to the Supreme Court, I once remarked that the rank-and-file union member who appeals to the Secretary against the union leaders feels that he is appealing to the ally of his enemy to protect him against his enemy. Justice Arthur J. Goldberg, who had only recently left the Labor secretaryship, leaned forward and pointedly asked: "Do you think that helps your case, Mr. Hall?" Obviously it did not—but the statement remains true and inevitably so. Yet, the law bars union members from complaining of stolen union elections to any court or agency other than this very friend of the officials he is complaining against. It is doubtful that legal recourse has ever been sought through less promising auspices. Nor have many reforms emerged.

For all these reasons and more, it is tempting to repeat the condemnation that Eugene V. Debs delivered in 1905. "To talk about reforming these rotten graft-infested unions," wrote Debs, "which are dominated absolutely by the labor boss, is as vain and wasteful of time as to spray a cesspool with attar of roses."[4] Debs, however, wrote at a time when it seemed possible to sweep all these "rotten graft-infested unions" aside and build a new labor movement entirely outside the existing union establishment. The Industrial Workers of the World had just been organized and was pledged not only to a revolutionary program but even more important, to a program of industrial and democratic unionism that would unite all the workers in each industry and, through a departmentalized structure, the workers in all industries. "It makes no difference what your color, creed or sex or kind," one of the more popular Wobbly organizing songs went: "If you're a worker then it's pitch right in and join!" (And this at a time when every major AFL union except the United Mine Workers either excluded Negroes absolutely or discriminated against them within its structure.) Debs could easily scorn the corrupt unions when he could hope—and urge workers to share his hope—to see them all replaced by the rank-and-file democracy of the IWW, a democracy so open that it would not permit corruption to exist.

That hope might have come true if the Justice Department in the fall of 1917 had not used the IWW's opposition to war and militarism as an excuse to raid its offices, to throw more than 300 of its leaders in jail and, by force and violence, to reduce it from a mass movement to a minor radical sect. Something approaching that hope actually did happen in the 1930s and early 1940s when millions of unorganized workers rebelled, demanding unionization, and were encouraged in their rebellion by the fact that the new CIO unions that came into existence during those years were genuinely different from and more decent than the old AFL unions.

But the fact is that today there is no similar prospect of a new labor movement growing up outside of or independent of the existing unions. This may be taken as the reason why, in the essays that follow, the authors do not express such grand and overpowering contempt for the "rotten graft-infested unions" as did Debs. Whether we think that there is or isn't any practical possibility of reforming them, we are compelled to remember that the struggle is inside them.

"Only one thing is certain," Sylvia Kopald wrote at the end of her book in 1923, after describing in painful detail how four major rebellions of the union rank and file—of miners, of railroad workers, of printers and of web pressmen—had been crushed by the power of entrenched officialdom. "The fight within the unions is on. . . . Behind the conservative officials is the power of official machines. Behind the radicals is the trend of the times. The outcome remains to be written."

The fight is still on and the outcome still remains to be written. Some reports on the progress of the struggle are contained in the essays collected here.

---

1. Sylvia Kopald, *Rebellion in Labor Unions* (New York: Boni and Liveright, 1924), p.2.

2. In his novel *Fontamara,* Ignazio Silone described how Italian peasants saw the coming of Fascism:
> At the Fucino they had put up the rents of the smallholders and lowered the rents of the big proprietors. That was clear. But the proposal to do this had been made by the representative of the poor peasants and that was not so clear.
> Each one of our misfortunes, examined separately, was not new, for similar misfortunes had often happened in the past. But the way they befell us was new and strange.
> The whole thing was absolutely beyond our understanding.

In mid-August 1971, President Nixon by Executive Order imposed an absolute 90-day freeze on all workers' wages—coupling it with the all-but-empty pretense of a like freeze on prices. Workers' incomes were thus kept down while in fact prices, and business incomes, continued to rise. Nixon's discretionary and almost unrestricted power to impose a freeze "as he may deem appropriate" on prices, rents, wages and salaries was given him by this very same "Economic Stabilization Act." That also was, and is, clear. But the passage of the "Economic Stabilization Act" had been advocated most energetically by George Meany and the AFL-CIO—i.e., by the representatives of the largest body of organized workers—and that is not so clear.

After the 90-day freeze was announced, Meany insisted that when he had called for a freeze (under the slogan of "wage-price control") he had meant something different, a freeze on profits as well. That appears to have been an afterthought on his part, since he had never mentioned "profit control" before and no suggestion of it is contained in the Stabilization Act. But even that token degree of opposition soon faded; Meany, along with the top officials of the Auto Workers, the Machinists and the Teamsters unions, even accepted membership on Nixon's "Phase 2" freeze board. And Meany has, since the freeze was imposed, publicly hinted that, under certain circumstances, he might support Nixon for re-election.

Such misfortunes as these—namely, frozen wages during a period of constantly rising prices—are not new. But the way they have befallen American workers this time seems new andd strange—though not so new or strange perhaps, to someone familiar with the matters reported in the essays that are contained in this book.

3. *New York Times,* June 26, 1968.

4. Quoted in Philip Foner, "The Industrial Workers of the World," Vol. 4 of his *History of the Labor Movement in the United States,* (New York: International Publishers, 1974) p. 62.

I: THE FIGHT WITHIN THE UNIONS

Miners for Democracy

CLARICE R. FELDMAN

Hundreds of miners gathered in the Immaculate Church in Washington, Pennsylvania on January 9, 1970 to bury Jock Yablonski, his wife, Margaret, and his daughter, Charlotte. But for them and the Yablonski family and friends, few others attended: Congressman Ken Hechler, who had supported Jock; Joseph Rauh, Jock's lawyer and friend; and Doctors Don Rasmussen and Hawley Wells, who had alerted miners in West Virginia to the dangers of coal workers pneumoconiosis and who had helped them in their battle to have legislation passed to reduce the incidence of the disease and compensate its many victims. Except for Marion Pelligrini, a subdistrict board member in District 5, Jock's home district in southwestern Pennsylvania, there were no United Mine Workers' of America (UMWA) officials present. Ken and Chip Yablonski, Jock's surviving sons, had issued a statement earlier that no UMWA officials were to attend the funeral. No labor organization bothered to send an official representative.

At the rear of the church before the mass, Joe Rauh consulted with the remaining miners who had joined Jock as co-plaintiffs in the suit filed the previous month which charged the UMWA's top officials with misappropriation and misuse of millions of dollars of UMWA funds. All but one of the men said they wanted to press on with Jock's fight, and even the lone dissenter changed his mind when his grief at this enormous tragedy had passed. Outside in the parking lot there were many cars bearing Jock's orange and yellow campaign stickers, "It's time for a change" and inside Msgr. Charles Owen Rice, Pittsburgh's "labor priest" who had married Jock and Margaret said, "There will always be evil men but there will always be men who dare. Idealism will not vanish. Peace shall come to the coal fields."

But on the icy hill where three caskets were lowered into the frozen ground and we all huddled together for warmth, the predominant feelings of shock, grief, anger and fear left little room for the hope and idealism Father Rice had meant to inspire. The killers had not been apprehended, and everyone who had worked for and believed in Jock was apprehensive. In the eight months prior to Jock's death we had come to know how insurmountable a struggle to reform a union can be when the union can utilize its manpower and tremendous resources to crush it—and when the government stands by in surrealistic indifference to pleas for assistance and protection. How much harder it would be now without Jock's leadership.

Later we returned to the church basement for hot coffee, and while most of the mourners ate a lunch prepared by the ladies of the parish, some 200 coal miners from Kentucky, Illinois, Ohio, Pennsylvania, Virginia and West Virginia met with Joe Rauh in a small classroom in the adjoining school to discuss the future of the reform movement which Jock had led. They talked about safety in numbers and about the importance of continuing what had begun on May 29, 1969, as the first real democratic challenge to the UMWA's leadership in over 30 years. More men asked to be named co-plaintiffs in the suit, and considering the fate of the man whose name had led the list and his family it was no small show of bravado.[1]

Afterward, Charles Washlack, a miner, was heard to say, "This movement is stronger now than when Jock was living. Joe opened the door. We would have been out of our minds to close it now."

So, in a sense, Miners for Democracy (MFD) was born on the day they buried Jock. But it wasn't until April 1, at a memorial service for Jock, that the group was officially organized and its officers elected. In the interim, Mile Trbovich, a miner who had been Jock's campaign manager, acted as its chairman. He filed the official challenge to the UMWA election with the Department of Labor. Later, on February 10, after the opening of the hearings of the Senate Labor Subcommittee, where Chip, and miners Louis A. Antal, Bill Savitsky and Karl Kafton testified about the election violations, kickbacks, blacklisting of dissidents, misuse of union funds and the violence and fear in the coal fields, Trbovich tried to win the support of organized labor. He sent a telegram to George Meany at the AFL-CIO convention in Bal Harbor, Florida, stating that the corruption and tyranny within the UMWA were now a matter of public record, that organized labor should "clean its own house without Senate or Administration interference," and asked to be allowed to send an MFD delegation to "appear before and enlist the aid of the AFL-CIO council in cleaning up the UMW."

He received no official answer, but the next day Walter J. Mason, legislative director of the executive council of the AFL-CIO's Building and Construction Trade Department, told reporters, "As a direct result of the controversy surrounding the recent United Mine Workers election and related events, it appears likely that the historical enemies of labor will use these events as a justification for an all-out effort against the labor movement."

Sometime later, when Stanley Levey of Scripps-Howard asked Meany about the Trbovich telegram,[2] he responded that he had not answered it because, "The AFL-CIO traditionally has refrained from intervening in the internal affairs of its own affiliates, let alone outside organizations."[3]

In this deliberate rebuff to Trbovich, organized labor made its position crystal clear: they would not help and they did not want the Senate or any government agency to do anything either. Only Walter Reuther dared to break this solid front. After the bodies were found, he declared that this was a horrible tragedy and the federal government should investigate immediately.[4]

About one month later, the Department of Labor announced that it was bringing suit to upset the Mine Workers election and filed a lengthy complaint, echoing the charges made many months before when we had repeatedly and unsuccessfully begged for its assistance. Most of the evidence to support those charges had been spoon-fed Labor by the dissident miners and the college students who had blanketed the coal fields in December to act as election observers. The Department of Labor had, at long last, been forced to act, but it would take its time in prosecuting this suit which was of vital importance to all of us. The case has yet to come to trial; indeed, the motion for a preliminary injunction to compel the UMWA to maintain adequate books and records which was filed on the same day, March 5, 1970, has not been heard although such proceedings are normally scheduled for hearing within weeks.[5]

In the meantime, as the Senate investigation plodded along, it became clear that in a union of about 190,000 members residing in 25 states and four Canadian provinces, there could be no opposition without an organized opposition party. So, on April 1, the Miners for Democracy Steering Committee was organized in Clarksville, in the basement of a church a few blocks from Jock's now-abandoned and boarded up home. The Steering Committee returned to the districts and organized district-wide MFD organizations. To sustain themselves and to finance the publication of their own newspaper, *Miner's Voice* (they have been excluded from the UMWA's official newspaper which still operates after the 1969 election as a Boyle campaign instrument), they organized raffles and fund-raising events. To supplement this, representatives speak at college campuses and elsewhere, turning over all honoraria to MFD.

Although the Mine Workers *Journal* was warning the men of dangerous "outsiders" trying to take over their union and of the necessity of pulling together behind their leadership, the first evidence that the UMWA leaders were frightened of MFD came in early 1970 when the District 5 officers announced the convening of a Constitutional Convention. Knowing that they would try to stack the convention with delegates from "bogus" locals—locals which contain less than the ten working coal miners required by the UMWA Constitution and which are solely or primarily comprised of easily intimidated pensioned miners who can be counted on to ratify the incumbent's wishes—MFD members went to court to attempt to force the District officials to disband those locals and to keep delegates from those locals from voting at the convention.

The Court refused to grant the injunctive relief we asked for, and with the votes from those delegates, the incumbents were able to have passed resolutions condemning MFD and those who had instituted the pre-convention suit, preventing the posting of "scurrilous or campaign material" on mine bulletin boards, and requiring local union officers to post all official communications from the incumbents on these same bulletin boards. In addition, the district was gerrymandered to load up rebellious subdistricts with passive, pro-incumbent pensioners, and, for the first time, the convention adopted a provision permitting absentee balloting.[6]

The International Constitution expressly forbids absentee voting except in very limited circumstances. The districts have always read this provision as applicable to district elections, and the members acting at International UMWA Conventions have consistently rejected efforts to amend the Constitution to permit it. On this ground District 5 dissidents sought Court intervention to enjoin the District officers from carrying out the absentee balloting provision which, inter alia, gave them the sole possession of the marked ballots for as long as a month. The Court rejected this effort on the ground that the Secretary of Labor had exclusive jurisdiction of the matter under *Calhoon* v. *Harvey*.[7]

Although it had lost this suit, MFD entered the important District 5 election—it is the largest UMWA district which elects its own officers—with a number of plusses. It had been able to bring about the withdrawal of the President's nominee for the position of the Director of the Bureau of Mines by demonstrating his close ties to the coal industry and the probability that he would not bring to the job the firm determination to enforce the new federal Coal Mine Health and Safety Act which the UMWA, the coal operators and the Department of Interior's own officials had succeeded in gutting.[8]

When it had become clear that the Bureau of Mines was not conducting the weekly spot inspections of "especially hazardous mines" as required by law, MFD informed the men of their right to have these inspections. Angry coal miners, who are presently dying in the mines at a rate of one every other working day (a rate higher than that in 1969 before the new Safety Act became effective), walked off their jobs. District 5 President Budzanoski said MFD was fomenting the strikes as a "political move to embarrass the union." This was not MFD's motive—it had merely wanted the new law enforced—but the union's response to the safety walkouts no doubt did prove an embarrassment to its leadership. District officers publicly ordered the men to return to work, and after the companies subpoenaed hundreds of men to appear in Court the following morning in order to stop the walkouts, the union's lawyers represented to the Court that there were no safety problems in the mines and tried to work out orders against individual miners and local unions whom they did not represent.

Chip Yablonski was asked by these men to represent them and he took an emergency appeal to the United States Court of Appeals for the Third Circuit where again the union's lawyers tried to undercut the case, claiming it was only a political move by the dissidents, that the mines were no more dangerous than they had ever been, that the Bureau of Mines was understaffed and its failure to inspect should be excused and that there was not even any reason to expedite the appeal. Within days, the Court indicated that it was rejecting the union's and the companies' contentions: it reversed the lower court's decision summarily and remanded the case for a full hearing on safety problems in these mines.

Shortly afterward, miners in West Virginia walked off their jobs in support of disabled miners and widows of miners who were receiving no benefits from the union's grossly mismanaged pension fund.[9]

When word of the announced strike reached the union's vice-president, George J. Titler, then picnicking on the lawn of District 29 headquarters, he said the disabled miners' demands were "like a child asking for the moon." One miner responded, "We done got the moon, what we'd like is a hospital card." The strike led by a disabled black miner, Robert Payne, was crushed in time by union scabs and dozens of injunctions. Payne and others were jailed for reportedly violating injunctions against picketing but not before tens of thousands of miners had joined the strike in its July through mid-August duration. When Payne was released after 14 days' detention, he said, "We are going to keep on fighting for the things that are right." MFD played no official part in this strike but had indicated its sympathy with the strikers and the disabled miners, and the strike, which was openly directed at Boyle, revealed miners' growing disaffection with his leadership.

In addition, the President and Secretary-Treasurer of District 5, Michael Budzanoski and John Seddon, had been indicted for conspiring with four members of the district's executive board to file false vouchers in order to obtain funds from the union's bank account. (The money was to go to Boyle for his 1969 reelection campaign, and we had brought this matter to the attention of the departments of Labor and Justice about a year before.)

But in spite of the strike, the union's bungling of the Lucas nomination and the safety walkouts, and the indictments, MFD had many problems with respect to the District 5 election.

Foremost among these was the fact that the International Executive Board had established a "dual unionism" commission to look into the affairs of MFD and had launched a major publicity campaign to the effect that MFD was a dual union and anyone supporting it could be expelled from the union. Given the fact that the organized coal mines operate under a union-shop policy, expulsion from the union would mean loss of employment, and consequently many miners feared to associate publicly with the MFD slate of candidates or even to distribute its literature.[10]

Second, Boyle had "maced" all of the UMWA's considerable staff for contributions to the Budzanoski campaign and, of course, all of the staff-heavy District 5 offices and personnel were put to work full time on the campaign. (MFD candidates, all working miners, had been forced to take off from work at no pay to carry on the closing stages of the campaign.)

Third, pensioned members outnumbered working miners in District 5 and could be counted on to vote for the incumbents to whom they feel they owe their pensions.

We complained repeatedly to the Department of Labor about the illegality of the dual unionism commission; the unlawful absentee balloting provision; the continued misuse of the UMWA *Journal* and the "macing" of UMWA officers and employees and asked them to enjoin these acts, but they again turned a deaf ear. Finally, on November 30, several MFD members paid an unannounced visit to District 5 headquarters. We knew that the District officers would tamper with the absentee ballots in their possession. Still, we never expected to catch them at it. But we did.

Sitting in Secretary-Treasurer John Seddon's office were a number of District employees and Mr. Seddon. The ballot box was open and the room stacked with marked and unmarked ballots, and on Seddon's desk were a paste jar and a razor blade. One of the men ran out of the room with a bag full of what appeared to be marked ballots. This time the Department of Labor did do something. As the request of the *incumbents,* they offered advice and assistance. They told the officers to place the marked ballots in their possession in a bank vault. As if this would somehow neutralize the ballot tampering which had already occurred!

On election night, December 8, we witnessed a miracle. Despite everything the incumbents had done, the MFD slate received a better than two-to-one majority of the working miners' votes and captured virtually every office in the District. But the almost 1,200 absentee ballots have not yet been counted, and the election may still be stolen. MFD has filed briefs with the Department of Labor, noting that if they follow their own precedents and rulings, they should impound the absentee ballots, enjoin their tabulation, and conduct a hearing to determine whether or not the ballots were tampered with and should be counted at all. As I write this I do not know whether the Department will take this action, but I do know that they can no longer continue to ignore MFD. Every working miner in District 5 knows that MFD won. It is impossible to mine coal with retired miners and to really win an election with tampered votes. The working miners have spoken. "It's time for a change." And their message has already been heard loud and clear throughout the coal fields, where other working miners who support MFD are fighting for control of this union.

Perhaps the message may also reach organized labor which, after the coal miners rebellion in 1969 resulted in the new Coal Mine Health and Safety Act, followed suit by pressing, at long last, for a federal occupational safety act. This is not the only autocratic and corrupt union—although we think it is the worst example—and perhaps it's time for a change elsewhere, too.

January 1971

1. A Pennsylvania miner, Steve Segedi, said at the time, "The men who signed to be added as plaintiffs are no different from the men who signed our Declaration of Independence."

2. By this time one UMWA local union president, Silous Huddleston, had been indicted in connection with the murders. Although the prosecutor, Richard Sprague, has publicly stated that he believes persons higher up in the union hierarchy were involved and subsequently will be charged, and the five federal indictments indicate that the murders were election-connected, the Department of Labor spokesmen still maintain that there was no connection between the murders and the 1969 UMWA election.

3. When Jock announced that he was challenging Boyle for the presidency of the UMWA, however, Meany was less shy about interfering in the UMWA's internal affairs. He reportedly commented that this was just a case of a man wanting to come out of the kitchen into the parlor.

4. Despite rumors to the contrary, in part disseminated by Assistant Secretary of Labor Willie J. Usery, this was the sum total of Reuther's or the UAW's "assistance" to the efforts to reform the UMWA.

5. The Department has ample precedent for this delay. Most of the UMWA's districts—19 out of the 23 U.S. districts—are under trusteeship. Six years ago, the Department brought suit to remove the trusteeship status of some of these districts. That case, too, has yet to come to trial.

6. Because the union requires the continued payment of membership dues as a condition precedent to obtaining a pension, the union has an extraordinarily high percentage of retired workers who still vote in all elections. Of its approximately 190,000 members, 70,000 receive Bituminous Fund pensions; 15,000 receive Anthracite Fund pensions; and approximately 10,000 retired or unemployed miners have maintained their membership in the UMWA in the expectation of receiving a pension at some date in the future. Several months ago, a charge was filed with the National Labor Relations Board to declare this practice of requiring retired men to continue paying dues unlawful, but the Board's General Counsel has yet to act on this charge. In addition, MFD has charged that the substantial Bituminous Fund pension increase which Boyle engineered in the pre-election period last year was designed to influence the result of the election and should be challenged by the Department of Labor which has refused to do so. The Senate Labor Subcommittee staff has noted that as a result of this increase in the Bituminous Fund pension, Boyle received almost 93 percent of the pensioner vote and the Fund is in serious danger of bankruptcy.

7. See "Meanwhile Back at the Labor Department" (1970), pp. 267 to 283 of this volume and "Law, Democracy and the Unions" (1965), pp. 109 to 120, for a thorough explanation of *Calhoon.*

8. In the UMWA *Journal* Boyle had urged the "immediate confirmation" of the President's nominee, Dr. J. Richard Lucas. Lucas had been handpicked for the job by a group of coal mine operators in Virginia who earlier, at the suggestion of a Department of the Interior official had brought suit to enjoin enforcement of the Act. After the facts concerning Lucas were made public and he withdrew, Boyle asserted that MFD's charges that he had supported this man were "an outright calumny against the union."

9. Over the years, the union has kept as much as $86 million dollars of the money of this purportedly independent fund in non-interest-bearing accounts at the National Bank of Washington of which it owns approximately 75 percent of the outstanding shares, thereby siphoning off into its own and others' coffers hundreds of millions of dollars which belong to the Fund's beneficiaries. A suit was brought last year to rectify this and other abuses and it is scheduled to come to trial in February. (Although the Department of Labor was invited to intervene by the attorneys who have brought this suit, it declined to do so.)

10. Not content with the free publicity he was getting in the official UMWA

Journal, Budzanoski began publishing with union funds a District 5 Newsletter which touted the incumbents and denounced the MFD slate. Finally, at election time, he got out an "Election Bulletin" similar in tone to the smear sheet he had published and distributed with union funds and personnel against Jock in 1969. This one charged, inter alia, that the Communists had donated $150,000 to MFD for its District 5 campaign.

UMWA Dictatorship
on the Defensive

FRED BARNES

W.A. (Tony) Boyle is unnerved. As president of the coal miners' 175,000-member United Mine Workers of America (UMWA), he is a national figure. But he rarely appears in public—except in court under subpoena. When speeches are to be made at major UMWA functions around the coalfields, Boyle usually doesn't deliver them. He assigns a subordinate to the task. The aging union leader doesn't like to leave his Washington office and come face to face with the angry miners whose destinies he controls.

Boyle has good reason to feel embattled. Up until 1969, his rule of the UMWA, one of the country's wealthiest labor organizations, was all but unchallenged. Then Ralph Nader began attacking him for his dictatorial practices, coziness with mine owners and neglect of the miners themselves. Ken Hechler, the crusading West Virginia Congressman, soon joined in criticizing Boyle. Finally, Joseph A. (Jock) Yablonski, a long-time UMWA official, broke with the Boyle regime and sought to unseat Boyle in the union's presidential election. Yablonski lost a disputed election and a few weeks afterwards he was found murdered in his Pennsylvania home along with his wife and daughter. The publicity surrounding the murders brought the Boyle administration under the scrutiny of the federal government, which had earlier shied away from doing anything about corruption in the UMWA.

21

It was this series of events in 1969 and 1970 which has led to Boyle's current troubles. Suits were filed by miners and their families and by the government. Investigations were launched. These suits and probes began to bear fruit in 1971 and the result was a significant loosening of Boyle's grip on the union. And with several strong cases against Boyle still pending, the prospects are great that his power will be further reduced or that he may be forced out of office entirely.

The most important court decision so far was delivered April 28, 1971 by Judge Gerhard A. Gesell of U.S. District Court in Washington, D.C. Judge Gesell ruled that Boyle and the other two trustees of the UMWA Welfare and Retirement Fund were guilty of mismanaging the fund's assets. He also found the union, the fund and the UMWA-controlled National Bank of Washington guilty of conspiracy. Both the mismanagement and conspiracy stemmed largely from the practice of keeping as much as $75 million of the fund's money in non-interest bearing accounts at the bank. Gesell postponed the decision as to what penalties he would assess, but he was expected to force the union, fund and bank to pay compensatory damages up to $30 million.

"The trustees well knew that cash deposits at the bank were unjustified," the judge said. "It was a continuous and serious violation of the trustees' fiduciary obligation for them to permit these accumulations of cash to remain uninvested." The effect of the practice, Gesell said, was to deprive the beneficiaries of the fund—retired and disabled miners and widows of miners—of income which investments would have earned. The judge said that reform of the fund is "urgent" and he ordered Boyle and another trustee to step down. He also instructed the fund to take all of its money out of the National Bank of Washington, where the UMWA owns 74 percent of the common stock.

Gesell's ruling came in a suit filed by a group of former miners and their families, mostly from West Virginia, who had been denied hospital benefits and pensions because of the arbitrary rules of the fund. They argued in their suit that they were denied because the trustees were using some of the fund's assets to build profits for the bank and thus indirectly enrich the UMWA's treasury. Left out in the cold, they said, were thousands like themselves with justifiable claims for financial aid from the fund.

UMWA patriarch John L. Lewis established the fund in 1950. He allowed coal mine owners to mechanize mining operations—and thus take jobs away from hundreds of thousands of miners—in return for their payment of a royalty to the fund for each ton of coal produced in a union mine.

Though he had failed to win an increase in the royalty since he became UMWA president in 1963, Boyle rammed through a boost from $115 to $150 in monthly pensions for retired miners. This occurred the day after Boyle became a trustee upon Lewis' death in 1969 and only a week after Yablonski announced his candidacy to unseat Boyle. The move was clearly a political one, designed to win the support of UMWA pensioners in the upcoming election. It was made without first studying what effect the increased payments would have on the solvency of the fund. Later, the United States Comptroller General found that the fund will run dry by 1975 at the new rate of spending. Gesell characterized Boyle's move this way: "His actions in forcing through the pension increase, partly by misrepresentation, in haste and without consulting the neutral trustee, reflect an insensitivity to fiduciary standards."

The judge was further critical of Boyle's failure to resign as a director of the National Bank of Washington and a member of its executive committee when he became a fund trustee. About 20 percent of the bank's assets came from the fund. Boyle's position at the bank, Gesell decided, created "a relationship which conflicted with that degree of independence required of a trustee under the circumstances."

Boyle's fast and loose handling of money in the welfare and retirement fund is matched by his questionable disbursement of money from the union's treasury. Boyle has passed out millions of dollars in UMWA money to his lieutenants without providing proper justification for the expenditures. Instead, these payments fall under the category of "organizing expenses."

Between 1963 and 1968, for instance, Boyle authorized "loans" of $3.7 million to a district in Kentucky and Tennessee and $1.8 million to a district in southwestern Virginia. During his campaign, Yablonski charged that the money was used by Boyle to assure his "political control" over the districts. "Loans of a similar nature and for a similar purpose have been made to other districts," Yablonski said. All of them were written in UMWA records as going for unspecified "organizing expenses."

Such vague justifications for expenditures violate the Landrum-Griffin Act's provisions on union record-keeping and the government went to court in Washington to force Boyle to keep proper records, ones in which illegal expenditures could not be easily masked. Shortly before Judge Gesell's ruling, Judge William Bryant ruled in favor of the government, instructing Boyle to quit the loose bookkeeping.

It was Yablonski's contention that thousands of dollars in union money were funneled illegally into Boyle's re-election campaign and he pointed particularly to an instance in Pennsylvania and another in Virginia. His charge has now led to the conviction of Boyle lieutenants in each of the cases. In their unsuccessful court defenses, the Boyle men said the money in question wasn't earmarked for the campaign, but was for "organizing expenses."

A federal court jury in Pittsburgh on May 6, 1971 found UMWA District 5 president Michael Budzanoski and district secretary-treasurer John Seddon guilty on one count of conspiring to falsify union records and three counts of actually doing so. District 5 encompasses southwestern Pennsylvania and was Yablonski's home district. Two former District 5 officials testified that they and two others were instructed to cash UMWA checks totaling $8,500 and return the money to Seddon. They said Budzanoski told them the money was to be funneled into Boyle's campaign coffers. To hide this illegal use of UMWA money, they said they were ordered to hand in fraudulent vouchers saying the money was used for "organizing expenses."

In the other case, Ray Thornbury, the second-ranking UMWA official in District 28 in southwestern Virginia was convicted on June 10, 1971, by a federal court jury in Washington of one count of embezzlement. The jury decided that Thornbury had illegally received a union check for $180 as reimbursement for expenses on a campaign trip in July and August of 1969, in the midst of the Boyle-Yablonski campaign battle.

Thornbury had escorted seven miners from Virginia on the four-day trip to Pittsburgh, where they met with Budzanoski, and then to Washington. The aim of the excursion was to persuade the miners against supporting Yablonski and to inspire them to campaign for Boyle on their return. Three of the miners testified that Thornbury promised them before the trip that they would be paid out of UMWA funds for their lost work time. And indeed Thornbury and the seven miners received union checks when they got back to Virginia. But it was merely a bookkeeper's mistake that the miners' checks were written on the union account instead of the account of Boyle's District 28 campaign committee, UMWA witnesses testified. Thornbury was chairman of the committee. The jury acquitted Thornbury on seven embezzlement counts stemming from the miners' checks. But it didn't accept his explanation that the check to himself, written at the same time as the other seven and marked as payment for the "Washington trip," was really for "organizing expenses."

The convictions of the Boyle lieutenants are significant for several reasons. They expose the kind of financial hanky-panky that is the hallmark of Boyle's regime. And they serve as a warning to others in the Boyle camp. The three face possible jail sentences and fines. But particularly important is the fact that if the convictions are upheld on appeal, as is expected, the three will be barred from holding union office for five years.

Boyle, too, faces the prospect of being forced out of office if he is convicted on either of two criminal counts stemming from allegedly illegal political contributions made by the UMWA from 1966 to 1969. A federal grand jury in Washington indicted Boyle on March 3, 1971 along with UMWA secretary-treasurer John Owens and James Kmetz, the head of the union's lobbying arm, Labor's Non-Partisan League. The league was the conduit through which $49,250 was channeled into political campaigns, the indictment said, with $30,000 of the money going to Hubert Humphrey's presidential campaign in 1968. Humphrey addressed the union's convention in Denver that year, telling the delegates that he envisioned a luncheon tête-à-tête with Boyle at the White House in the near future.

The grand jury charged Boyle with one count of embezzlement of union money, one count of conspiracy to embezzle and make illicit campaign contributions and 11 counts of actually making illegal donations. The two embezzlement counts come under the Landrum-Griffin Act and carry with them the five-year ban on holding union office. By merely being indicted, Boyle was forced to resign as a director of the National Bank of Washington. But even if Boyle is convicted and loses all his appeals, ouster from union office as a result of the political donations could be years away. If union attorneys are competent at nothing else, they are experts at delaying cases, if only by lodging groundless appeals when all else fails.

Nearly seven years ago, the federal government filed suit against the practice of UMWA leaders of preventing miners from electing officials in their regional districts. Instead, the districts are kept in "trusteeships" and the district officials are appointed from Washington. The trusteeship setup, which is used in 23 of the union's 27 districts, is blatantly illegal but Boyle's attorneys have capitalized on the indifference of the government lawyers handling the case and have managed to stave off a trial until July 1971. Finally forced to present their case in court, government attorneys acted in the same perfunctory manner that allowed the trial to be delayed so long in the first place. On its merits, the case against the Boyle "trusteeship" system was overwhelming, but after the government finished its prosecution there was some doubt that the case would be decided against Boyle. Judge Joseph C. Waddy was expected to issue his ruling early this fall.

The trusteeship case is perhaps the most far-reaching one pending against the Boyle regime, for it strikes at the very heart of the Boyle dictatorship. Boyle maintains his ironclad hold on the districts because he can hire and fire the officials who run them. The officials naturally follow Boyle's orders, which are often at variance with the interests of the miners they are supposed to represent. The setup neatly averts the possibility of potential foes building up a power base and challenging Boyle. Yablonski came from the only major coal-producing region, District 5, in which miners have "autonomy," the right to elect their district officials. Miners there had been electing Yablonski since the early 1940s.

In another delaying move, Boyle's attorneys were able to put off until the fall (1971) a trial in the government's challenge of Boyle's re-election over Yablonski. Delay is the only tactic left to the union lawyers since the government is almost certain to win the case in court. In fact, the government is basing its case on only a portion of the potential grounds for overturning the election. Among the grounds cited are the use of the union's biweekly publication, the UMWA *Journal,* as a campaign tool for Boyle and various instances of vote fraud.

The most potential damage to Boyle appears to stem from the trials of the defendants in the Yablonski slayings. One of the alleged murderers, Claude E. Vealey, pleaded guilty in June and said that "a man named Tony" was behind the plot to kill Yablonski. Vealey said he didn't know the identity of "Tony" and Boyle denied any involvement in the murders. But prosecutors remain convinced that the culpability for the killings extends to the upper reaches of the UMWA hierarchy. Vealey has promised to testify against the other four defendants, one of whom is a UMWA local president in Tennessee, and his testimony appears certain to convict them. With the prospect of a sure conviction facing him, one of the defendants could conceivably end his silence, turn state's evidence in hopes of mercy and tell the real story of who ordered the death of Yablonski. The chief prosecutor in Pennsylvania has said he thinks Boyle was somehow involved in the murder plot. So revelations in the upcoming trials of the remaining defendants could have a shattering effect on the Boyle regime.

Despite his setbacks in court and the expectation of more in the future, Boyle remains firmly entrenched. He has a union treasury of $50 to $100 million to fiddle with. He has whatever prestige is left in the office of UMWA president. He has control of the *Journal*. Even in autonomous District 5, the Boyle forces were able to beat back, at least temporarily, an election challenge by Miners for Democracy, the organization of reform-minded miners who are carrying on Yablonski's crusade. The Boyle men violated the UMWA constitution repeatedly in the process and ultimately had to "disqualify" the votes from locals sympathetic to the insurgents. The United States Labor Department investigated the election and may file suit to overturn it but meanwhile Boyle's allies, Budzanoski and Seddon, stay in office. While the Boyle forces would probably lose a rerurn in District 5, Boyle himself seems assured of winning a rerun, probably next summer, of the union-wide presidential election. One reason for Boyle to be confident is that no new leader of Yablonski's stature has emerged from the reform forces in the union.

The role of the *Journal* cannot be underestimated. While the readers of newspapers and liberal journals may think of Boyle as an evil man, many miners who read only the *Journal* think otherwise. Boyle is routinely portrayed in the publication as a labor leader cut in the mold of his predecessor, John L. Lewis. He is a selfless champion of the miners and it is simply because he is so ardent in his efforts on behalf of the miners that the suits against him come rolling in. And when the court cases go against Boyle, who is responsible? "Reactionary judges," responds the *Journal*. Yablonski won a court order barring Boyle from using the *Journal* to boost himself, but that ban applied only during the closing months of the campaign.

Issues of the *Journal* are larded with snippets from letters supposedly written by miners. "Thank our President Tony Boyle and others for the good work they are doing for the miners," said one. "President Tony Boyle is a John L. Lewis disciple and has done a wonderful job for the benefit of all members," said another. In others, the welfare and retirement fund is fulsomely praised.

Distortion is one of the trademarks of the *Journal*. According to its version of Judge Gesell's ruling, the judge found that Boyle "was too militant" when he pushed through the pension increase. Gesell's decision is "a dangerous, ill-thought-out ruling that can do irreparable damage not only to the United Mine Workers of America—and we mean the coal miners—but also to all of organized labor in America," it added. And what of the indictment of Boyle for the campaign contributions? It is "an attack on the basic right under our Constitution of working men to petition their government for a redress of grievances," the *Journal* said. Then in a flight of pure fancy, it said, "So what it seems to us to boil down to is: How much is a coal miner's life worth?" No mention was made of the federal law which bars union officials from making campaign contributions out of the union treasury.

Each issue of the *Journal* invariably prints an attack on the reform forces in the union. Printed in full was an April 1 speech by Edward L. Carey, UMWA general counsel and the heir apparent to Boyle. Carey's picture took up the entire front page of the issue. "Unseen forces," he said, "were behind Yablonski's campaign. This campaign of terror, vilification and character assassination was the work of well-educated and very shrewd manipulators. . . . Honesty is not a part of their system and honesty will never be part of their system. These villainous men with evil in their hearts don't know the meaning of honesty, decency and integrity. . . . So I say to you, let us not get into a situation where these fakers, the new-left, if you wish; communists, if you wish; members of the new-right; or fascists, if you wish; deceive us. Don't let them destroy your union so that the coal operators can walk in and have you work for lousy wages, with the lousy working conditions that you had years ago before you had a union. . . ."

If there is to be a free presidential election in the UMWA, it is imperative that Boyle be restrained from using his union position to insure re-election. Miners for Democracy asked the Labor Department on May 9, 1971 "to move promptly and forcefully for a monitorship over the affairs of the union until the miners can themselves choose different leadership in a new election." The department could seek a government monitorship of the union in its suit to overturn Boyle's election, the reform miners said. But the Labor Department, which failed to heed Yablonski's pleas during his campaign, refused to consider the idea. Peter G. Nash, department solicitor, went so far as to say that the murder of Yablonski wasn't connected to his bid to defeat Boyle.

The response angered the attorneys for Miners for Democracy, Joseph L. Rauh, Jr. and Joseph A. (Chip) Yablonski, the slain insurgent's son. They called it a "whitewash of Tony Boyle and his crowd." If it did nothing else, the department's timidity insured that the reform-minded coal miners have an uphill fight in their attempt to topple Boyle and sweep away his dictatorship.

June 1971

The Painters' Union:
Autocracy and Insurgency

BURTON HALL

Bureaucratism is a deformity in any organization but to a labor union it can be slow (sometimes rapid) death. Seen from inside the union, it means the repression of rank-and-file opposition and the rigging of union elections; seen from outside, it involves the betrayal of union standards and the first steps toward racketeering. It has become the prime menace to unionism. That is why rank-and-file workers who struggle against bureaucratism within their unions are today the best hope of the labor movement. Yet, of all the struggles which go to make up the labor movement, these intra-union efforts at reform are the least known and understood. Their history is rarely recorded; they take place in isolation from each other; and each effort must encounter anew all the problems and difficulties of untutored rebellion.

One notable exception to this pattern has been the long struggle inside the New York painters' and paperhangers' union, District Council No. 9. It is illuminating because it has raised the issues of bureaucratism and democratic reform to their most universal level. Though not impressively successful (for New York painters and paperhangers suffer from bureaucratism and its attendant evils today [1964] much as they did 30 years ago), the painters' rebellion has already proceeded a long way toward opening the road to union democracy throughout the labor movement—and may soon open it a great deal further.

It began in the early 1930s, when the painting industry in New York City was a minor fiefdom in the empire of "Lepke" Buchalter and "Gurrah" Shapiro, a fiefdom efficiently policed by Murder, Inc. District Council No. 9, composed of local unions in Manhattan and the Bronx and headed by Philip Zausner as Secretary-Treasurer (i.e., chief officer), was a well-controlled cog in that fiefdom. And painters' and paperhangers' wages and working conditions were at gangsterism's abysmal level.

It was against this system that the painters rebelled. Most active in the early stages of the rebellion was a factional caucus known as the "Painters' Rank and File" which, though Communist-controlled, kept up a militant and consistent attack throughout the pre-war years upon the racketeer domination of the industry. It contested the District Council elections of 1933, 1934 and 1935, each of which the racketeers stole for Zausner by the most primitive, strong-arm methods. It fought the election-stealing in court and, though it won no judicial relief, established that the elections of 1933 and 1934 had in fact been stolen. ("This was a riot," declared the judge after hearing the 1934 election case, "not an election.") And after Zausner stole the 1935 election in the same way, the rackets were driven from power. Faced with a barrage of newspaper publicity, a Citizens' Committee investigation and a vigorous pursuit by the newly-appointed Special Rackets Prosecutor for New York County (Thomas E. Dewey), Zausner resigned in December 1935. In the special election which followed, the "Rank and File" swept its leader, Louis Weinstock, into the Secretary-Treasurership. It seemed as though a new day had dawned for the painters' union.

Weinstock and the victorious Rank and File promised to free the union from gangsterism. Indeed, the Rank and File leaders in office, with the help of the newly-reformed office of the District Attorney for New York County, stopped the beatings and killings that had kept "order" in the industry in the past. They led a long overdue organizing drive into the previously neglected field of alteration painting. If the union still suffered a lack of internal democracy, its public stance was militant. But when Nazi Germany invaded Stalinist Russia on June 22, 1941, the Rank and File show of radicalism disappeared. The administration proclaimed a "No Strike Pledge." It abandoned enforcement of union standards on "war" work. (And, of course, virtually all painting work promptly moved into the war

work category.) It called for victory workdays, with wages contributed to the "war effort." Union militancy was replaced by
chauvinism.

The painters, by and large, felt that they had been betrayed. The
opposition, or "Progressive" caucus, radicalized by an infusion of
angry, anti-Stalinist militants, called for democratice reform and
effective unionism. Soon after the war, Weinstock's structure of
power in seven of the District Council's twelve affiliated local unions
was split beyond healing and Weinstock himself was not long for
office. In 1947, the Progressive caucus removed him and elected a
loud-spoken ex-Trotskyist named Martin Rarback as Secretary-
Treasurer of the District Council.

For the next five years the District Council remained electorally
divided almost equally between the two caucuses. Both spoke in the
name of militancy and democracy. The membership of the two
caucuses meant it: for the next several years the membership of the
Progressive caucus regularly voted down any bureaucratically-
inspired proposal that smacked of bad unionism or of
anti-democracy—so long, at least, as the voting itself was secret.

But the balance of power between the caucuses fell into the hands
of those bureaucratic elements—specifically, the foreman, the
business agents, and their hangers-on—who, then as now, represented
the seamier side of the union's politics (and who of all factions and
strata stood closest to the employers). The Progressive administration and its Secretary-Treasurer soon courted their electoral support
and persuaded most of them to join the Progressive caucus itself.
Once in, they proceeded to take over.

Business agents and foremen, acting together with the Secretary-
Treasurer, have virtual control over the ordinary members' employment tenure and job possibilities. And each tends to use his power to
build his own following in union politics. Whenever the membership
of the Progressive caucus could be forced to vote by show of hands
with Rarback and the business agents watching, it would vote as a
rule whatever way the bureaucrats favored. Thus it was that, by
open hand vote, the Progressive caucus committed itself to such
proposals as the replacement of voting machines by paper ballots in
local elections, and the expulsion of administration opponents from
the union, and the systematic job discrimination against non-
supporters of the administration. With the adoption of each such

proposal, militant reformers became disgusted and drifted away from the Progressive caucus. Step by step the bureaucrats gained unchallenged control of it and of its machinery.

Soon the scandals symptomatic of bureaucratism appeared in the Progressive administration. In 1949, one of its pillars—Samuel Lemkin, Progressive president of Local Union 442—was indicted and convicted for having conspired with a painting contractor to defraud the City of New York. (Rarback, when asked about the indictment at a meeting of his own Local Union 892, explained that the "capitalist press" had distorted the facts.) This was just one such scandal. By the time of the 1951 elections the opposition could accuse Rarback himself and certain named business agents of specific instances of collusion with employers—collusion to stifle valid grievances, to break a strike to prevent unionization of a non-union shop, to remove a militant steward, and to permit paint-spraying (this last barred by the union contract for health as well as other reasons.)

With such scandals in the air the bureaucracy was pressed to the brink of electoral defeat. In the June 1951 elections, Rarback fell far short of a majority, his plurality (in the three-way race that year) being a mere 127 votes out of a total of 5636 cast. It was too close for comfort for a bureaucrat, who had come to love the perquisites of office.

To stay in office, Rarback hit upon a stratagem that has guaranteed the bureaucracy its grip on power ever since. He arranged with the officials of four local unions not affiliated with the District Council (locals composed of workers in specialized crafts—glaziers, signwriters, scenic artists, etc.) to come into the District Council for voting purposes only, on an "autonomous" basis. Though the District Council is, to painters and and paperhangers, their local labor organization itself (the affiliated local unions having no substantial power or autonomy whatever), the autonomous locals' members would henceforth vote for its officers and yet not be governed by it or represented by it to any degree at all. During the ensuing years close to a dozen autonomous locals drifted into and out of the District Council on this basis, as their officials' alliances with Rarback waxed and waned. In District Council elections they cast their votes overwhelmingly for Rarback and the bureaucracy.

With the votes of the autonomous locals propping him up,

Rarback was electorally unbeatable. And the opposition was shattered. After 1951 the Rank and File caucus withered away; after 1953 it never again ran a candidate in a District Council-wide election. From 1953 to 1961 Rarback was electorally unopposed. The two-party system was ended and the bureaucracy's power within the union was at last absolute.

But the power of the union itself steadily declined. During the 1950s the District Council bureaucracy bargained away most of the powers that had made the District Council a union. Its collective bargaining agreements established a Joint Industry Board composed of employer representatives and union bureaucrats, half and half, financed entirely by employer contributions. To the Joint Industry Board the District Council surrendered its power to adopt and to enforce safety rules, its power to limit the ratio of apprentices to journeymen in each shop, and even its power to appoint and discharge shop and job stewards (i.e., the workers' representatives on the job). The result, of course, was that conditions on the job returned to those of the Zausner era.

Even more startling was the relative decline in wages. When Weinstock had left office in 1947 the District Council had been the wage leader for painters and paperhangers throughout the New York area. Painters' wages within its jurisdiction were a full 50 cents per hour higher than laborers' in New York's building trades. They were far higher than painters' wages anywhere else in New York City or in surrounding areas. But by the end of Rarback's uncontested fifties the situation was exactly reversed. District Council No. 9 painters received, by 1961, the rock-bottom *lowest* wages in the New York City building trades—$3.77 per hour. Their wage rate was 48 cents per hour *less* than the wage rate of painters in Brooklyn and Queens and far less than that of painters in all the surrounding areas.

Rarback sought to overcome the disparity by abolishing higher wages! He demanded that all local unions of painters in Brooklyn and Queens and Staten Island affiliate (non-autonomously) with the District Council and that their members work thenceforth for the lower, District Council wage rate.

Needless to say, Rarback's demand aroused more enthusiasm among employers than among working painters. Nevertheless, it found an echo in the General Executive Board of the Brotherhood of Painters which, in the summer of 1961, ordered the Brooklyn,

Queens and Staten Island locals to affiliate on Rarback's terms. They, of course, refused. They formed a joint committee, prepared to go to court, and vowed never to succumb to Rarbackism. To force them in, the General Executive Board had to come to New York and hold public hearings on the issue—and, in private meetings, to twist the arms of recalcitrant local union officials.

By mid-1962 the local officials were won over; what remained was to break the members' resistance. To do this, Rarback needed the appearance (not necessarily the reality) of a higher District Council wage rate, so that the Brooklyn, Queens and Staten Island painters would not regard affiliation as necessarily implying a wage cut. He achieved that appearance with the District Council's new (1962) collective bargaining agreement, which (in flat defiance of Gresham's Law) established not one but *two* wage rates for painters. It never became clear how the lower wage rate (for "old" work) was to be kept from swallowing up the higher wage rate, but clear or not the curious scheme broke the resistance to affiliation and Rarbackism was spread throughout New York City.

In order to win his (however chimerical) wage increase, Rarback surrendered most of the union protections that had not already been given away. The new agreement allowed free, unrestricted use of several applying devices previously banned as dangerous to health. This, in short, was the employers, *quid pro quo* for the "higher" wages under the new agreement.

No sooner had Rarback conquered the Brooklyn, Queens and Staten Island painters than he was faced with a new embarrassment. The Nassau County (Long Island) painters' union bordering on the District Council's new jurisdiction, refused the employers' demands to surrender their ban on the harmful devices. On April 1, 1963 they struck for a higher wage rate, six-hour day and the continuance of the ban. And it looked as though they might win.

Rarback met the danger in characteristic fashion: on his personal proposal the District Council bureaucracy sent strikebreakers to work on jobs within New York City which had been struck by the Nassau painters. The strike was crippled. At the end of April, the Nassau painters' local union settled for a slightly higher wage and a continued ban on the harmful devices. Under the circumstances, the Nassau painters counted it a victory.

Rarback next singled out the paperhangers for special betrayal.

These men were the members of the small (less than 400 members) Paperhangers' Local Union 490. Paperhangers were comparatively well paid. Rarback took the view that they were too well paid. In 1959, after negotiating a three-year collective bargaining agreement covering paperhangers as well as painters, he made special agreements with special employers to undercut those wages—and forced the lower-than-contract wages upon the paperhangers. Then late in 1960, he agreed with the employers to a straight, across the board, 20 percent wage cut on certain work and forced that cut upon the paperhangers. When Local 490 unanimously protested, Rarback brought six of its members (including its three chief officers) up on charges of "slandering" him and suspended them from all union rights.

This was only a first step. In 1962, the earlier agreement expired. Rarback negotiated a new one—but for painters only. He prohibited the paperhangers from negotiating an agreement for themselves and he refused to negotiate one for them. As soon as the contract expired, the employers dictated terms to the paperhangers which added up to a cut in wages.

Being union men, the paperhangers refused to work without a contract, or on conditions worse than those of the expired contract. Rarback declared that they were on an unauthorized strike and ordered them back to work (without a contract). When they refused, he called upon painters to take their jobs and do the paperhanging themselves.

But he failed. Less than 40 painters responded to his scab appeal. His subsequent attempt to recruit strikebreakers from out of town was foiled by timely recourse to New York City's newly enacted ordinance forbidding the importation of strikebreakers. The work stoppage ended when the employers agreed (informally) to abide by the expired agreement. Local 490, by its own efforts, managed to enforce that informal understanding for a year and a half. Finally, early in 1964, in return for Local 490's dropping certain legal action (including a $5 million libel suit against him personally), Rarback relented and negotiated with the employers an agreement to cover paperhanging work.

The painters' rebellion was reborn slowly, and reluctantly. For one thing the painters were growing old: by 1960 their median age was 59 years. At that age a union member's thoughts turn largely around his pension rights: few sexagenarians are inclined to risk those rights by rank-and-file rebellion. Pension plans, in a sense, are the opiate of the aging union rank and file.

For another reason, rebellion seemed hopeless. By the end of the fifties the bureaucracy was formidably entrenched, with the District Council's newspaper, treasury and disciplinary apparatus at its disposal. It had increased its own terms of elective office from one to three years. Above all, it had two weapons which made it virtually unchallengeable: its power to discipline its intra-union opponents by depriving them of all union rights and its power to rig, flood or otherwise control the union's elections.

Still the painters had little choice but to return to their unfinished revolution. Life in the building trades even under good conditions is by no means as pleasant as those seemingly high hourly wage rates would suggest. It means irregular work at best and virtually no work at all during a large portion of the year. A few days' pay must often tide a worker's family over days or weeks between jobs. And under conditions of bureaucratism, life becomes harder still, for jobs tend to be distributed on a patronage basis. When such conditions get bad enough, even the oldest and tiredest workers are driven to fight back.

In Local Union 1011 a group of painters known as the Active Painters' Club set itself to reform the District Council. It aimed at this extraordinary task by challenging the bureaucracy to bring all its weapons into the open—the better to neutralize them or to knock them from the bureaucracy's hands.

The Active club asked one of its members, Frank Schonfeld, to effectuate its challenge by making the hopeless race for the Secretary-Treasurership. Schonfeld, one of the early leaders in the Progressive caucus (he had served as the inter-local Secretary for the Progressives and as editor of the caucus newspaper from 1946 to 1949), had withdrawn from caucus affairs when the bureaucrats had taken over. He set himself the task now of forming a new, insurgent inter-local caucus to bring two-party politics back into the District Council.

Schonfeld won the nomination of his local union (with the help of a court order restraining Rarback from flooding it immediately in advance of the nominating election) and attempted to mail his campaign literature to the members of the various locals. He was allowed, in time, to send his material to the members of only eight of the District Council's 12 affiliated locals—in the final voting he carried these eight locals by an aggregate vote of 1,464 to 1,281. In the other locals (in which he was denied access to the mailing lists) Rarback's lead piled up. In the 12 affiliated locals Schonfeld won a respectable 42 percent of the aggregate vote, 1,800 votes to Rarback's 2,529. But the autonomous locals added another 1,333 votes to the total, 1,222 of which went to Rarback. So with their help Rarback won his expected landslide.

In advance of the elections, the bureaucracy had brought a handful of oppositionists up on charges, most of them for "slander" of union officials. Among them was Solomon Salzhandler, Financial Secretary of Local Union 442 since 1953, whose "crime" was distributing a leaflet criticizing the way in which Isador Webman, President-Business Agent of that local, handled checks drawn on the local's account. Webman, of course, never explained his mishandling of the checks. As a typical pillar of Rarbackism, he simply brought Salzhandler up before a District Council trial board on charges of "slandering" him—and Salzhandler was promptly suspended from all union rights for five years.

As soon as the election was over, these early victims were joined by others. Rarback himself filed charges against Schonfeld and 12 of his campaign supporters. Some were charged with having gone to court to protect their electoral rights, some with having "slandered" him by campaigning against him, and others with having improperly participated in union affairs by campaigning against him.

Nor was this the end. In the next two years, other members were brought up on charges and deprived of all union rights for various periods of time (three to five years) for having criticized, at union meetings, such hallowed institutions as the election procedures used in some of the affiliated locals and the receipt of salaries by union officials (specifically, by District Council President Caputo and by the president of Local Union 892) paid by the employer-financed "Joint Industry Board."

But this merry game of repressive discipline ended suddenly, in April 1963. Salzhandler's case had finally reached the United States Court of Appeals. That court ruled[1] that a union member is protected in his right of free speech under the Bill of Rights title of the Labor Reform Act—and that no union bureaucracy may discipline him for his criticism. The result was instant victory for the members charged with having slandered officials and/or having intimated that elections were stolen. The federal courts granted them immediate injunctive relief against the carrying out of their discipline. (In December 1963 the United States Supreme Court made members' protection even more certain by denying the District Council's petition for review in Salzhandler's case.)

And so one of the bureaucracy's chief weapons was knocked from its hands. But only one. There remained the power to rig and flood elections. This, too, came under attack when Schonfeld brought suit to challenge the right of the bureaucracy to count the votes of autonomous local members in District Council elections, alleging that such election-flooding debased the rights of painters and paperhangers to vote in their union elections. Another unionist, Harold Robins, who had been deprived of union rights for criticizing his local's election procedures, also went into court to enjoin his repressive discipline, the intimidation of voters, the deprivation of voting secrecy and to prevent non-member and repeater voting in future Local Union 892 elections.

Both these cases raised a legal issue which is still in dispute: whether a union member may sue in advance of an election to enjoin procedures which so debase and infringe his right to vote as to render balloting a vain act. To this question different federal courts have given different answers. Robins is currently petitioning the United States Supreme Court to consider the question, on which both his and (probably) Schonfeld's suit will ultimately depend.[2]

It is beyond reasonable hope that the legal issue can be resolved before the end of 1964. Meanwhile, the District Council will hold its first general election since 1961 (its last until 1967) in June of this year. In advance of it—in March and April 1964—District Council repealed its by-law provisions which had required the identification of voters preliminary to voting. (Rarback explained that his counter-reform would make it "easier" for people. The result, of course, is to open the door wide to election flooding.)

In a fair election, which side would win? It is hard to say. Like all workers' rebellions, the painters' reform movement ebbs and flows, reexamines itself and continually rebuilds. But its message, by now, has permeated the general membership and the newest fruits of Rarbackism add new force to its arguments for reform. In a fair election it might well topple the bureaucracy. But a fair election it is not likely to get.

The painters' rebellion thus poses—for the courts and the District Council—the final and crucial question that insurgent democracy poses ultimately to bureaucratism everywhere, whether the bureaucrats can be required to submit to a democratic vote. The question goes to the heart of union bureaucratism. It challenges the bureaucrats' continued enjoyment of their piecards—and it defies them to do their worst. It is a question which sooner or later the rank and file of the labor movement as a whole must pose to the "new class" of union bureaucrats; and on its resolution rests the future of trade unionism.

March 1964

1. *Salzhandler* vs. *Caputo,* 316. F.2d 445, (2nd Cir. 1963), 1 *cert. den.* M. 375 U.S. 946 (1963).

2. This hope was shattered by the *Calhoun* decision [see "Law, Democracy and the Unions" in this volume (*New Politics,* May 1964)] cf. also *Robbins* vs. *Rarback,* 325 F.2d 429 (2nd cir. 1963), *cert. den.* 379 U.S. 974 (1965).

The Painters' Union: A Partial Victory

BURTON HALL

When Martin Rarback, the up-til-then chieftain of Painters' District Council No. 9 in New York City, walked out of Manhattan Center on September 16, 1967, he was followed close at the heels by a rank-and-file member who shouted at him, over and over, "You're dead, you thief! You're dead, you son of a bitch!" Apparently Rarback agreed; he was virtually incommunicado for close to a week thereafter.

The last chapter in the Rarback story began last October, when Rarback was at long last indicted by a New York Grand Jury for receiving some $840,000 in bribes from employers in return for discriminatory enforcement of the painters' collective bargaining agreement. The indictment came after a nearly two-year investigation, in the course of which Rarback, when called to testify, had refused to waive his statutory immunity. And it came on the heels of charges, some of them upheld by the federal court, of "sweetheart" dealings on Rarback's part with employers and of close financial relationships with the labor racketeer, Jack McCarthy. To all of these earlier disclosures, the top officials of the Brotherhood of Painters had lent a deaf ear, just as they did whenever rank and file members complained of Rarback's dictatorial practices inside the union. But the indictment, and the publicity surrounding it, threatened to shake Rarback's throne. So, to shore up the Rarback regime, the Brotherhood placed a trusteeship over District Council 9 the day after the indictment was handed down.

In a telegram appointing General Representative Damery as Trustee, General President Raftery explained that "widespread publicity" given by the newspapers to "allegations" of corruption had "tended to create an atmosphere of dissension and controversy among the membership of the District Council. . . ." So he was moved to impose a trusteeship—not to investigate the "allegations" of corruption but rather to stifle the membership "dissension and controversy." To a newspaper reporter, Raftery once again praised Rarback and emphasized that he didn't care whether the "allegations" were true or not.

The Trustee did as instructed by Raftery without any attempt to investigate the "allegations," or even to find out what they were; he re-appointed all of Rarback's cronies to the offices they had held under Rarback and soon thereafter appointed Rarback as "Coordinator" of "Organizing and Educational" activities. In practice, under the trusteeship, Rarback continued to exercise all his former powers, including the assignment and direction of business agents. Nobody, certainly not the Trustee, made any attempt to aid the District Attorney's investigation or to find out why it was that, in Damery's words, the painting trade in New York City, and especially in City Housing Authority work, had become a "jungle" and a "cesspool" and that blatant violations of the collective bargaining agreement had been going on "for years and years and years and years." In fact, the Trustee's only accomplishment was to cancel the election for Secretary-Treasurer that was scheduled for June 1967—thus leaving Rarback in power without the necessity of submitting to membership approval.

It wasn't long before the insurgent rank and file members began to get the drift. On behalf of some of them, I appealed to the Secretary of Labor to set the trusteeship aside, pursuant to Title III of the Landrum-Griffin (née Kennedy-Ervin) Act. The Secretary refused, and to avoid giving formality to the refusal the appeal was withdrawn. So, on behalf of 19 rank and file members, I brought suit directly in federal court under a curiosity in the law that permits either the Secretary *or* rank and file members to challenge a trusteeship as unlawful. The members charged that, as the court later put it, "the trusteeship amounted to a 'front' or 'cover' for retaining control by the discredited—or at least seriously suspect—Rarback regime."

The case went to a seven-day evidentiary hearing, in all respects equivalent to actual trial, before Judge Marvin E. Frankel. Rank and file union members testified at length about the corruption of the Rarback regime, about Damery's servility toward Rarback's cronies, about their own unsuccessful efforts to interest Damary in combatting the obvious corruption in which Rarback and his henchmen were involved, and about the outright repression and electoral fraud that continued to exist under Damery, as it had under Rarback. For their own part, the top Brotherhood officials played it mum. Neither Raftery nor any other top official came forward to explain why the trusteeship had been imposed (and be cross-examined by plaintiffs). The only important witness they produced was Damery himself, and Damery's testimony was so self-contradictory and so contrary to the proven facts that the court later described it as "a train of evasive, misleading and plainly untrue testimony." But even Damery admitted, at the end of his testimony, that the real reason for the trusteeship was to suppress what he called the "power struggle" of rank and file members who were seeking to oust Rarback.

But if the Brotherhood's big guns didn't appear in the courtroom, they were active outside it. They got George Meany to announce to the newspapers, while the hearing was still in process, that the Brotherhood's trusteeship over District Council No. 9 was fine and perfect and that the Brotherhood's top officials were all sterling characters. They induced Secretary of Labor Willard Wirtz to come into the case as a "friend of the court" and to submit a memorandum at the close of the hearing in support of the trusteeship. According to Wirtz's memorandum, Damery had testified that he sought the good of the Council and that resolved all doubts as to his and the Brotherhood's good faith. The court, in weighing it, was moved to remark that "the weakest area of the Secretary's brief . . . is in its thin treatment of the facts, largely and uncritically rested upon the testimony of the Trustee."

The court rejected Secretary Wirtz's argument and, in a 62-page opinion handed down several weeks later, found the proof "clear and convincing" that Raftery had created the trusteeship in bad faith and that Raftery's real purpose was to maintain Rarback in power, not to correct corruption. As the court put it, "The Trustee's stance of 'impartiality' between Rarback and his opponents, the bland re-installation of the Rarback team, the new assignment to Rarback and the false and evasive testimony about it, the whole pattern of inconsistent and equivocal explanations—all point to the conclusion that there has been bad faith, not good faith, that the trusteeship was imposed to keep the entrenched group in power rather than for one of the allowable purposes." The court held the trusteeship invalid and ordered an election for the office of Secretary-Treasurer. Moreover, because the evidence had shown, as the court delicately put it, that the practice of electoral fraud had "continued into the period of the trusteeship," it directed that the election should be impartially supervised. When the Brotherhood and the Trustee appealed from these rulings, the U.S. Court of Appeals affirmed the district court on all points, holding that the evidence "amply justified" Judge Frankel's findings.[1]

The result is that, for the first time within the memory of modern man, the members of District Council No. 9 had a genuinely fair and honest election. There were, of course, further attempts to rig it. Immediately after Judge Frankel's decision was handed down, Damery sent out to all members, under the letterhead (and at the expense) of the District Council, a letter in which he completely twisted the court ruling, implying that the court had exonerated him and Rarback and the other officials of all charges. When the letter was produced in court, the attorneys for Damery and for the Brotherhood admitted that it was misleading, wrongful and likely to have an improper effect upon the election that was then in process. The court asked Damery's attorney to prepare a new letter correctly summarizing the court's decision and to send it out to the members. After two months of wrestling with this problem, Damery's attorney said that he didn't want to do that, because any such letter would require Damery to say, in effect, "Dear Brother: I am a liar." Damery asked the court for permission to send out instead, to every member, a copy of the court's full opinion, and the court agreed that he might do so. Perhaps Damery expected that ordinary working painters would not read the long and careful opinion in its entirety. If so, he was mistaken; the court's opinion, with its painstaking analysis of the true situation inside the District Council, was read and discussed in every one of the Council's 27 local unions.

The election proceeded, with a field of six anti-Rarback candidates being rather painfully reduced to one, namely Frank Schonfeld of Local Union 1011, so that when election day came around on September 16 the fight for the Secretary-Treasurer's office became a straight fight between Schonfeld and Rarback. Although Rarback's machine of foremen, superintendents, stewards, business agents and the favored "job trust" remained intact, it wasn't enough to stem the enormous wave of membership hostility toward his corrupt regime.

What has happened since then is anti-climactic. When Schonfeld was formally installed a few days after the election, he promised publicly to let "bygones be bygones" and to "work" with those rather numerous remnants of the Rarback regime who remained in office. And this was not mere oratory. He began an aggressive courtship of Raftery, Damery and such remaining Rarbackites as Assistant Secretary-Treasurer Morris Arber (whom he kept in his appointive office) and the other Rarback-allied business agents, one of whom he had defeated for re-election but actually re-appointed to serve as acting business agent. And to avoid conflict with these new-found friends, he began dumping the more outspokenly militant reformers among his allies and supporters.

There is at least some practical logic for his turnabout. Of the Council's 21 business agents, only two are anti-Rarback men. The delegates to the Council from the locals are almost all their pawns. The top officials of the Brotherhood were and are allied with Rarback and with the business agents against the rank and file reformers. The employers and such strategically placed sister unions as the Teamsters and Carpenters are much friendlier to the remnants of the Rarback regime than to the subsersive spirit of union democracy. Add to all this the absence of any organized group behind the new Secretary-Treasurer and you present a somewhat timid, though high-minded, new office-holder with cause for fear.

Before September 16 the future looked simpler. Militant union reformers were (as they still are) in the leadership of the large painters' local unions in the San Francisco area; rank and file movements were flourishing (as they still are) in such cities as Cleveland, Chicago, Pittsburgh and Washington. The insurgents in New York naturally looked to these fellow-reformers as their allies and hoped with their aid to democratize the Brotherhood and turn it into a genuine labor union. Solidarity seemed to be simple common sense, until Schonfeld came into office himself. It was not until the new Secretary-Treasurer was elected that the dangers of his newly-responsible position became so frightening.

Where does this leave the reformers in other cities? That matter is not clearly determined as yet, except perhaps in Schonfeld's own mind. Accommodation to one's former enemy necessarily puts into question any continued alliance with one's former friend. It also puts some doubt upon the continued backing of one's former supporters. There is already an indication that Schonfeld has broken with, or intends to break with, the Active Painters' Club in Local 1011, which first set him on the path toward the Secretary-Treasurership; why shouldn't he also break with the militants on the West Coast? And when troubles break out within the District Council, in which direction will the new Secretary-Treasurer look for support?

Such questions may be troubling, but they are not the end of the story. Nor are they the whole of it thus far. In throwing Rarback out, and in thereby making full and dramatic use of the unique opportunity that Judge Frankel's decision had given them, the rank and file painters scored one of Labor's few genuine victories in recent decades. Even if the corrupt Rarback regime were to be replaced by another bureaucratic regime, almost as bad as it, the victory would remain an important one. We can only hope that the painters' continued struggle will lead, with or without the help of (and maybe against) the current administration, to a much more complete and significant victory.

October 1967

1. *Schonfeld* v. *Raftery,* 271 F. Supp. 128 (S.D.N.Y. 1967) affd. 381 F. 2d 446 (2nd Cir. 1967).

Rebel Voices in the NMU

HENRY SPIRA

The Land of Propaganda is built on unanimity. If one man says "No," the spell is broken and public order is endangered. The rebel voice must be stifled.

Ignazio Silone

Joseph Curran has been president of the National Maritime Union (NMU) since its inception 30 years ago; his name is hewn into the rock of the $7,200,000 Joseph Curran Building and the $5,900,000 Joseph Curran Annex; he is protected by an army of private guards; he draws an annual salary that has ranged, during the past few years, from $71,135 to $102,637, in addition to expenses; he has a telephone-equipped limousine bearing the license plate NMU-1, chauffered by a $15,688-a-year NMU "field patrolman"—and all this is taken from the pockets of 38,000 NMU seamen. But Curran is in a state of agitation because he hears rebel voices.

At the front entrance of the Joseph Curran Building, one of the monuments that Curran has dedicated to himself, there hangs a plaque which reads:

Joe Curran is a seaman who came ashore to lead the fight of seamen for a better life. He has dedicated his strength, courage and skill to this task. He has done more than any one man in history to give all seamen the chance for human dignity, economic security and first class citizenship.

NMU seamen rarely see that inscription, since the platoons of blue-uniformed guards they pay for keep them from entering through the front door; but it is there nevertheless, and so is the rumbling that comes from the seamen, who enter by the *back* door.

They are aware that Curran is spending money as if it were going out of style; he draws $280 a day while a skilled, able-bodied sailor earns $13. He is an absentee boss, remaining for the most part, in his "winter residence" in Boca Raton, Florida, or in his "summer residence" in Dutchess County, New York; except for occasional NMU-paid junkets to Europe and elsewhere; but he is "covered" by an Assistant to the President, who does the president's job for an additional NMU salary of $30,637. Curran's favorite saying is "I've made mine."

But seamen are not making theirs. NMU is currently [1967] tied to an eight-year no-strike contract, signed in 1961 and running to 1969, which has permitted only two, almost negligible, wage increases: one in 1963, the other to come in June 1967. The best it offers to seamen is a parasite "me-too" clause, allowing NMU the right to seek benefits that other unions have already won. It is a contract much praised by the employer-oriented press. The *Daily News* called it an "admirable contract" that others "would be smart to study"; the *Times* hailed it and hoped for "similar statesmanship" in other maritime unions. Curran called it "unprecedented"—and it remains that. But NMU seamen, noticing that West Coast seamen are making far higher pay than they—the differential runs as high as $120 per month—suspect that they may be victims either of a deliberate sellout or of merely inefficient leadership.

Even more menacing to seamen is the NMU's failure to take any trade union action aimed at protecting their jobs. At the NMU Convention in October 1966 the Under Secretary of the Navy, Robert H. B. Baldwin, told the delegates that by 1979 there would be 75 percent fewer berths for United States seamen than there were in 1954. Gingerly, Baldwin remarked, "I would be surprised if you did not look askance at proposals for automation which might cause employment to dwindle still further." But though a seamen's leader might indeed look askance, Curran clearly doesn't. The *Times* reported (May 21, 1966), that "Some industry executives privately concede that Mr. Curran has been 'given a snow job.' . . . He agreed to drop manning demands, while other unions accepted less in reductions."

Curran, it would seem, is fearful of mobilizing the ranks to protect their jobs and their economic standards; instead, he relies on posturing and on letter-writing campaigns. Eight years ago, the NMU "unfroze" its $1,800,000 strike fund to allow its use in building Curran's mausoleums and that has been the fund's principal purpose ever since. In the last fiscal year, the NMU's expenditures on "negotiation expenses" totaled $563. But because a $100,000-per-year labor leader is expected to do something to protect his duespayers' jobs, Curran writes letters. On January 25, 1966 he wrote to President Johnson, accusing Johnson of having "turned your back on us who have so loyally and conscientiously supported you" and hinting darkly that "the Republican Party is, in contrast, vitally interested in the well-being of this industry and of those who sail American ships. . . ." So far, however, Curran's implied threat has produced no sign of panic among the White House staff.

As to the men on the ships, their role in the union becomes steadily narrower. From the founding of NMU in 1937 until 1966, NMU patrolmen, the officers (or business agents) who handle seamen's grievances, were elected by the membership; now they are appointed by Curran. The change was made by resolution at the 1963 Convention. Discussion on the resolution takes up three pages in the record; the vote was taken by counting those opposed to the resolution and then subtracting them from the total number of delegates, who are accordingly listed as in favor of the motion. The matter was then sent out for membership referendum. According to the official figures, one-third of the membership voted: 7,604 are listed as voting in favor and 3,368 against. NMU balloting, however, leaves something to be desired. In the last (1963) dues referendum, for example, the dues increase is officially reported as passing nationally by a three to two margin; but that success was made possible by returns from the port of Baltimore which purport to show that more than 1,100 members there voted for the dues increase and that *only one* voted against it. (In more recent balloting, the votes from all ports are scrambled together, possibly under the theory that what you don't know. . . .)

Traditionally, the patrolmen have been the direct link between working seamen and the Union and, because of their role, the officers most sensitive to the feelings of the rank and file. As Curran's appointees, however, they concentrate on collecting dues

($120 a year) and peddling "fighting fund" stamps. These "sucker" stamps cost the members $5 each and go into a slush fund; among the expenses charged to the fund are $10,000 for a university banquet honoring Curran and $5,000 for a schoolroom named in Curran's honor. But even if a patrolman wanted to fight for the seamen he couldn't accomplish much without backing from the NMU leadership. And that he would not get, because the Curran machine wants, most of all, peaceful coexistence with the ship-owners.

It has been reported that on many ships nobody will accept a post as ship's delegate since, without backing from the Union in settling grievances, a delegate is reduced to performing clerical services for the company. One ship's crew recently came out in favor of paying its delegates. At many shipboard meetings it is even impossible to find someone to take the job of recording secretary. At the 1966 NMU Convention a proposal was made to pay $2 for every hour of picket duty performed; convention delegates voted themselves $350 for three and one-half days of convention, plus first class transportation, cab fares and subsistence. The atmosphere in NMU encourages the notion that everything is bought and paid for; the Curran machine, a collection of hustlers and rubber stamps, is destroying trade union consciousness.

The leaders of the machine, after parking their NMU limousines in an underground garage, take a private elevator to their sixth floor suites in the Joseph Curran Building. If they are curious, they can turn on the closed circuit television in those plush, penthouse chambers and get a quick look at what is going on in the hiring hall downstairs, where the working seamen congregate. They are pleased to be so far removed from the reality of the seamen's life, but concerned nonetheless—not with the needs of the seamen but with the stifling of rebel voices.

The clearest rebel voice of late has been that of James Morrissey who, in running as an independent candidate for the post of National Secretary-Treasurer in the spring of 1966, wrote and distributed a six-page leaflet discussing some of the facts about the Curran regime. In the port of New York, where half the NMU membership is based and where there was an element of outside supervision of the election, he piled up an impressive 47 percent of the vote; nationally, he and Joseph Padilla, who ran for Vice

President, were both officially credited with one-third of the vote. Following the election, and with the NMU's triennial convention scheduled for October 1966, Morrissey, with Padilla's help, began to publish and distribute a four-page newspaper entitled *The Call for NMU Democracy*. And that is when the calm within the Union was broken.

Morrissey published and distributed the first issue of *The Call* in mid-August 1966, calling on NMU members aboard ship to send delegates to the convention sworn to "re-democratize" NMU's constitution by restoring the election of patrolmen, providing limits to officers' salaries, cutting terms of office from four years to two, and so on. A few days after that issue first appeared, photographs of Morrissey and Padilla, cut from the NMU *Pilot* (the union's official journal), were posted in the security shacks on piers in the ports of Newark and New York, with instructions that they be barred from access to vessels.

That was only the first incident to follow *The Call*'s publication. On August 20, when Morrissey picked up mail in *The Call*'s post office box, he found an envelope containing marijuana. Had he kept it, he would have faced a criminal prosecution and would have been automatically barred from the maritime industry. But he turned it in immediately to the postal inspector—and learned that the Post Office and the *New York Times* had received anonymous tips complaining that *The Call*'s post office box was a narcotics drop. As soon as the inspectors looked into the matter they found it to be an obvious attempted frame-up.

Then, on September 14, 1966 as Morrissey was leaving the NMU hall after distributing leaflets to members, he was attacked less than half a block from the Joseph Curran Building by three men armed with lead pipes wrapped in brown paper bags. His skull was multiply fractured and his leg badly injured.

The NMU officers, asked for a statement on these occurrences, expressed the opinion that Morrissey had fractured his own skull. The American Civil Liberties Union wrote Curran a letter, indicating disbelief in that theory and asking Curran to condemn the "substituting [of] physical assaults or intimidation for legitimate debate" within the union; Curran never deigned to reply. He had expressed his views on rank-and-file debate as long ago as 1950, when two leaflet distributors were set upon by 12 goons outside the

NMU's headquarters. "They were handing out leaflets," he told reporters. "They knew what they were doing and apparently got what they were looking for."

Yet the NMU itself was born out of rank-and-file rebellion against the bureaucratic, sellout policies of the old International Seamen's Union (AFL), and Curran's role in it began in the latter phases of that rebellion. Curran was a boatswain—that is to say, a foreman. In those days, a boatswain had to be a pusher, a slavedriver, a rump-licker, and Curran was every bit of that. He earned the nickname "No Coffee-Time Joe," because he refused to give the men under him the customary 15-minute coffee break. But he was a gifted speaker and a colorful personality, and the Communist Party, which controlled the rank-and-file movement, carefully groomed him as a seamen's leader during the strikes of 1936. For the next ten years, Curran dutifully did their bidding.

The arrangement worked well for Curran; as he has remarked, "If it weren't for the Union, I'd still be a goddam, good-for-nothing bum." He marched in the Stalinists' May Day parades and he toed the Communist line. When that line called for a "Popular Front" (i.e., until the Stalin-Hitler pact of September 1939), he popular-fronted—he even went so far as to support the anti-labor Maritime Commission up and down the line. At the August 1939 NMU Convention, one of the Chair-supported resolutions began, "Whereas, Our democracy demands the support of all democracies in the fight against aggression. . . ."

But after Stalin signed the pact with Hitler, Curran and the NMU were busy trying to "Keep America Out of War!" Curran wrote in his official report to the NMU National Council in 1940, " 'The Yanks Are Not Coming,' the slogan . . . which has caught on all over the country, should be our slogan too." On June 20, 1941, two days before Hitler's attack on Russia, he wrote in his column in the NMU *Pilot,* "big business is utilizing the present hysterical war situation throughout the world to smokescreen its efforts to destroy the American labor movement."

As soon as Hitler attacked Russia, Curran changed his tune again. At the July 1941 Convention, Curran pledged support to the Russians because "they, as workers, are fighting the one foe that democracy has and that is fascism."

Curran's column in the *Pilot* was now headed "Keep 'Em Sailing."

He organized an NMU "leadership school," where seamen were trained to get along with the shipowners and indoctrinated to support a postwar no-strike pledge; some companies sent their Port Captains and agents to the school. As late as the 1945 NMU Convention held after V-E Day, Curran forced a unanimous vote supporting continuation of the no-strike pledge. During this period, men who turned down ships or overstayed their time on the beach were turned over to the draft board by the Curran machine.

Curran's pro-employer policies of those days seem, looking back, to be his true leanings; they are continued today in his eight-year, no-strike contract. But his connections with the Communist Party lasted only so long as the Communist Party was strong. At the end of 1945, five top NMU leaders (Jack Lawrenson, Charles Keith, Hedley Stone, Thomas Ray, Harry Alexander) were expelled from the Communist Party. In the same period, with the beginning of the Cold War, the Communist Party's strength began to disappear.

A "Rank-and-File Caucus" was organized at the 1947 NMU Convention to vote out the Communist Party machine, democratize the NMU Constitution and give control back to the membership; it was headed by Lawrenson, Keith, Stone, Moriarity . . . and Curran. Its democratizing amendments were passed by margins of fifteen-to-one; its slate of candidates was elected by three-to-one and two-to-one in the July 1948 NMU elections, in a record turnout of 41,000 members. The Communist Party which, with Curran at its forefront, had had a decade to prove its leadership, suffered a total defeat. In the struggle against Communist Party control there was no red-baiting, no flag-waving—just a continuing debate on union issues, on the record of the Communist Party machine. Curran declared himself in Jeffersonian terms: "I am against, and will always be against any type of repression, discrimination, or any brand of witchhunt."

But as soon as the July 1948 elections were over, Curran began to expel his former friends, first individually, then in mass purges where political opponents were lumped with knife-wielders. By the time the next convention was held in September 1949, hundreds of NMU members had been expelled for pro-Communist sympathies. And Curran's new line became a demagogic anti-Communism. In April 1949 he tried to ram through, by referendum, a series of McCarthyite constitutional amendments; one would have taken

NMU membership away from seamen who "subscribe to, support, sponsor or otherwise follow a course of action consistent with and demonstrating membership in or adherence to the policy and program of the Communist Party or any other subversive or totalitarian doctrine."

At the 1949 Convention, the Curran machine pushed for motions expelling members guilty of "issuing, distributing or mailing literature" which in any way, "vilifies" NMU leaders. One hundred and fifty of the delegates organized themselves into an "Independent Caucus" to protect NMU democracy against Curran's new onslaughts. The new caucus, headed by Jack Lawrenson, Dave Drummond and Charles Keith, excluded the Communist Party. Despite Curran's packing of the Convention, it defeated Curran's proposal to expel Communist Party members.

Almost as soon as the 1949 Convention was over, Curran bureaucratically removed Drummond, the elected New York port agent, from office and, without membership approval of any kind, appointed an "administrator," H. B. Warner. Nevertheless, the Independent Caucus continued to outvote Curran at New York membership meetings by resounding majorities. Curran responded by taking over the meetings with the assistance of the New York police and imported supporters. Seamen who protested Curran's phony counts were beaten right at the microphone. A citizens' committee headed by Norman Thomas, Dorothy Day and George Rundquist objected to the use of violence in the intra-union struggle and asked the police not to act as agents of any faction or leader; Curran, however, refused to see or talk to them.

On Thanksgiving Day, 1949, Curran instituted a putsch. All but one entrance to the union hall were sealed off; the area was surrounded by police. Seamen entering one at a time were forced to surrender their union books at the door. Those identified with the Independent Caucus were pointed out to the police, their books taken, and they were forcibly ejected. The dragnet gained momentum in 1950, when the Coast Guard, in cooperation with Curran, denied "emergency clearance" to some 500 militant seamen who were thus screened out of maritime without any prior hearing. Many of the victims had helped Curran wrest control from the Stalinists two years earlier.

A few years later, the officials who had helped Curran defeat the

Independent Caucus were themselves ousted. One of them, former Vice President and New York "administrator" H. B. Warner, accused Curran of bureaucratic dictatorship. Warner, who was in a position to know, charged that "In the port of New York the votes are stolen from the membership. You haven't got a rank-and-file Union anymore, you have a businessmen's machine."

Since then, Curran has bureaucratized the union even further. In 1959 he turned the strike fund over to the financing of buildings named for himself; in 1960 he forced a constitutional amendment giving him the power to appoint convention committees; in 1963, he forced through amendments giving him power to appoint patrolmen, depriving the membership of the right to a secret referendum on major policy decisions and constitutional amendments, and barring from running for national office any member who has not served a full term as a salaried official. He has built a powerful machine based on the big money paid to NMU officials who see the union as a means of personal enrichment. He has been able to buy off many shipboard militants by appointing them to jobs.

And he keeps a blacklist. When a seaman applies for a job, his name and seaman's number are sent over a teletype machine to the Marine Index Bureau, with files on three million seamen—files collected by shipowners with NMU cooperation since 1957. In addition, the NMU has its own dossiers. The *Times* reported in 1964 that "Some of the dossiers are pretty thick and there are some seamen who are now . . . finding it increasingly difficult to find a berth."

Despite all this, Curran has reason to be fearful, for rebel voices have occasionally been heard these past ten years. During and after the 1960 NMU elections, several members complained that Curran had used a numbered-ballot device to deprive members of a secret vote, that he had sent patrolmen aboard the vessels to campaign for his machine during their working hours, that he had barred oppositionists from campaigning aboard the vessels, that he had used the *Pilot* as his private electioneering organ. Under the then-new Landrum-Griffin Act, Secretary of Labor James P. Mitchell investigated, found the charges valid, and brought suit (in October 1960) to compel NMU to conduct a new, fair election. In 1961, Mitchell was replaced by Arthur Goldberg, and the suit was dropped in return for a stipulation by which Curran admitted some of the charges and

promised "that future elections of officers of defendant [the NMU],
including the nomination, balloting, and counting procedures, will
be conducted in accordance with the provisions of Title IV of the
[Landrum-Griffin] Act. . . ." So ended what the *Times,* in October
1960, had editorially described as "a major test of the guarantees of
democratic procedures in the Landrum-Griffin Act."

Then in 1966 the same drama began again. Morrissey, Padilla and
other opposition candidates contended that Curran had stolen the
April-May 1966 NMU elections by some of the same means and that,
in addition, rank-and-filers had been barred, by the 1963 constitutional amendments, from running for national NMU office and from
electing patrolmen. The Landrum-Griffin Act requires the Secretary
to act on such a complaint within 60 days, yet Secretary of Labor
Willard Wirtz spent nearly four months in secret negotiations with
Curran, trying to get a verbal concession or two, a promise not to
commit the same electoral violations in future elections, that might
excuse him from bringing suit. But Curran was obstinate. So at the
end of December 1966 Wirtz brought suit, demanding a new NMU
election at which patrolmen, as well as other officers, would be
elected, at which rank-and-filers could run for office, and which
would be supervised by the Secretary. The suit will come to trial, in
all likelihood, early next fall [1967]; it could lead to a new NMU
election before the end of the year.

But what is most frightening to Curran is that the newer rebel
voices are not dying out but growing. Morrissey's fractured skull did
not silence him; while he was still in the hospital, Morrissey's wife,
friends and supporters were distributing a second number of *The
Call,* which attacked Curran on the wage issue. A third number has
come out and a caucus is beginning to group itself around Morrissey
and *The Call.* If a new NMU election is held next winter it will not
be a cut-and-dried affair; even if it is not held, the basis for a
movement to re-democratize NMU over the next few years is already
in existence.

Boss Tweed, long ago, delivered the classic challenge of the Big
Man to the Many: "What are you going to do about it?" Boss Curran
repeats the same challenge, but with less and less confidence—
because it is beginning to be answered by a chorus of rebel voices.

March 1967

Curran Dictatorship Under Fire

JAMES MORRISSEY

More than two years ago, five rank and file members of the National Maritime Union (NMU) began the long and tortuous process of appealing the undemocratic procedures by which our union's 1966 election had been conducted. That process took us through appeals to the National Office of NMU, protests to the Secretary of Labor and trial in federal court. As expected, the machine in control of the NMU responded with a fierce onslaught against us, against the Labor Department and against the court; two of the protesting members were expelled from the union on rigged charges, others were harassed on the ships, and several members identified as our supporters got similar treatment. In both regular and "special" issues of the NMU *Pilot*, the union's official journal, the incumbent officers and their spokesmen blasted away at this writer and Joseph Padilla, two of the protesting members, and at everyone else who had anything to do with "outside interference" in the affairs of the NMU.

Then on April 19, 1968 Federal Judge Constance Baker Motley handed down a 57-page decision in which she struck down the most undemocratic electoral provisions of the "Curranized" NMU constitution and directed an election, under the supervision of the Secretary of Labor, in which NMU members would have an opportunity to elect *all* officers of NMU, from patrolmen (who are currently appointed by the National President) up to National President. (In her opinion, Judge Motley noted that because of the strict restrictions on candidacy that have been inserted into NMU's Constitution over the past six years, "it now takes a *minimum* of 10 years to become eligible for national office. No other union studied, except possibly the International Ladies Garment Workers Union required so much time for its members to qualify for national office.")

Curran's response was, at first, more of the same. He boasted that the election would never take place, that the NMU would appeal Judge Motley's decision, that the whole matter would be ironed out shortly. He sent his patrolmen aboard the NMU-contracted ships to round up showings of support for his administration and declared war once again on the opposition.

But his posturing backfired. On April 24, Patrolman Quinones sent a telegram in the name of the crew of the S.S. *Argentina* praising Curran and denouncing Judge Motley's decision—but no sooner did the crew hear about it than they denounced it boldly and clearly. On April 26, the *Argentina's* NMU crew passed three resolutions by a vote of 114 to 0 (with four abstentions), in which they "disassociated" themselves from Quinones's telegram, praised Judge Motley's decision, and resolved to send a telegram to Judge Motley telling her so. "We are very much in favor of electing our officers from patrolmen up," they declared, "and for the election to be supervised by the government."

The *Argentina* was only the first of the big ships to declare itself. A few days later the NMU crew of the S.S. *Constitution* passed a similar resolution. On May 6, the crew of the S.S. *Independence* passed a resolution, by a vote of 175 to 0, declaring that the crew "goes on record as supporting the decision to have a free election of *all* union officials, and to send a telegram to the *New York Times*, notifying them of our position, that we do not support the National Office [of NMU]. We support Judge Motley's decision." The resolution was signed before the ship's meeting by 67 of the crew's members and then adopted unanimously by a show of hands of the 175 members present.

On the same day the crew of the S.S. *Santa Paula*, at their ship's meeting, voted unanimously to send cablegrams "hailing the Court's decision on the new elections" to the *New York Times*, to a Spanish-language paper and to the Labor Department; in a companion resolution they demanded "that N.M.U. stop the practice of intimidation of its members on ship or ashore, (Union Hall) in particular." At the same meeting, it was reported that $229 had been collected from the crew members for the insurgent newspaper, *The Call for NMU Democracy*, and that more had been pledged.

Since then, similar resolutions have been adopted by the NMU crews of the S.S. *Brasil*, the S.S. *Santa Mariana* and a variety of others.

Curran's efforts backfired in other ways as well. The newspapers pointed out that federal law provides that an appeal from a district court decision ordering a union election may not delay the election; Curran therefore reversed his position and declared himself in favor of an early election—at the same time continuing his threat to appeal.

Curran made it clear, however, that he expected to fight this election in the same way he had fought the past ones: by heavy use of strong-arm tactics. A good example occurred on April 29, when Gaston Guyon and I passed out a leaflet—headed "Victory! New Election!"—to members as they arrived at the "Joseph Curran Annex" to attend the New York Port Meeting of NMU: Curran's appointed patrolmen waited by the door of the building and grabbed the leaflet out of the hands of members as they entered. Guyon and I told the members to put the leaflet in their pockets; the two patrolmen responded by demanding that members produce their membership books—and relinquish the leaflet before allowing them to enter the meeting. In the course of half an hour the two patrolmen had confiscated more than 200 copies from cowed members. Inside the meeting hall things went in their usual manner: members were barred from discussing any controversial matter and in particular from discussing the election. One rank-and-filer, Joseph Lutz, got up and remarked that the officials had failed to say anything whatever about the federal court's order, adding that he wanted to discuss it; he was told to sit down. (The matter had been "fully discussed," it seems at a "special" meeting, in which the New York Port Agent had denounced the writer and other oppositionist members and then read the NMU's official press release, which denounced Judge Motley's decision. Of course, ordinary members were barred from saying anything at this "full discussion" of the matter.)

When Lutz was ruled out of order, Ralph Ibrahim demanded the right to be heard; other members began chanting "Discussion, discussion" and "Let him speak!" Ultimately he was allowed to approach the floor microphone, but after a minute or two the microphone was switched off so he could not be heard. (When he sat down it was switched back on again.) And so the meeting was brought to an end.

Curran's technique, of course, involves more than rigging meetings. One of his methods is much more direct: Guyon, Ibrahim, myself and numerous other members have faced physical beatings in or around the NMU hall in the course of campaigning against the officials. Joseph Padilla and I have had our pictures posted in the security shacks of the company piers, with orders not to let us on the ship; both the companies and the union have denied having anything to do with it, but we are still barred from going on board to campaign—while incumbent officials have been going on board regularly to campaign against us. Padilla has been forced repeatedly to go through all manner of medical and physical examinations every time he takes a job out of the NMU hiring hall, as a device to keep him from working—and has been fired by companies in alliance with the Curran machine on charges of "insubordination" that, upon the Coast Guard's investigation, turned out to be totally unfounded. Guyon has been barred from even going to the hiring hall for a job ever since last September. The officials' excuse for barring him is that one of their supporters, a waitress aboard ship, asserted some time ago that Guyon had "pointed his finger" at her in a manner which she said worried her.

As recently as April 16 [1968], a rank-and-filer named Clarence Walter Reed, who had recently recovered from a shipboard injury, went to the NMU hiring hall to register for shipping; while he was registering, one of the officials recognized him as an oppositionist member. He was taken into Port Agent Labaczewski's office and Labaczewski proceeded to berate him for being "one of the Morrissey bunch." Labaczewski seized his membership book and had him forcibly removed from the hiring hall.

Meanwhile, the United States Attorney was taking steps to protect the rank and file members. The issue was brought before the court as soon as Judge Motley's decision was handed down on a demand by the government to enforce a subpoena served on the union more than two months before. The NMU's lawyers argued for more than an hour and a half that the court had no power to protect rank-and-filers from the officials' vengeance. But on April 30, Judge Motley ruled that the court did indeed have power to protect them. Quoting from the federal statute, she remarked that "the Secretary [of Labor] has the power to determine whether anyone 'has violated or is about to violate' the LMRDA [the statute] which guarantees NMU members the right to vote for or otherwise support candidates of their choice in that new election 'without being subjected to penalty, discipline, or improper interference or reprisal of any kind' " and added that "It would be proper for the Secretary . . . to seek any relief which may be necessary." And she added that the court had unquestionable power to protect members who had testified before it from reprisals (this last applied to such members as Padilla, Guyon and myself, who in addition to having protested the 1966 election had been witnesses in the trial of the election case).

The enforcement of the subpoena is only one step in the process of protecting rank and file members, but almost immediately its effect began to be felt. The NMU's attorneys began to hint to the National Labor Relations Board (NLRB), which was pressing Reed's protest against being barred from the hiring hall, that it might give back his membership book. When Reed inquired what they meant, the attorneys replied that his book had been picked up and he had been barred from shipping because of a "mistake"; it seems, they said, that they weren't sure whether he was fully paid up in his dues and had kept him out of employment and out of union membership on the basis of that "uncertainty." (Reed's membership book, as well as his dues receipts, make it clear that he has been continually paid up in dues.)

Just how effective the protection of NMU rank-and-filers will be is not certain as yet, though it is apparent that members will get more protection than they have ever had in the past. The Manhattan office of the NLRB, which has never acted affirmatively on an NMU member's unfair labor practice charge against the union (despite floods of charges made by discriminated-against rank-and-filers) appears ready to act on behalf of Guyon and, very likely, other members. Meanwhile the United States Attorney's office, as representative of the Secretary of Labor, is prepared to ask the federal court for further protection of members in order to ensure a fair election.

But Curran and his administration continue more or less in the same manner as before. Since Judge Motley's decision, Curran himself has flown to NMU outports at NMU expense to campaign for re-election, and his administration has proceeded to publish at NMU expense two pieces of campaign literature in addition to the NMU *Pilot* (which for years has been an organ of glorification for Curran and the other officials). One of the two leaflets not only attacks the Secretary of Labor and all rank and file oppositionists—it goes further and condemns by name those members (including myself) who are expected to be opposition candidates in the coming election. All this—and all manner of additional literature glorifying Curran—is posted in the union halls and distributed to members at the union's expense. (When a member comes to the union hall with anti-Curran literature he is still stopped at the door and relieved of it.)

If the new NMU election is to be a fair one, it is obvious that the Secretary of Labor must do more than provide the merely nominal supervision that is usual in such cases. But whether fair or not by ordinary electoral standards, it will plainly be the nearest approach to a democratic election that NMU members have enjoyed in 20 years. It is the best chance that NMU members have ever had—and, likely, the best chance we ever will have—to rid ourselves of Curran's bureaucratic regime and build NMU into a real working seamen's union.

April 1968

Rule and Ruin in the NMU

HENRY SPIRA

What can be done within a job trust such as the National Maritime Union, where Joseph Curran (its first and only president) and his apple polishers feast and fatten themselves by milking the working seamen? When seamen are bound, gagged and helpless, when all their rights have been taken away, when a labor organization has been transformed into a racket for the enrichment of one man and his "yes men," then those who would return the union to the membership are forced to utilize the legal process to assert their constitutional rights. Publicity is necessary for physical protection. When hoodlums know that the press is watching, the terrorizing of oppositionists tends to be restrained. Reprints from the press are useful in making the membership aware that their leader is not God, rather that he is a mortal who can be challenged.

But the courts and the press can, at best, only open up the possibilities for the ranks to intervene, to express and assert themselves. It is only through the organization and education of the seamen that any meaningful change can take place. The mobilization of seamen so that they themselves can freely discuss and decide issues which affect their lives, is the key to moving seamen to control their own union.

Challenging Curran within the NMU is the Committee for NMU Democracy, organized by James M. Morrissey, publisher of *The Call*.

Morrissey came on the scene as the result of a series of grievances. NMU officials used a technicality to keep him from his pension unless he sailed another 15 months. Then he was ousted from a steady job aboard the S.S. *United States* to make way for a Curran machine man. Morrissey decided to even the score by running for secretary-treasurer in the 1966 election. He decided to expose the Curran machine for its backdoor shipping and its contempt for seamen.

At the same time another seaman, Richard "Dutch" Haake, was not permitted to run for president because he had not held prior office. Morrissey put out one leaflet and Haake's campaign for the "ghost candidate" sent mailings to all ships. Both campaigns were run by people who had no previous political experience. Haake's campaign was a one shot affair, brainstormed by a maverick writer-adventurer who decided Curran needed to be shaken off his luxuriant, rusting posterior. He wrote a dozen lively exposé leaflets after he found Haake, a likely candidate, willing to run. The Haake campaign gave full support to Morrissey.

In the 1966 election, Morrissey was credited with an impressive 47 percent of the New York vote. There was an element of outside supervision in this home base for half the NMU membership. Nationally he was credited with one third of the vote. Following the election, Morrissey published a four page edition of *The Call,* in preparation for the NMU convention, calling for the democratization of the NMU. He was thereupon barred from access to vessels, an attempt was made to frame him on a narcotics charge and on September 14, 1966 after distributing *The Call,* he was attacked within half a block of the Joseph Curran Building by three men armed with lead pipes. Morrissey's skull was severely fractured and he was placed on the critical list. Weeks later he signed himself out of the hospital, against the doctor's orders, to distribute *The Call* at the convention. With fear pervading the convention, not a single delegate, including Haake, spoke up. Morrissey, not a delegate, was the only one who challenged Curran, by his presence.

Meanwhile opposition candidates filed complaints that Curran had conducted an unfair election. The Secretary of Labor filed suit and a new election was ordered.

During the pre-election period, much time and energy were consumed by legal matters. *The Call* was published and mailed out as funds permitted. Its general line was the necessity for rank and file control in order for the NMU to meet the needs of seamen. Unless the seamen can oust a leadership which doesn't produce, unless the ranks have a voice and the final say in decision-making, the NMU is nothing but a trough for the enrichment of the Curran machine.

Seamen wrote to *The Call's* mailbox with their grievances, ideas and contributions; resolutions were passed, newsletters were exchanged, collections were taken aboard ship; all passenger ships supported Morrissey, phones were kept busy, a few meetings were held in New York. The Morrissey campaign received favorable publicity, portraying David taking on Goliath, from the *Wall Street Journal* to the *New York Post.*

Personally Morrissey is an heroic figure. At the height of the terror he boarded the S.S. *Brasil,* which was filled with NMU officials and their strong arm squad, because "we had to go on that ship, to show the crew that these NMU hoodlum officials are only people, not little gods." He spoke at the ship's meeting, distributed *The Call* and was escorted off the ship by company security guards.

Morrissey was and remains the recognized leader of the opposition. Unfortunately, he did not run for the Presidency, which meant that the strongest man was not pitched against Curran. An argument appeared that "you can't defeat a legend, you can't run against George Washington, father of the country." He apparently felt that more good would result from getting into the secretary-treasurer's office and splitting the monolith than from running against Curran and being on the outside.

An election campaign can be the springboard for establishing a viable opposition movement within the NMU, organizing a basic cadre of committed, dedicated seamen in ports and on ships, providing the nucleus for an organization. It can establish a tradition, a precedent for challenging the NMU officialdom on issues, as they come up, with a perspective of taking on the Curran machine in a long drawn-out fight.

With a mobile membership, scattered throughout the world, it is a formidable task to build an organization. It was only just before the election that a quick trip to the outports was made by Morrissey and another leading oppositionist, Gaston Guyon. Thus the slate was, at best, a haphazard affair. It included Ralph Ibrahim, fearless and incorruptible, highly respected aboard ships where he is invariably elected ship's chairman, organizer of the 1958-1961 NMU Rank and File Committee for Democratic Action, publisher of the *Lookout*, and who, in the course of his struggle against Curran's one-man rule was severely assaulted 13 times. On the other hand, the Morrissey slate also encompassed a significant number of opportunists, including two candidates for patrolmen who on June 5 moved and seconded the motion to increase the officers' salaries by 33 percent. Haake was willing to offer his name as presidential candidate. The results of the January-February 1969 election, which has not at this date (June 1969) been certified by the government, credited Morrissey with 43 percent of the seamen's vote nationally, 54 percent in New York, in his campaign against Shannon Wall, Curran's chief puppet.

To keep the seamen's vote at a rock bottom level, the NMU National Office jumped the 200-day seatime requirement for getting an NMU book to 400 days on April 1, 1966 (before the 1966 election), and to 800 days on August 15, 1968. Thus about 40 percent of NMU seamen were deprived of voice and vote by the 1969 election, though they are forced to pay $120 a year to the NMU in "service fees."

Meanwhile, shoreside workers were corralled into the NMU by the thousands right up to and during the election. They were given NMU books on the spot. Thus handbag and brassiere workers were voting for the men who would bargain for seamen's contracts and conditions. While shoreside workers were permitted absentee ballots, the 3,000 Great Lakes seamen who were home, far from NMU halls, because the Lakes were frozen, could not use absentee ballots and were thereby deprived of their vote. While a majority of seamen in New York, where there was significant surveillance by insurgents, voted for Morrissey (Wall 2,950; Morrissey 3,499), Panamanian shoreside ballots credited Wall with 98 percent of the votes (Wall 3,284; Morrissey 84).

Now that the election is over, with the Curran machine filling all posts, there remains the possibility that the voting results may not be certified thus calling for a new election. Meanwhile the following issues are on the agenda: a federal criminal grand jury investigation of NMU officials; contract negotiations; NMU convention; flooding the NMU with shoreside workers; fighting for jobs in the wake of containerization, automation, transfer of ships to scab flags, construction of 200,000-ton leviathans; threat of pension fund bankruptcy with job cutbacks (the pension fund has only 19 percent of its obligations covered); opening the NMU records as a result of a recent court order; fighting against the 33 percent raise for NMU officials.

It is to be hoped that Morrissey and *The Call* will maintain their opposition over the long haul by building a leadership, cadres and an organization that can maintain itself. It takes much time and energy to develop a nucleus of thinking, conscious, dedicated seamen. Cesar Chavez, leader of the grapeworkers, spent three years before the organized strike patiently gathering a core of vineyard workers.

Workers are cautious; they've been taken for a ride by the Communist Party with Curran acting as its spokesman and by Curran without the Communist Party, all promising them pie in the sky. Since over one quarter of seamen's earnings go directly in a non-vested pension fund, they are doubly hesitant of voting for the unfamiliar. What appears obvious to the leadership does not necessarily correspond to the consciousness among seamen; otherwise Morrissey would have run against Curran and won. It's necessary to utilize every favorable condition in order to mobilize the seamen. Taking as a starting point the seamen's level of understanding, they must be propelled forward.

Curranism and the problems faced by an opposition are dramatized by the attempted $100-a-year shakedown of voiceless, voteless pensioners. On December 26, 1966 when NMU halls were deserted because of the Christmas holidays, two resolutions were allegedly adopted. The first provided for increasing the NMU officers' fringe benefits. The vote to appease the officials' voracious appetites was 4,209 to 4 against. Pay and fringe benefits for Curran and his cronies come out of the NMU General Fund. Since the NMU is a small union there is insufficient revenue to meet these new, unspecified increases. Thus a second resolution was railroaded, to extort $100 a year from pensioners, under threat of withholding their pension checks. This $500,000 a year would be funneled through the NMU General Fund until it lined the officials' pockets. The vote on the resolution was 4,099 to 4 against. These counts are not the products of just one hallucinatory experience, but several. Thus the count was originally announced as 3,497 to 95, by the time it reached the March 1968 NMU *Pilot* the vote was 4,099 to 4.

Angry port meetings, leaflets, press releases, a picket line of pensioners around the Joseph Curran Building, court actions and complaints to the Labor and State Banking departments followed in rapid fire order. The pensioners received significant support from the Morrissey group. There were numerous well-attended meetings of pensioners where strategy was hammered out after a great deal of discussion.

By the end of February, Curran capitulated to the pressure, called a special meeting and announced the pensioners' tax was unnecessary because unspecified shipowner allocations were being reallocated. Shortly thereafter the court ruled the hijacking of pensioners illegal. During the 1969 election Curran had the gall to send letters to pensioners requesting their support for his election campaign.

Later it was revealed that the reallocation involved the switching of the 15 cents per man per day which the companies paid into the Automation Fund. This money was now being funneled into the NMU General Fund. Thus the members were in effect paying an extra $4.50 a month dues on top of the $10 a month official dues. All these shenanigans took place behind the members' backs. Currently the NMU officials are negotiating for another 15 cents a day for the Automation Fund, which can once again be switched to the General Fund to pay for the 33 percent increase which the NMU officials are railroading for themselves. Funds intended for seamen's benefits are used by the officials. When the Curran apparatus is checked on one front it gets similar results with new gimmicks.

The pensioners were able to win their victory because they combined legal and publicity activities with organization. Unlike seamen, pensioners are stationary, they meet informally, they can speedily rally together. Nevertheless, since their fight they have been inactive in the struggle for rank and file control, with a few notable exceptions. The pensioners are the one stable element in maritime. A recent "Newsletter" to *The Call's* activists, noted that continuity in the fight against the Curran dictatorship could be provided by including pensioners on port steering committees now in formation.

The latest Newsletter reported a communication from "Scotty" Edwards, West Coast spokesman, which suggested active participation of all seamen associated with the insurgents in "making decisions, planning activities and strategy." The Committee for NMU Democracy agreed "that in order to be effective, we must organize."

Ports and ships were urged to elect port and ship steering committees. Local committees were urged to send minutes of their discussions, resolutions and proposals to New York for distribution to all other committees.

The committees, besides being involved in deciding policy, were urged to protect rank and file leaders aboard ship, distribute *The Call*, organize tarpaulin musters to pay for *The Call*, raise issues affecting seamen wherever sailors congregate. This could indicate a new stage in the development of an NMU opposition.

At this point Curran can well ask the NMU insurgents: Do you think that your small group of seamen, lacking experience, cadres, organization, apparatus and funds, stands a chance of defeating the multimillion dollar Curran machine entrenched for 32 years with trained personnel covering every isolated crew in all American ports?

The oppositionists can paraphrase the words spoken to the French colonialists by an Algerian underground leader: We have a better chance of defeating the Curran machine than the Curran machine has of defeating history. Times are changing. The spirit of rebelliousness against exploitation and manipulation is sweeping from Columbia University to the mine pits. The days of the Czar are numbered.

June 1969

SIU: The Shortchange Artists

JOHN COLE

The history of The Seafarers' International Union (SIU) of North America, chartered by the AFL in 1938, is dominated by three strong personalities: the late Harry Lundeberg of the Sailors' Union of the Pacific; Hal Banks of the Canadian District; and Paul Hall of the Atlantic, Gulf, Lakes and Inland Waters' District. Lundeberg, the stormy petrel of West Coast unionism, was constantly embroiled in waterfront beefs, yet preserved membership regard by his firing line effectiveness in the bread and butter issues. Banks, committed to a compulsive strong-armism, is now a fugitive from Canada. Seamen north of the border will not soon forget his Don't Ship List, which deprived more than 3,000 of them of their livelihoods. Dominion authorities, too, have reasons for remembering him, including: an unserved five-year jail term, $26,000 jumped bail and some $80,000 in union funds only 10 percent vouchered.

The paradoxical Paul Hall has tossed many a towline to distressed unions during a glamorous career, as the plaques on his corridor walls confirm, but counterbalancing inconsistencies leave a shocking residue of injury to individual SIU members. It is in the area of internal performance that primary consideration should be given if a true assessment of his worth is to be made. Hall's political ambition is inordinate, which accounts for a public build-up of press-agent proportions, while his guilt complex keeps growing because of his unceasing oppression of a splendid membership in order to pay the burdensome costs.

Up to 1948 his District was going through growing pains which had it hustling for jobs for its members, and toward that end, undercutting the competitor union, the National Maritime Union (NMU), at every turn in the open market. In January of this year [1967], safety director Joseph Algina let slip an open secret at a headquarters' meeting when he confessed to engineering cut-rate deals in the forties to get companies under contract. In the organizational rivalry of that period, SIU held the decided advantage since its campaigners were hungry while NMU's volunteers had grown soft from a seasoned job security. This explains SIU victories in Isthmian and Cities Service as well as the upsurge of company signings.

But those practices, devised when SIU was hungry, became a standard feature of SIU bargaining under Paul Hall. In 1955, before the Labor Committee of the House of Representatives, Hall had pinpointed his ideas on the subject. His candor was almost naïve, as this testimony showed:

A number of years ago, we adopted the so-called Lundeberg attitude and the Lundeberg attitude was one of responsibility, that when we signed an agreement we didn't care how much we bled, how much we sweated, but we lived up to that agreement. . . . This particular agreement was not binding on any boss—as a matter of fact even those bosses on the Committee could not bind their own companies for which they worked but instead, after we had developed this pattern then the Union would go in and sign or negotiate terms which were not acceptable before signing with each of these particular companies. That allowed us the personal touch. It made that contract the responsibility of the individual boss. Yet, if the boss had a particular problem which was not an industry problem, it allowed us then the opportunity to give him relief on his particular problem or vice versa.

On the administrative level there were stickier problems. Hall labored to weaken outport autonomy in order to centralize control in New York. Resistance was understandably stubborn, for local cliques did not want to surrender their privileges any more than local officials wanted to defer to the order that went down the line to accept gracefully arbitrary ousters from their posts. One incident representative of this hectic phase of reorganization had "Punchy" McLaughlin traveling to New York to intercede for Boston agent Mogan's job. He was greeted at Hall's door by "Slug" Siekmann (previously tapped as Mogan's successor) and beaten to a bloody pulp with a baseball bat. The victim was then hung from the window by his feet as an object lesson to all other dissenters. As for Siekmann, soon after his installation in Boston, he resigned as agent following an encounter with McLaughlin in the union hall. Apart from isolated flare-ups, the port-by-port takeover was thoroughly accomplished.

Membership discontent was still to be disposed of, so the articulate opposition was weeded out systematically, and its more forceful ringleaders drummed out of the Union. Union membership was made to seem contingent on official sufferance. Refusal to give unstintingly of one's time in extra-organizational commitments or unwillingness to yield to extortionate monetary demands too often came under the vague constitutional offenses: "deliberate and unauthorized interference with regard to the execution of any office or job" and "refusal or negligent failure to carry out orders of those duly authorized to make such orders at any time."

With potential "trouble-makers" contained by the parliamentary steamroller, the establishment encouraged brazenness in its legmen. Larger contributions were exacted from crews at payoffs, and disputed overtime was settled on a "take a little, give a little" basis. Members' rights under the rotary hiring system were repeatedly violated, and there was an era when protesters found themselves stopped at headquarters' entrance by doormen Siekmann and Cardullo, relieved of their union credentials, then shoved unceremoniously out on the street.

Seamen, in the last stages of desperation, banded together for outside redress; in 1951, 22 men had the Union cited by the New York State Commission Against Discrimination, and were reinstated in a ceremony of shammed contrition; in 1956, the National Labor Relations Board (NLRB) issued a cease and desist order against the SIU for unfair labor practices involving hiring irregularities, and directed that complete restitution be made. Agency watchdogs were taken on ritualistic Moscow Tours to prove the Union's good faith, but at meetings the complainants were inveighed against, spokesmen raging bitterly that "stool pigeons" had to "blow the whistle" on the long-suffering union. Since bad publicity grew out of these investigations, the modus operandi was altered to silence critics. Elaborate trial procedures were staged and their results published. One kangaroo court recommended penalties for a defendant who had "knocked SIU's scholarships and art contests"; another committee's finding was "blasting officials on numerous occasions"; whereas, in a third, hapless PB 124 allegedly was "overheard in a Union hall pay phone telling somebody that the SIU was engaged in a labor dispute." It was further charged that "he would call each day with information of plans that might affect the sailing of SIU ships." Obviously, the accused did not challenge this trumped-up indictment, because the charge of treason, unfounded or not, always carried with it an implied threat of bodily harm. Not caring about disproving his guilt, he simply abdicated his rights. And so it was with many who found themselves at odds with high-handed officials backed by a muscular machine.

But federal law seems to have slowed down the effect of these rigged hearings. In 1963 I was expelled for having introduced at a headquarters meeting a resolution calling for a reform of the shipping rules and criticizing, in a number of "Whereas" clauses, Hall's practice of senselessly raiding other maritime unions. The charge against me was "malicious vilification" of Paul Hall. But the matter went to a judicial decision in the federal courts and the judge, in his findings of fact, found my alleged "vilifications" to be, in reality, reasonable criticism of Hall's policy. In his formal decision, ordering SIU to reinstate the writer in full membership, [1] the judge cast the following light on the SIU administration's integrity: "The facts as set forth do not support the high tone taken for the union's policy, the trial committee's determinations, or the subversive content or tendency of plaintiff's utterances. Rather, the [defendant's] argument reiterates the union officers' position as if that position was necessarily and because it was theirs, true."

Corroborating the Court's view is the narrowly one-sided scope of SIU publications. Officers dictate news stories, suppressing opposing views with the excuse that the *Seafarers' Log* has "refrained from publishing articles deemed harmful to the Union or its collective membership."

Although a backward tide was setting in for his hierarchy, Paul Hall kept right on using union lawyers to put down rank-and-filers who had been defrauded of their basic rights. But a new balance marked the contest, panicking SIU's privileged elite. In suits which charge union officers, individually, with depriving members of their rights or with misappropriating union funds, the union's salaried counsel are barred from providing legal services to the officers. (The issue came up in my case, when Hall tried to use SIU counsel to defend himself personally and was slapped down.)

The SIU leadership responded with a new organization, to be financed by the members, which would provide legal services to officers charged with robbing or oppressing the rank and file. It is to be called "Maritime Defense League," and it is to be run by SIU and International Longshoreman's Associations (ILA) officials. The plan was presented to the SIU membership as a protection for seagoing members. The officials lamented: "Under such laws as the Landrum-Griffin Act of 1959, and various court decisions and interpretations, unions can no longer help their members in this way." To get around paying the cost of lawsuits themselves they offered this solution at a series of general meetings: "The League has established an office in Brooklyn in One Hanson Place, and is establishing the necessary machinery to provide the type of help that SIU men need when they are in trouble. The Maritime Defense League is going to set about collecting the funds that are needed for the defense of SIU members who can't turn to their Union for help—because the law is set up to deny them the help they need."

Ostensibly created as a counter-thrust at class legislation, this expedient will find high-salaried labor leaders the chief recipients of its services. Visualize ordinary Union members pitted against Union officials in tests under the Act's "Bill of Rights." With top SIU functionaries heading the League, preferential treatment is not about to be given to working seamen. Even more unlikely to be gratified is a grassroots appeal for free legal aid now that the Supreme Court has ruled that members may sue unions for allowing them to be shortchanged at payoffs. Nonetheless, the instrument intended to nullify labor's newly-won legislative equalizer will be wholly financed by SIU's rank and file. And so it goes, in the Atlantic and Gulf District of the SIU.

An administration that openly scorns even the most elementary principles of union democracy can be expected to treat the various funds and financial plans that come within its control as the private property of the administrators themselves. It is hard to say precisely how the SIU's funds are managed, since itemized breakdowns are not made available and we have little to go on except the officials' cocky boasts that the SIU programs are the "best" in the industry.

Nevertheless, more than a decade ago, New York State, in making a probe of union funds, came up with a revealing analysis of SIU practices. Deputy Superintendent of Insurance Adelbert G. Straub reported that a building corporation wholly owned by SIU purchased ten parcels of land adjacent to SIU headquarters for the erection of a hotel for SIU members. The building corporation bought them at a total cost of $125,416; it resold them to the SIU welfare fund, which agreed in 1952 to take over the project, for $185,000, creating a profit of $59,584. A man who had been administrator of the plan until December 1952, and is currently an employer trustee, was not aware that a profit had been made. He understood that the corporation had purchased the property on behalf of the welfare plan and turned it over to the plan for the original purchase price. Another employer trustee was not even aware that the fund had purchased the property from the union.

Straub's investigation also revealed that the welfare plan was furnishing almost the entire subsidy for the SIU's cafeteria and that in 1952 and 1953, at least, the subsidy (which totaled $303,000) was based on the assumption that the cafeteria had met requirements for a full subsidy: that is, it had served at least 500 unemployed members per meal. In fact, it had served many fewer than 500 per meal; Straub calculated the overpayment at $102,000.

Straub found also that the plan paid $1,500 per week in rent to the building corporation for a portion of a floor in the SIU headquarters building, using that portion for union members' recreational purposes. Those quarters had previously been made available without charge. And as Straub's report put it, "In addition to the impropriety of transferring the cost of this function to the welfare plan, the rent charge was manifestly disproportionate to the space occupied and the facilities available."

And Straub found that, in 1953, the welfare plan had paid $7,000 for expenses incurred by its administrator "in connection with country club memberships and luncheon club dues." Such factors had contributed to an increase estimated by Straub to be "almost

100 percent in operating expenses between 1952 and 1953," although the amount of contributions remained "about the same."

Further, there were such curious stories as that of the SIU's training ship, the *Andrew Furuseth,* which was Paul Hall's exclusive yacht from 1951 to 1956, with his brother Don in charge of the crew. Expenditures for the boat in 1952 and 1953 eluded detection, but the welfare plan was burdened with costs of $31,179.29 in 1951 and $70,165.63 for the period from February 2, 1954, to August 31, 1956.

Although New York State's investigation addressed itself principally to monies channelled for personal use or to union activities in no way related to the purpose and function of the welfare fund, SIU administrators were unabashed by its charges and disclosures. The SIU continued to maintain officially that the disbursements were "necessary" and "proper," a new low water mark in protective brotherhood.

The welfare plan, between 1958 and 1965 was burdened with a variety of management functions, thereby creating the impression, on paper at least, of fringe benefits. These now include physical check-ups, safety programs, a lifeboat school, a food plan, even legislative lobbying. Far from conferring any benefits on the seamen, they simply made possible strengthened enforcement of onerous rules and unsatisfactory conditions.

In the area of genuine fringe benefits, the SIU set up a vacation plan in 1952 which gave to seamen an annual vacation payment totaling only $140. It is noteworthy that at that very time, SIU allegedly spent $900,000 trying unsuccessfully to organize Atlantic Refining sailors, who were already enjoying two months' vacation each year with full pay. Expediently, SIU added to its vacation pay through the years until it reached $1,000—roughly the equivalent of the two months' vacation with pay that the industry had already accepted. For this, the vacation plan administrators appropriated from the vacation fund an annual fee in the neighborhood of half a million dollars as administrative expenses.

But the most notable feature of Paul Hall's brand of unionism is the wage structure for unlicensed seamen—a structure that has steadily become geographically more and more unbalanced these past 20 years. During and immediately following World War II, unlicensed seamen on the East and West coasts enjoyed substantially identical wage rates. To this day, marine officers—organized apart from both SIU and NMU into separate unions for masters and mates, engineers and radio operators—enjoy an industry-wide uniformity of standards. The government declared that parity in wages between East and West Coasts was the national maritime policy and appointed a single federal arbitrator to maintain it. Yet, with SIU and NMU engaged in perpetual rivalry on the East and Gulf coasts, and facing the more powerful employers to boot, East Coast seamen have fallen far behind the West Coast. Deck and steward department wages on the West Coast are already some $200 a month ahead of deck and steward rates in Paul Hall's SIU Atlantic & Gulf District, while West Coast engine room rates are $45 to $80 above the SIU's Atlantic and Gulf rates; overtime rates in the SIU Atlantic and Gulf district run 57 cents to 83 cents per hour behind the Pacific Coast. And the further increases called for by the present West Coast contracts promise to widen the differential still more.

The differential was already sizeable in 1958, when Hall imposed on his members a seven-year wage freeze. And during that barren stretch, manning scales were cut—sacrificing quartermasters, deck engineers, water tenders, wipers, cooks and messmen. The freeze came to an end in September 1965 with only a nominal increase, ranging from $18.18 per month on the deck, $11.86 to $37.17 in the engine room, and $18.04 to $31.32 in the stewards' department, plus an overtime boost of 11 cents to 14 cents.

Hall gave SIU members a variety of explanations for their low wage rates. He told them repeatedly that a wage raise "would put some of our companies out of business"—implying that low wages would keep them in business. That this was not so was demonstrated when the Bull Line went out of business along with many shoestring operators, despite the SIU's substandard contracts. When the West Coast/East Cost differential was mentioned, Hall quite erroneously declared that "West Coast standards historically have been far ahead of the East Coast."

In 1963, the NMU negotiated a paltry wage increase, placing their members (also East and Gulf seamen) ahead of the SIU. In September 1965, in breaking its own seven-year wage freeze, the SIU brought its rates up to the NMU settlement of 1963—and no higher, despite proof that the shipowners could pay a great deal more. Then the leaderships of both unions relaxed again into a wage freeze which, for the NMU, had been continuous since 1963. SIU's contract had expired in 1964, only to be extended tacitly at the same terms prevailing in 1958; by contrast, longshoremen working on SIU ships got a $32 per week package increase in 1965 on top of the $12 a week raise they had received two years earlier. Yet the SIU seamen pay $100 more per year in fees than the longshoremen (who are not SIU members), being required to pay a lump $70 on the opening day of every year.

Toward the end of 1966, however, NMU's long-run contract became a source of embarrassment. In the wake of a contract reopener, bargaining was spiritless. But when the crews of 18 ships halted sailing for 24 hours, pleading "safety-of-vessel," the bargainers were galvanized to a speedy decision. Arbitrator Theodore W. Kheel gave NMU seamen a modest pay boost with the rationalization that it "does not create an inequity, but eliminates old ones. It is aimed at achieving stability in the field." Aware that the formula was far from closing the breach between West and East Coasts, Kheel added that NMU would have the right "to seek additional increases above those granted herein," the contractual guide being the percentage of changes in the total cost of wages and overtime rates as well as fringe benefits in the seagoing maritime industry after June 15, 1965.

Kheel's determination pegged NMU a bit higher on the seagoing unions' totem pole and, conversely, reduced the Seafarers' Atlantic and Gulf district to the status of sub-substandard again. And a campaign was launched against "me-too opportunism," meaning by that any attempt to bring SIU wage rates up to the new NMU levels.

One month before Kheel handed down his judgment, I presented a written resolution to the SIU membership in New York, requesting "parity with West Coast unions in wages and working conditions," a proposal which would eliminate the longstanding inequities with a single stroke. Such rashness was instantly crushed by the parliamentary juggernaut and space was again denied in the *Seafarers' Log* for an expression of these views. But in the light of Kheel's decision, Hall, who had earlier declared that "if members want a raise they must upgrade themselves in order to get it," shifted his ground on February 6, 1967 and promised "to talk money matters with the bosses."

But even his pretense of militancy remains weak. Nobody has

been fooled by the crocodile tears being wept around the banquet circuit by SIU officers, lamenting that their seagoing members finished a poor last in the contract derby because of honor-bright adherence to President Johnson's guidelines. Even if they were to go so far as to demand parity with NMU, their position would still fail to satisfy rank-and-file common sense. Any return to stability and sanity in the maritime wage structure must begin with removal of the disparity between West and East Coasts; anything short of equalization means continued unrest on the waterfront. This objective is difficult to obtain in a union where free speech, democracy and fair play persistently take second place to administrative policy, negating liberties and rights that Seafarers have so long been battling to maintain for everybody else. To leave them stranded in this backwater is to render democratic principles academic and economic advances painfully inadequate.

March 1967

---

1. *Cole* v. *Paul Hall,* 56 LRRM 2606 (E.D.N.Y. 1964), affd. 339 F. 2d 881 (2nd cir. 1964).

The ILWU:
A Case Study in Bureaucracy

STANLEY WEIR

I: THE MYTH OF ILWU DEMOCRACY

There is a deeply ingrained myth among workers and liberals in and even beyond the borders of the United States, that Harry Bridges, President of the International Longshoremen's and Warehousemen's Union (ILWU), despite his shortcomings, is responsible for democracy in the ILWU and for excellent working conditions enjoyed by West Coast stevedores.

The persistence of this myth is due to many factors, but primarily to the refusal of the working longshoremen to air the problems of their union in public. They have felt that the ensuing scandal would create a reactionary offensive against the job-hiring process which the ILWU controls jointly with the stevedoring companies of the Pacific Maritime Association (PMA) rather than an attack on the scandalous corruption of internal union democracy and the rigged auctioning of working conditions and job security through collusion between the union's international leadership and the employers.

This feeling has been so strong in the past that even individual longshoremen who were driven out of the industry accepted their victimization silently. They either hoped that the rank and file would establish its former control and right the injustice, or they simply gave up the fight.

But this debilitating silence in the face of thoroughly undemocratic procedures on the part of the union, aided and abetted by the employers, ended when the ruling employer-union Joint Labor Relations Committee in the port of San Francisco notified 82 registered longshoremen on June 17, 1963, that they no longer had the right to earn a living on the waterfront.

Why were these men ousted from the industry? There are a number of answers suggested, but basically the question must be answered by pointing to the crisis in the industry created by automation, anti-labor legislation and irresponsible union leadership.

All of the deregistered men entered the industry in June 1959. They were part of a group of over 700 who were the first to become registered longshoremen since the ILWU closed its membership books in 1948. These men were not formally made probationary members of the union. They were given an industry classification new in West Coast longshore history—B men, or men with a B (second-class) registration status. They were made to work under the union's jurisdiction, but were not allowed full union membership rights, although they paid their share of the cost of the hiring hall operation and paid assessments to send union delegates to conventions.

The union segregated the jobs to be worked daily and gave the B men the heavier and more onerous cargoes—hides, bones, frozen meats, asbestos, coffee, rubber, etc. Worse still, neither their jobs nor working conditions were union protected.

The stevedoring companies thrived. Working without the benefit of union protection, without established conditions, the B men could be driven to top the tonnage of men doing the same work by up to, and even over, 50 percent. For the first time since the birth of the ILWU during the maritime strikes of the 1930s, the employers enjoyed the luxury of having almost total power over a portion of the men working the ships. (They still lacked this control over the A men, but the B men were decisive because they did most of the work in the ship's hold which is the point of production in this industry.) This was to create a major change of course for both the PMA and the ILWU. After several years of studying the effects of automation in the industry since the end of World War II, the ILWU negotiated a one-year pilot contract in 1958, which taxed the specific use of new machines and cargo handling methods. This tax was meant to create a fund to be used to compensate longshoremen for lost work opportunity and job displacement. When the contract went into effect in 1959, the employer, as required, placed one and a half million dollars into this fund as a starter, until a method of taxation could be devised.

During 1959, no method was arrived at; the introduction of new machinery was insignificant and there was very little increase in the use of vans to containerize cargo. (Containerization is the main source of loss of man-handled cargo and jobs in the industry.) Instead, the attention of the ILWU-PMA was turned to the efficient utilization of the new source of hold labor—the B men.

Since no new men were accepted into full membership in the ILWU in the Port of San Francisco after 1948, more and more union members took over the skilled jobs. The union job dispatchers filled the hold jobs with casual workers, off the streets, or with workers from other maritime unions on a day-to-day basis. The introduction of the B men in 1959, presented the employers with over 700 men who, by threat of discharge, could work only on the waterfront and had to be available for any job for 70 percent of the seven-day week. Within one year, the companies comprising the PMA, with the help of the union, turned these men into a disciplined work force to do the hold work and act as cadres on days when there were so many ships in port that it became necessary again to hire casuals.

Toward the end of 1959, the ILWU went into negotiations to extend and enlarge upon its pilot one-year contract. At the outset of these negotiations, the PMA announced to the union negotiators, headed by Harry Bridges, that it was not willing to discuss an extension of the 1959 contract that would tax new machines and handling methods. The PMA stated that they simply wanted to purchase all the working conditions won by the men during the strikes of the 1930s. The only question they would discuss with the union was the price of this purchase. Harry Bridges was willing. With some difficulty, he sold a majority of the longshoremen on the employers' proposal.

The work practices of 25 years were to disappear immediately, including the tonnage limit per load on cargo to be stowed or discharged by hand. The employer could introduce new machines and methods—the only restrictions being that each operation was to be "safe" and not "onerous."

In return, Bridges guaranteed the men that this new "Mechanization and Modernization Contract" would "take the sweat out of longshoring," while simultaneously giving the A men early retirement and old-age security through a fund into which the PMA was to pay $29,000,000 over the six-year life of the contract. Each man with 25 years in the industry could collect a $7,900 bonus at age 65, or use the money to retire early. For the younger men, it would create a guaranteed annual wage. On a few occasions, Bridges was forced to add that the only people who could be hurt by this contract were the B men.

Again and again, Bridges appealed to the ILWU members whose average age in 1959 was over 50. His line was: better to sell these conditions while we can still get a price for them; in a few years the employers will take them anyway! The only alternative to his program, he said, was to strike.

On the job, Bridges' supporters would tell the younger men that the presence of the older men in the ranks made strike impossible. The older men were told that the young men were still shortsighted and that, one day, they too would see the advantages of the bonus.

By coastwide vote, the Bridges contract won. Characteristic of the last 15 years, there was a sizeable opposition vote. This opposition was unorganized, fearful and without an alternative to Bridges' program.

Only a few months after the "M and M" contract went into effect, its real nature became apparent to everyone. Most loads to be built or stowed had doubled in size, rest periods were fewer, the speedup was on and the accident rate in the most dangerous industry in the nation was up 20 percent over the previous year in San Francisco and up 16 percent on the West Coast. (On the East and Gulf coasts the accident rate had declined.)

Gone was the right to take direct action on the job to correct contract violations, except in matters involving "safety." The phrase in the contract that said the men must "work as directed" blunted every attempt to act.

The contract, hailed in government and industrial circles as an example of Bridges' labor statesmanship runs contrary to the militancy of the ILWU's earlier traditions. The PMA is paying the $29,000,000 into the fund at the rate of $13,650 per day. However, if any port has a work stoppage, the contribution stops until work is resumed and the fund can be penalized. This has created an atmosphere in which the PMA can victimize an ILWU local in one port without the locals in other ports coming to its aid. (Port Los Angeles Local 13 has been burdened with a special restrictive contract because it took job action in 1960. No other ILWU local objected.)

True to Bridges' prediction, the B men were the longshoremen burdened most by the big loads. Additionally, the contract froze their status as B men. Immediately prior to the negotiation of the "M and M" agreement, Local 10 in San Francisco had started to process B men for union membership and A status. The contract eliminated the autonomy of the locals in such matters as deciding the size of their memberships.

Not until February 1963, did Local 10 resume the processing. During the wait of over three years, the B men tried to obtain an end to the freeze and some immediate concessions. They were granted the right to elect three representatives to the Local's Executive Board. They were never allowed to fulfill this function. Two of these representatives were driven off the waterfront. The victimization of their elected leaders silenced any further open criticism among the B men about their working conditions. They could only bide their time and wait for union membership.

In June 1963, when the "processing" that started in February was completed, the union and the employer upgraded all but 82 of the B men. Instead of allowing the 82 to remain B men, they were locked out for "infractions" of rules during their four years as longshoremen. The rules not only were never posted, but were never rumored to exist until 1963. Bridges and his selected screening committee, headed by William Chester, International Representative and prominent Negro civil rights leader, told a meeting of Local 10 that the 82 were "chiselers, ne'er-do-wells, and men who paid their dues late."

It was impossible for Bridges to justify the lockout to the union's ranks. Many of the victims have fathers or relatives in the union. At a meeting of Local 10 prior to the deregistration, the ranks objected to the methods of the Bridges committee which screened the men for membership. Bridges immediately took the floor and threatened to stop the promotion of the 500 B men recommended by the committee if its findings were challenged. The membership voted against his committee's report and the very next day Bridges went to the PMA and made good his threat. All promotions to A status for B men were stopped until "you quit letting a few stand in the way of the many." Temporarily defeated, the ranks gave in at the next meeting, only to make a future try at a meeting in July.

As for the 82 men who were deregistered, the notifications they received did not tell them why the action was being taken against them. It simply cited the existence of all rules governing the deregistration (firing) of longshoremen; stated that the recipient had violated these rules which were "applicable"; and hastily concluded:

> In the event that the Joint Labor Relations Committee receives within 15 days a signed and detailed written statement satisfactorily demonstrating that there is no ground for your termination and requesting a hearing, you will be given a hearing, at which time you may show cause, if any you have, why such termination should be rescinded. Pending the hearing you cannot work in the industry.

It must be added that these letters contained no signature. But they were, indeed, official, as the 82 men quickly found out.

Since it was necessary to act, the men went to the California State Department of Employment and filed for unemployment insurance benefits. They were shortly notified of the denial of payment because the Department accepted the word of the PMA that these men were "cheats, delinquents and irresponsibles." This further increased the shock. To be denied unemployment benefits and publicly libeled simultaneously, before ever having been heard, was not only a monstrous violation of due process, but indicated that the men controlling the PMA-ILWU policy intended to blacklist these men and make it impossible for them to get employment anywhere.

On July 10, 11 and 12, the Joint Labor Relations Committee held "appeal hearings." Each of the deregistered appeared individually and upon entering the hearing room above Pier 24 was informed of his "rights": he could have no counsel, produce no witnesses, would not be told the specifics of the charges against him, would be shown no evidence in connection with the charges. He could make any statement in his defense that he desired, would receive the verdict in ten days to two weeks, could learn the specifics of the charges in a private confrontation with two clerks at the industry's Joint Records office a week after the hearing.

Seventy-seven men were heard. By July 25, 71 received letters reaffirming their deregistration. In spite of the right to further

appeal offered by the Master Contract and promised by Harry
Bridges before a membership meeting of San Francisco Local 10, the
applications of the 71 for another hearing were ignored. They were
also informed that they were being denied their accrued vacation
pay and that their paid-up membership (through April 1964) in the
longshore industry's Health and Dental Plans were cancelled without
refund.

It was at this point that most of these men sought each other out
and organized the Longshore Jobs Defense Committee (LJDC). This
Committee immediately began investigating ways of using the law to
get back their jobs. (Any hope that the union ranks might help them
disappeared during the course of the hearings. On July 11, Local 10,
led by its President, James Kearney, overwhelmingly demanded the
return of the frame-up victims. This demand was swiftly killed when
it reached the area committee of the ILWU-PMA apparatus. Robert
Rohatch, the union official at that level, who incidentally was one of
the prosecutors at the appeal hearings, simply voted with the PMA
against the demands of the men who elected him.)

The Steering Committee of the Longshore Jobs Defense Committee started its operation by visiting the National Labor Relations
Board (NLRB) and stating the case of the deregistered men. It
quickly rejected filing a complaint with the government for several
reasons: (1) That agency was rigged for primarily suing the union
rather than the employer and the LJDC wanted to sue both parties,
(2) the NLRB procedure looked as though it would be slower than
the civil courts, (3) once having made a complaint with the NLRB
the filer has very little control over the manner in which the agency
conducts the case—if it accepts the case. There was no guarantee that
during the course of the litigation the NLRB would not seek to use
the case to create an atmosphere for the passage of new laws which
would harm the rank and file by putting further restrictions on the
hiring hall. The risk was too great and (4) there were strong rumors
that the PMA has very close personal connections with top staffers
in the NLRB locally and in Washington.

The LJDC sought a lawyer who would represent them. The
Committee was faced by two enormous obstacles: how to find
counsel which was unafraid to take on Harry Bridges and the PMA in
San Francisco and how to find someone whose price would not be
exorbitant given the amount of work involved. The lowest fee
mentioned by any firm during the search was $25,000.

The Committee agreed to pay this price but then met the problem of being unable to raise more than $4,000 against the $10,000 down payment requested. Almost every source of jobs or quick money had been cut off. This problem was finally solved when a very able Los Angeles attorney, Sidney Gordon, heard of the case and volunteered his services on a basis that the men could afford to pay.

Since their deregistration, only five men have obtained jobs that can be called steady. Ninety percent of these men are Negroes and none can list his four years as a longshoreman on a job application. Some are forced back to shoeshine stands and bellhop uniforms; any kind of work to live and pay the LJDC lawyer who will shortly start the necessary proceedings to regain the men's rights.

Bridges and the PMA have achieved a far-reaching success, for the moment. When the 500 B men who achieved A status entered the union, they did so as a demoralized and intimidated group. They had seen their friends deregistered without cause and feel that the same can still happen to them, despite their A status. The men who work in the hold have traditionally been the militants in the union. At the present time the hold men, these new A men, are silent, as are the 700 men on the second B list who were brought into the industry several months ago. Little criticism of the "M and M" contract reaches the union floor.

The ILWU international leadership appears ready to do anything to defeat the efforts of the Committee. At the first LJDC press conference, last August, Morris Watson who edits the ILWU West Coast paper, used red-baiting in his attempts to smear the Committee!

The cause of the Bridges leadership's anxiety is twofold: a victory for the LJDC could hasten the destruction of the Bridges-ILWU myth publicly, and the sympathies of the bulk of the rank and file are with the expelled men whose return would end intimidation by the leadership.

II: THE UNION GOES TO COURT

Harry Bridges' anxiety over his public image and prestige within the ILWU has increased steadily during the last few months despite the continued ability of his guilt-ridden public relations staff to obtain what they obviously consider a good press. To a large extent this anxiety is due to the persistent efforts of the LJDC to regain its members' jobs on the San Francisco waterfront, jobs they held over four years before being locked out by the action of the PMA and the ILWU.

On May 27, 1964 Bridges and PMA President, Paul St. Sure, were guest speakers at a University of California-sponsored conference where they planned again to describe the success of the 1960 Mechanization and Modernization Fund Agreement. With only overnight preparations, 12 unemployed members of the LJDC picketed Bridges and St. Sure with signs and leaflets explaining the case of the 82 men deregistered in June, 1963.

Four large television stations gave full coverage to the picket line in all evening news reports. Cameras showed the pickets, and the captains of the line made statements about the reason the LJDC was picketing. Viewers then saw a visibly shaken Bridges being asked to comment on the pickets outside the hotel. Asked about the fact that most unions have six-month probationary periods while the pickets claimed to have worked four years as probationary men, Bridges replied that the ILWU had a six-month probationary period like many other unions but that the 82 men were "crooks and chiselers [who] should have been kicked out after six months, but we were lenient and let them stay another three and a half years. They broke the rules. We had to kick them out." Bridges hastily added that the decision to kick the men out was jointly made by the union and the employer, and that none of the 82 had ever been union members.[1]

Six weeks before this incident, on April 15, Sidney Gordon, lawyer for the LJDC, filed suit in Federal District Court, San Francisco, against the PMA-ILWU in the name of 45 members of the Committee. The plaintiffs seek full registration in the industry, full union membership, lost wages and $600,000 in damages. The bulk of the damages are sought from the PMA. No damages are sought from the union, but from a list of union officials who locked out the 82 against the wishes of the union membership. The list is headed by Bridges who militantly led the fight against the ranks when they sought to defend the 82. (The LJDC has publicly announced that half of any damages won will be used to establish a scholarship fund for the sons and daughters of all ILWU longshoremen.)

One of the actions by which the PMA sought to damage the deregistered men has boomeranged. Made to serve the maximum penalty waiting period of five weeks before drawing their first unemployment checks because the Unemployment Insurance Department in this state accepted the employers' word that these men were "delinquents, cheaters, and irresponsibles," they appealed the penalty and a 15-day hearing was held. More than 40 appellants had the experience of standing up under cross examination by PMA lawyers aided by a lawyer from the State Attorney General's office. With their own attorney, Sidney Gordon, forcing the issue, they heard the employers' admission for the first time, that the rules by which they were fired and four years of their conduct judged, had been devised in informal discussion between Bridges and St. Sure only four months before their discharge. No written rules were ever adopted. The employer was able to produce only one longshoreman to testify against these men, a Tom Silas, member of Bridge's appointed B List Committee who, from the first, had led in the carrying out of the plan to victimize the 82. A Negro himself, he earned a reputation for being harshest when prosecuting Negroes.

The June 4 decision of the Appeals Board Referee was emphatic: The discharge of these men was not for their misconduct and they should not have been penalized.

Contrary to its threat, the PMA did not appeal this decision. Instead, without giving proper notice to the LJDC attorney, the PMA and ILWU officials, defendants named in the Federal suit mentioned above, sent almost all LJDC members notice to appear for a hearing to decide whether the San Francisco Joint Labor Relations Committee (LRC) would give them another hearing on the matter of their discharge. The notice explained that the Joint LRC had waited almost a year to hold hearings because it felt the transcript of the Unemployment Insurance hearing would "expedite the actual disposition" of the fired men's claims of injustice. At Gordon's request, the Federal Court issued a restraining order against these hearings. The PMA-ILWU claim was that by calling these hearings they were making a sincere attempt to "arbitrate." In October, the question of whether or not to "arbitrate" the case is scheduled to be argued before the court.

Shortly, the ILWU-PMA lawyers will be appearing in Federal Court on yet another case. The May 15 Bulletin of ILWU Local 13, Port of Los Angeles, contains a statement signed by the President and Secretary-Treasurer announcing that the Local has filed suits in the United States District Court against the Coast Labor Relations

Committee to obtain relief from a special restrictive contract imposed upon that Local for allegedly conducting a wildcat strike. During the period when Bridges was trying to sell the Mechanization and Modernization Fund Contract in 1960, this most militant of ILWU ports was victimized by a contract which, among other things, legalizes the blacklisting of union members. As a member of the Coast Committee, Harry Bridges participated in this victimization without alerting any of the other ports about the injury occurring to one of the union's leading locals.

In still another port, a scandal that has been developing for over eight years is about to be aired. In Stockton, a small port less than 100 miles from San Francisco, the pilot program for the B man system started in 1956, three years before it was inaugurated in all West Coast ports. 110 of the men who became B men at that time, many of whom had already been on the front for five years, are now, eight to thirteen years of work later, still B men. They pay union dues and assessments, do the hard work and are allowed no voice in the union, no equal union protection. During strikes they are expected to walk the picket lines. In July 1963, they filed grievances with the Joint Coast LRC against the Stockton Joint LRC under the guidance of attorney John O. Fugazi. They seek upgrading to an A status and full union membership. They have been told that the Coast Arbitrator will hear them very soon.

It is obvious that the caste system or job trusting that already existed in Stockton was facilitated by the introduction of the B Man System. In other ports free of job trusting, the introduction of this sytem made an aristocracy of union members. It was with great resistance that the ILWU rank and file finally gave in to Bridges and allowed the formation of the first B List in San Francisco in 1959. They voted to bring in 400 and Bridges and the PMA registered over 700.

By June 1963, there were about 550 remaining of the original 700. After a long and exhausting fight, that B List was disposed of through promotion and deregistration. The port was without a B List, and the ranks showed resistance to carrying out what Bridges had committed them to—a second B List of about 500 men. Bridges' answer was publicly to accuse the San Francisco Local of "job trusting." He won this fight and 750 new B men were registered.

The original enthusiasm among the new B men for the Bridges

leadership in the ILWU was even more noticeable than it had been among the men of the first B List. The new B Men are now ending their first year as longshoremen. They have averaged one day of work per week. Promises and unemployment insurance have kept them going. They do only the hardest, dirtiest work, while the A men get full pay checks. Already there are signs of an impending campaign for equal rights.

It is easy to see why Bridges and St. Sure decided against allowing the men on the first B List, not promoted to A status, to remain on as B men. That would have hastened the disillusionment and rebellion of the second B List. The LJDC's campaign, however, will clarify and facilitate their fight.

Matters of this sort, once known only to members of the industry, their families and friends, are more and more topics of interest in labor, liberal and minority group circles in the Bay Area. The coverage in *The East Bay Labor Journal*, the AFL-CIO weekly with a circulation of over 40,000, is largely responsible for this. Then too, the first part of this essay was reprinted almost in full by a militant local Negro newspaper, *The Mallet*. This plus press and TV coverage received by the LJDC on several occasions has started what is really the most effective communication . . . word of mouth.

The basis for a successful drive was made possible when Rowland Watts, President of the Workers Defense League, announced that his organization was sponsoring the formation of a special WDL defense committee to aid the LJDC. Thus far, this committee is composed of Herman Benson, Dr. Thomas N. Burbridge, Matthew Clarke, Herbert Gold, Michael Harrington, Gordon Haskell, Nat Hentoff, Herbert Hill, Norman Hill, Paul Jacobs, Julius Jacobson, S. Martin Lipset, Bayard Rustin, Dr. Phillip Selznick, Rev. William Shirley, Harvey Swados and the WDL's Honorary President and Socialist Party leader, Norman Thomas.

The men of the LJDC are much less alone. Gone is the despair out of which they originally organized. Circumstances have forced upon them the necessity and privilege of fighting to root out the entire B List system. Their success would again allow the ILWU to restore to its banner the slogan long-removed: An Injury To One Is An Injury To All.

September 1964

1. This incident and the speeches made by both St. Sure and Bridges at the above mentioned conference were given much fuller coverage in an excellent, hard hitting article by Paul Jacobs, titled, "Harry, The Gag Man," *The New Leader,* July 6, 1964.

The Retreat of Harry Bridges

STANLEY WEIR

The process by which Harry Bridges, president of the International Longshoremen's and Warehousemen's Union (ILWU), has been destroying the myth of himself as a radical and progressive labor leader grinds on, dimming a career already in twilight. The latest episode in this saga of self-destruction began in August 1965 when Bridges sued 15 of the 18 members of a special defense committee, formed with the aid of the Workers Defense League in order to raise funds to help finance the deregistered longshoremen's struggle. This latest episode ended on December 18, 1969, four and one-half years later, when Bridges dropped that suit rather than go to trial with it—a suit that had served only to harass the committee, the Workers Defense League and the fired longshoremen.

For reasons unknown, Bridges never got around to suing three members of the special defense committee, namely Daniel Bell, Norman Hill and the late Norman Thomas. The 15 he did sue included such people as sociologists Philip Selznick and Seymour Martin Lipset; writers Herbert Gold, Nat Hentoff, Paul Jacobs and Harvey Swados; Herbert Hill, the NAACP's National Labor Secretary; Thomas Burbridge, former president of the San Francisco NAACP; Julius Jacobson, the editor of *New Politics* and Bayard Rustin of the A. Philip Randolph Institute.

In the first four years of lawsuit, Bridges's lawyers took

depositions from only two defendants, Burbridge and Rustin—the only blacks among the 15 defendants. And unlike most libel suits, in this one those being sued for libel were pressing for trial while the plaintiff, Harry Bridges, constantly sought to postpone it.

During the course of the libel suit, Bridges claimed that the defendants were "made up of a few professional 'revolutionaries,' writers and professional men, plus a few characters like Paul Jacobs, a man who has been an openly declared self-confessed enemy of the ILWU all the way back to the late 1930's."[1] The accusation that some are professional revolutionaries is revealing, coming from Bridges. It fits in with the attack by Morris Watson, former editor of *The Dispatcher,* against the 51 longshoremen at a press conference in 1963, claiming that many of the men were fired because of their "subversive backgrounds." It may also be related to the fact that Philip Selznick and Paul Jacobs have supported a number of militant movements in the Bay Area, such as the Berkeley Free Speech Movement (1964-1965), which Bridges failed to do.

Specifically, what were the allegedly libelous acts committed by the 15 sponsors of the longshoremen? They had allowed their names to be used in an appeal for funds to cover the legal expenses incurred by the men in trying to get their day in court. Bridges claimed that the appeal accused him of "practicing autocracy" and of colluding with the employers. It can be proved that Bridges and the employers did in effect collaborate to lock out these longshoremen and that Bridges did autocratically play a leading role in the frameup. Bridges also alleged that he and the ILWU were accused of racial discrimination. That allegation is a lie. The accusation was never made. The lie was circulated at the 1965 AFL-CIO convention in San Francisco by friends of Bridges in order to drain off support the framed men had obtained among unionists. While the lie was exposed, some harm may have been done to the longshoremen; it is still too soon to tell. The ILWU of San Francisco is anything but a "Jim Crow" local union. Nevertheless, 90 percent of the fired longshoremen are black and were thrown off the waterfront into a society with racist employment policies. What is more, their efforts to get decent jobs were further hampered by Bridges' televised accusations that they were "liars, chisellers and cheats."

What reason did Bridges give for withdrawing the libel suit? One big lie demands another. Thus, in *The Dispatcher* (December 16,

1969), he claims that the sponsors have admitted they were wrong and that changes made in the law by the Supreme Court in "recent years" make winning a libel suit impossible. That the defendants "admitted they were wrong" is a pathetically feeble lie. The truth is that the defendants were pressing hard to get the case tried in court and, in fact, had made arrangements to appear in court as scheduled in January. This is hardly symptomatic of defendants admitting to error.

Bridges' swipe at "recent" Supreme Court decisions, widely hailed by civil libertarians, which undermined his libel action has about it the aroma of Birch Society propaganda. The big lie here is easily nailed down. The Supreme Court decision to which Bridges refers—*New York Times* vs. *Sullivan*—was rendered in March 1964. Bridges filed his libel suit in August *1965*. What is more, the Supreme Court decision "that an extra heavy burden of proof" is needed to establish libel where public officials and personalities are involved, was based in important part on a Supreme Court case—*Bridges* vs. *California*—based on an appeal by Bridges from a charge of criminal contempt of court for criticizing a judge. Bridges took the case all the way to the Supreme Court to establish the principle of a person's privilege to criticize public figures and institutions.

Legally, to drop a libel case is to lose it. But one aspect of the libel suit remains. Bridges must now pay the court costs of the defendants. (It remains to be seen who is going to pay the costs: Bridges or the ILWU.)

With the libel suit obstruction eliminated, the 51 longshoremen are free to go into Federal District Court in San Francisco for the trial that the Ninth Circuit Court of Appeals and the U. S. Supreme Court have said they must have.[2] It took six and one-half years to win this right to a trial. Bridges is busy propagandizing the ILWU membership in an effort to rationalize the existence of this suit. For a long time *The Dispatcher* implied that the case was dead but now that it is coming to trial, Bridges barrages the members with the urgent news that it will cost them money. And it well may if the members allow Bridges to pass the costs on to them since some of the fired men, if they win the suit, may get a wage differential between what they have earned since being fired and what they would have earned working as longshoremen.

Bridges continues to tell the ILWU members that he does not know the identity of the deregistered men and yet he singles out this writer: "Funny part of it is I never met the bum in my life, never heard of him until the case came along, and, in fact, wouldn't recognize him right now if he turned up in my soup." (*The Dispatcher,* December 16, 1969.) The wisecrack is reminiscent of old Hollywood "B" gangster movies in which the suspect attempts to establish an alibi. But although a little humor and a gag can be a temporary salve for fear, Bridges can hardly expect the ILWU membership to take it seriously. Most members remember the confrontations on the floor at B meetings and know that I was the elected representative for the B men for three years. What is more, it is now well known that for some time the name "Weir" was a swear word in the offices of the international union headquarters, especially after the receipt of a letter to Bridges from James Baldwin in which Baldwin said that if I am "anti-progressive and anti-labor" then he [Baldwin] is "a dues-paying member of the Birch Society."

But more to the point, the gag is in bad taste because there is no humor in the destruction of people's lives. After all, men who can rig ship's gear and move cargo do not take lightly a return to shoeshine and busboy jobs. And wives who were at home caring for children now find themselves working as domestics or at home husbandless and on welfare. Then, too, we have learned that Ed Reed is dead. Maybe Bridges "never met the bum." He was a quiet, gentle man. We are told that exhaustion from long commutes to jobs far out of town brought death at a railroad crossing. This destructive process must be stopped and it can be stopped the day we return as first class citizens to the hiring hall that Bridges has said we are trying to destroy.

What a monstrous and cynical lie that is—that we would destroy the hiring hall! Bridges learned his tactics in a bad school and his own victimization did not lead him to help others avoid like treatment. Instead, he has used police state tactics to create victims of his own. Bridges, at least, had a public trial, was represented by lawyers and had the right to face unfriendly witnesses and produce friendly ones. We do not know where and when we were tried and found guilty, and at our appeal hearing on the afternoon of July 11, 1963, we were not even told the charges against us. The appeal jury was the same one that had found us guilty, in secret. This did not take place in a totalitarian society in the 1930s but in an office above Pier 24 in San Francisco in 1963. The truth is Bridges and his supporters saw in our victimization a way to intimidate others who might one day pose a vague challenge to his power. To remain in power has become Bridges' end and he has used any and every means to serve that end. Herbert Gold said it well on learning that Bridges had dropped the libel case. Gold, who as a teenager had donated his lunch money to defend Bridges against government attempts to deport him, said, "It's sad that a man who has been persecuted by the government, and defended by artists and intellectuals, should have spent his union's money and many men's time and money in four and one-half years of legal persecution of writers, artists, ministers and teachers whose offense was that they sought to help a group of longshoremen deprived of their jobs. It's as if, secure in his power, he wished to imitate bureaucratic tyranny."

We feel that our crime consisted in openly daring to criticize the so-called "mechanization" contract negotiated by Bridges in 1961. We have not changed our minds about that. Because we were subjected to "trial" in a Kafkaesque world does not mean we are willing to live in it. We will not recant. That contract is destroying the hiring hall. It has created a permanent non-union group of registered longshoremen who cannot afford to stand up for their rights on the job or in the hall. It has alienated young and old, and ranks from leaders. It is the existence of that contract and the weakened hiring hall that is Bridge's problem. Attempts to use the fired longshoremen to divert the attention of the membership from the state of the union are in vain because we cannot be separated from the question of the contract and the hiring hall; we are simply one of the manifestations of Bridges' dilemma.

March 1970

1. From Bridge's column, "On the Beam," in the ILWU publication *The Dispatcher*, July 30, 1969.

2. *Williams* v. *Pacific Maritime Ass'n et al.* 384 F.2d 935 (9th Cir. 1967), *cert. den.* 390 U.S. 981 (1967).

An Exchange:
Was Fred Ferrara Slandered?

FRED FERRARA / BURTON HALL

Editor's note: The exchange that follows between Fred Ferrara, President of the 10,000-member Chain Service Restaurant, Luncheonette and Soda Fountain Employees' Local 11 in New York City (affiliated with the Hotel and Restaurant Workers Union, AFL-CIO), and the editor of this collection, resulted from an article published earlier in *New Politics* (Spring 1967). The article, entitled "The Coalition Against Dishwashers," is omitted from this collection to avoid repetition; its arguments are expressed in much the same terms in other essays that are included here.

In "The Coalition Against Dishwashers," I discussed the practice of sweetheart dealing between employers and corrupt union officials. My essay reported that Ferrara had accepted employer bribes of at least $36,606, that testimony before the McClellan Committee indicated that Local 11 officers had looted the union's welfare funds of hundreds of thousands of dollars, and that these expressions of corruption were linked in some way to the absence of union democracy in Local 11—a union in which all rank-and-filers who had not previously served either as officers or on the executive board were barred from running for any office and in which the president had (and still has) power, without ratification from anyone, to bind the union to collective bargaining agreements negotiated with the employers by him and him alone.

I also briefly discussed the three-year contract that Ferrara had signed on October 1, 1966 with the huge Schrafft's restaurant chain to cover some 4,000 workers in New York and northern New Jersey. At the time the contract was to be signed, Ferrara was hiding out in St. Clare's Hospital to avoid testifying before the McClellan Committee, which was then investigating the racketeering activities of labor "consultant" Jack McCarthy. However, he managed to leave the hospital long enough to sign the contract, and then returned.

The contract—which served as a model for Ferrara's subsequent contracts with the White Tower and Bickford's chains—purported to bar all strikes and work stoppages not only for the duration of the contract but *forever*. It allowed the employer to discipline any worker who participated in a work stoppage or a slowdown (even after the contract's expiration), and further provided that the employer's discipline, whatever it might be, would be "final and binding." All disputes that might arise other than such "final and binding" disciplinary matters were to be disposed of by the "impartial arbitrator," who turned out to be none other than Jack McCarthy's partner in the labor "consultancy" business, J. Kenneth O'Connor. O'Connor would even have power to arbitrate any disputes arising in the negotiation of a new contract after the expiration of the current one—in other words, to write the new contract himself.

Mr. Ferrara wrote to the editor of *New Politics,* protesting my comments about him. The following exchange includes his letter and my reply.

I: FRED FERRARA PROTESTS

In his article entitled "The Coalition against Dishwashers" Burton Hall rambles far and wide, violently condemning the constitution, organizational structure, eligibility rules and general conduct and philosophy of most of the American labor movement. Such vast topics are perhaps for historians and legal experts and would certainly require much more space for opinions than you would appreciate.

Mr. Hall's complaints are vague and obscure and suggest no remedial substitutes. A curious reader might inquire from Mr. Hall as to which organizations, labor or otherwise, he has been associated with, where there are such things as leadership, rules and regulations and procedures governing the conduct and affairs of members?

As one of many former dishwashers, now holding positions of leadership in local unions in the hotel and restaurant industry, I should like to comment on Mr. Hall's very grave charges against our union, its officers and myself in particular, as these appeared in *New Politics.*

Hall makes some shocking charges in his article:

1. Local 11's leaders have looted the Welfare Fund of hundreds of thousands of dollars.

2. Local 11 has negotiated sweetheart agreements with employers in return for thousands of dollars in bribes.

3. Fred Ferrara, President of Local 11 accepted some $36,606 (at least) in bribes from employers in return for negotiating sweetheart agreements.

4. Ferrara was hiding out in St. Clare's Hospital during the McClellan Committee hearings, presumably to avoid answering questions.

If Mr. Hall is slyly reporting these charges as possibly having been suggested by the McClellan Committee, then the best that can be said about him is that he is a poor reporter. If, on the other hand, Mr. Hall is presenting these charges as facts, then Hall is guilty of sheer and unadulterated slander!

For the record, I categorically deny the truth of any of these allegations. I challenge Mr. Hall to present evidence and facts: which "sweetheart contracts"? what companies bribed union officials or myself? when and where? how and where have Local 11 leaders "looted the local's welfare funds of hundreds of thousands of dollars"? what illness, exactly, necessitated my being in the hospital during the McClellan Committee hearings?

If Mr. Hall is prepared to tell us something to substantiate his charges, we will be happy to hear from him. Since we know that these statements are entirely without foundation, we ask Mr. Hall to apologize to our officers and myself and to retract the specific accusations as they appear in his article.

As for Mr. Hall's impressions of the no strike—no lock-out clause, and his apparent conviction that he, alone, is working to assist and free the down-trodden restaurant employees—Hall is pitifully ignorant of the history of hotel and restaurant union organizations in New York City, of the millions of dollars spent, of the bitter strikes and long sacrifices, of court injunctions and elections and of the remarkable standards achieved for the employees through our unions.

Especially is Hall totally ignorant and unaware of the provisions of the no strike—no lock-out clause he refers to and with the experience and operation of the institution of permanent arbitration, as it has applied in our industry, to the tremendous satisfaction, benefit and greater security of our members.

We don't recall when Hall was chosen to protect the dishwashers or when he was elected to office in Local 11. In our own defense, we deeply resent his blind, malicious interference in our affairs. We look forward to finding the apology and retraction in your next issue.

Fred Ferrara, President, Local 11
Hotel & Restaurant Workers Union

II: BURTON HALL REPLIES

The McClellan Committee, or more accurately the Permanent Subcommittee on Investigations of the Senate's Committee on Government Operations, subpoenaed Fred Ferrara, alias Fred Gladstone, to testify before it at its hearings commencing September 27, 1966, in connection with an investigation formally entitled, "Labor Racketeering Activities of Jack McCarthy and National Consultants Associated, Ltd." On the day before Ferrara was to appear, a doctor acting on Ferrara's behalf submitted to the Subcommittee an affidavit dated September 26, 1966 which, after identifying the doctor, stated:

I admitted Mr. Fred Gladstone to St. Clare's Hospital on September 25, 1966, under my professional care for a medical condition. Mr. Gladstone's physical condition is such as he is unable to appear as a witness before the Subcommittee.

The doctor's accompanying letter identified "Mr. Fred Gladstone" as Fred Ferrara. But neither it nor the affidavit explained what Ferrara's supposed "medical condition" was, or what there was about his "physical condition" that prevented him from testifying before the Subcommittee.

The Subcommittee's hearings began on September 27 and continued on September 28 and October 4; the subpoena served on Ferrara remained operative as to all dates on which the hearings were held. Yet Ferrara failed to appear. His "medical condition" did not stop him from leaving St. Clare's Hospital on October 1, 1966, to sign the permanent no-strike Schrafft's contract; one wonders why it should prevent him from appearing before the Subcommittee on October 4.

Because of Ferrara's failure to appear, and because most of Jack McCarthy's other associates who did appear pleaded the Fifth Amendment to the questions put to them, the Subcommittee had to get most of its information from employers and from public officials who had investigated one or more aspects of McCarthy's racketeering activities. As a result, the information it adduced is uneven. But the Subcommittee learned, among other things, that Ferrara had been closely associated with McCarthy for at least six years; that in 1960 Ferrara had "recommended" to the president of the huge Restaurant Associates company that they hire McCarthy as labor "consultant"; and that the company thereupon hired McCarthy and also hired McCarthy's close associate, J. Kenneth O'Connor, as its attorney for labor relations matters. The company paid McCarthy $7,800 per year from early 1961 to mid-1963, when it had to drop him because of publicity arising from the New York District Attorney's investigation into McCarthy's activities. Whatever services McCarthy performed for the company were so mysterious that Austin Cox, the company's labor relations representative (who had also been hired upon Ferrara's recommendation), didn't learn of McCarthy's existence until April 1963, when the District Attorney demanded certain documents in connection with the investigation.

While all this was going on, Ferrara, as president of Local 11, continued to represent the employees of luncheonettes operated by Restaurant Associates, including the Rikers' and Zum-Zum chains, as well as the Brasserie and Trattoria, in collective bargaining with the company.

That much, all by itself, would make Ferrara's role as bargainer on behalf of employees represented by Local 11 more than a little suspect. But the matter is made more than suspect by the revelations that Ferrara, as "partner" of Jack McCarthy's brother-in-law, Joseph Maake, received $36,606 from two cleaning and waxing firms known as Purity Maintenance Co., Inc., and Preferred Maintenance Co., Inc., from 1960 to 1965. In 1965, Ferrara sold his stock in the two companies to McCarthy's mother for an additional sum. Meanwhile,

McCarthy was busy "recommending" to employers who retained him as a labor "consultant" that they hire the two firms and pay them large sums of money—and Ferrara was busy negotiating as the representative of employees with firms that retained McCarthy.

Ferrara had ample opportunity to appear before the McClellan Subcommittee and explain his relationship to McCarthy; instead, he pleaded that his "physical condition" prevented his appearance. His partner, Maake, also had ample opportunity. But Maake, upon being called to the stand, merely gave his name and, when asked whether he was represented by counsel, said that he was (his attorney was J. Kenneth O'Connor); from then on he pleaded the Fifth Amendment to every substantive question that was put to him.

Typical of Maake's performance were the following exchanges:

Senator Jackson. Mr. Maake, will you please inform the subcommittee concerning the background of the Purity and Preferred Building Maintenance companies?

Mr. Maake. I refuse to answer that question on the grounds that it may tend to incriminate me.

Senator Jackson. Is this to say that if you were to give a truthful answer to that question, that it would tend to incriminate you?

Mr. Maake. It might.

Senator Jackson. It is the subcommittee's understanding, Mr. Maake, that Fred Ferrara, president of Local No. 11, Hotel & Restaurant Workers Union, was a partner with you in these two companies from 1960 to 1965.

Testimony has indicated that he received in excess of $36,606 from these companies from 1960 to 1965. What services for your company did he perform?

Mr. Maake. I refuse to answer that question on the grounds that it may tend to incriminate me.

Senator Jackson. Are you aware that Ferrara would recommend to employers that they hire McCarthy as a labor consultant?

Mr. Maake. I refuse to answer that question on the grounds that it may tend to incriminate me. . . .

Senator Jackson. Was this method the one utilized by Mr. Jack McCarthy to pay off Fred Ferrara as president of Local No. 11 for favorable treatment during the contract negotiations with employers that hired McCarthy as labor consultant?

Mr. Maake. I refuse to answer that question on the ground that it may tend to incriminate me.

Senator Jackson. In 1965, Mr. Ferrara sold all his stock in Purity and Preferred Building Maintenance companies to Jack McCarthy's

mother who put the stock in the name of McCarthy's children.
Would you furnish details concerning this transaction?

Mr. Maake. I refuse to answer on the grounds that it may tend to
incriminate me.

It seems apparent that Ferrara's "physical condition" consisted in
his disinclination to face the kind of questions that Senator Jackson
put to Maake. And he had good reason for that disinclination.

The story of the "depletion" of Local 11's Welfare Trust Fund
was given to the Subcommittee by James J. Higgins, supervising
insurance examiner for the New York State Insurance Department,
which has jurisdiction over the Fund. Higgins's testimony was
lengthy and detailed; he described how the Fund's administrator
(Local 11 Business Representative Murray Solomon) and its trustees
(half of whom were Local 11 officers) had depleted the Fund
through three separate avenues: through the medical plan, the dental
plan, and the optical plan. Through the optical plan alone, said
Higgins, the Fund's assets were depleted of the sum of $156,564.72
from 1960 to 1965, through the device of paying out an average of
$46.21 per pair for single-vision eyeglasses that should have cost the
Fund only $6.19 per pair.

The Fund also paid some $340,000 under its medical plan to a
certain Dr. Epstein from April 1, 1957 to April 1, 1966 without
having made cost studies, comparisons or requests for competitive
bids and without keeping any records of utilization or requesting
access to Dr. Epstein's records. When the Insurance Department,
investigating the matter, asked Dr. Epstein to make his records
available to it, Dr. Epstein said he needed the trustees' authorization,
and they failed to give such authorization. The Insurance Department thereafter subpoenaed Dr. Epstein to testify, but he refused to
answer pertinent questions or to divulge any information as to
utilization, ultimately basing his refusal on the doctor-patient
privilege. In other words, he asserted the privilege as his reason for
refusing to say whether he performed any services at all!

The third avenue by which the Fund's assets were depleted, its
dental plan, is tied up with the colorful story of the Amalgamated
Dental Plan, Inc. (ADP); on a now-defunct outfit to which the Local
11 Welfare Trust Fund paid $60,000 per year for the two years of its
existence. All that ADP did in return was to furnish a list of
"participating dentists." ADP announced in its circular that the

dentists would provide free mouth X-rays and free tooth cleaning (once a year), but even this "fringe benefit" was provided by the dentists themselves as a come-on: ADP did not pay them and it appears that they did not know that ADP was receiving large amounts of money in connection with the scheme. The Insurance Department's examiners found that "Actual utilization by the [union] members appeared to be so negligible as to be virtually non-existent."

ADP received a total of $200,200 from Local 11's Fund and from three other union welfare funds. Out of this it paid five convicted bookmakers total salaries of $16,800 and it paid the ubiquitous Jack McCarthy $20,800, or $900 per month from October 1962 to August 1964. The testimony before the McClellan Subcommittee indicates that the payments to McCarthy constituted a kickback for his influence in bringing welfare funds with which he was associated, either as "consultant" or otherwise, into ADP. Senator Jackson summed up the testimony in examining McCarthy:

Senator Jackson. We have heard evidence, Mr. McCarthy, that you have been successful in receiving union welfare funds through a phony dental plan called the Amalgamated Dental Plan that received approximately $200,000 for nothing more than referring union members to certain dentists.

The plan was run by Dr. Goldin and Sam Kushner. You received from that plan in excess of $20,000 during the 2-year period that this plan was in existence. It is interesting to note the local unions connected with this plan.

.... Fred Ferrara, president of Local No. 11 of the Hotel & Restaurant Workers Union, was a major factor in bringing that local union into the dental plan.

Ferrara was a business partner of your brother-in-law, Joseph Maake, in a cleaning and waxing firm.

Can you tell us, Mr. McCarthy, if any of these officials received kickbacks from you or the dental plan for bringing their unions into this racket?

Mr. McCarthy. Senator, I refuse to answer that question on the grounds that the answer may tend to incriminate me.

The evidence in the Subcommittee's record does not clearly indicate how much of a "major factor" Ferrara was in bringing Local 11's Fund into the ADP; Senator Jackson's conclusion on that point would appear to be based on the obvious fact that Ferrara effectively dominates the administrative machinery of the local union and of its Fund. But the evidence as to improprieties and depletion of the Fund's assets is overwhelming. The Subcommittee, in its formal "Findings and Conclusions," found the Fund's Administrator, Local 11 Business Representative Murray Solomon, "guilty of gross irregularities and improprieties in the administration of [the Fund's] dental, optical and medical plans"; it found as well that Solomon had "demonstrated a complete disregard of the fiduciary responsibilities of [his] office"; and it declared that Solomon "should be summarily removed" from his position. Those findings and conclusions, embodied in the Subcommittee's report, were handed down almost a year ago. Solomon continues to hold office both as Fund Administrator and as Business Representative of Local 11.

Shortly before the Subcommittee held its hearings, the New York Insurance Department brought an administrative proceeding against Solomon and the trustees of the Local 11 Welfare Trust Fund, charging wrongful depletion in the sum of $156,564.72, basing the proceeding solely on the expenditures through the optical plan. Actual hearings held by the Department in 1967 have since been completed and the hearing officer's decision is awaited.

But while the Insurance Department's hearings were still going on, in September 1967, Ferrara distributed to the members of Local 11 a letter in which he boasted that "there is absolutely not one single charge of any description now pending or ever made in the past, by any agency, against any officer of Local 11." The letter was signed by 15 officers of Local 11 in addition to Ferrara; six of the officers who signed it were at the time and still are individually-named respondents (i.e., defendants) in the proceedings brought by the New York Insurance Department involving depletion of the Fund's assets. Ferrara's boast, in other words, was less than candid; but that, it would seem, is his style.

The apparent complicity of employers and union officials, as trustees of the Local 11 Welfare Trust Fund, in arranging the depletion of the Fund's assets to the tune of several hundreds of thousands of dollars suggests—even aside from the omnipresence of Jack McCarthy in Local 11's affairs—that complicity in the mishandling of all that money may have had something to do with the negotiating of soft contracts by Local 11. Just what bearing it had or may have had is unclear—but it is plain and obvious that Ferrara, as president of Local 11, has negotiated and continues to negotiate extraordinarily soft contracts. The notorious Schrafft's contract, now applied to the employees of Bickford's and White Tower, and prospectively to be applied to all other employees represented by Local 11, may serve as an example. Aside from its other peculiarities (mentioned in the introduction to this exchange), it provided for a wage rate that for some nine months in 1967 was actually *below* the New York State minimum wage for restaurant industry employees. It permitted the employer to fire any employee for any reason upon 24-hour notice to the union and permitted the employer to fire an employee even without notice for such reasons as "gross insubordination" or "offensive language or conduct" or for leaving the work place without his supervisor's permission. And the employee's only recourse was to appeal to the "impartial arbitrator," J. Kenneth O'Connor, who figured as "director" of Jack McCarthy's "consultant" firm, National Consultants Associated, Ltd.

The mere mention of facts such as these, says Fred Ferrara, amounts to "blind, malicious interference in our affairs." Ferrara complains that I was not chosen by anybody—not by Ferrara anyway—to protect dishwashers, nor was I elected to office in Local 11. In other words, Ferrara is opposed, with all the fervor of an Alabama sheriff, to "outside agitators." He has reason, just as an Alabama sheriff has reason.

April 1968

Postscript: On April 3, 1968, the Deputy Superintendent of Insurance for New York State who served as trial examiner in the proceeding concerning Local 11's Welfare Trust Fund, handed down his decision. It found that the Fund's assets were depleted through excessive payments for single-vision eyeglasses in the sum of $138,130.90 during the years 1960 through 1965. Among the 12 trustees whom it finds responsible for the depletion (the whole or varying parts of it, depending on their terms of office as trustees) are Local 11's Executive Manager, William Donovan; the Local's Secretary-Treasurer, Arthur Russell; its General Organizer, Elmer

Hauck; its General Business Agent, George Papalexis; and Business Agents John Leonidas and Murray Solomon. It orders that Solomon be removed both as trustee and as Administrator of the Fund, and that he be fined $2,500, the maximum fine authorized by the New York Insurance Law. It seems almost unbelievable but, as this book goes to press, Ferrara is still President of Local 11 and the main pillars of his machine—George Papalexis, Julius Kriedman, Elmer Hauck and William Donovan—are still in office with him. This is so despite the fact that:

1. In November 1970 Ferrara and retired Local 11 Secretary-Treasurer Arthur Russell were convicted in federal court on three counts of embezzlement from the union (the sums embezzled amounting to approximately $36,000), four counts of filing false financial reports with the government, plus counts charging an illegal loan to another union officer and failure to report the loan. In December Ferrara was given suspended sentences on these various counts totaling 14 years in prison, plus an unsuspended sentence of six months, plus three years' probation and an order to make restitution to the union in the sum of $17,000. Russell got an eight-year suspended sentence plus a restitution order of $5,000. Execution of the sentences is delayed pending their appeals.

2. Ferrara, Russell, Papalexis, Hauck and a former Local 11 business agent are awaiting trial in federal court, currently scheduled for August 26, 1971, on charges of receiving some $15,000 in bribes from the Walgreen drug chain. The background is that in 1964 Ferrara signed a contract with Walgreen which reduced employee benefits: in particular, it cut out the free meals allowed to employees under the earlier contract and gave the employees only a $3 weekly wage increase.

3. Donovan has been convicted in New York's criminal court for perjury in connection with testimony to the grand jury in which he denied knowledge of a plot to bribe an employee of the New York State Insurance Department. Originally sentenced to five years in jail, he is awaiting re-sentencing.

Law, Democracy and the Unions

BURTON HALL

Should unions be democratic? The question seems pointless. Unionism is a struggle for democracy, a struggle to democratize the industrial regime. But what—and here is the rub—if democracy inside the unions is suppressed? Who, if anybody, shall step in and correct the situation—and in what manner shall it be corrected?

There are two possibilities: either protect the right of rank and file members to participate in governing the unions, or turn the supervision and ultimate control of the unions over to some government (or other) official and entrust the unions' future course to his "special knowledge and discretion," whatever it may be. The first means to restore unions to that democracy which is their purpose and their strength; the second means to compound union bureaucratism with government bureaucratism and render the unions subservient to government manipulation.

Over the past six years these issues have been fought out in Congress, in the courts, and in the conference rooms of the United States Department of Labor. The results are frightening. For in December 1964, at the urging of the AFL-CIO and of the government of the United States, the Supreme Court announced in *Calhoon* v. *Harvey*,[1] with Justice Douglas dissenting, that the *second* of the alternatives is now the law of the land. Union members' democratic rights are *not* to be protected, said the Court, and the rank and file is *not* to be trusted to govern the unions. Instead, the "special knowledge and discretion" of the Secretary of Labor is to be "utilized" in order to determine when, where and to what degree the choice of officials is to be subjected to the approval of the union membership.

To a generation of radicals, liberals and rank and file union reformers who have struggled to find a way of bringing democracy back into the unions, the new dispensation cannot fail to appear as the blighting of their hopes. In 1959, it seemed that Congress had at last established the democratic rights of union members, by enacting a "bill of rights" which guaranteed their rights within their unions and enabled them to protect those rights themselves. How could an honest effort at union reform be turned into the subjection of unions to manipulation by the government? And what, after this victory-turned-defeat, is left of the demand for union reform, the demand for protection of union members' democratic rights?

In seeking an answer, let's first go back a few years. The Wagner Act of 1935 included a formal prohibition on employer-domination of unions; other than that it made no provision as to internal union democracy. Instead, one of its unintended side-effects was to encourage such bureaucratic and sweetheart tendencies as existed in the legitimate unions; for, by protecting each employer-recognized or National Labor Relations Board-certified union against displacement and competing representation, it made the established union leadership less dependent upon the support of the rank and file workers. Bureaucratism hardly needed any such encouragement. It had already appeared to one degree or another in many unions. Its characteristic expressions—an over-friendly attitude toward employers and public officials; the suppression and repression of the union rank and file—have been familiar and notorious since the end of the last century. But not until recent decades has bureaucratism—and the consequent struggle, within the unions, between the rank and file membership and the union officials—become the central issue of the labor movement.

So it was that, in the 1940s and 1950s, one current of liberal opinion led a campaign for union reform. The American Civil Liberties Union (ACLU), beginning in 1942, called for legislation (including a labor union "bill of rights") that would protect the democratic rights of union members inside the unions. Its arguments were articulate and specific: they boiled down to the proposition that only a union which is itself democratic can bring democracy into the industrial regime. At first, there was little response. But when the McClellan Committee's investigation, in the later 1950s, brought union bureaucratism, sweetheart agreements and the suppression of union members' rights to the attention of the mass public, the ACLU's arguments took on overwhelming force.

"Much that is elicited in the Committee's findings of misconduct by union officials," said the McClellan Committee in its Interim Report, "can be substantially improved, in the Committee's view, by a revitalization of the democratic processes of labor unions." Obviously, the first step was to protect the democratic rights of union members. But the original bill, sponsored by Senators Kennedy and Ervin, as reported out of the Senate Committee on Labor (of which McClellan was not a member) contained only the mildest provisions regarding union democracy and no protection of union members' rights. Its emphasis was upon financial "disclosure" and reporting; other matters were treated almost as afterthoughts.

The only provision dealing with union elections—now contained in Title IV of the Labor Reform Act (i.e., the Kennedy-Ervin bill as amended and enacted)—did set down some of the minimal standards of democracy in elections. It did not even pretend to protect the rights of members or enforce these standards. Instead, it authorized the Secretary of Labor to use them in determining, *after* an election had been conducted, whether violations of those standards had been so extreme or widespread as to have affected the outcome of the election. If he should find that they had, he was directed to bring suit to set the results of the election aside and order it to be re-run. This procedure was to replace (and, under the Act, does replace) the rights that union members had previously enjoyed to bring suit in state courts to challenge the results of elections already completed. But it was not to foreclose members from challenging election procedures in future elections, whether by suit in state courts or anywhere else.

Whether good or bad in itself, that "reform" was most certainly a weak one. When the Kennedy-Ervin bill reached the Senate floor for debate, Senator McClellan (joined by a curious mélange of mostly conservative Republicans and opposed to a man by Establishment liberals) attacked it as inadequate. McClellan urged the Senate to adopt a "bill of rights" to protect union members' democratic rights within their unions.

Senator McClellan's proposed "bill of rights" was anything but a polished product of careful draftsmanship. For one thing, it relied for protection upon the Secretary of Labor, surely as weak and indifferent a reed as could have been chosen. But the "bill of rights'" more fiery opponents—chiefly, the AFL-CIO hierarchy and its political satellites—produced an uproar as soon as the Senate adopted it, and the uproar enabled the Senate, a few days later, to replace Senator McClellan's "bill of rights" with a rewritten and stronger "bill of rights" proposed by Senators Kuchel, Clark, Neuberger, Church and five others. The "Kuchel Substitute," among other improvements, made the rights of members enforceable by the members themselves, through suit in federal courts. As Senator Clark remarked, "it takes the Federal bureaucracy out of this bill of rights and leaves its enforcement to union members, aided by the courts." And the rights it guaranteed to union members included not only freedom of speech and assembly but also the equal rights to nominate candidates, to vote in union elections and referendums and to participate in union meetings—and to do so "subject to reasonable rules and regulations" in the unions' own constitutions and bylaws.

This occurred during the early consideration of what is now the Labor Reform Act. Before the bill became an Act it suffered many changes, even a change in popular name (which occurred when Congressmen Landrum and Griffin tacked onto it a string of Taft-Hartley "tougheners" which had nothing to do with union reform or union democracy). But as enacted, the new Act retained in curious juxtaposition the two proposals concerned with union democracy: the provisions of the original Kennedy-Ervin bill (Title IV of the Act) which authorized the Secretary of Labor to challenge the results of completed elections under certain unusual circumstances; and the union members' "bill of rights," now Title I of the Act, which the Senate had added to the bill.

The two titles could not (it would seem) conflict with each other since they approach the matter of union elections from different directions, one attacks the results of elections already completed (when it is too late to protect union members' rights with regard to them) while the other seeks to protect union members' rights in the future—specifically, in future elections. But they represent opposing political attitudes and vastly different political tendencies. Title IV places the power and responsibility to reform the unions in the hands of the Secretary of Labor—while Title I places that power and responsibility in the hands of the union rank and file. And between those contrary political tendencies there has been a very substantial conflict in recent years.

The principal victories for reform, under the Act, have been won under Title I (the "bill of rights") with regard to those rights not directly related to union elections. In a series of cases presenting fact-situations typical of conditions inside most bureaucratized unions the courts have (and, with increasing consistency, still do) enjoined union officials from expelling or otherwise disciplining members for having criticized them. Thus a federal court enjoined the officials of the Seafarers' International Union (SIU) from expelling a member for having introduced a resolution at a union meeting calling for reform of the union's shipping rules.[2] Similarly, another federal court enjoined the New York Painters' District Council No. 9 from depriving a member of his union rights as discipline for having criticized, in a leaflet he distributed to the membership, a local union President-Business Agent's mishandling of checks drawn on the union's account.[3] So, too, with expulsion of members from the American Bakery and Confectionery Workers Union for having called their local union's president a "dictator."

But the nerve center of union democracy is the electoral process and it is here that the contrary political tendencies of the two titles come into conflict. Should union members be enabled to protect their rights to nominate candidates and to vote? Should they be entitled to challenge any rules and regulations which unreasonably interfere with their exercise of those rights, or which totally negate those rights? Or should their only protection be to challenge the results of an election *after it has been completed* and to hope that the Secretary of Labor will conclude that the election results should be set aside?

That issue was presented by the argument that the two Titles "contradict" each other, that the ability of the Secretary of Labor to cause the results of completed elections to be set aside must necessarily foreclose the courts or the members themselves from protecting their rights in current or future elections. On its face, the argument seems almost childish. But it has been championed by some rather imposing social forces. First, by the separate union officials; next by the AFL-CIO itself; then by spokesmen for the government of the United States; and finally by the Supreme Court of the United States.

The issue arose in several cases, in which rank and file members sought to challenge electoral rules and regulations which effectively deprived them of their rights under Title I. But the case in which the issue has been decided—and as a result of which union members have been stripped of all directly enforceable democratic rights regarding elections—arose in regard to a small union of what might be called "labor aristocrats," the Marine Engineers Beneficial Association (MEBA). That union was beset, from 1949 to 1959, with an intensive attack pressed against it by the Seafarers' International Union. After two major MEBA strikes had been broken and MEBA's jobs and contractual rights on three major shipping lines had been lost to the SIU affiliate, MEBA's officials surrendered. They "merged" MEBA with the SIU's subsidiary, allowing the SIU to take control of the new, "merged" MEBA. To make the surrender safe against the MEBA membership, the "merged" MEBA abolished all local unions and divided itself into three more easily manipulable "districts." The SIU's subsidiary became one of the three districts, District No. 2; the other two—District 1 and the Pacific Coast District—comprised the old MEBA membership on the East (Atlantic and Gulf) and West Coasts respectively. Officials were appointed to govern the districts and they "promulgated" bylaws under which they did the governing.

The conversion to district structure became effective January 1, 1961; meanwhile, the chief purpose of the "merger"—to facilitate the wholesale transfer of former MEBA jobs and bargaining rights to what now became District No. 2 (the SIU's subsidiary)—proceeded apace: the SIU subsidiary had numbered not more than 300 members at the time of the "merger"; by 1964 it exceeded 3,000 members.

The former MEBA members began to protest. In the Pacific Coast District they even won some support from their appointed officials, who conducted a running opposition skirmish against the national officials of the "merged" MEBA and against the SIU's domination. But on the Atlantic and Gulf Coasts the members' protests were suppressed by national officials who had conveniently appointed *themselves* to serve as President and Secretary-Treasurer of District No. 1.

This happy arrangement could proceed only for a limited period, since the law requires that every local labor organization conduct elections every three years. So the districts' first elections were scheduled for the fall of 1963, to follow the National MEBA elections which were to be held in the summer of 1963. But the officers took precautions: in March 1963 they met in convention and amended MEBA's constitution to make rank and file electoral opposition virtually impossible. Already, the districts' "promulgated" bylaws limited each rank and file member's nominating rights to the right of nominating *only* himself. The new amendments extended this limitation to national offices as well—and, in addition, prohibited most rank and file members from nominating even themselves. This latter prohibition was imposed via a series of eligibility restrictions, one of which required that a candidate for any national office or district presidency must have already served as a full-time paid official and members who had been ashore for any considerable period of time in recent years were prohibited from running for any office at all.

It was then that suit was brought. Three District No. 1 members challenged the nominations-and-eligibility requirements on the ground that they prohibited most rank and file members from nominating any candidate at all, surely a complete infringement of their rights under Title I to nominate candidates. MEBA's attorneys countered with the argument that nominations and eligibility requirements were "Title IV rights," since nomination and eligibility were both mentioned in the election standards adverted to in Title IV, and that the members should be barred from protecting such rights under any other title. Surprisingly, the district court accepted that argument and declared that it had no jurisdiction over the members' suit. But on the members' appeal, the federal Court of Appeals unanimously reversed and held that—regardless of whether an election in which members were deprived of their right to nominate candidates might or might not be subsequently upset under Title IV—the members were entitled to assert and protect those rights in advance of the election under the "bill of rights" Title I. Having held that there was jurisdiction to consider the plaintiffs' claim, the Court went on to find that the members' rights to nominate candidates in fact had been infringed; indeed, said the Court, the infringement was so extreme that it "would have been deemed invalid at common law, long before the LMRDA [the Labor Reform Act] ."

But all this was preliminary to the main event. The MEBA officials raised the claim once more of a "contradiction" between Title I and Title IV—and they raised it to the Supreme Court of the United States. They asked the Supreme Court to review the case—not on the merits, but only on the question of whether the federal court did or did not have jurisdiction to consider the members' complaint—and the Supreme Court agreed (in January 1964) to hear it. The case was argued in October 1964 and on December 7, 1964, the Court dropped its bombshell: it declared that union members could not protect their democratic rights in or with regard to union elections by any method other than the politically and bureaucratically tortuous, post-election path that leads to the Secretary of Labor's door.   The issues argued—between the MEBA members and the MEBA officials—were simple: whether or not the fact that nominations procedures and eligibility requirements are mentioned in Title IV must necessarily preclude any pre-election remedy for infringement of members' rights to nominate candidates that might be brought under Title I. What made the case of interest—before the final decision—was the alignment of forces as amici curiae (or "friends of the court"). Shortly after the Supreme Court had determined to consider the case, the ACLU and the Workers Defense League decided to enter the case as amici curiae on the side of the union members. On the side of the MEBA officials, as amici curiae, were the AFL-CIO and then, somewhat later, the government of the United States.

The AFL-CIO submitted a brief, as "friend of the court," which called for a "compartmentalized approach" to the Labor Reform Act. Title IV—and under it, the Secretary of Labor—was to be assigned a full jurisdictional monopoly on the protection of any and all electoral rights that were to be protected at all. Union officials, said the AFL-CIO, should be encouraged "to police [their] own election standards and procedures" and to do so without "intrusion" by members' suits in the courts. Such a liberal, laissez-faire approach would "ensure the knowledgeable and responsible union leadership needed to advance the best interests of the union's membership." If some outsider had to poke his nose into the way in which union elections are conducted, after the election was over, it had best be, said the AFL-CIO, the Secretary of Labor—because his "expert's appraisal" could be counted on "to avoid improper interference."

The Secretary, it turned out, agreed with this flattering view of his "expert's appraisal." His viewpoint, translated into legal argument by the government's Solicitor General (on behalf of the United States, as amicus curiae), was that the Court should "center in the Secretary control over litigation involving the substantive rules under which union elections are conducted" by nullifying the "bill of rights'" protection of members' electoral rights. And the Court went along with that argument.

According to the Court, "Section 402 of Title IV . . . sets up an exclusive method for protecting [electoral] rights, by permitting an individual member to file a complaint with the Secretary of Labor challenging the validity of any election because of violations of Title IV." Thus, all electoral rights become "Title IV rights," which can not be protected except by the procedures of Title IV. "It is apparent that Congress decided to utilize the special knowledge and discretion of the Secretary of Labor," said the Court, "in order best to serve the public interest."

Now let's take a look at that "special knowledge and discretion" and the manner in which it is exercised. Of all politically appointed government officials, the Secretary of Labor is the closest to the union officialdom. His appointment is, as a rule, conditioned upon his political acceptability to those union officials who support the administration and his role, largely, is to round up "labor support" for the administration. Small wonder, then, that among the most important of the suits brought by the Republican Secretary of Labor, in the early days of the Labor Reform Act, were those brought under Title IV against certain former CIO union officials allied with the Democratic Party. Small wonder, too, that when the Democratic administration took office shortly thereafter, those suits were voluntarily dismissed before trial. And it should occasion little surprise that the Democratic labor secretaries have concentrated their attention, so far as Title IV suits are concerned, upon (a) the Teamsters' Union and other independents, (b) those few, former AFL unions whose officials are or were allied with the Republican Party and (c) rebellious or maverick locals of AFL-CIO unions with whose national officials the administration is on friendly terms.

Influence in politics is a two-way street. The government official who, for reasons of political friendliness, uses his "discretion" to go easy on a union official today will quite probably ask for a proof of the official's political friendliness tomorrow. Indeed, over the past few years, more has been asked of union officials and more has been given by them. To travel much further down that path would mean total surrender of the unions' political autonomy and their submission to outright government manipulation.

The deprivation of union members' electoral rights and the violation of the electoral standards prescribed by Title IV are widespread throughout the union establishment—in those segments which are politically "friendly" as well as those which are "unfriendly" to any given administration. The Secretary, therefore, has ample scope to make political hay out of his "special knowledge and discretion." Especially so if recourse to the Secretary of Labor is to be—as, under the Supreme Court's ruling in the *Calhoon* case, it is—the rank and file union member's *only* protection against unfair election procedures. For under those conditions, the Secretary has—in his "special knowledge and discretion"—the sole power to impose or desist from imposing "democracy" (in measured doses) upon any union officialdom.

On this issue, too, the case of the marine engineers is illustrative. The Court of Appeals' ruling that District No. 1's combination of nomination and eligibility requirements infringed the rights of members to nominate candidates made it clear that each of MEBA's 1963 elections was invalid, since substantially the same combination of nomination and eligibility requirements was in force in all of them. Particularly so in the National MEBA election—for the national MEBA constitution, in addition to limiting each member to the right of self-nomination only, declared that any member who had not previously served as a full-time, paid official could not be eligible for candidacy to *any* national office. As a result, only 47 of National MEBA's 10,000 members were eligible for office (and most of them were incumbent officials). Regardless of what the Supreme Court ultimately said as to jurisdiction under Title I, it was and is apparent that the restrictions on nomination and eligibility violated the standards prescribed by Title IV.

Shortly after the National MEBA elections of 1963, three members protested to the Secretary of Labor, pointing out, among other things, that they had been denied their rights to nominate candidates and to be candidates. (One of these protesting members, the Treasurer of New York's former Local 33, the largest in MEBA, had been barred for nominating himself because his had not been a salaried office.) The result was a series of conferences, from which the protesting members were excluded, between the Department of Labor's officials and the MEBA officials. After many delays and extensions of time (which were not even communicated to the protesting members), the Department indicated that it would not bring suit with regard to the National MEBA election—but would bring suit instead with regard to the maverick Pacific Coast District, whose officials were once more feuding with national officials. As the protesting members' attorney I telephoned the Department to find out why. I was told, by an assistant solicitor in the Department, that the Labor Department had "talked with Mr. [Lee] Pressman [the MEBA's 'National Counsel']" and "we agreed to do it this way." Thereafter, the protesting members each received a letter from the Assistant Solicitor, full of administrative gobbledygook, which told them that, "Taking into consideration all the factors . . . it was our conclusion that the Pacific Coast District case presents a more promising prospect for successful litigation." And that—surely an edifying example of the Secretary's "special knowledge and discretion" (or, perhaps, of his "expert's appraisal")—was the only explanation that the protesting members ever received as to why the Secretary refused to protect their democratic rights.

That example could be duplicated many times over; every union member and every member's lawyer who has ever brushed up against the Secretary of Labor in a Title IV protest can recount a similar tale of political and bureaucratic wheeling and dealing. However heart-warming or even inspiring such displays of political friendliness may seem to those who regard all friendliness as a blessing, to rank and file trade unionists they are apt to be distasteful. And even more distasteful may be the quid pro quo required for such shows of friendliness.

Is this what reform of the unions must mean in practice? If it is, then trade unionists might well regard all labor relations legislation, from the Wagner Act on, as a trap and a snare. Professor John R. Commons pointed out years ago, that "if the State recognizes any particular union by requiring the employer to recognize it, the State must necessarily guarantee the union to the extent that it must strip it of any abuses it may practice." His conclusion need not follow in its entirety, but it is largely true: once the government "certifies" or gives to a particular union special powers with regard to workers and protections against rival unions, it must take some measure of responsibility for the internal affairs of that union. Does this mean that unions must submit to government manipulation in the name of "reform?"

Even a dictatorial union officialdom is apt to be better, from the workers' standpoint, than one which is merely the patsy for the political administration in Washington. It is a bastard "reform" which is used as a manipulative device for the bureaucratic subjugation of free trade unionism. Is there no escape from that subjugation—no new course for the unions, which can lead to union democracy *and* to independence from the governmental apparatus?

In the light of the *Calhoon* decision, the hope that rank and file trade unionists, through the simple exercise of their democratic rights within the unions, might transform bureaucracy into *de facto* democracy now seems an empty one. "Reform," in the wake of *Calhoon*, means the wheelings and dealings of the Secretary of Labor, the intrusion of the government bureaucracy into union affairs and the closer growing together of the unions and the state power. It means the government's use of Title IV proceedings—or, the threat of their use—to keep union officialdoms in line; and it means one more barrier to any independent social or political role on the part of the unions.

January 1965

1. 379 U.S. 134 (1964), reversing *Harvey* v. *Calhoon*, 324 F.2d 446 (2nd Cir. 1963).

2. The member was John Cole. See his "SIU: The Short-Change Artists," pp. 70 to 79 in this volume.

3. See "The Painters' Union: Autocracy and Insurgency," pp.30 to 40.

An Exchange:
Law and the Unions

JAMES YOUNGDAHL / BURTON HALL

I: JAMES YOUNGDAHL OBJECTS

"Advocates" said Mr. Justice Frankfurter, "are like managers of pugilistic and election contestants in that they have a propensity for claiming everything."[1] Burton Hall, in his essay "Law, Democracy and the Unions,"[2] bemoans a lost lawsuit,[3] characterizes his clients as "reformers," the prevailing legal view as "childish," and the result as "frightening."

This response to Hall neither disputes the desirability of democracy in trade unions nor evaluates the complaints of members of the Seafarers' Union. It does take issue with three of his primary conclusions: 1) that the Supreme Court was wrong in *Calhoon* v. *Harvey*, 2) that union members have insufficient opportunity to challenge conduct of internal union affairs and 3) that the central issue of the labor movement in recent decades has been "suppression and repression of the union rank and file."

At the very least, the claims of an able advocate need to be placed in perspective. *Calhoon* v. *Harvey* was the first major interpretation of the Labor-Management Reporting and Disclosure Act (LMRDA) of 1959 by the United States Supreme Court. Title I of the Act establishes a "bill of rights." Title IV regulates elections. Hall's clients alleged election irregularities. The court held that their allegations are governed by Title IV.

The Thrust of this inescapable syllogism to Hall is that he has less chance of convincing the Secretary of Labor, who administers Title IV, than the courts, which administer Title I, that his clients are right. The historical attitude of courts toward the labor movement has not exactly been one of objective understanding. But to Hall, a remedy through the Secretary of Labor is bureaucratic intrusion, whereas a remedy through the courts is the democratic ideal.

Remedies have had a prominent role in the development of American labor law. Time and cost have special meaning in fast-flowing combat in which there is marked disparity between financial resources of the combatants. Complaint to administrative agencies, with resort to the courts to enforce the administrative determination, has been the fundamental method of applying federal statutes dealing with the employment relation. This National Labor Relations Act procedure, though criticized especially by employers, has survived almost 30 years of reasonably successful operation. It is cheapest for the employee, allows him to invoke the expertise of representatives trained to contend with the best employer money can buy, and probably is faster than direct resort to the courts.

With this background, Congress provided for administrative enforcement of many portions of the LMRDA or Labor Reform Act. Certain specific rights are enforceable directly in the courts by complaining members, but union elections are covered by an extensive regulatory scheme in Title IV, in which most complaints must first be addressed to the union itself, then to the Secretary of Labor, and then, if meritorious but unremedied, taken by the Secretary to the courts. The purpose of this sequence, said Senator John Kennedy on the Senate floor, is to correct, not punish, with minimum interference in the internal affairs of essentially private institutions.[4]

Particular care is needed for interpretation of a statute with the painful genesis of LMRDA. Many observers believe that its Titles I through VI were designed as a vehicle for the restrictions on union economic strength imposed by its Title VII.[5] In any event, as the Supreme Court has said about other labor legislation, the Act:

> . . . was, to a marked degree, the result of conflict and compromise between strong contending forces and deeply held views on the role of organized labor in the free economic life of the Nation and the appropriate balance to be struck between the uncontrolled power of management and labor to further their respective interests.[6]

The decision of Congress to correct, not punish, by Department of Labor regulation of elections was honored by *Calhoon*. Speaking through Mr. Justice Hugo Black, never reluctant to defend the right of individual dissent, the Court held that reasonableness of qualifications for candidacy, the principal complaint involved, must be challenged in the manner Congress established.

Reliance on the discretion of the Secretary is in harmony with the general congressional policy to allow unions great latitude in resolving their own internal controversies, and where that fails, to utilize the agencies of government most familiar with union problems to aid in bringing about a settlement through discussion before resort to the courts.[7]

"Et Tu, Hugo!" cried *Union Democracy in Action,*[8] a publication edited by H.W. Benson and sponsored by Hall.[9] The Supreme Court, it said, has "reduced the right of union members to nominate to the same status as the right of citizens of Soviet Russia to vote." *Calhoon* was a "bombshell," argues Hall, which subjugates union democracy to outright governmental manipulation.

These outbursts must be dismissed as lamentations of zealous advocates who lost a case. The decision was not wrong, as it merely honored express Congressional intent. It was not "surprising," as it had been reached by a vast majority of the courts that had passed on the issue.[10] It was not "frightening," as it turned in no respect on the merits of union democracy.[11]

The gravamen of the Hall-Benson contention is that a gigantic conspiracy, including the Supreme Court, Congress, the Department of Labor, the Democratic Party and most of the labor movement, is persecuting Hall's clients. Such conspiracy smacks of the fantasy in the assassination scheme being promoted by Mark Lane,[12] and must also fall of its own fantastic weight.

Unfortunately, however, cries such as these give unwarranted significance to a problem which, in perspective, is of a minor importance in the complex of issues facing the contemporary American labor movement.

There is special irony in criticism of the United States Supreme Court for failure to protect the rights of union members. The Court consistently has upheld rights of dissenters, even when in tension with hallowed traditions of the labor movement.

Two landmark cases deserve attention. In *Brotherhood of Railway Clerks* v. *Allen,*[13] a 1963 decision, the Court warned the labor movement that it would not permit use of union dues, exacted as a condition of employment, for political purposes to which a member objects. In successive decisions on the point over the past few years, the Court has used stronger and stronger language, based on "congressional concern over possible impingements on the interests of individual dissenters from union policies," and judicial concern over the danger of subordinating First Amendment rights of the minority to decisions by the majority.[14]

Allen places the responsibility for setting up the mechanics of dues-excusal or rebate on unions themselves; the Court suggested as a guide the English statutory system of voluntarily "contracting out" payments into a special fund for political purposes. The response of the labor movement has been sluggish, but it is clear that the Court will, in an appropriate case, cut deeply into traditional ideas of union security unless dissenters are permitted to use their money for whatever political purposes they choose.

In *Humphrey* v. *Moore,*[15] decided last year, the Court stamped authoritative approval on a "duty of fair representation" by labor unions. Collective bargaining agents must deal with individual rights in good faith, employing procedural due process of law. This duty is essentially a judicial creation; its expression by the Supreme Court was of vital importance.

Allen and *Humphrey* are symbolic of efforts of the Court to preserve individual rights *vis-à-vis* trade unions.[16] Their expansiveness has been echoed in decisions of the key administrative agencies in the labor-law field. The National Labor Relations Board enforces an obligation for unions to represent their constituents without regard to race.[17] In applying the hotly contested *Miranda*[18] rule, the Board has found in very general statutory status a prohibition against unions "taking *any* action against *any* employee upon considerations or classifications which are irrelevant, invidious, or *unfair.*"[19]

Hall again relies on his experience with his *Calhoon* v. *Harvey* clients to conclude that the Department of Labor refuses to protect the democratic rights of dissident unionists. He complains, for example, because the Secretary chose to challenge a national

Seafarers' International Union (SIU) practice in one court instead of in another because of the agency's evaluation of its best chance of legal success.

The most recent survey of the activities of the Department of Labor with respect to union election challenges was published in January 1965.[20] It dealt principally with a period between 1959 and 1963, spanning the various political manipulations ascribed to the Department by Hall. There were 211 enforceable complaints filed during the period, and the agency's investigations disclosed 136 violations. Of the 136, 71 were technical and did not, as required by the Act, affect the results of the election; 65 may have affected the results. Of the 65, 52 were settled by voluntary compliance (usually rerun elections), and 13 were taken to court.

The facts do not support Hall's accusations against the Department of Labor. There are over 33,000 local unions which report to the agency. A four-year total of 211 colorable attempts to use a well-publicized procedure is inconsistent with Hall's conclusion that "deprivation of union members' electoral rights and the violation of the electoral standards prescribed by Title IV are widespread throughout the union establishment. . . ."

His conclusion that the Department does not take the complaints seriously is refuted by statistics that in the second and third years of the operation of the Title, violations were found in more than 70 percent of the cases. His conclusion that bureaucratic favoritism is shown to certain unions is also inconsistent with the facts. Most unions support Democratic Party candidates; yet in recent years, under Democratic administrations, violations have been found in an *increasing* percentage of complaints; during the year 1963-64 it rose to 80 percent in those filed. The United Auto Workers (UAW), a leading supporter of the Democratic Party, has 1,189 reporting locals. Of the eight UAW cases closed during the period surveyed, violations were found in six, and only one of the six was found not to have affected election results. The Teamsters, in consistent political disfavor, had eight out of 11 violations declared not affecting the results.

Examination of the actual operations of government, from the Supreme Court to the Office of Labor-Management and Welfare-Pension Reports, reveals a plethora of legal channels for complaints of members about union internal affairs. The facts, as distinguished from disappointment arising from a particular case, show that the need for "reform" is small, but satisfiable.

Hall's most seriously erroneous conclusion is a classic example of the failure of labor's critics to distinguish between criticism and analysis. "But not until recent decades," he claims, "has bureaucratism—and the consequent struggle, within the unions, between the rank-and-file membership and the union officials—become the central issue of the labor movement."[21]

Clearly the American labor movement has problems, not the least of which is membership participation. Clearly these problems beg for informed assistance. But to say that the struggle between the union members and their officials is the central issue of the labor movement is to ignore the critical economic context and political reality.

Engaging in a little of the polarization by association employed by Hall, it is no accident that Senator McClellan is the primary legislative source of his clients' cause of action. The last time the Senator was re-elected, the voters of his state also expressed their attitude toward working people by refusing to amend a minimum wage law providing for $1.25 an hour—for a day of nine hours work by experienced women! Problems for labor unions in LMRDA are not surprising, comments one leading labor attorney;

... when we recall that the Bill of Rights' proposal first came from such great friends of the Trade Unions as Senator McClellan from Arkansas and Congressman Landrum of Georgia. This sounds a little like Krushchev being concerned about granting more democratic rights to the stockholders of General Motors.[22]

This is not to say that no portion of LMRDA has proved to be of any value. It is to doubt that its proponents were politically naive enough to sponsor a law which would make unions more, rather than less, effective. The election regulations themselves, Philip Taft observed, were "the result of a strange alliance of conservatives who either wished to reform or weaken unions, and left-wingers and doctrinaire democrats who believe that the new rules will make it easier for their followers to penetrate and capture them."[23]

The operation of the Act does illumine "the central issue of the labor movement." But that issue continues to be effectiveness in fulfilling economic needs of its members. In fact, as well as in the expectations of its sponsors, the legislation has weakened this effectiveness.

A necessary consequence of LMRDA has been internal bureaucratization of trade unions.[24] The number and autonomy of separate locals are being reduced and the power of officers is being concentrated at higher levels because of its onerous reporting demands and technical procedures. In some locals in Arkansas or Mississippi, for example, a majority of the members cannot read and write, let alone be responsible for the complexity of paper work which the Act requires.

Some subtle consequences are more massive. The publicity surrounding the McClellan Committee disclosures and passage of LMRDA has encouraged members to be rebellious for the sake of rebelliousness, whatever may have been its effect on the exercise of their proper democratic rights. Refusal of the rank and file to accept negotiated settlements has been a major characteristic of strike problems in recent years; the New York International Typographical Union (ITU) strike and the International Longshoremen's Association (ILA) dispute which drags on at this writing are familiar examples.[25] Offices of local unions are difficult to fill, as responsible leaders become heartsick from harassment stimulated by fair and unfair legal obligations. Grievances, whether or not meritorious, are being forced to higher and more expensive levels because of fear of litigation and agitation.[26]

Effects of LMRDA are substantial on the continuing economic struggle between labor and management which Hall chooses to ignore. Employers now can and do look at union books to evaluate their ability to finance a strike at crucial points in bargaining. Reports filed by unions are regular sources of information for employers fighting the most bitter kinds of battles against unionization. Typical is an anti-union leaflet distributed to employees during a recent organizational drive at an aircraft plant in Western Oklahoma, headed:

To Paul Russo, United Automobile Workers' Union:

Hey, Misser Russo, you wanna pusha de pencil. We like to pusha de pencil too!

This information has been compiled from the United States

Department of Labor, Office of Labor Management and Welfare Pension Reports, Washington, 25, D. C.

There follows a list of the salaries and expenses of union officials, particularly of the organizers working on the plant, and selected union contributions to the NAACP, Martin Luther King, American Association for the United Nations, Afro Asian Institute, etc.[27] Senator McClellan knew what he was doing.

If Hall has a complaint about elections in the SIU, he now knows where to take it. If he has genuine worries about union membership participation, *constructive* suggestion is needed. His thesis that *the* crucial struggle concerns rank-and-file democracy is inaccurate and irrelevant to historic—and continuing—crises of the labor movement.

II: BURTON HALL REPLIES

Mr. Youngdahl tells us that all criticism of the Supreme Court's decision in *Calhoon* v. *Harvey*—the case in which the court declared that union members have no legally-enforceable democratic rights in regard to the governing of their unions—is merely the sour grapes of the lawyer who lost the case. What else, he implies, could it be? For good measure, he suggests that people who press for democratic unionism and for the protection of workers' rights in their unions are either anti-labor conservatives or "left-wingers" or "doctrinaire democrats" or borers-from-within or all of these at the same time. His verbal darts appear to be aimed, primarily, at the American Civil Liberties Union and the Workers Defense League, the two organizations that campaigned for enactment of a union members' "Bill of Rights" and that appeared as *amici curiae* on the side of the union members in the *Calhoon* case. But they are aimed, as well, at anyone else who sides with rank-and-file workers struggling for democracy in their unions.

On whose behalf does Mr. Youngdahl toss his darts? He does not say. But his comments are permeated with the traditions and outlook of modern labor statesmanship. And these are worth a careful examination.

"The need for 'reform,' " declares Mr. Youngdahl, counting the several hundred formal complaints of election abuses filed with the Secretary of Labor, "is small, but satisfiable." The fact that only a few hundred complaints have pursued, to the end, the cumbersome and largely fruitless procedures for filing such complaints "proves," to Mr. Youngdahl's satisfaction, that there is nothing really wrong with the internal life of the union.

The substance of the modern labor statesmanship comes through most clearly, perhaps, in Mr. Youngdahl's comments on the *Allen* case. He tells workers, in essence, "You don't need democracy in your unions because you can prevent your unions from making political contributions!" Peasants don't need bread because they can always eat cake. He seems unable to imagine that workers might want their unions to be politically active while at the same time wanting the leadership of those unions to be responsible to them.

The modern labor statesmanship does not want to be responsible to ordinary workers. It would far rather be responsible—and even subservient—to government bureaucrats. For that reason it dreams of ever-larger and more elaborate bureaucratic constellations, in which it allows government bureaucrats the upper hand. No shortcoming in its statesmanlike policies can be acknowledged; if unpleasant facts obtrude they are blamed upon labor's enemy, Senator McClellan, and promptly forgotten. Thus, Youngdahl tells us, unionism's reserves in the South are not the fault of the bureaucracy's unwillingness to mount an aggressive organizing campaign—they are simply the result of the reporting-and-disclosure requirements contained in Title II of the Labor Reform Act. And even rank-and-file rebellions against the bureaucracy's negotiation of sweetheart contracts (admittedly, "a major characteristic of strike problems in recent years") are not, says Youngdahl, indicative of a rift between the bureaucracy and the rank and file: they are simply the product of "publicity surrounding the McClellan Committee disclosures" of 1957 and 1958!

In almost the same breath, Mr. Youngdahl talks of the "continuing economic struggle between labor and management." Mr. Youngdahl's hostility toward even the most elementary expression of labor militancy—toward rank-and-file rejection of sweetheart contracts, toward vigorous prosecution of job grievances, toward all manifestations of "rebelliousness"—leaves one wondering which side of the "continuing economic struggle" Youngdahl is on. One is tempted to conclude that modern labor statesmanship has more in common with management than with working people.

But the real question at issue concerns those provisions of the

Labor Reform Act which impinge upon union election procedures. These provisions can be briefly summarized. Title I of the Act (the "Bill of Rights" title) guarantees to union members certain democratic rights and makes those rights enforceable by suit in federal court. Among these rights are the rights to nominate candidates, to vote in elections and referendums and to participate in membership meetings. Thus, under Title I (prior to the *Calhoon* v. *Harvey* decision), union members could challenge the validity of any practices or restrictions which unreasonably deprived them of any of these rights, and by so doing could overcome any such barriers to democracy in the future. Until the Supreme Court's decision in *Calhoon*, every United States Court of Appeals which had ever passed on the question had held that union members could, in this way, challenge and strike down any unreasonable restriction upon their rights to nominate, to vote or to participate in meetings.[28]

Parallel with Title I, Title IV of the Acts provides a *post*-election remedy for fraudulent election practices, by which the Secretary of Labor may, if he believes that a specific election has been grievously affected by fraud, bring suit in federal court to set the election results aside and to direct a rerun. That remedy is a matter not of the member's right but of the Secretary's "discretion." And more important, it has no prospective effect: it cannot prevent the deprivation of democratic rights in future elections. All it can do is to cause a specific, already-conducted election to be run again.

The difference between such pre-election protections as those (supposedly) guaranteed by Title I and such post-election remedies as are made available by Title IV was described by Clyde Summers, on the basis of his exhaustive analysis of the State court cases preceding the enactment of the Labor Reform Act.[29] Said Summers:

> Lawyers who have been involved in these cases agree that pre-election remedies are the only ones of practical value. Correction of defects prior to the voting gives the members that to which they are entitled—a fair and honest election in the first instance. It also protects the union from the instability of an unsettled election and the cost and disruption of a new election. Post-election remedies provide too little protection for the members and too much burden for the union.

The *Calhoon* decision abolishes the Title I *pre*-election protections, leaving only the "exclusive" *post*-election remedy of Title IV.

Under it, union members who are deprived of their democratic rights in union elections (so long as they are equally deprived) can do nothing whatever about the deprivation except wait until each election is over and then complain to the Secretary of Labor. If the Secretary, in his "discretion," decides that it would be politically advantageous to himself to do so, he may (or he may not) bring suit to set the election results aside—which suit will come to trial two, perhaps three years after the election has been completed.

To put the matter differently, the *Calhoon* decision declares that working people have no rights in regard to the governing of their unions that a bureaucratic official is bound to respect. The official may, years later, have his wrist slapped by another bureaucratic official if he goes too far along the avenue of electoral fraud, but the rank and file have little if anything to gain in that event.

But if the official is not subject to the members' control, then what, exactly, is his social role? And how does he fit into the "continuing economic struggle between labor and management"? Already, one United States Court of Appeals, following *Calhoon*, has suggested that—since "most unions are honestly and efficiently administered"—the officials who administer them need not and should not be responsible to the membership.[30] Union officials are, it would seem, to become a caste of mandarins who, freed from control on the part of the rank and file, will administer the unions in accordance with their own, caste consciences. Union members are thus placed in the same category as minor children and mental incompetents: instead of being enabled to govern themselves, they are to have their union affairs administered for them, without their participation, by guardians not responsible to them.

All this is, of course, to the liking of the modern labor statesmanship. Youngdahl accordingly praises the *Calhoon* decision and expresses an abiding faith in the Secretary of Labor, the bureaucrat empowered (by the *Calhoon* decision) with *exclusive* power to oversee the union bureaucracy. Why such faith in a government bureaucrat? One might put it down simply as the class consciousness of a union bureaucrat who knows that his class brothers staff the government bureaucracy, except that it represents an historically new attitude even for union bureaucrats. The older labor statesmanship was suspicious of government and hostile to governmental manipulation. But the modern statesmanship embraces both. Youngdahl gives articulate and eloquent expression to that feature also of the modern labor statesmanship. In doing so, he provides an illuminating illustration of contemporary bureaucratic attitudes.

Let us consider but one example. Youngdahl suggests that in bringing suit to set aside the election results of the Pacific Coast District of MEBA while pointedly declining to bring suit with regard to the National MEBA elections, the Secretary was merely choosing "to challenge a national SIU practice in one court instead of in another because of the agency's evaluation of its best chance of legal success." Aside from his curious slip in substituting SIU for MEBA, Youngdahl takes an altogether sanguine view of the Labor Department's integrity. The suit that could have been brought against National MEBA was a far stronger one than that which actually was brought against the Pacific Coast District, since in National's election more than 99.53 percent of National's members were *totally* deprived of their rights to nominate candidates and/or to be candidates, while the Pacific Coast District's restrictions were far more lenient. And there is not the slightest reason to suppose that suit in the Northern District of California would be more promising than suit in New York. To accept Youngdahl's view of things, one must refuse with all the bones in one's head to entertain even the slightest suspicion of hanky-panky in the secret and private discussions between the Labor Department's officials and National's officials. Surely it is more reasonable to suppose that the explanation for the Department's behavior in the MEBA case lies in the fact that the Pacific Coast District's leadership had embarked upon a feud with National's officials—and the latter had Washington's ear.

Youngdahl's faith in the goodness of government officials seems naive at best. And his corresponding contempt for rank-and-file workers is disheartening. But one need not surrender hope that his attitudes might change, as time goes on. There does appear to be an operative psychological law, by which the union bureaucrat who has lost his grip on the reins of power suddenly becomes converted to the principles of union democracy. Thus David McDonald, never before noted for too ardent a devotion to democratic principles, became a "doctrinaire democrat" as soon as he realized that I. W. Abel, rather than he, controlled his union's election machinery. However much we may question the causes of McDonald's conversion, all true "left-wingers" and "doctrinaire democrats" will join in welcoming McDonald to the side of union democracy.

And who knows? Perhaps with the next turn of the wheel

Youngdahl, too, will find himself an ally of "doctrinaire democrats."
One waits and hopes.

December 1965

1. *First Iowa Hydro-Electric Coop.* v. *F.P.C.*, 328 U.S. 152, 187 (1946).

2. Burton Hall, "Law, Democracy and the Unions," pp. 109-120 this volume.

3. *Calhoon* v. *Harvey*, 379 U.S. 134 (1964).

4. *Legislative History*, LMRDA of 1959, Titles I-VI 699 (1964).

5. *E.g.*, Previant, "A Union Commentary on the Impact on Collective Bargaining of Titles I through VI of the Landrum-Griffin Act," *N.Y.U. Sixteenth Ann. Conf. on Labor 157* (1963).

6. *Local 1976, United Bro. of Carpenters* v. *N.L.R.B.*, 357 U.S. 93, 42 LRRM 2243, 2246 (1958).

7. 57 LRRM at 2563-64. The "equal protection clause" included in the bill of rights of Title I was not violated in that the right of Mr. Hall's clients to nominate was precisely equal to that of other members of the union. See Dunau, "Some Comments on the Bill of Rights of Members of Labor Organizations," *N.Y.U. Fourteenth Ann. Conf. on Labor* 77, 81 (1961).

8. "Et Tu, Hugo!" *Union Democracy in Action*, No. 14 (Jan. 1965), p. 2.

9. See *Union Democracy in Action*, No. 9 (May 1963), p. 4.

10. *Calhoon* v. *Harvey*, 221 F. Supp. 545, 54 LRRM 2131, 2134 (S.D.N.Y., 1963); *Report of the Committee on the Development of Law on Union Administration and Procedure*, Proceedings, Sect. of Lab. Rel. Law, A.B.A., 1963, Vol. I, pp. 133, 138.

11. The merits of the claim of Mr. Hall's clients are not easy to resolve from its face. Two of the Supreme Court Justices thought the courts should take jurisdiction under Title I, but that the wrongs complained of did not violate the Act. Requiring a candidate for union office to have recent and active union membership and job experience seems reasonable. The Department of Labor has treated it as such, except when its actual effect has been to disqualify all but a handful of the members. Part 452, *Statements of General Policy, Secretary of Labor*, Lab. Rel. Exp. 7131 (Supp. 1965).

12. See Lieber, "The Faithful and the Fact-Mongers," *The Realist*, No. 56, p. 3 (Feb. 1965).

13. 373 U.S. 113, 53 LRRM 2128 (1963).

14. See, *e.g., International Association of Machinists* v. *Street*, 367 U.S. 740, 48 LRRM 2345 (1961).

15. 375 U.S. 335, 55 LRRM 2031 (1964).

16. See also *Steele* v.*Louisville & N. R. Co.*, 323 U.S. 192, 15 LRRM 708 (1944) (racial discrimination under the Railway Labor Act); *Syres* v. *Oil Workers Intl. Union*, 350 U.S. 892, 37 LRRM 2058 (1955) (racial discrimination under the National Labor Relations Act); *Elgin, J. & E. R. Co.,* v. *Burley*, 325 U.S. 711, 16 LRRM 749 (1945) (right of employee to participate in the processing of his own contract grievance).

17. Local No. 1, Independent Metal Wkrs. Union (Hughes Tool Co.), 147 NLRB No. 166, 56 LRRM 1289 (1964).

18. Miranda Fuel Co., 140 NLRB No. 7, 51 LRRM 1584 (1962), *enforcement denied* 54 LRRM 2715 (2nd Cir. 1963).

19. 51 LRRM at 1587 (emphasis added).

20. Riche, "Union Election Challenges Under the LMRDA," *Monthly Labor Review* Vol. 88, 1 (1965).

21. Rosen, "Labor's Critics and Labor's Crisis," *New Politics*, Vol. III, No. 3, pp. 54-55 (Summer 1964).

22. Previant, "Have Titles I-VI of Landrum-Griffin Served Their Legislative Purpose?" 14 *Labor Law Journal* 28 (1963). The regulation of internal union affairs by LMRDA goes beyond extant regulation of internal corporate affairs, although both are affected with a public interest. See Philip Redding, "Democracy, Collective Bargaining and LMRDA," *Symposium on the LMRDA of 1959* 158 (Slovenko ed. 1961).

23. Taft, "Comments on Title IV," *Symposium on the LMRDA of 1959* 495 (Slovenko ed. 1961). See also Dunau, *supra* note 7, at 78.

24. Previant, *supra* note 5.

25. See *Fifteenth Ann. Rpt., Fed. Med. & Concil. Serv.*, 1962, which notes an increasing tendency of the membership to reject contracts negotiated by their bargaining committees, resulting in "uncertainty and instability in negotiations which are detrimental to the bargaining process."

26. Taking advantage of the trend, management spokesmen demand more. See Rose, "Do the Requirements of Due Process Protect the Rights of Employees under Arbitration Procedures?" *Labor Law Journal* Vol. 16, 44 (1965).

27. *Report on Objections* (Appendix 52), Aero Commander Division of Rockwell-Standard Corp., NLRB Case No. 16-RC 2781 (1965).

28. *Beckman* v. *Local No. 46*, 314 F. 2d 848 (7th Cir. 1963); *Harvey* v. *Calhoon*, 324 F. 2d 486 (2nd Cir. 1963); *Libutti* v. *Di Brizzi*, 337 F. 21 216 (2nd Cir. 1964). To the same effect but holding the specific restrictions upon membership rights at issue to be reasonable is *Mamula* v. *United Steelworkers*, 304 F. 2d 108 (3rd Cir.), cert. den. 371 U.S. 823 (1962). And see *Young* v. *Hayes*, 195 F. Supp. 911 (D.D.C. 1961) and *Gurton* v. *Manuti*, 235 F. Supp. 50 (S.D.N.Y. 1964).

29. Clyde W. Summers, "Judicial Regulation of Union Elections," 70 *Yale Law Journal* 1221, 1248 (1961).

30. *Gurton* v. *Arons*, 339 F. 2d 371, 375 (2nd Cir. 1964). The Supreme Court's decision is, of course, binding upon all other courts. As a result, the post-*Calhoon* decisions have uniformly denied protection of union members' rights with regard to elections, referendums and membership meetings.

II: WHITE LEADERS
AND BLACK WORKERS

Black Caucuses in the Unions

CHARLES DENBY

The whole new stage of black revolt that has now moved directly into the factories has to be seen as part of the long, long history of black caucuses. To understand both today and tomorrow, you first have to know what the black caucuses were yesterday when they sprang up spontaneously at the end of World War II.

I remember the first strike I ever led. It was over the discrimination against black women workers in our shop. It was during World War II, when I was at Biggs and I was so new in the shop that I didn't even know what a strike was. I was working in the dope room, where you put glue on the airplane wing. You had to paint on so many coats of glue and then it was baked and painted again. The room was sealed and ventilated through some kind of fans in the ceiling. The fumes and odor were so bad we had no appetite left by lunch time.

When I was first hired, there were all white men in the room. But as they hired blacks, the whites were transferred to better jobs. One day they brought in the first black woman. By the end of that week they had brought in about five black women, and there were only one or two white men left. That's when we decided to get those girls out of there. The women had been talking about their husbands who were in the service in Germany—and here they couldn't even get a job in the sewing room next door. That was for white women only. These things just burned us up.

None of us knew anything about the union, but I finally got to talk to our white Chief Steward, who told me the reason there were only white women in the sewing room was because they had so much seniority—ten or 15 years. We knew they were lying, because some of those girls were just out of high school. So we told the steward that if he didn't do something about it we were all going to quit at the same time, on the same day. We didn't know it would be called a strike. All we knew was that every factory had "Help Wanted" signs up and if we quit and went together to some other factory, we'd be working the next day.

On the day we walked out, they locked the gates on us. (That was the first time we realized that the huge fence around the shop wasn't so much to keep saboteurs out, as to keep us in.) By that time, other workers inside the factory were coming out with us. We didn't even know what they were coming out for. I thought maybe they just had a problem like we did. It wasn't until the company sent for me as the "strike leader" that I realized what we had actually done.

We learned a lot in that strike, including what to expect from the union leaders. It was a Negro committeeman who, after the company had agreed to transfer the black women to the sewing room, talked them into going to a Mack plant where they would make 15 cents an hour more—but be separated from the rest of us. They didn't know until the fifth day they were there that Mack didn't even have a sewing room and that they were going to work on a press.

One stage in the black workers' revolt, in fact, arose because workers began to realize that we would have to fight the union bureaucracy as much as we had fought management up to then. This unrest was what led A. Philip Randolph to organize the Trade Union Leadership Council (TULC) in 1959. What workers didn't know was that there was some sort of "gentlemen's agreement" between Walter Reuther and Randolph.

United Auto Workers' (UAW) members all over the country were attacking the bureaucrats—much as the black caucuses are doing today, except that there was no exclusion of whites such as you find in some of the current black caucuses. Randolph came to Detroit to hold his little convention and ran it just like the UAW convention: from the top, evading all the questions the rank and file wanted to discuss.

After the convention, we kept pressing Randolph about the question of discrimination in the shop and he told us plainly that this was not going to be an organization to take up grievances of black workers on the shop level. All TULC was going to do, he said, was to raise the question of discrimination; writing grievances would have to be done through regular channels. A lot of the workers said, "Hell, this is what we've been doing all the time and nothing has ever happened." But, because they made a big splash in the papers, many black rank-and-filers came around, in the beginning.

The leaders always emphasized that it was not a "black organization." Yet that is just what the black workers wanted to make it—not by excluding whites but by blacks controlling it, for themselves, not for the UAW. As TULC developed, it played around more with community problems than shop problems and when it did raise shop questions, it was more concerned with the building trades or things outside of the UAW than inside it. Reuther has always been a master of substitution—and he managed to teach Randolph the same trick.

After two years there was a tremendous drop in membership, and today, no matter how urgently a meeting is called, you seldom see a rank-and-filer around. Recently they called a meeting and sent letters to every older black activist they could think of. They said they called it to discuss how they could protect themselves from the "vicious racist extremists"—like the Dodge Revolutionary Union Movement (DRUM). But there were more young black workers outside picketing the meeting than older blacks inside attending it.

The whole situation was summed up pretty well when 26 young black workers were fired after a wildcat strike at the Eldon axle plant and went down to picket Solidarity House, early this year. The UAW sent a black official, Sheldon Tappes, to meet with them. Tappes had to admit that if TULC had done what it was organized for there wouldn't have been any such development as DRUM. And one of the young black pickets answered, "And if Reuther and the other bureaucrats had done what the *union* was organized for, there wouldn't have been any need for TULC."

An entirely new stage was born with the appearance of groups like DRUM within the auto shops. The Dodge Revolutionary Union Movement was organized after Chrysler fired seven of the black workers who had struck the Dodge main plant last year [1968] to protest a speedup on the line, while the UAW Convention was being held in Atlantic City. In July, when DRUM called for a strike to support a list of demands against racism, both by Chrysler and the UAW, the call brought thousands of workers out of the plant and shut down production for two days.

In February 1968, several months *before* the Dodge strike in Detroit, 500 workers at the Mahwah, New Jersey, Ford plant had shut down production for three days after a racist foreman called a production worker a "black bastard." Out of that spontaneous wildcat, the United Black Brothers of Mahwah Ford was organized. This caucus has just led another wildcat strike over continued racism at that plant.

What is new about these caucuses is that they represent a much more basic opposition than any Reuther has ever before faced. The UAW had, until the appearance of these new caucuses, pretty much eliminated any organized opposition—by any means, ethical or unethical. The bureaucracy has not really had to be concerned about rank and file problems in the shop for years. Now they are facing some real opposition, from below.

In the early stages of the black caucus at Dodge, DRUM raised a proposal that amounted to "dual unionism." They proposed in their paper that all black workers stop paying dues to the UAW and pay them instead to DRUM, to be used in the black communities. Many black workers I spoke with, who were very sympathetic to DRUM's activities in the plant, were opposed to this idea completely. They were all for a black caucus that would fight racism and inhuman working conditions in the plants. They were all for militant black workers taking over leadership in the unions for the purpose of making a complete change at the point of production. But they became skeptical of the objectives behind a proposal like this.

Black workers at Sparrow's Point, a Bethlehem Steel mill in Baltimore, on the other hand, formed a group outside the union, called the Committee for Equality, rather than forming a caucus within the union. They had a specific situation there, in which they could apply pressure on the government to end its multi-million dollar contracts with the company unless the company stopped discriminating. These workers created a "dual union" of a sort but it was tactical in their case. They felt they had to find some way to shake everything up—the racist company as well as their racist union. And it worked.

The opposition of the black worker is part of the opposition of black people as a whole to white racist America, a movement that has been gaining in momentum ever since 1961. In 1964, a mass picket line of about 500 got world headlines by surrounding the General Motors building in Detroit with signs saying "Racism Hurts All Labor," "Automation Layoffs—Lily White Departments—Slow Upgrading—What is my job future?" The demonstration had been called by the NAACP and was distinguished from traditional labor picket lines by the presence of student youth and the singing of freedom songs. General Motors agreed to negotiate even without the threat of a demonstration; Chrysler and Ford did the same. What happened after the talks is another question.

In 1965, SNCC helped to organize a Mississippi Freedom Union and later a Tennessee Freedom Union. They had found, while trying to work on voter registration, that what black people in the South wanted most was to do something about their $3-a-day wages and miserable working conditions. From organized labor all they got was evasion.

Later that same year, the grape workers in California began their strike for a farm workers' organization with the help of CORE and other civil rights groups. By March of the next year, 1966, the Freedom Union idea moved to northern cities when CORE organized a pilot project in Baltimore—and the Maryland Freedom Union was born. The greatest victory there was the manner in which the unorganized black workers of Baltimore took matters into their own hands when nursing home workers walked out first and then called to tell the "organizers."

That same year, *organized* black workers were also taking matters into their own hands. When the UAW convention delegates met in Long Beach, California in the summer of 1966, they found black workers from Local 887 of the North American Aviation (NAA) plant picketing the convention to protest discrimination by their local union against Negroes, women and Mexican Americans. They said, simply: "We've written lots of letters to Reuther. We even sent them return receipt requested. We have a pocketful of receipts. But no answers."

By September, these same NAA workers held the first "civil rights strike" of its kind to protest the discriminatory practices of the company. They wrote me that, "One Negro worker who had been trying to be a drill press operator for two years was finally accepted the day after the strike. Another worker who had been told a few months earlier that he had failed (by one point) the test for machine operator's apprentice was told he had been accepted. Another was promoted to assistant foreman, whatever that means. And the company even announced that a Negro top brass was promoted to a $30,000 a year job. Long live tokenism!"

One of the most significant developments out of that NAA situation was the appearance of a mimeographed shop paper, edited by these black workers themselves, which they called *The Protester*.

In Detroit, a group of auto workers at the Highland Park Chrysler Plant had come out that same year with a mimeographed shop paper called *The Stinger*. Another *Stinger* has just appeared this year at the Mack Avenue Chrysler Plant.

The richness and diversity of the black workers' group is constantly growing. Moreover, there are significant differences between the various black workers' groups that are springing up everywhere. The Mack Avenue *Stinger*, for example, though it is edited by black workers, makes a distinction between the "whitey" who is a rank and file worker, and the "whitey" who is either a company representative or a union bureaucrat. The black editor puts it this way: "It's true that we are fighting discrimination against black workers in the shop as one of the most important questions of our lives. But that isn't the only question. The reason many of the white workers in our shop also read—and even support—*The Stinger*, is that we are raising the question of the *inhuman conditions* of all workers in production. Automation speed-up and the inhumanity of the company and union bureaucrats is against workers as a whole. That is what *The Stinger* is fighting, and why white workers have told us they are glad we are distributing it."

There is nothing more stupid than to think that all black workers think alike, or that there is only one face to the whole new phenomenon of the black caucuses. This was one of the most important points discussed at a conference sponsored by *News & Letters* in Detroit in January of this year, where black youth, workers, women and intellectuals had a chance for the first time to confer with each other.

One black auto worker at the Detroit Conference felt that "too much of the activity of some black caucuses is pointed to getting on supervision rather than elevating labor on the line. The company doesn't care whether it's a white man or a black man as long as they get the production out. The company is getting very expert at using black supervisors to fight black workers."

Some younger auto workers felt that "trying to get a coalition with white workers is impossible because they are hung up in their racist bag." But a steel worker from the East described the black workers' organization in his mill which was so effective in ending some of the racist practices there that it was recognized by white workers who had their own problems with the union. When the black workers invited a group of white workers to come with them on one of their marches, the same white workers who hadn't wanted to associate with "those raving black militants out to destroy everything" suddenly decided maybe it wasn't such a bad idea, after all, and couldn't wait for the next march.

The United Black Brothers at Mahwah have also made it a point to appeal to all the workers in the shop. A leaflet issued in their wildcat two months ago put it this way:

Why We Ask Your Support?—Because the same thing can happen to you. The company has been laying off men by the dozens, but lines have not slowed up a bit. You have been given more work, and if you can't do it, you lose your job or get time off. The supervisors are harassing the men and calling them all kinds of names such as 'Dirty Guinea Bastard', 'Black SOB', and 'Stinking Spick', to name a few. . . . We, the United Black Brothers, demand an end to this now and those guilty of these charges be removed. . . . We ask all of you to stay out and support us in this fight!

The greatest difference between the new caucuses emerging today and those that appeared before is that most of us who were in black opposition groups up to now thought that the most important thing to do was to throw out the leadership, or change the union structure or something of that nature. The young people today aren't thinking that way. They are thinking in terms of a complete change—of revolution.

They are just filled up to their necks with racism. And with the war. One professor from Cornell, during the recent revolt there, reported talking to one of the black students about their use of guns. He had sympathized with their demands but he had been trying to point out to them how powerful this country is and to warn them that they were facing tremendous oppression if they continued using such tactics. The black student had just laughed in his face: "You're talking about oppression coming upon me? I've been oppressed all my life. It's you and the people who call themselves liberals who are going to feel the oppression that's coming." It shocked the professor, because he knew the black student was right.

Young blacks today aren't joking about the complete change they are out to get. When the group at Dodge named themselves the Revolutionary Union Movement, it was very significant. Years ago if workers called themselves "revolutionaries," other workers would have shied away from them. Today the very word can attract workers.

It is too early to draw any sweeping conclusions about what will happen next with many black groups that exist independently and spontaneously in shops throughout the country. No national caucus is on the horizon yet and to give the impression that one already exists, much less to imply that DRUM is it—as the *Guardian* did in its March 8, 1969 special supplement on the black workers' revolt—is futile self-deception.

In the recent shop elections, DRUM lost badly at Dodge Local 3, despite the fact that the membership there is overwhelmingly black. It is true that the union bureaucracy is not telling the whole truth when they claim that *they* won everywhere. At the Eldon axle plant, for example, where 65 percent of the workers are black, Eldon DRUM ran candidates for only a few positions, and although they lost, black workers are in complete control of the local for the first time. Doug Fraser, Executive Board Member-at-Large for the Chrysler Division, claims that these workers are the "moderates" he was supporting. But Eldon DRUM supported them, too. And, most important of all, workers know that black workers have never controlled that local before.

The most honest way to judge the response of black workers is to compare the manner in which thousands responded to DRUM's call for a wildcat last year and the way they reacted at a mass meeting called after the 26 workers were fired at the Eldon axle plant. The Eldon meeting was held in a large church and about five or six hundred workers crowded inside. The majority was younger workers but there were many older workers, too. The first thing that struck me was that those in control of the meeting were not workers in the plant or in any plant.

The speakers went on at great length attacking white racism—with the most vulgar name-calling possible. They spent a lot of time clowning and trying to be comedians. Once in a great while they touched on the vital issue of shop problems. Finally, the principal speaker was called. As soon as he got up, he raised his little red book above his head and said, "My Comrades of the Black Revolutionary Movement, how many of you have this book?" He had to ask several times before four or five raised their books in reply. The speaker told the audience that this was what the movement was all about and gave the address where everyone should go after the meeting to get his copy of "Comrade Mao's Thoughts." When he went on to call Mao "our closest ally" many of the workers in the audience began squirming and I felt that this sort of meeting was what labor bureaucrats need to destroy the movement.

The one thing the young black workers may not fully realize is that every time a black independent movement has appeared, the "politicos" who have rushed in to take it over, have helped reactionaries like Reuther to kill it before it can get off the ground. It was true in the first black organization within the union that I was involved with as early as the forties. There were about 200 of us, and we "stormed" Lansing and every black worker I knew was enthusiastic about where we were going. But the Communists and Trotskyists moved in and began a naked fight over control of our organization. It is not so much that the so-called "radicals" come rushing in, but every time they come rushing in they want to take control and direct it. The same thing is happening today. The only thing the Maoists do differently is to send blacks instead of whites to take control.

It is clear that the labor bureaucracy will try either to crush the movement or to kill it by "joining" it. It has done that with every spontaneous movement that ever arose, including the unemployed movement of 1959. Many workers are already sure that Reuther's activity with the black hospital workers in Charleston, South Carolina, was forced on him by what has been happening in his own union. DRUM has not only attacked Reuther and called him a "racist pig"—but has told *why* they call him that. He has to try to remove that stigma from his image.

He has not fooled black workers. Of course, they are only too happy to see him give $10,000 to the hospital strikers. But when they see him marching on a picket line in Charleston or Selma or anywhere else, they know that he hasn't been on a picket line with his own UAW workers for so many years he's forgotten what it's like. Reuther is always glad to integrate anything—outside of his own UAW.

Everyone in the shop is laughing at the Alliance for Labor Action, which they consider just some more of Reuther's power politics against George Meany. They know that Reuther is hoping the black workers in the South will save his neck. Reuther forgets that they have brothers in the North who insist he has to prove his Labor Action at home, in his own union. The black workers have made it clear that they want to stick to shop problems, not get diverted to Reuther's latest schemes for "community organization." That is the message of the wildcats and the shop papers that have appeared in such diverse forms.

The question at this point is: Will the momentum of the movement be great enough to see the black caucuses become a national force separated from the labor bureaucracy and strong enough to keep control in the hands of the rank and file? Or will the bureaucrats and the Maoists succeed in nipping it in the bud?

June 1969

The ILGWU Today:
The Decay of a Labor Union

HERBERT HILL

The evidence established in the course of my investigation of the status of nonwhite workers in the garment industry of New York City makes it clear that Negro and Puerto Rican workers are the victims of a broad pattern of racial discrimination and segregation and that there is a direct connection between the permanent condition of semi-poverty experienced by these workers and discriminatory racial practices. The factual record discloses that Negro and Puerto Rican members of the International Ladies' Garment Workers' Union (ILGWU) are discriminated against both in terms of wages and other conditions of employment and in their status as members of the union.

There are two faces to the ILGWU. One is the public image of a union fighting against sweatshops, bringing stability to the industry, securing educational and recreational services for its members, building housing projects and generously contributing to worthy causes. This image has been carefully nurtured for many years by an extensive and well financed public relations campaign. But there is another face to the ILGWU, one that is the daily reality for the Negro and Puerto Rican members of the union in New York City and elsewhere.

The other face of the ILGWU is of a trade union controlled by a rigid bureaucracy that long ago lost contact with its rank and file members; a bureaucracy that has more in common ethnically and socially with the employers than with the workers it is supposed to represent. The clearest and sharpest manifestation of this serious internal degeneration is to be found in the treatment of the nonwhite worker within the union.

All the available evidence indicates that in the admission of Negroes into local unions affiliated to the New York Dress Joint Board of the ILGWU there is a clear pattern of racial segregation. Thus there are virtually no Negro and Puerto Rican members in the locals that control access to the well paid jobs where there is a high degree of employment stability. These are Local 10, the Cutters local; Local 60, the Pressers; and the Pressers Branch of Local 89. It is further established that, as a matter of practice and policy, Negroes and Puerto Ricans are barred from membership in these locals and from the high paying stable jobs within their jurisdiction. Thus, for all practical purposes, Locals 10, 60 and 89 are "lily-white." Negro and Puerto Rican workers are limited to membership in Local 22 and in the unit known as 60A, which is the "Jim Crow" auxiliary of Local 60.

The racial practices of the ILGWU are seen most clearly in the Cutters and Pressers locals. Local 60, the Pressers local, controls jobs within its jurisdiction that on an hourly rated basis are the highest paying jobs in the entire garment industry in New York City, the average wage being almost $5.00 an hour. Local 60 has an all-white membership. On the other hand, there is 60A which is simply an appendage to Local 60 with a membership almost entirely Negro and Puerto Rican. The members of 60A are shipping clerks, push boys and delivery men. These workers earn in the vicinity of $50.00 per week. Yet, 60A with twice the membership of Local 60 has never been chartered by the International as a separate local and the manager of 60, who is a presser, functions also as the manager of 60A. One must ask, why should a local of shipping clerks and push boys, whose members are paid extremely low wages, be attached as an auxiliary unit to the pressers local whose members make the highest wages in the garment industry? It is interesting to note that on occasion the ILGWU refers to 60A as a separate local although the International has never issued a local union charter to 60A and in the annual reports filed with the Bureau of Labor-Management Reports of the U.S. Department of Labor, a joint report is filed for

60 and 60A as one unit although every other local affiliate of the ILGWU files an individual report.

To anyone acquainted with the realities of the union's operation the reason for denying a separate local union charter to 60A is that, given the ethnic composition of the membership, there would inevitably be a Negro or Puerto Rican local union manager. This is obviously unacceptable to David Dubinsky, President of the ILGWU, and his colleagues on the General Executive Board who have resorted to the unusual practice, repeated nowhere else in the entire union, of joining the low paid Negro and Puerto Rican workers in 60A with the high paid pressers in Local 60.

Another example of the same discriminatory pattern is to be found in the exclusion of Negroes from Local 10, the Cutters local. Local 10 controls job opportunities in the well paid cutters' jurisdiction. Through a variety of devices, the leadership of Local 10 prevents Negroes and Puerto Ricans from securing membership in this desirable craft local. Over a period of years, Negroes, who are members of other locals of the ILGWU, have attempted to secure admission into Local 10 but are almost without exception denied membership upon a variety of pretexts. On July 2, 1962, the New York State Commission for Human Rights, which administers the state's fair employment practices statute, found "probable cause" against Local 10 in the case of Ernest Holmes, a Negro who was repeatedly denied membership in Local 10 although he worked on the cutting tables of a union shop. Furthermore, the State Commission found, after a 15-month investigation, that there are virtually no nonwhite persons in this local union. This decision also confirmed the charge made in the Holmes case and in so many other instances that private "deals" are made by the ILGWU with favored employers at the expense of Negro and Puerto Rican workers.

A device that is used by Moe Falikman, the manager of Local 10, and his colleagues to prevent the admission of nonwhite persons into that local union is the rigid control of admission into various training programs. Local 10 exclusively decides who shall be referred to on-the-job training opportunities created as the result of informal arrangements made by the union and employers operating with ILGWU contracts, or into the Grading School operated by Local 10 in its headquarters, or in the referral of young persons to the Fashion Institute of Technology High School. It is essential to understand that there is absolutely no objective criteria, no established standards by which a person is accepted or rejected for admission into any of these three forms of training programs. When Moe Falikman was recently questioned as to how persons are chosen for these programs, Falikman arrogantly stated, "I choose them." It is quite possible that for public relations purposes the ILGWU will produce one or two Negroes or Puerto Ricans who claim to be members of Local 10 or Local 60. But the presence of one or two nonwhite persons does not alter the racial pattern and must be regarded as less than even a token of integration, especially in New York City where Negroes and Puerto Ricans constitute so large a part of the labor force.

According to the Division of Labor Research of the New York City Department of Labor:

> The proportion of the city's population accounted for by Puerto Ricans and nonwhites increased from 13 percent in 1950 to 22 percent in 1960. Their 1960 share of the labor force was 21 percent. By 1970, based on projections of the Department of City Planning, Puerto Ricans and nonwhites will account for 30 percent of the population.

The ILGWU leadership simply refuses to adjust to these facts and continues to operate the union in the interests of a small and declining number of white garment workers with high seniority in the industry. A Harvard University study noted that Negroes and Latin Americans

> [. . . were largely to be found in the less skilled, lower-paid crafts and in shops making the lower price lines, and in this industry their advancement to higher skills was not proceeding very rapidly. In the higher-skilled coat-and-suit industry the new ethnic groups have hardly made an appearance.]

In short, Negro and Puerto Rican women, who are on the lower rungs of the city's economic ladder, have become important in the New York garment industry, but they work mainly in the more standardized branches, and with few exceptions, unlike the Jewish and Italian men of earlier days, they do not become highly skilled tailor-system workers on dresses or "cloaks." As a result, a shortage of skilled sewing machine operators is developing.[2]

The leadership of the skilled crafts locals of the ILGWU must bear a major share of the responsibility for this development.

The ILGWU operates two local unions in Puerto Rico. These are designated as Local 600 and Local 601 of which the entire membership are Spanish-speaking Puerto Ricans. However, both of these locals are denied Puerto Rican leadership as they are managed by one Jerry Schoen, a former business agent from Local 62, who was sent from New York City by the International union to manage these two Puerto Rican locals. Obviously, the more than 8,500 Puerto Rican members of the union were not consulted as to who would be the principal officers of the locals, as Schoen was arbitrarily imposed by Dubinsky upon the Puerto Rican membership.

It is clear that Dubinsky's practices in this matter have little in common with the practices of modern American trade unionism.

These are but a few of the examples that illustrate the attitude of the ILGWU leadership regarding the Negro and Puerto Rican union members wherever it operates. Nonwhite workers are denied an effective voice in determining the union's policies and practices. Furthermore, they are denied even the slightest measure of internal union democracy that might result in a Negro or Puerto Rican rising to a position of real leadership within the union. Thus, the voice of more than 130,000 members of the ILGWU, that is, almost a third of its members, is throttled. This includes the membership in New York City where more than 52 percent of the workers are nonwhite, and this is the pattern throughout the union. Of necessity the question is asked: How are these more than 130,000 workers denied an effective voice in the leadership and policy-making functions of the union? The answers are to be found simply by a careful analysis of the constitution and bylaws of the ILGWU.

First of all, members of the union are not permitted to engage in any internal political activity, and are not permitted to have clubs, groups or caucuses within their union except for a designated period of three months before conventions every two years. How can workers gain support for choices contrary to those of the administration unless they are permitted to organize to discuss their own interests and to press for the election of candidates to union office responsive to their needs? The answer is that they are specifically forbidden to do so as the ILGWU constitution prohibits all membership caucuses, groups and clubs.[3] This incredible denial of democratic rights of the workers prevents the discussion of matters vital to every union member in an organized fashion and prevents the offering of rank and file candidates for union office. Dubinsky's spokesmen will answer that this is done to prevent Communists from taking over the union. This response is not worthy of a serious and dignified answer. One can only compare it to the argument that we should suspend the United States Constitution and the Bill of Rights because they endanger the country in fighting subversion.

Although the rank and file membership of the ILGWU is denied the same right to internal political activity that is accepted as commonplace in the United Automobile Workers union, the Typographical Workers Union and in other major labor organizations, the Dubinsky administration caucus functions every day using the dues money of all of its members to maintain control and to congratulate itself on its power and achievement. I propose to examine the requirements for important leadership positions in the ILGWU.

In order to be eligible to run for President or General Secretary-Treasurer, a member must be a delegate to the convention, which immediately reduces the number eligible to approximately 1,000 out of 450,000 members. The member must be a member for ten years and a paid officer for five years. This means that no member who is not on the paid staff is eligible for these offices.

In order to run for the General Executive Board a member must be a delegate to the convention, a member for five years and a paid officer for three. This means that no member who is not a paid officer is eligible for the General Executive Board of the ILGWU. Page 14, Article 3, Section 6 of the ILGWU Constitution reads as follows:

> No member shall be eligible to hold a general office unless he or she has been a member of the ILGWU in continuous good standing, with respect to the office of vice president, for at least 5 years prior to the convention, during three years of which he has held a full time, paid elective or appointive office, and with respect to the offices of President and General Secretary-Treasurer, for at least 10 years prior to the convention, during 5 years of which he has held a full time, paid elective or appointive office.

An analysis of the composition of the delegates to the last two ILGWU conventions would show that of the 450,000 members of the ILGWU, the number of members eligible to run for the General

Executive Board, given the requirements for nomination, is reduced to less than 300. Those eligible for the post of President or General Secretary-Treasurer are less than 200.

In other words, of the membership of the ILGWU, less than 1/15 of 1 percent is eligible to run for the General Executive Board less than 1/20 of 1 percent is eligible for the Presidency or the General Secretary-Treasurership.

The particular condition of the more than 130,000 Negro and Puerto Rican members of the ILGWU is even worse than the general condition. No more than four or five nonwhite persons would be eligible to run for the General Executive Board of the union and virtually none at all for the top leadership positions. This explains why there is not a single Negro or Puerto Rican on the 23 member General Executive Board, not a single Negro or Puerto Rican Vice-President of the union and why there are no Negro or Puerto Rican local managers who are usually hand-picked by the Dubinsky-controlled administration.

These fantastic restrictions on political activity within the union and the incredible eligibility requirements for top offices are obviously violations of the Bill Of Rights For Members Of Labor Organizations contained in the Labor-Management Reporting and Disclosure Act of 1959 (Section 101-A2 and Section 401-E). These operational procedures, together with Dubinsky's practice of requiring a signed undated resignation from all officers of the International union and from members of the General Executive Board, absolutely guarantee the perpetuation of what really amounts to one-man rule of the ILGWU. Thus, it is easy to understand how Negroes and Puerto Ricans are discriminated against and relegated to second-class membership when the rigid monolithic structure of the ILGWU is closely examined.

The systematic exclusion of Negro and Puerto Rican members from effective participation in the leadership and policy making procedures of the union, together with the general suppression of democratic membership rights within the ILGWU, and the pattern of segregation and discrimination, all directly contribute to the economically disadvantaged position of Negro and Puerto Rican workers in the industry itself. Thus we find that in the locals where there is a major concentration of nonwhite workers, ILGWU contracts provide for only a few cents above the bare minimum required by law. For many locals in New York City, where the overwhelming membership is Negro and Puerto Rican, the wage schedules provided in collective bargaining agreements made with such locals as 23, 25, 32, 62, 66, 91, 98, 105, 132 and 142 are a shame and a disgrace to the entire American labor movement. In these union agreements, where jobs are filled largely by Negroes and Puerto Ricans, the so-called minimum wages are in fact the maximum wages. In this category are floor girls, shipping clerks, trimmers and sewing machine operators in the low priced dress field and in the so-called miscellaneous locals.

I cite the basic contract between Local 98 and the Manufacturers' Association in effect until August 14, 1963. The contract provides the following minimum wages (Page 7, Article 4 (a)):

```
Floor Girls  . . . . . . . . . . . . . . .$1.15 per hour
Operators  . . . . . . . . . . . . . . .  1.20 per hour
Shipping Clerks  . . . . . . . . . . . .  1.20 per hour
Cutters  . . . . . . . . . . . . . . . .  1.20 per hour
```

In September 1961, the Federal Minimum Wage was increased to $1.15 an hour. The current minimum for floor girls is $1.25 an hour at the end of seven months (only ten cents above the minimum wage required by law) and $1.30 an hour for the other classification at the end of nine months.

The minimum scales for learner-floor girls shall be as follows: (Page 8, Article 4 (b) (i))

During the first month of their employment, they shall be paid not less than the then effective Federal minimum wage, and in any event not less than one ($1.00) dollar per hour.

Commencing with the beginning of the second month of their employment, they shall be paid not less than five (5c) cents in excess of the then effective Federal minimum wage, and in any event not less than one and 05/100 ($1.05) dollar per hour.

Commencing with the beginning of the seventh month of their employment, they shall be paid not less than ten (10c) cents in excess of the then effective Federal minimum wage, and in any event not less than one and 10/100 ($1.10) dollar per hour.

Commencing with the beginning of the tenth month of their employment, they shall be paid not less than ten (10c) cents in excess of the then effective Federal minimum wage, and in any event not less than one and 15/100 ($1.15) dollar per hour.

The minimum scales for learners-operators, learner-shipping clerks and learners at the cutting table, shall be as follows: (Pages 8-9, Article 4 (b) (ii))

Commencing with the beginning of the second month of their employment, they shall be paid not less than five (5c) cents in excess of the then effective Federal minimum wage, and in any event not less than one and 10/100 ($1.10) dollar per hour.

Commencing with the beginning of the seventh month of their employment, they shall be paid not less than ten (10c) cents in excess of the then effective Federal minimum wage, and in any event not less than one and 15/100 ($1.15) dollar per hour.

Commencing with the beginning of the tenth month of their employment, they shall be paid not less than fifteen (15c) cents in excess of the then effective Federal minimum wage, and in any event not less than one and 20/100 ($1.20) dollar per hour.

In those jobs where there are virtually no Negro or Puerto Rican workers the stated minimums have no relationship to the actual wages received. The wages are much higher than the contractual minimums. In this category are the cutters, pressers and skilled sewing machine operators in the expensive lines. Thus, Negroes and Puerto Ricans today are the manpower source for the garment industry's "sweatshops," as the union does nothing to move workers from low paying jobs into the skilled classifications. There is virtually no mobility of workers within the ILGWU.

Recently I made an on-the-spot investigation of these conditions. I cite the Fine Art Pillow and Specialties Company at 37 West 26th Street in Manhattan, as a typical example of conditions in firms under contract to Local 98 of the ILGWU. Here, virtually all nonwhite workers, male and female, who are union members are paid $1.15, $1.20 or $1.25 an hour, the very minimum or near minimum wage required by law. This does not include those workers who are designated as "learners" who may be employed for as long as ten months under the union contract and receive less than the lawful minimum wage. An appalling fact disclosed during this investigation was that there was no perceptible difference in wage levels in Local 98 shops and in non-union shops in the same industry. In shop after shop visited in New York City one can observe at first hand the fact that nonwhite workers are invariably the lowest paid in each firm, and where the general wage pattern in a particular shop is extremely low the work force is almost exclusively nonwhite.

I wish to stress again that there is a direct and functional connection between the unassailable fact that Negro workers are concentrated in the low-wage sectors of the industry where there is a high vulnerability to unemployment and the fact that Negro and Puerto Rican members of the union are excluded from top policy making positions, although they comprise a very large section of the union membership. Indeed there is not one Negro or Puerto Rican local union manager despite the fact that the membership of many locals is overwhelmingly Negro and Puerto Rican, including several where the membership is almost 100 percent Negro and Puerto Rican.

A typical example of the callous and bureaucratic manipulation of workers by the ILGWU leadership is to be found in the Haffkine Company case which has become a classic example of a union "sellout." In this case the ILGWU completely organized a group of Negro and Puerto Rican workers employed by a "sweatshop" employer whose workers engaged in a two-day ILGWU strike for union recognition. However, these striking workers were turned over to a local of another international union, one well known for signing "sweetheart agreements" and generally with an unsavory reputation. This was done by Herbert Pokodner, the manager of Local 98, who in the local headquarters and in the presence of the employer and of one Julius Isaacson, President of Local 118 of the Toy and Novelty Workers Union, told the workers that it really didn't matter which union they belonged to and arranged for them to be transferred to Local 118 even though the ILGWU had just recently signed into the union all the Haffkine Company employees. This is simply one more example of how Negro and Puerto Rican workers are viewed by the officers of the ILGWU, as commodities in commerce, to be bartered off in trade between "sweatshop" employers, racket unions and the ILGWU itself. The Haffkine case is just one shocking example of the practices of those who are in the "union business" and this, too, is a face of the ILGWU rarely revealed to the public. This explains why an analysis of the data provided by the Bureau of Labor Statistics of the U.S. Department of Labor concludes that only 11 percent of the unionized garment workers in New York City can realize the basic earnings necessary for the "modest but adequate" standard of living established by the Bureau for the 1960 Interim City Worker's Family Budget.

This budget is based upon a "family of four persons, consisting of an employed husband aged 38 with a wife, not employed outside the home, and two children, a girl aged eight and a boy aged 13 who live in a rented dwelling in a large city or its suburbs." It was designed to estimate the dollar amount required to maintain such a family at a level of living described as "modest but adequate."

The budget does not portray how an average family actually spends its money; rather "it is an estimate of the total cost of a representative list of goods and services considered necessary by four-person city families of the budget type to maintain a level of adequate living according to standards prevailing in large cities of the United States in recent years." In New York City the total cost of this budget is $5,048.

On the basis of a 52-week work year it would be necessary to earn $3.28 per hour for a 35 hour week or $2.87 per hour for a 40 hour week to earn the yearly amount stated by the City Worker's Family Budget for a "modest but adequate" standard of living in New York City. In the garment industry, women's and misses' dresses' section (that is the ILGWU Dress Joint Board) regular inside and contract shops, as of August 1960 and assuming a 35 hour week, approximately 47,644 (83 percent) workers earned less than $3.30 an hour. Taking a 40 hour work week base, there were 40,251 (70 percent) workers earning less than $2.90 an hour.

It may be assumed that the typical four-person family exists among the 47,644 (83 percent) workers cited in the study of the New York City garment industry. It is, therefore, clear that on the basis of the City Worker's Family Budget these families cannot possibly secure a "modest but adequate" standard of living in New York City. Only 9,255 (11 percent) of New York City garment workers can achieve the necessary income level to reach standards established in the City Worker's Family Budget. In addition, it must be noted that the very modest figure of 11 percent has been reached by assuming that these workers will be employed uninterruptedly for 52 weeks. However, given the seasonal character of the New York City garment industry this is highly unlikely.

The available data clearly indicates that the wages of workers in the New York City ladies' garment industry have declined relative to the total manufacturing average. The average hourly earnings of employees in the dress industry have not kept pace with the average hourly earnings of workers in other manufacturing industries in the New York City area. In addition, the "customary upward push of wages upon prices" has not been evident. Indeed, a price decline has occurred.

According to the U.S. Bureau of Labor Statistics the garment manufacturing industry provides the single greatest source of manufacturing man-hours of employment in New York City. Thus, conditions in this industry will be a decisive factor in determining the general income level for the entire city. At the present time the annual median income for all male workers in New York City is $4,396. The annual median income for nonwhite males in New York City is $3,336. Thus the white male worker earns at least 30 percent more than the nonwhite male worker.

Extensive investigation and direct interviewing of persons in the New York City garment manufacturing industry over a long period of time clearly demonstrate that there is an attitude among the employers and among union officials that a "little bit of chiselling is okay" and most often it is chiselling at the expense of the Negro and Puerto Rican workers who are threatened with loss of jobs if they protest too much.

Although it is very difficult to prove in terms of substantive legal evidence, everyone connected with the industry knows of shops that do not get organized because they have bought protection from union organizing campaigns; and they know of contracts not enforced because the union business agent is regularly accepting money from the employer.

There is an atmosphere of venality and corruption that permeates the industry. Workers who take home $49.00 a week tell each other jokes about the greed of union business agents or of the ILGWU manager who places bets of thousands of dollars a day on basketball games among the "bookies" operating in the Seventh Avenue barber shops, but they feel powerless to protest against conditions. They know all too well what happens to troublemakers. The real corruption, the real dry rot, however, is to be found in the discriminatory racial practices which victimize tens of thousands of Negro and Puerto Rican wage earners and their families.

These workers now look to their government for relief. These workers, who have already experienced such a profound sense of alienation and rejection from American society, who have been forced into a condition of silence and mute acquiescence, now ask for help from the Congress of the United States.

These are my recommendations:

First, all appropriate Federal agencies and indeed the entire community must inform the Dubinsky-controlled leadership that the private bureaucratic power which has controlled the ILGWU for so many years can no longer be immune from justifiable regulatory observation by responsible government agencies.

Second, the violations of the Labor-Management Reporting and Disclosure Act of 1959 by ILGWU, specifically Title I, Section 101, A-2 and Title IV, Section 401-E, should be immediately referred to the proper enforcement agencies of the federal government, and continuing and vigorous action must be forthcoming to protect the democratic rights of ILGWU members.

Third, the protection which a union receives for "exclusive representation" rights under the National Labor Relations Act and the "contract bar" to decertification proceedings and representation elections must be examined in the light of the practices of the ILGWU.

A union that is discriminating against members and denying them basic democratic rights within the organization or is not providing at least minimal standards of performance should be denied "exclusive representation" power under the law as well as the "contract bar" provision when such a "contract bar" provides no meaningful benefits to the workers involved.

I believe that if a union is entering into agreements with employers who provide little more than the minimum wages required by law, it should not have the protection of federal law to be the exclusive bargaining agent; nor should federal laws protect such a union against a decertification petition by the workers involved or from an organizing campaign by another union.

The affected sections of the National Labor Relations Act should be carefully reviewed so as to require standards of performance by unions as a necessary requirement for maintenance of exclusive bargaining rights.

Fourth, I urge that the National Labor Relations Board be empowered to refuse and/or to revoke certification of trade unions as exclusive bargaining agent if these unions engage in discriminatory racial practices and

Fifth, I urge the passage of a federal fair employment practices act which will include trade unions as well as employers within the coverage of the law.

The rapid implementation of these and related proposals is not only necessary to safeguard the rights and protect the welfare of working people throughout the United States, but in the final analysis is in the best interest of the organized labor movement itself. The struggle against racial discrimination and for internal union democracy must be understood as an effort to stop the further stagnation and decay of trade unions and to regenerate the entire American labor movement.

September 1962

1. This chapter is based upon testimony presented by Herbert Hill before the Special Subcommittee, House Committee on Education and Labor, August 18, 1962.

2. *Made in New York: Case Studies in Metropolitan Manufacturing* (Harvard University Press, 1959).

3. Page 52, Article 8, Section 16 of the ILGWU Constitution.

The Truth About the ILGWU

GUS TYLER

On August 17, 1962, the Labor Secretary of the National Association for the Advancement of Colored People, Herbert Hill, began to read "testimony" to the House Education and Labor Committee investigating the "extent" of discrimination, exploitation and corruption in the garment industry and the union. Hill never had a chance to finish his statement. Committee members objected to its inclusion in the record because it was not factual testimony but "opinions, conclusions, and characterizations." (*New York Times,* August 19, 1962.)

Unable to have his "testimony" accepted by the committee (to which he was a special consultant) as submitted, Hill used the facilities of the NAACP to circulate the statement widely.

When David Dubinsky, President of the ILGWU, appeared before the committee to refute charges, he was repeatedly told that the Committee would not entertain replies to Hill since the Hill statement was not part of the record.

On October 8, Hill's "testimony" became the basis for a resolution passed by the NAACP Board of Directors demanding further Congressional investigation of the ILGWU. The resolution stated that "the union leaders have as yet made no adequate answer to charges."

Since the Hill testimony is the basis for a widening rift between the NAACP and the progressive labor movement, it may be worthwhile to see how much truth there is in this basic body of charges.

To set the Hill charges in perspective, here is the ILGWU policy and record:

1. The doors of the union are open to all workers, regardless of race, creed or color. Among members it counts Negroes, Puerto Ricans, Cubans, French Canadians, Portuguese, Japanese, Chinese, and the older ethnic groups of Jews, Italians, Irish, Poles, Russians, Germans and Scandinavians. Just how many the union does not know since it does not put a racial or religious tag on dues-payers. But Negroes and Spanish-speaking members alone—relative new-comers—run into the tens of thousands.

2. The union admits all races, creeds and colors to its skilled craft locals, the cutters and pressers. These add up to hundreds of Negroes, Puerto Ricans, plus other Latins, Japanese, etc.

3. The union runs extensive training and placement programs to upgrade skills and teach new skills especially for newcomers. In the skilled operating category, this program in the union's greatest center—New York, with about half the union membership—is attended by workers, 90 percent of whom are Negroes and Puerto Ricans.

4. The union runs an unusual leadership training program to recruit and train leadership from all groups, with special care to find present staff and future top leadership reflective of the composition of the industry and the union.

5. All union facilities are integrated: locals, meetings, summer camp, health centers. This is true of the union everywhere.

6. The union has, for years, been a force in civil rights movements—and has been recognized as such.

And now to the details.

Hill Charge: "As a matter of practice and policy, Negroes and Puerto Ricans are barred from membership in these locals:—Local 10, Cutters; Local 60, Pressers; and the Pressers Branch Local 89."

The Truth: In Local 10, there are 199 known Negro and Spanish-speaking members (the ILGWU has many Cubans, Panamanians, Colombians, Dominicans, Salvadorians, Mexicans, etc., as well as Puerto Ricans) as of the summer of 1962. There are probably more. An exact count is difficult since the union does not tag its membership by racial categories. The 199 names were found in a shop count. (The count rose to 239 by November 1962.)

The 200 or more Negroes and Spanish-speaking members of Cutters' Local 10 are an impressive demonstration of integration, since in this trade where there is very little "turnover" of employment, the total number of jobs covered by Local 10 has fallen in the last decade. Despite a diminishing number of available jobs, there are at least 200 Negroes and Spanish-speaking members in the cutters' union.

Hill Charge: "Local 60 has an all white membership."

The Truth: One out of every five pressers (a skilled craft) in Local 60 is either Negro or Spanish-speaking, mainly Puerto Rican. This, too, was accomplished in the face of diminishing jobs for pressers in the New York market.

Hill Charge: "Locals 10, 60 and 89 are lily white."

The Truth: The charge is pure fabrication, as we have seen, in the case of Locals 10 and 60. The charge is comical in the case of Local 89. This local was created at a time when dressmakers' Local 22 conducted its meetings in Yiddish, because the members could not speak English. The newcomer Italians did not understand Yiddish, so they set up a parallel local to conduct the union's business in Italian. Local 89 still does so, with the result that it is not "lily white," but pure Italian, with no Negroes, Jews, Puerto Ricans or other non-Italians in the membership. To put Negro pressers in Local 89, as Hill seems to suggest, would be to disenfranchise them completely from union participation unless they were Italian-speaking Negroes.

Negro dress pressers (who work in the same shops as Italian Local 89 dress pressers under the same contract with the same wage rates) are members of Local 60—where the business is conducted in English, a language more convenient for most of the Negro pressers.

Hill Charge: "Negro and Puerto Rican workers (in the New York Dress Joint Board) are limited to membership in Local 22 and in the unit known as 60A which is the Jim Crow auxiliary of Local 60."

The Truth: The locals of the Dress Joint Board are 10, 22, 60 and 89. There are Negro and Puerto Rican members in every single one of these locals except 89, the Italian affiliate of the Joint Board. Local 60A is not Jim Crow, it contains all races, religions, etc. It is composed of dress shipping clerks no matter what their race, creed or color. It is a craft affiliate of Local 60 and not a racial grouping.

Most of its members are Negro and Puerto Rican, but to call it a Jim Crow local for that reason would be the same as calling the Sleeping Car Porters' Union a Jim Crow union because all or most of its members are Negro.

Hill Charge: "To anyone acquainted with the realities of the union's operations, the reason for denying a separate local union charter to 60A is that, given the ethnic composition of the membership, there would inevitably be a Negro or Puerto Rican local union manager."

The Truth: In the ILGWU, around the country, shipping clerks do not have separate locals, whether they are white, Negro, Gentile, Jewish or Mexican. Generally, ILGWU locals are industrial, not craft. The cutter and presser locals in New York and a few other areas have an historic basis that does not apply to parts of the country or even to the trades in New York that have been more recently organized.

More important: a majority of the combined members of Local 60 and Local 60A are Negro and Puerto Rican. Each member has an equal vote—whether in 60 or 60A. If the present manager is not a Negro or Puerto Rican, it merely indicates that the members of this union prefer not to cast a "racial" vote.

Hill's suggestion that a separate local of shipping clerks would elect a Negro manager is both inaccurate and vicious. It is inaccurate because Local 60A is "mixed" with no one ethnic group—Negro, Puerto Ricans, Cubans, Irish, Jewish or Italian—in a simple majority. What is more, if a predominantly Gentile labor movement could elect a Jew, Samuel Gompers, as its president for more than three decades; and if a Protestant United States could elect a Catholic as President; and if the NAACP could choose a white Jew as its labor secretary, there is no reason to believe that the members of Local 60A would elect a manager on a racist rather than unionist basis. The proposal is socially vicious because to create a separate Local 60A just to guarantee the election of a Negro or Puerto Rican manager is to create a Jim Crow local—separate but equal. ILGWU members prefer integration: craft and color.

Hill Charge: "These workers (members of Local 60A) earn in the vicinity of $50 a week."

The Truth: This may have been true before Local 60A organized the shipping clerks into a union. A study of 536 shops, employing 1,220 members of 60A, shows:

3%	earn from	$46	to	$49 a week.
13%	earn from	50	to	60 a week.
21%	earn from	60	to	70 a week.
22%	earn from	70	to	80 a week.
17%	earn from	80	to	90 a week.
9½%	earn from	90	to	100 a week.
14½%	earn more than $100 a week.			

This means that about two-thirds (63 percent) earned from $70 a week up to more than $100. The truth is that the shipping clerks owe a vote of thanks to the pressers local, whose relatively stable membership, high dues rate (more than twice that of the shipping clerks) and experienced staff made these gains possible. Standing by themselves, the clerks would have great difficulties primarily because of the very high turnover of workers in their craft. The clerks enjoy all benefits of being united in industrial union fashion with a more highly skilled craft. No student of labor relations has to be told why—and to destroy these advantages to create a Jim Crow local is bad economics and worse intergroup relations.

Hill Charge: "Over a number of years, Negroes, who are members of other locals of the ILGWU, have attempted to secure membership in Local 10 but are almost without exception denied membership."

The Truth: Among the more than 200 members of Negro and Spanish-speaking origin (including Puerto Ricans) there are members of Local 10 who were transferred from Locals 23, 66, 91, 105 and even 60A.

Hill Charge: "It is quite possible that for public relations purposes the ILGWU will produce *one* or *two* Negroes or Puerto Ricans who claim to be members of Locals 10 and 60."

The Truth: The actual count in Locals 10 and 60 of members from these ethnic groups is well over 500. They do not "claim" to be members; they *are*. They have been for years.

On a November 9, 1962, broadcast, Hill stated "there are in the vicinity of 50 (Negro) cutters of Local 10 in the city."

Here it is clear that when Hill said "one or two" he had no regard for the truth. Now when he says 50 he still has no regard for the truth. This is the old McCarthy numbers game: a couple of thousand Communists in the State Department; a couple of hundred Communists in the State Department; maybe a couple in the State Department.

Hill Charge: Local 10 had been found "guilty" of excluding Ernest Holmes from membership because he was a Negro.

The Truth: On November 4, 1962, WNBC-TV broadcast the following:

On September 9, 1962, in the second half of a broadcast of "Our Protestant Heritage," over this station, a guest, Herbert Hill, Labor Secretary of the National Association for the Advancement of Colored People, made certain spontaneous and unrehearsed remarks concerning the International Ladies' Garment Workers' Union and two of its leaders.

Mr. Hill stated that, in the Ernest Holmes case, Local 10 of the International Ladies' Garment Workers' Union had been found guilty of discrimination by the State Commission for Human Rights.

The fact is that this case is still being investigated by the Commission and no final determination of guilt has been made.

The full story will be available when the investigation is completed.

Hill Charge: "To prevent the admission of nonwhite persons into that local union (Local 10)," the leadership exerts "rigid control of admission into various training programs . . ." including the "referral of young persons to the Fashion Institute of Technology High School."

The Truth: Local 10, of course, does *not* prevent the admission of Negroes and Puerto Ricans. They are members of Local 10.

"The Fashion Institute of Technology High School" is non-existent. There are two separate schools of major importance to the needle trades in New York where the trade is taught. The first is the High School of Fashion Industries, run by the New York Board of Education. The other is the Fashion Institute of Technology, a two-year college-level school, licensed by the State of New York. Despite the fact that these two schools have been the great training-ground for the industry since 1933, Hill has done so little research into the way people are trained and placed in the New York garment trades that he does not even know the names of these schools.

Neither Local 10 nor any other union controls admissions, formally or informally, to the High School of Fashion Industries or to the Fashion Institute of Technology. Any grammar school graduate who wishes to may enroll in the high school. If that high school discriminates against any student, then the NAACP ought to denounce the New York Board of Education. The truth of the matter is that in the High School of Fashion Industries, the student body is presently about 40 percent Puerto Rican and about 30 percent Negro. The school graduates cutters as well as operators and has for years been successfully placing its graduates.

Hill Charge: "The ILGWU . . . continues to operate the union in the interests of a small and declining number of white garment workers with high seniority."

The Truth: In the New York metropolitan area as in almost 95 percent of the ILGWU shops, there is no seniority clause in contracts. The ILGWU contracts call for equal division of work when there is not enough to go around.

The terrible irony is that the ILGWU is one of the few, perhaps the only, major union calling for equal division of work. In the ILGWU, the Negro or Puerto Rican in New York, or Mexican in the Southwest, or Japanese on the West Coast is not the last hired and the first fired. Once a member of the union, any worker—regardless of origin—shares the work equally. No union in America—or anywhere in the world—has a greater job security clause for newcomers to the trade and union.

Hill Charge: "A shortage of skilled sewing machine operators is developing (in New York). The leadership of the skilled craft locals of the ILGWU must bear a share of the responsibility."

The Truth: There is a shortage of skilled sewing machine operators. Nobody knows this better than the ILGWU. Some employers have either closed shop in New York or threatened to fold up for lack of skilled operators. Hill's charge implies that the ILGWU prejudice is so deep that rather than teach Negroes and Puerto Ricans these advanced skills, the union would prefer to lose the industry and lose its strength at its prime center in New York.

The truth is that as far back as 1938, the ILGWU worked with Max Meyer to set up the Central Needle Trades High School (now the High School of Fashion Industries) to train skilled workers. The school is a huge establishment, advertising its existence in subway car cards pleading for increased enrollment. Its student body numbers about 2,000. Its ethnic composition: 40 percent Puerto Rican and 30 percent Negro.

In addition, the high school runs evening sessions. Here there is open enrollment for any worker in the trade to learn any skill: operator, cutter, pattern maker. Last year, more than 700 ILGWU members attended. 90 percent were either Negro or Puerto Rican.

In addition, to encourage ILGWU members to upgrade skills, New York locals run special union-sponsored classes—advertised by and recruited by the locals. The high school teaches the classes on its premises. Of the 532 ILGWU members who attended last year, 90 percent were Negro or Puerto Rican. These have been run for years.

Hill Charge: The two Puerto Rican locals "are denied Puerto Rican leadership."

The Truth: The entire leadership of the Puerto Rican locals— Director of Organization, Business Agents, organizers, local Presidents and Executive Board members—is Puerto Rican. The sole exception: Jerry Schoen, a stateside man with many years of experience who serves as manager. (Schoen was appointed only after Alberto Sanchez, Puerto Rican Director of Organization, turned down the job as manager to stay with organizing.)   Perhaps more pertinent for those who prefer the "color-blind" approach to this problem is the letter submitted by Hipolito Marcano, President of the Puerto Rican Federation of Labor, to the subcommittee of the House Committee on Education and Labor, on this matter:

The workers in Puerto Rico never look at the national origin, color, race, religion or political ideas of their leaders with the only exception of communist affiliation which is barred by our State Federation Constitution. A labor leader's worth cannot be measured by his religious beliefs, his origin or color of his skin but by his service, dedication and devotion to the cause of the working people whom he represents. We learned that lesson at the turn of the past century, when our labor movement was founded—not by a Puerto Rican—but by a native born Spaniard, Mr. Santiago Iglesias.

The workers in the garment industry in Puerto Rico were earning 2 cents an hour in 1940, when President Dubinsky and other "continentals" representing labor were appointed as part of the first Wage & Hour Committee to investigate this industry. Today those workers average over $1.00 an hour and their wages are constantly increasing in addition to very reasonable fringe benefits. A great change has taken place and is going on. Organized labor has done a substantial part to win that battle for the enrichment of our life as a free and democratic community. We don't care about the color, origin or religion of the leaders who have done that task of constructive leadership. The credit goes to the Union and in this particular industry the credit goes to the ILGWU for a job well done and for which we are grateful.

Hill Charge: "In the locals where there is a major concentration of nonwhite workers . . . the so-called minimum wages are in fact the maximum wages."

The Truth: ILGWU members, with rare exception, work on a piece work system. This means that a rate is set for a given operation and workers are paid for what they produce. The minimum is set so that the *slowest* worker will, on the set rate, make the minimum; the faster worker makes proportionately more—some twice as much or more. The average wage and the maximum wage in an ILGWU shop on piece work are never the minimum or even near the minimum.

In addition, ILGWU contracts provide for supplementary benefits—medical care, hospitalization, optical care, vacations with pay, holidays with pay, death benefits, retirement benefits, severance payment, etc.—that automatically add 10 percent, 15 percent or 20 percent to the money wage. This does not exist in similar ways in non-union shops.

ILGWU contracts provide that the union minimum shall not only be above the Federal minimum but shall automatically rise whenever the legal minimum rises.

ILGWU policy is to set union wages as high as possible without jeopardizing the jobs of unionized shops that must meet non-unionized competition in one of the most fiercely competitive industries in America. To pave the way for higher *union* wages, the ILGWU has successfully spearheaded repeated campaigns to raise the Federal legal minimum.[1]

Hill Charge: "I cite the Fine Art Pillow and Specialities Company of 37 West 26th Street in Manhattan as a typical example of conditions. Here, virtually all nonwhite workers, male and female, who are union members are paid $1.15, $1.20 or $1.25 an hour."

The Truth: According to a payroll check, 54 of the 104 employees are paid more than $1.25 an hour. These are overwhelmingly Negro and Puerto Rican. Of the top ten earners—with a range from $1.53 an hour to $3.23 an hour—seven are Negro or Puerto Rican.

The further truth is that Fine Art Pillow is about as typical of

ILGWU conditions as Mississippi is typical of America. This is a rubber and plastic shop in a trade where union jurisdiction is contested by dozens of legitimate unions plus dozens of racket unions. Of the thousands of ILGWU shops in New York, Hill chose this one for an on-the-spot check. And even then, Hill got the facts all wrong.

Hill Charge: There is "systematic exclusion of Negro and Puerto Rican members from effective participation in the leadership and policy making procedures of the union." Hill refers specifically to the fact that the ILGWU constitution sets up rules on caucuses and qualifications for holding top offices in the International union.

The Truth: The caucus clause dates back to the 1920s, when the ILGWU was in a battle with the "standing" caucuses of the Communist Party. Whatever the merits of the clause—a good subject for a full set of articles—it certainly is no bar to Negroes, Puerto Ricans, Mexicans, Cubans, Portugese, French and other minorities running for and winning office in the union. Dozens out of these backgrounds presently hold both appointed and elected office. If this "clause" is a sign of the "Decay of a Labor Union," then the ILGWU has been decaying ever since it beat the Communists several decades ago and increased its membership ten-fold.

Other qualifications provide that to run for President a member must be elected as delegate to the ILGWU convention. Hardly a disqualification! If a member can not be elected by his own local, he is hardly Presidential timber. In any event, this clause applies to all members—regardless of race, creed or color.

To run for the General Executive Board (top legislative body of about two dozen elected at the convention) a candidate must have served as a paid officer with the benefit of three years of experience. Hardly a disqualification! Virtually every paid officer of the ILGWU has seen three years of service, including the dozens of Negroes and Puerto Ricans on staff.

Most important: Every Convention of the ILGWU is a Constitutional Convention. At any convention, a simple majority may remove all these qualifications to elect anyone the delegates want under any qualifications they set up.

The truth is that the ILGWU has made labor history by a most extensive and expensive program for leadership development, unparalleled in the world labor movement, with a conscious concentration on the development of leadership that would reflect the newer ethnic groups in the industry and the union.

In 1938, the ILGWU set up an Officer Qualification Course to prepare candidates for elective union posts. Enrollment was open to all members of two years standing. Of the 832 applicants, 19 were Negro and eight were Spanish-speaking—a total of 27 in 24 years.

Why so few? The answer is the composition of the union, where 80 percent of the members are female, with little interest in and less time for full-time union jobs. Of the 832, only 106 were women.

Because of the predominantly female composition of the ILGWU, especially among the newer ethnic groups, the union set up a full-time, full-year Training Institute in 1950 to reach outside the trade, if necessary, to recruit leadership talent. (The only such program in the entire American labor movement.) In the first 11 years of its existence, the Institute graduated 30 trainees of Negro or Spanish-speaking origin. Of the 90 applicants, one out of three was graduated, a higher percentage than for the Institute as a whole.

Some idea of the philosophy of the Institute and of the ILGWU can be obtained from a letter written by an ILGWU Vice President when one Spanish-speaking graduate left the union staff. The letter was addressed to a Puerto Rican social agency in February, 1960:

> No one knows better than you that in the last few years many Spanish speaking workers, especially Puerto Ricans, have entered our industry and union. To develop staff and leadership from this community of working people we have a special Training Institute, a full year course. We look forward with keen interest to the growth and maturation of such new personnel so that in the coming years they may be able to play a major role in our union.
>
> To us, C . . . . represented more than an individual. He represented a trend. His progress, we felt, would be an encouragement for other young men and women with his interests to serve in the labor movement.
>
> To put it bluntly, we feel that C . . . .'s departure represents a setback to our program of developing Spanish-speaking staff and leadership in our union.

In the report of the General Executive Board of the union to its 1959 convention, progress was reported. "The call for the development of such leadership in the ranks of the ILGWU, on the basis of merit only, has taken the form of numerous appeals in the Spanish language press and in *Justicia* for Spanish-speaking ILGers to enroll in the ILGWU Training Institute. The results of the recent ILGWU elections indicate that a corps of such leaders is already emerging from the ranks."

The report went further. "President Dubinsky urged that the Puerto Rican government establish a training institute for developing community civic and labor leadership for the thousands of islanders who are in transition. This would be the greatest preventive to their being exploited by misleaders and charlatans taking advantage of language and initial cultural confusion in the slum environment, as well as in the homeland island itself."

The ILGWU offered to provide on-the-job training on the mainland for these Puerto Rican trainees and pledged to place them on ILGWU staff immediately after graduation.

Without appearing to be superior or self-righteous, may I ask whether there is any other union in the world that can show a comparative record of trying to develop new leadership—with a specific eye on new ethnic groups?

Hill Charge: "Workers who take home $49.00 a week tell each other jokes about the greed of union business agents."

The Truth: The ILGWU has one of the tightest systems ever devised by a union to check on the conduct of its officers: an army of accountants with a special corps of accountants to check accountants. In the last 30 years, the union has had occasion to drop some 40 of its officers for improper conduct.

The Hill charge is trial by rumor and humor. It is an anonymous smear: the kind of smear used to characterize races, religions, the NAACP or the labor movement by reference to some piece of gossip embedded in jokes. Just a report on alleged jokes.

To characterize a union or any body of humans by the anonymous smear—the great mark of McCarthyism, of the anti-Semite, of the white racist, of the bigot—is hardly "evidence." This is the lynch spirit.

December 1962

---

1. See Gus Tyler, *A Legislative Campaign for a Federal Minimum Wage–1955,* (New York: Holt, Rinehart, Winston 1959). Also see Gus Tyler, "Marginal Industries; Low Wages, High Risks," *Dissent* (Summer 1961).

The ILGWU:
Fact and Fiction

HERBERT HILL

In "The ILGWU Today: The Decay of a Labor Union," I charged that: "In the International Ladies' Garment Workers' Union in New York City, the Negro and Puerto Rican members are concentrated in the low-paid job classifications and with very little employment mobility." This was my main charge. I further stated that:

... there is a direct connection between the permanent condition of semi-poverty experienced by these workers and discriminatory racial practices. The factual record discloses that Negro and Puerto Rican members of the International Ladies' Garment Workers' Union are discriminated against both in terms of wages and other conditions of employment and in their status as members of the union . . . .

These charges were and remain justified. No statement or explanation by officials of the ILGWU or their apologists refutes the major points of my arguments. On the contrary, their defense of the Union essentially confirms my criticism of the ILGWU's policies and practices.

The most serious effort made to counter my charges was the reply by Gus Tyler, Educational Director of the ILGWU, which appears in this volume.[1] Much of Tyler's material had previously appeared in a widely circulated document by Harry Fleischman, Director of the American Jewish Committee's National Labor

Service, entitled "Is the ILGWU Biased?" November 5, 1962. The Jewish Labor Committee distributed the same material in the form of a memorandum from Emanuel Muravchik, National Field Director, dated November 16, 1962.

Tyler's technique was to quote me (Hill Charge: . . .) followed by his answer (The Truth: . . .). After almost 12 pages of rapid-fire dialogue between "Hill Charge" and "The Truth" I can readily understand the reader falling under a semi-hypnotic spell. Tyler, the "Truthsayer," writes with such seemingly inviolable "facts" that one might think he is really giving a point by point refutation of my charges. Aside from the failure to refute my charges, his is *not* a point by point discussion of my article. A number of the most important specific charges I made are not commented upon at all, others are obviously distorted or treated so perfunctorily that he might well have omitted any comment and, most seriously, his "fact" sheet fails completely to come to grips with the basic charges I directed against the ILGWU concerning the source of discriminatory practices suffered by nonwhite garment workers in New York City.

At no time did I charge the ILGWU with discriminatory practices emanating from a conscious racist ideology. What I have argued is that the social fact of discrimination is rooted in the ILGWU today because of the interaction of the old union leadership with the changing social composition of the membership and the nature of the industry.

In the first place, there is the sheer weight of numbers of the Negro and Puerto Rican minorities. They comprise nearly one-third of the national membership and more than a half of the membership in the New York area, the heart of the International Union's operation. Given the rapidly increasing number of Negroes and Puerto Ricans in the garment industry in New York, they have a unique status within the union which the all-white top leadership clearly sees as a growing threat to its monopoly of control.

A second factor contributing to discriminatory practices relates to the garment industry itself. The industry is made up of many small, highly competitive firms, further threatened by low priced imports. It therefore seeks to draw workers from a large, cheap labor market, one that in New York consists largely of nonwhite workers. This directly encourages discriminatory practices as the unskilled, lowest paying jobs are the only jobs available to Negroes and Puerto Ricans.

The many problems that the ILGWU faces in the industry are very real. To improve the living standards of its members and particularly those who are doubly victimized by a sick industry because of their color would pose a problem to the best of unions. The issue is *how* to meet the problem: to resist or acquiesce to the employers' demand that the ILGWU maintain a cheap labor market for the garment industry in New York City.

It is clear that some years ago the ILGWU leadership made a fundamental decision to keep the industry in New York City on the basis of maintaining low wages and minimal standards for tens of thousands of unskilled workers, i.e., Negroes and Puerto Ricans. Thus, the union provides itself with a vast dues paying membership which also constitutes the base of its extensive political operations in New York City and State. In this manner the ILGWU has chosen to operate as a stabilizing force in the industry.

The present wage rates of the unskilled and semi-skilled garment workers, most of whom are nonwhite, are below the subsistence levels indicated by the 1960 Interim City Workers Family Budget established by the Bureau of Labor Statistics of the U.S. Department of Labor. (Data given in my previous article.)

A detailed report of wages in New York City, released by the Bureau of Labor Statistics on June 27, 1962, clearly indicates that New York City has become a low-wage area. One of the major reasons for this development is the wage policies of the apparel unions.

This United States government report found that between 1950 and 1960, wages for the city's apparel workers fell from second place among 16 industrial categories to 11th place, and dropped below the national average for all manufacturing.

The tacit collusion between employer and union to maintain a cheap labor market was revealed by the ILGWU's opposition to a bill introduced in the New York City Council in 1962 to establish by law a minimum wage in New York City of $1.50 an hour. The ILGWU representative on the Mayor's Citizens' Commission on the City Economy, E. Howard Molisani, manager of Italian Cloakmakers' Local 48 and a Vice President of the ILGWU, originally voted against the Commission's report which recommended prompt enactment of a law establishing a $1.50 minimum hourly wage in New York City, but, for the public record, later changed his vote to an abstention.

This is evidently "the philosophy of the ILGWU" to which Tyler repeatedly alludes and which Fleischman and Muravchik defend.

Arnold Witte, general manager of the Commerce and Industry Association of New York City, writing in the October 5, 1962, New York *World Telegram & Sun,* cited the ILGWU's opposition to the city minimum wage bill. Mr. Witte noted that "the garment workers, the largest union of the largest industry in the city, has refused to endorse this legislation."

On February 12, 1963, a mass demonstration was held in Albany in support of passage of a $1.50 minimum wage law for New York City. Several major trade unions participated, as did the NAACP, the Negro American Labor Council, and many other groups. The ILGWU was conspicuous by its absence.

There is a third factor behind the discrimination suffered by nonwhite garment workers. It pertains to the ingrown quality of the union leadership. Again, I do not charge that the ILGWU leadership is motivated by a deliberate racist ideology. But it is evident that the top all-white leadership has grown contemptuous of the younger, less educated, the less sophisticated—*the altogether different*—newer members who are overwhelmingly Negro and Puerto Rican.

That many of the older leaders of the ILGWU have nothing in common with their radical past is beside the point; that they have a certain past in common is very much to the point. (Talk about discrimination in his union and David Dubinsky will recount *ad nauseum* how he was imprisoned under the Czar for his socialist activities.) The picture which would emerge from any detailed study of the leading personnel is of an old, conservative, ingrown bureaucracy. It has become an elite club which seeks to preserve for itself the leading power positions in the International, the local unions and the best jobs in the shops for those most closely identified with its own history and nostalgia. It passes these desirable, well-paying positions on from father to son, and from father to son-in-law. The "business" is kept within the family.

Daniel Bell of Columbia University commented on this serious problem:[2]

. . . .The fact is—and this is the "bite" in Hill's charges—that the Negroes are underrepresented in the leadership of many of the unions where they form a significant proportion of the membership. In the case of these unions, what the Negroes want is "recognition" at the level of top leadership and a growing share of the spoils of office. . . . For one thing, the realistic political process in the United States, at least in the northern urban centers, has been one of ethnic groups advancing themselves precisely in this fashion; by organizing on bloc lines, electing their own kind, and using the patronage system to enhance the wealth and status of their group. . . .

Bell concludes by noting that:

. . . .In economic and educational opportunity, the Negro is in a position of inequality, and the government is bound to help him move ahead. But doesn't the trade union movement have a *special* obligation to help redress the balance? . . .

Tyler knows that crucial to my argument is my characterization of the ILGWU leadership as being rigidly bureaucratic. Yet, his "discussion" of this documented charge is so feeble and unresponsive as to be an unwitting admission of its truth.

I sought to establish that the ILGWU leadership, as is the case with virtually every bureaucracy, has tried to legitimize its privileges through constitutional provisions. While these provisions make everything "legal," they also paralyze initiative from below, prevent an influx of new life into the leading policy making bodies of the organization and transform conventions into tedious rituals. For example, I pointed to the clause in the ILGWU constitution which prohibits a democratic internal life in the organization. Here is what Tyler has to say on the matter:

. . . The caucus clause dates back to the 1920s, when the ILGWU was in a battle with the 'standing' caucuses of the Communist Party. Whatever the merits of the clause—*a good subject for a full set of articles*—it certainly is no bar to Negroes, Puerto Ricans, Mexicans, Cubans, Portuguese, French and other minorities running for and winning office in the union . . ." (Emphasis added.)

This will not do. Frankly, I do not know if the clause was justified at the time by the struggle against the Communists. And this might make for a full set of articles by labor historians. But it also makes for a full set of articles by the Labor Secretary of the

NAACP and others on the character and practices of the ILGWU today. While the clause deprives the entire membership of democratic rights today, it takes on the added edge of discrimination against those minorities which are thus deprived, in addition, of their right to organize within the union to press for their special needs and rights.[3]

Other constitutional provisions reduce the number eligible to run for the top offices in the union to a few hundred out of a total of over 400,000. This is bad enough. Worse yet, it reduces the number of Puerto Ricans and Negroes eligible to run for the General Executive Board to proportionally a very small number (Tyler says "dozens"!) and those eligible to run for the offices of President and General Secretary to even less. (Tyler doesn't give a number.)

In the same vein he writes of these constitutional restrictions on democratic rights: "At any convention, a simple majority may remove all these qualifications [from the Constitution] to elect anyone the delegates want [to the General Executive Board] under any qualifications they set up." Getting a "simple majority" at an ILGWU convention is not quite that simple. To do that would require a long, arduous campaign against the solidly entrenched leadership, a campaign which would require far more time than the three-month pre-convention limit on caucuses. And there's the rub. The ILGWU constitution itself, through the extreme limitation and control placed on opposition, is the best, built-in, guarantee that Tyler's "simple majority" will never materialize.

It is revealing to see what sections of my article completely escaped Tyler's roving but very selective eye.

Hill Charge: ". . . there is not a single Negro or Puerto Rican on the 23 member General Executive Board. . . ."
Tyler Answer: *Silence.*
Hill Charge: ". . . not a single Negro or Puerto Rican Vice-President of the union. . . ."
Tyler Answer: *Silence.*
Hill Charge: ". . . there are no Negro or Puerto Rican local managers who are usually handpicked by the Dubinsky controlled administration."
Tyler Answer: *Silence.*
Hill Charge: ". . . Dubinsky's practice of requiring a signed undated resignation from all officers of the International union and from members of the General Executive Board, absolutely guarantees the perpetuation of what really amounts to one-man rule of the ILGWU."

Tyler Answer: *Silence.*

Hill Charge: "I cite the basic contract between Local 98 and the Manufacturers' Association in effect until August 14, 1963. The contract provides the following minimum wages (Page 7, Article 4 (a)):

Floor Girls	$1.15 per hour
Operators	1.20 per hour
Shipping Clerks	1.20 per hour
Cutters	1.20 per hour

In September, 1961, the Federal Wage was increased to $1.15 an hour. The current minimum for floor girls is $1.25 an hour at the end of seven months (only 10 cents above the minimum wage required by law) and $1.30 an hour for the other classifications at the end of nine months."

Tyler Answer: *Silence.*

(Tyler does try to answer some of the other charges made about wage scales. All the worse for his case, as we shall see.)

Hill Charge: "In this case [of the Haffkine Co.] the ILGWU completely organized a group of Negro and Puerto Rican workers employed by a 'sweatshop' employer whose workers engaged in a two-day ILGWU strike for union recognition. However, these striking workers were turned over to a local of another international union, one well known for signing 'sweetheart agreements' and generally with an unsavory reputation. This was done by Herbert Pokodner, the manager of Local 98. . . ."

Tyler Answer: *Silence.*

Hill Charge: ". . . an analysis of the data provided by the Bureau of Labor Statistics of the U.S. Department of Labor concludes that only 11 percent of the unionized garment workers in New York can realize the basic earnings necessary for the 'modest but adequate' standard of living established by the Bureau for the 1960 Interim City Worker's Family Budget."

Tyler Answer: *Silence.*

Hill Charge: "In addition, it must be noted that the very modest figure of 11 percent has been reached by assuming that these workers will be employed uninterruptedly for 52 weeks. However, given the seasonal character of the New York City garment industry this is highly unlikely."

Tyler Answer: *Silence.*

Hill Charge: The available data clearly indicates that the wages of workers in the New York City ladies' garment industry have declined relative to the total manufacturing average.

Tyler Answer: *Silence.*

These are, among several others, omissions of major points in my article that Tyler, Fleischman and Muravchik make no attempt to answer, although they create the illusion they are "answering Hill item by item."

In his article, Tyler writes:

> Hill Charge: "To prevent the admission of nonwhite persons into that local union (Local 10)," the leadership exerts "rigid control of admission into various training programs . . ." including the "referral of young persons to the Fashion Institute of Technology High School."

If we substitute my words for Tyler's three little dots, the quotation would then be that the leadership exerts:

> "rigid control of admission into various training programs. *Local 10 exclusively decides who shall be referred to on-the-job training opportunities created as the result of informal arrangement made by the union and employers operating with ILGWU contracts, or into the Grading School operated by Local 10 in its headquarters,* or in the referral of young persons to the Fashion Institute of Technology High School."

Thus, there are *three* training programs mentioned in my article and Tyler dots his way over the first two: 1) the informal arrangement made between employer and union for on-the-job training and 2) the Grading School operated by Local 10 in its headquarters. Why? The answer is clear enough. My charges in these two instances are incontrovertible. Where the union exercises its control, the number of Negroes and Puerto Ricans is so embarrassingly small that Tyler discreetly resorts to his dots. He discusses, instead, only the third form of training, that offered by the New York City Board of Education where the ILGWU, fortunately, does *not* exercise control—and here I stand corrected—about who is admitted. Tyler then rests his case on the non-discriminatory policies of the New York City Board of Education and tacitly concedes that he has no case where the union is concerned.

What is more, the figures Tyler gives of the number of Negroes and Puerto Ricans trained by the Board of Education contradicts any claim that the extremely small number of nonwhite workers in the skilled trades is due to a shortage of skilled Negro and Puerto Rican labor.

The *New York Times* of August 18, 1962, reporting on the testimony of Moe Falikman, business manager of Cutters' Local 10, before a hearing of the Subcommittee of the House Committee on Education and Labor states that "Mr. Falikman explained that Local 10 had no formal training program for cutters and no apprentice system." That led Congressman Roosevelt to observe that "with the changing pattern of population in New York it seems to me you would have gone to some lengths" to provide training and jobs for members of racial minorities.

"We are not an employment agency," Mr. Falikman replied.

"But you are," Mr. Roosevelt declared. "I'd have greater faith in you if you would face this situation honestly and say, yes, this needs looking into."

After consulting with a union attorney, Falikman did agree that he would look into it.

The *New York Times* of August 25, 1962, in reporting Mr. Dubinsky's appearance before the House Subcommittee stated that "Mr. Dubinsky denied that it was the union's responsibility to upgrade Negroes and Puerto Ricans, as much as we would like to see them go to higher brackets. 'The union,' he said, 'is not an employment agency.' " Other ILGWU officials appearing before the Subcommittee insisted that upgrading and promotion "was not the union's responsibility." "We are not an employment agency," they all said.

But in Dubinsky's testimony reprinted in the October 1962 issue of the ILGWU newspaper *Justice*, in reply to a question as to why Negroes and Puerto Ricans do not advance in the union or in the industry, Dubinsky is quoted as saying, "We are doing everything under the sun on this score."

Either the ILGWU is "doing everything under the sun," or "we are not an employment agency, it's not our responsibility." The union cannot have it both ways.

Then there is the following sleight-of-hand. According to Tyler:

Hill Charge: Local 10 has been found "guilty" of excluding Ernest Holmes from membership because he was a Negro.

Tyler incorporates this alleged "Hill Charge" in what purports to be an answer to my article in *New Politics*. Here is what I actually wrote:

... On July 2, 1962, the New York State Commission for Human

Rights, which administers the state's fair employment practices statute, found "probable cause" against Local 10 in the case of Ernest Holmes, a Negro who was repeatedly denied membership in Local 10 although he worked on the cutting tables of a union shop . . . .

Tyler's dishonest practice consists of using the word "guilty" attributed to me in an unrehearsed television interview but nowhere stated in the article he is presumably answering. In this way, he relieves himself of the responsibility of answering why, after an eight-month investigation, the New York State Commission for Human Rights found "probable cause" (the first stage in a finding of guilt) against Local 10 of the ILGWU. On September 14, 1962, Ruperto Ruiz, Investigating Commissioner, New York State Commission for Human Rights, in a letter to Emil Schlesinger, attorney for Local 10, stated that the Commission had "repeatedly requested and for a period of eight months tried to obtain data pertinent to a resolution of the charges of discrimination against the Amalgamated Ladies Garment Cutters Union—Local 10. These efforts were unsuccessful. The failure of representatives of that local to cooperate in the investigation, despite their promises to do so, left me no alternative but to find 'probable cause to credit the allegations to the complaint.' "

Sixteen years ago the ILGWU entered into an agreement with the New York State Commission Against Discrimination (the predecessor to the State Commission For Human Rights) that it would not bar Negroes, Spanish-speaking or other persons from membership in the all-Italian locals. (*Elsie Hunter* v. *Agnes Sullivan Dress Shop,* September 4, 1946.) This was an action brought by a Negro member of Local 22 who was barred from higher paying jobs controlled by Local 89. Today 16 years later, not a single Negro or Spanish-speaking person holds membership in the two Italian locals which have control of some of the highest paying jobs in the industry and no action has been taken to comply with the state law forbidding such practices.

Yet in the recent statement prepared by Mr. Tyler, the ILGWU asserted that the NAACP charge that Locals 48 and 89 discriminate is "comical." What Mr. Tyler must explain is why, if the NAACP charge is "comical" today, the ILGWU agreed to go along with the comedy years ago.

Tyler makes such a grand production of his comedy; so much joshing. He good humoredly tells us that the reason for all-Italian locals dates back to the days when Italian immigrant unionists who spoke no other language needed their own locals to conduct union business. Being Italian language locals, only those speaking Italian can belong. Not only Puerto Ricans and Negroes are excluded (unless, as Tyler wittily thrusts, they are "Italian-speaking Negroes") but all other non-Italian groups are excluded. What could be more fair? And, if all non-Italians are excluded, how can Hill claim that Negroes and Puerto Ricans are thereby specially victimized? The Jewish Labor Committee and the Director of the National Labor Service also defend this practice in a similar manner.

I submit that it is not "comical" that the largest local in the ILGWU (Italian Dressmakers' Local 89) and the largest local in the coat and suit industry (Italian Cloakmakers' Local 48) bar Negroes and Spanish-speaking persons from membership. I submit that it is not "comical" that as a result of being barred from membership in Local 48 and Local 89, Negro and Spanish-speaking persons are further denied access to certain high paying jobs in the two branches of the garment industry of New York City where such jobs are concentrated.

Other national and religious groupings, all of them white, have access to skilled jobs via other locals which are virtually closed to Negroes and Puerto Ricans on the basis of tradition and practice. That is the point. The practical effects of the operation of Italian language locals is to further keep Negroes and Puerto Ricans concentrated in the low paid unskilled classifications with little opportunity for advancement.

While it appears that all are equally unequal where the Italian locals are concerned, some are actually far more unequal than others.

It is obvious that the ILGWU's humorous rationalizations and glib assertions completely fail to answer the charge that these locals discriminate against Negro and Spanish-speaking persons. Indeed their admission of the facts is the proof of the charge. I further submit that the barring of Negroes, Spanish-speaking and other persons from Locals 48 and 89 is a violation of the AFL-CIO Constitution and a violation of the nondiscrimination pledge which the ILGWU recently signed in the Office of the President of the

United States. We of the NAACP do not think, moreover, that it is "comical" that the ILGWU subscribes to no-discrimination pledges for public relations purposes when in reality it fails to put an end to such discriminatory practices. Sixteen years have passed since the ILGWU entered into the stipulation agreement with SCAD concerning the Italian locals, but these locals are still "lily-white." Shall this, too, be hailed as "an impressive demonstration of integration"?

Tyler is not above borrowing a trick or two from management associations which, when pressed by unions for higher wages, place statistic-ridden ads in The *New York Times* and other newspapers to prove to the world that their employees never had it so good. One such gimmick is to advertise workers' wages without corresponding figures on how many hours of work the payroll represents. Tyler commits the same patent and deliberate fraud.

My report, for example, indicated that "push-boys" and shipping clerks in the "Jim Crow" auxiliary known as 60A—mainly Negroes and Puerto Ricans—receive extremely low wages. Tyler "refutes" this charge by arguing that some of these workers earn from $70 to $100 per week. Of course, by working long overtime hours at time-and-a-half wages, by working 60 or 70 hours a week and more, they can earn $80 and $90. But my report, as Tyler knows, describes straight hourly wages, not overtime wages earned at time-and-a-half pay. I am describing one week's pay for one week's work, that is, a regular week's earnings for the "normal work week" of 35 hours.

The wages set forth in the section of the union agreements that cover members of 60A are as follows:

The following minimum rates of pay for the *normal work week*, as hereinafter defined, shall apply to the following employees: Group I—Assorters, piece goods workers, push boys, porters, delivery boys, packers and errand boys. Minimum wages of $46.00 per *normal work week*. Group II—Shipping clerks, receiving clerks, chargers, order pickers, checkers. Minimum wage of $50.00 per *normal work week*. (Emphasis added.)

The overwhelming majority of members of 60A are employed in the job classifications contained in Group I as described above and receive a minimum wage of $46.00 ($1.31 an hour) for 35 hours, a normal work week.

I cited the pay of workers—almost all Negroes and Puerto Ricans—in a particular unionized shop as an example of an ILGWU substandard negotiated contract. Tyler takes up the "Hill Charge" and then proceeds to demolish only himself with "The Truth" as follows:

Hill Charge: 'I cite the Fine Arts Pillow and Specialties Company of 37 West 26th Street in Manhattan as a typical example of conditions . . . . Here, virtually all nonwhite workers, male and female, who are union members are paid $1.15, $1.20 or $1.25 an hour.

The [Tyler] Truth: According to a payroll check, 54 of the 104 employees are paid more than $1.25 an hour. These are overwhelmingly Negro and Puerto Ricans. Of the top ten earners—from $1.53 an hour to $3.23 an hour—seven are Negro or Puerto Ricans.

Tyler's truth is that "54 of the 104 employees are paid more than $1.25 an hour." But this means that *50* workers, approximately half the work force, in a unionized shop receive less than $1.25 an hour. That is not all. Tyler boasts that the ten top earners receive from $1.53 to $3.23 an hour (how many earn that miserable $1.53 or only a few cents more he doesn't say). What this figure further reveals is that at least *45* additional workers receive between $1.25 and $1.53 an hour (how many are just slightly above the $1.25 scale he doesn't say either). Thus, at least 95 out of 104 workers earn from less than $1.25 an hour to $1.53 an hour.

To cover himself in the event that some readers might work out the arithmetic presented by his "Truth," Tyler argues that the shop under discussion in any case is "as typical of ILGWU conditions as Mississippi is typical of America." How typical it really is can be seen in the following exhibits of ILGWU-negotiated contracts in New York City where there is the heaviest concentration of Negro and Puerto Rican workers, in some cases as high as 90 percent.

"As typical of ILGWU conditions as Mississippi is typical of America"? The United States has only *one* Mississippi. The ILGWU, as the above figures indicate, has a whole flock of them!

It is evident from the data above, that new workers do not even receive the contract minimum for "skilled" workers, but must work a considerable period before they even receive this low wage. Indeed, in the case of Local 62, for example, workers must work eight weeks at the federal minimum wage and a full 15 weeks before they receive the contract minimum of $1.30 or $1.33 an hour. At the same time, of course, these workers are required, as a condition of employment,

JOB TITLE	PROGRESSION RATES FOR "UNSKILLED" WORKERS *Time Intervals and Rates*				CONTRACT MINIMUM FOR "SKILLED" WORKERS

Corset and Brassiere Workers' Union of N.Y., Local 32 (6,632 members)

	1-8	*9-10*	*11-13*	*14-16*	
Weeks					
Operators	1.15	1.20	1.25	1.30	1.36
Weeks	*1-8*	*9-10*	*11-12*		
Pressers	1.15	1.20	1.25		1.30
Cleaners	1.15	1.20	1.25		1.30
Examiners	1.15	1.20	1.25		1.30

Beltmakers' Local 40 (4,504 members)

	1-8		
Weeks			
Machine operators	1.15		1.38
Operators	1.15		1.43
General Help	1.15		1.43
Shipper	1.15		1.30
Floor Girls	1.15		1.30

Undergarment and Negligee Workers' Union, Local 62 (16,592 members)

Weeks	*1-8*	*9-10*	*13-15*	Class R Shops	Class S Shops
Operators	1.15	1.25	1.30-1.33	1.30	1.33
Ironers	1.15	1.20	1.25-1.25	1.30	1.30
Examiners	1.15	1.20	1.25-1.25	1.30	1.30
Finishers	1.15	1.20	1.25-1.25	1.30	1.30

Childrens' Dress, House Dress & Bathrobe Makers' Union, Local 91 (11,943 members)

Weeks	*1-12*	
Operators	1.20	1.41
Ironers	1.20	1.38
Cleaners	1.20	1.35
Finishers	1.20	1.35

Rubberized Novelty & Plastic-Fabric Workers' Union Local 98 (4,403 members previously cited)

Months	*1st.*	*2-6*	*7-9*	
Operators	1.15	1.20	1.25	1.30
Shipping Clerks	1.15	1.20	1.25	1.30
Cutters	1.15	1.20	1.25	1.30
Floor Girls	1.15	1.20	1.25	1.25

Plastic, Molders & Novelty Workers' Union, Local 132 (5,460 members)

Months	*1st.*	*2-6*	*6-9*			
All workers other than Molders	1.15	1.20	1.25			1.30
Months	*1st*	*2-4*	*5-7*	*8-10*	*11-13*	*11-13*
Molders	1.20	1.25	1.30	1.35	1.40	1.45

Unit 60A Sect. of Dress Joint Board Agreement (1,943 members)

Assorters, Piece Goods Workers, Pushboys, Porters, Delivery Boys, Packers and Errand Boys   1.31

Chargers, Order Pickers, Checkers, Shipping Clerks, Receiving Clerks   1.43

to become members of the union after 30 days and pay an initiation fee and dues.

Tyler's explanation for the creation of the "Jim Crow" auxiliary 60A is completely fraudulent. 60A is a unit composed of "push-boys," packers, piece goods workers, porters and shipping clerks. It has about 2,000 members, of whom more than 90 percent are either Negroes or Spanish-speaking persons. The existence of 60A is, in keeping with the tradition of the "old-line" AFL craft unions, an auxiliary to another local, Dress Pressers' Local 60, with less than 1,300 members.

60A is a new unit in the ILGWU. While the women's garment industry in New York City has had "pushboys," packers, piece goods workers, porters and shipping clerks for as long as the industry existed, the ILGWU did not consider these workers, virtually all Negroes and Puerto Ricans, worthy of union membership until a few years ago, and then only because other unions began organizing activities among these workers. The ILGWU, for the sole purpose of preventing another union from getting a toehold in the garment industry, and not because of the urgent needs of the low-paid, exploited Negro and Puerto Rican workers, then reluctantly organized these workers. Rather than granting them a separate charter, however, the ILGWU made them an auxiliary to Dress Pressers' Local 60.

The NAACP has charged that this was done among other reasons to prevent a Negro or Spanish-speaking person from rising to the position of local union manager.

It should be noted that the collective bargaining agreements negotiated between the Dress Joint Board and the employers' associations covering the members of the Dress Joint Board locals has two sections concerning wages, hours and conditions of employment: one section covers the members of Locals 10, 22, 60 and 89, and the other covers the members of 60A. Aside from the question of wages, there are other striking and illuminating differences concerning conditions of employment between the two sections which are described below. Here are two clauses in the collective agreements between the Dress Joint Board and the employers' associations:

Fifteenth—Hours of work (covering members of locals 10, 22, 60 and 89)

A regular week's work shall consist of thirty-five hours in the first five days of the week. *Work shall begin at 9:00 A.M. and end at 5:00 P.M.*, with one hour interval for lunch. There shall be no more than one shift of workers in any day.

During the season, when the inside shop and each of the contracting shops of the manufacturer or jobber for whom a member of the Association is registered or designated as fully supplied with at least a full week's work, and when there are no vacant accommodations in the said shops for additional worker or additional workers cannot be secured, *overtime may be worked by all the workers therein except the cutters, provided the member of the Association notifies Joint Council in writing, in advance of the period during which overtime will be worked. In no event shall overtime worked beyond the first five days of the week exceed one hour per day.* All week workers, when working overtime, shall receive pay at the rate of time and one-half. (Collective Agreement 1961-1964—United Better Dress Manufacturers' Association, Inc., with International Ladies' Garment Workers' Union and Dressmakers Joint Council.)

Compare the above (emphasis added) with below, which covers 60A:

Sixty-ninth—The normal work week for the purpose of this agreement, shall be deemed to mean a 35-hour week. *Each employer shall, in his discretion, be free to fix the hours of the day within which each employee in the unit shall work,* but work in excess of 7 hours performed in any one day shall be compensated for at the rate of time and one-half. Saturday work shall likewise be compensated at the rate of time and one-half. *All overtime shall be performed in the discretion of the employer.* (Collective Agreement—United Better Dress Manufacturers' Association, Inc., with International Ladies' Garment Workers' Union and Dressmakers Joint Council.)

It is clear from the foregoing that members of 60A are considered by the ILGWU as different than, and inferior to, the members of the other locals affiliated to the Dress Joint Board. With respect to members of 60A, unlike the members of the other Dress Joint Board affiliates, the *employer* has full discretion both as to hours within which they will work and how many hours they will work. It is clear, too, how members of 60A can earn more than $50.00 per week: many long hours beyond the so-called "normal work week."

How does Tyler discuss the status of those consigned to 60A? In the first place, according to him, their segregated position is for their own good. Tyler writes: "The clerks (in 60A) enjoy all the benefits of being united in industrial fashion with a more highly skilled craft. No student of labor relations has to be told why . . . ." I'm afraid that Mr. Tyler takes too much for granted. The supposedly self-evident advantage of the unskilled workers being affiliated to a skilled craft local as argued by Tyler is simply an exercise in fantasy. What, concretely, have been the benefits for the members of 60A getting $46.00 to $50.00 for a normal work week of being affiliated to a craft local with pay scales ranging up to close to $5.00 an hour (the highest in the industry)?

Then there is Tyler's ludicrous analogy designed to counter my charge that 60A is a "Jim Crow" affiliate:

Most of its (60A) members [over 90 percent to be more exact] are Negro and Puerto Rican, but to call it a "Jim Crow" local for that reason would be the same as calling the Sleeping Car Porters' Union a Jim Crow union because all or most of its members are Negro.

In the first place, 60A is not a local. It is an *auxiliary* to Local 60. Quite a difference there. In the second place, the Sleeping Car Porters' union would be a Jim Crow organization if it had a parallel construction to that of 60A. If the Sleeping Car Porters' union were an auxiliary to, say, the Brotherhood of Railroad Trainmen and, if instead of A. Philip Randolph there were the equivalent of a white local manager, selected in reality by the international office of the Brotherhood of Railroad Trainmen to service the needs of the Sleeping Car Porters' local, then the Sleeping Car Porters' Local would be a segregated auxiliary just as 60A is a Jim Crow unit.

Then we have Tyler the expert on ethnology:

Hill's suggestion that a separate local of shipping clerks would elect a Negro manager is both inaccurate and vicious. It is inaccurate because Local 60A is "mixed" with no one ethnic group—Negro, Puerto Ricans, Cubans, Irish, Jewish or Italian—in a simple majority.

It is Tyler who is inaccurate and vicious. Inaccurate, because I did not say that a separate local would "elect" a Negro manager but that "there would inevitably be a Negro or Puerto Rican manager." While the ILGWU constitution provides for the formal election of local managers they are not really elected. In practice they are selected by the International and confirmed by the local! In the second place, I said "Negro *or* Puerto Rican," and not just "Negro." Tyler decided to omit the Puerto Ricans in his reference in order to make his sly point that no one ethnic group is in a simple majority in 60A. (To be sure, in a previous quote from Tyler on this matter, the reader can clearly see that he says "most of its members are Negro and Puerto Rican." Suddenly, in an effort to fudge over the question we are introduced to Cubans, Irish, Jewish or Italian as though they represent a significant part of the membership of 60A.) Now, it is true that Negroes and Puerto Ricans constitute a separate group. But they are coupled in my discussion and in Mr. Tyler's—except when inconvenient to him—because they are both the victims of economic, political, ethnic and racial discrimination different in kind and degree from other ethnic groups which comprise less than 10 percent of 60A.

Tyler goes even further:

". . . there is no reason to believe that the members of Local 60A would elect a manager on a racist rather than unionist basis. The proposal is socially vicious because to create a separate Local 60A just to guarantee the election of a Negro or Puerto Rican manager is to create a Jim Crow local—separate but equal. ILGWU members prefer integration: craft and color."

Most damaging here (aside from the "elected" managers) is Tyler's sophistry, that pseudo-liberal conception that for Negroes and Puerto Ricans to seek their own leadership is racism in reverse. Of course, I think that Negroes and Puerto Ricans would take special interest and justifiable pride in electing a Negro or Puerto Rican manager or joint board chairman or president of the international union.

I might ask Tyler whether he uses the same standards in judging political gerrymandering when it is done to deny Negroes representation in Congress. Does he then virtuously declare that it is "socially vicious" to speak of allowing Negroes to have Negro congressmen? Or does he, good liberal that he is, protest this kind of gerrymandering—another form of "craft and color"—because it specifically denies Negroes their representational rights?

How vicious it is, he writes "to create a separate Local 60A just to guarantee the election of a Negro or Puerto Rican . . . ." However, Negroes and Puerto Ricans are already separate. Who is responsible for this? The NAACP or the ILGWU? They are separated, not as an independent local as are other crafts in the Dress Joint Board, but as an auxiliary of a skilled local. Thus, they are separate and *unequal*. It is also interesting to note that 60 and 60A have separate executive boards but one manager for both units.

The NAACP claims that when the boundary of separation is drawn at the point where *autonomy* begins, this is evidence that discrimination is a hard fact. As against this affiliated status, local autonomy would, indeed, be a step in the right direction. And not "just to" guarantee the election of a Negro or Puerto Rican, but as a means of better protecting the rights of both groups and offering the enormous educational and training advantage of self-leadership.

Tyler says as against local autonomy for 60A, "ILGWU members prefer integration: craft and color." Bravo! The NAACP looks forward to seeing Negro and Puerto Rican ILGWU members on the General Executive Board, as local union managers, given a more equitable share of the better-paying jobs and that the union conduct a vigorous union campaign against exploitation.

One final quotation from Tyler on 60A:

> . . .a majority of the combined members of Local 60 and Local 60A are Negro and Puerto Rican. Each member has an equal vote—whether 60 or 60A. If the present manager is not a Negro or Puerto Rican, it merely indicates that the members of this union prefer not to cast a "racial" vote. . . .

I am again obliged to point out that whether the manager of Local 60 is or is not a Puerto Rican or a Negro has little to do with normal elections. The manager is actually selected by the General Executive Board and ritualistically confirmed at a local union meeting. Apart from this little detail what Tyler is suggesting is completely demagogic. Everyone knows that given the situation as I have described it—and as Tyler unwittingly confirms—the "equal vote" that he boasts of is non-existent because of the lack of involvement of these minorities in the union. Their apathy and the refusal to use their "equal vote" is an indication of the controlled, undemocratic atmosphere in which they are treated with contempt as "things" to be manipulated by an arrogant bureaucracy.

Am I exaggerating when I say that the ILGWU is contemptuous of Negroes and Puerto Ricans? A comparison of the clauses in the same collective agreement concerning discharge of workers, first that covering members of Locals 10, 22, 60 and 89, then covering members of 60A, is in order.

Thirty-eighth—Discharge [of members of Locals 10, 22, 60 and 89]

(a) No member of the Association shall discharge a worker, except for misbehavior sufficient to justify a discharge, before a notice in writing is served on Joint Council of the reason for the intended discharge. In case of a discharge for alleged misbehavior, and it be determined that the worker be reinstated, he is entitled to receive pay for all the time he stayed out.

(b) Joint Council shall investigate the notice of the intended discharge within forty-eight hours of the receipt of same. If Joint Council does not consent to the proposed discharge, the question shall be referred to the Impartial Chairman, whose decision shall be final. Pending such decision the employee shall continue working at full pay. Collective Agreement (1961-1964—United Better Dress Manufacturers' Association, Inc., with International Ladies' Garment Workers' Union and Dressmakers' Joint Council.)

Seventy-four [on discharge of members of 60A]

The employer may discharge regular employees for any just and reasonable cause including the following:

Incompetence,
Insubordination,
Dishonesty,
Intoxication,
Soldiering on the job,
Repeated lateness or absence,
Assault or attempted assault on the job,
Repeated breach of reasonable rules established by the employer.

In the event that the Union questions any discharge as not being for just and reasonable cause, it shall so inform the Association within five (5) days after the discharge. Representatives of the Union and the Association shall attempt to settle the grievance by negotiation. If no settlement can be reached, Joint Council may invoke the arbitration machinery provided in this agreement. (Collective Agreement 1961-64—United Better Dress Manufacturers' Association, Inc., with International Ladies Garment Workers' Union and Dressmakers' Joint Council.)

In the discharge of members of Locals 10, 22, 60 and 89, the burden is on the employer, not the worker.

In the discharge of a member of 60A, the burden is on the worker. It is significant that specific reasons for which a member of 60A can be discharged are set forth, while with respect to members of Locals 10, 22, 60 and 89, they are not.

What do Tyler, Fleischman and Muravchik have to say about these specifics contained in a contract negotiated by the ILGWU?

Are "dishonesty," "intoxication," "soldiering on the job," "assault or attempted assault" on the job the characteristic habits of Negroes and Puerto Ricans? Or do they recognize in this listing the hallmark of the bigot enthusiastically perpetuating the sickening stereotypes of racial and national minorities? If Tyler does not understand this, his stint with the ILGWU has served to corrupt his sensibilities completely. Tyler and the other apologists for the ILGWU neglect to state that the "integrated" members of 60A are covered by a separate union agreement from that covering members of Locals 10, 22, 60, 89.

Further evidence of discrimination is documented in Tyler's own discussion of the ILGWU's Officer Qualification Course and the Union's Training Institute. The Officer Qualification Course was set up in 1938 "to prepare candidates for elective office." A total of 832 applied. Of these 832, only "19 were Negro and eight were Spanish-speaking—a total of 27 in 24 years." An annual average of *one* (and one-eighth)!

Tyler then tries to compensate for this failure with the reputed success of the union's Training Institute. We are told that in 11 years, 30 Negroes and Puerto Ricans were graduated by the Institute. An excellent record. Certainly it is better than the Officer Qualification Course showing. However, far from proving the ILGWU's concern with promoting Negro and Puerto Rican leadership, the greater success of the Institute reveals just the opposite when placed side-by-side with the failure in the Officer Qualification Course. The reason lies in the difference between the two programs which Tyler deliberately tries to gloss over. The failure was in recruiting trainees within the union for officers with the (theoretical) right to participate in formulating and influencing the policies of the union. On the other hand, where the ILGWU achieved some success, in the Institute, it has been with individuals who are not necessarily even members of the union, who are to become employees and not officials of the union and who have no voice in determining union policy. Also, the ILGWU must employ some Negro and Spanish-speaking organizers given the changing racial and ethnic composition of the industry.

As an example of discrimination, I mentioned in my article the fact that two locals in Puerto Rico—locals 600 and 601—were placed under the managership of an official from New York, one Jerry Schoen. Here is how Tyler discusses my charge:

Hill Charge: The two Puerto Rican locals are "denied Puerto Rican leadership."

Now, the words are mine, but the period after the quoted phrase belongs to Tyler. What I wrote was: "However, both these locals are denied Puerto Rican leadership *as they are managed by one Jerry Schoen*, a former business agent for Local 62, who was sent from New York City by the International union to manage these two Puerto Rican locals." (Emphasis added here.)

By trimming my sentence as he does, Tyler thinks that all he has to do is rattle off a list of Puerto Rican "officials" in these locals, although the point I am making, seen clearly in the omitted words, is that the two locals are denied self-leadership "as they are managed by one Jerry Schoen."

And as Tyler knows, as I know, as anyone who knows anything about the ILGWU knows, it is the manager who wields the power in ILGWU locals. It is Schoen who represents the International in Puerto Rico. His is the real power.

More than a year and a half ago, officers of Local 10 claimed before representatives of the New York State Commission for Human Rights investigating a complaint of racial discrimination that there were 400 nonwhite members of this local of skilled, higher-paid workers. I offered to withdraw the complaint if this were proven. The figure was then reduced to 300 by the union representatives. Harry Fleischman later said that there are "250 Negro and Spanish-speaking cutters in Local 10."[4] In Fleischman's other article "Is the ILGWU Biased?" he refers to "Negro ILGWU member Ernest Holmes." *Holmes was never, at any time a member of the ILGWU.* This was precisely the charge of his highly publicized complaint, that he was refused admission into Local 10 of the ILGWU. This falsehood is typical of Fleischman's frequent distortions.

In Gus Tyler's article we are told that there are 239 Negro and Spanish-speaking workers in Local 10—only slightly more than one-half of what the ILGWU originally claimed.

On the basis of these figures, either the ILGWU lied one and a half years ago, or it has dropped nearly 200 Negro and Spanish-speaking people from Local 10.

Of the 239 figure in Tyler's article, it would be interesting to know how many are Negro and Puerto Ricans, since his count embraces "Cubans, Panamanians, Colombians, Dominicans, Salvadorians, Mexicans, etc., as well as Puerto Ricans . . ." I, of course, am not discussing "Cubans . . . etc.," but Negroes and Puerto Ricans, over 120,000 strong, with problems quite distinct from those presumably located by Tyler in his quest for as large a number as possible. It would also be interesting to know how many Negroes and Puerto Ricans have been brought into Local 10 in the past 18 months—i.e., since the NAACP focused national attention on the status of Negroes and Puerto Ricans in the ILGWU.

Tyler says that when Hill claims in a television broadcast "that there are in the vicinity of 50 (Negro) cutters of Local 10 in the city" that he "still has no regard for the truth."

However, if one makes a modest deduction for "Cubans . . . etc.," from Tyler's strained-for 239 his number of Negroes and Puerto Ricans would no doubt go below 200. Since it is most likely that there are considerably more Puerto Ricans than Negroes in Local 10, I suggest that Tyler take out his slide rule and let the reader know how far off my estimated "vicinity of 50 (Negro) cutters" is from his "regard for the truth."

Now, even less than 200 skilled Negro and Puerto Rican workers would not be too bad in a local of one or two thousand craft workers. But, if Tyler wants to play the numbers game, why does he hide the most revealing figure, "239 Negroes, Puerto Ricans plus "Cubans . . . etc.," out of *7,531* members. Slightly more than 3 percent! This, Tyler tells us "is an impressive demonstration of integration."

The NAACP finds this impressive evidence of discrimination, especially when over one-half the New York membership of the ILGWU is composed of Negroes and Puerto Ricans.

Tyler tells us that what makes the over 200 figure such an impressive demonstration is that "there is very little 'turnover' of employment; the total number of jobs covered by Local 10 has fallen in the last decade." While this might explain a disproportionately fewer number of Negroes and Puerto Ricans, it cannot explain the excessiveness of that disproportion.

Though they tell us that Negroes and Puerto Ricans never had it so good, as in Local 10, ILGWU spokesmen usually feel compelled to explain that the union is not responsible for hiring cutters; it is all the employer's fault. This won't do. In the first place, if there is impressive integration no one is really at fault. In the second place, if it is only the employers who discriminate in hiring, it is the responsibility of the union to combat that policy. In the third place, the union *does* have considerable control in the hiring of cutters.

In the November 1, 1962, issue of *Justice*, the official ILGWU publication, there is a news story which would seem not only to substantiate the Union's placement role, but to boast of it. The article states: "A total of 576 members of Local 10 have been placed on permanent jobs during the year since last October, Vice-President Moe Falikman, manager of the organization reported at its membership meeting on October 29. This was disclosed by a tabulation based on reports submitted by officers and business agents functioning in the various trades in which cutters are employed."

The report continues with reference to the Local's placement activity over a three-year period and says that placing its members in permanent jobs "is a major continuing activity."

Thus, it is clear beyond doubt, despite the ILGWU's public denials, that Local 10 has considerable control in the placement of cutters in all branches of the women's garment industry in New York City.

On the total number of Negroes and Puerto Ricans in all the skilled craft locals, Tyler makes a boast of what is actually a confession of moral bankruptcy. He writes that the number of Spanish-speaking and Negro members "runs into the *tens of thousands*"[5] and in the next breath he takes pride in his reference to "*hundreds* of Negroes, Puerto Ricans, plus other Latins, Japanese, etc., who are in the skilled craft locals." [Emphasis added.]

A further analysis, employing the ILGWU's own figures, discloses the following: out of a total of approximately 14,500 members of Cutters' Local 10, Pressers' Locals 35 and 60 and the Pressers' branches of the two Italian Locals, 48 and 89, there are some 550 Negroes, Puerto Ricans and "Cubans . . . etc." This constitutes about 3.7 percent of the total membership of the locals controlling the highest-paying jobs in New York City. 96.3 percent white and 3.7 percent Negro, Puerto Rican, Cuban . . . etc., cannot be considered "an impressive demonstration of integration." I submit that the ILGWU figures are greatly inflated; 2 percent is closer to the truth.

Why does the NAACP single out the ILGWU? Aren't there unions with far worse records than this one? These questions are usually asked by those who will candidly acknowledge that the charges against Dubinsky's union are justified in large measure, but bridle at concentrating so much fire on a "progressive" union which passes fine resolutions on civil rights, and contributes to worthy causes.

I believe that this approach is unwarranted for the following reasons:

1. The ILGWU is the largest union in the largest manufacturing industry in New York City. It affects the economic welfare and dignity of hundreds of thousands of Negro and Puerto Rican men, women and children in New York. Is the NAACP supposed to refrain from presenting the truth about this union because it passes good resolutions on integration in Mississippi?

2. The "go-soft-on-Dubinsky" line has the disagreeable connotations of "Uncle Tomism": it is suggested that the liberal and Negro community should be appreciative of small favors and not attack its "benefactors" even if those friends aren't completely perfect. This is of course nonsense and is rejected by responsible and serious elements in the Negro community.

3. It implicitly fails to give credit to the NAACP for its work in combatting the anti-Negro practices of blatantly discriminatory unions, North and South. A part of my time for the past 16 years as a staff member of the NAACP has been devoted to exposing and combatting the vicious racial practices of the railroad unions, the building trades unions and other labor organizations where discriminatory practices are blatant and open to new job opportunities for Negro workers in the craft jurisdictions. Most of the major breakthroughs in the past decade made by Negro workers in the "old-line" AFL-controlled craft occupations as well as in industrial union jurisdictions are the direct result of NAACP exposure and pressure.

4. Those who say "Hill is really right but why make such a fuss over a progressive union" substitute sentimentality for thought, myth for reality. Judging the ILGWU by its current practices and not by its past, the "progressive" label is a nostalgic hangover. The word suggests militancy, internal democracy and social vision. On none of these counts does the ILGWU qualify.

5. The ILGWU leadership is greatly concerned with presenting a

progressive liberal public image, without critically examining the social consequences of its policies and practices. This is perhaps the most dismal factor in the entire situation, their incapacity to admit that anything at all is wrong. But they do care obsessively about their public image. The concern, I believe, increases the possibility that the pressures applied by the NAACP might have salutary effects. I think that as a result of the activity of the NAACP there may be more Negroes and Puerto Ricans in better-paid jobs, that the operational bar against Negroes and Puerto Rican local managers might be raised slightly; Dubinsky will perhaps allow a Negro or Puerto Rican to find his place on the General Board and the ILGWU might feel obliged to do something about the substandard wage levels in the industry which victimizes, primarily, the Negro and Puerto Rican worker. Already one notes perhaps a little less arrogance on the part of ILGWU officials in the daily treatment of Negroes and Puerto Ricans in the shops and within the unions.

I anticipated that my analysis of the ILGWU would be met with the fury with which any powerful and entrenched bureaucracy retaliates when challenged. The attacks upon me for telling the truth are characterized by a viciousness and hysteria that tells much about the institution defending itself. Among a variety of other personal attacks the ILGWU leadership has charged publicly and in corridors that I am a Jewish anti-Semite, a kind of McCarthyite and in the camp of the Birchites.

No less incredible than the anti-Semitic smear was the abortive attempt to discredit me by Evelyn Dubrow, an ILGWU staff member who together with other union representatives went to several Congressmen and other public officials and "explained" that Hill was a Communist stirring up racial strife, an anti-Semite, etc.

If I am incensed at the anti-Semitic smear, the reader will surely understand. I am, after all, a "white Jew" as Tyler so delicately puts it.

Had I committed a gross injustice in my charges, the Dubinsky leadership's reaction would never take such grotesque forms. That it struck out so wildly, with such malevolence, is evidence that my criticism pierced a bureaucratic shell and pricked what there is of a sense of guilt among those who have led the ILGWU from what it was yesterday to what it has become today.

While Tyler does not make this charge—at least, not in his

article—he must accept responsibility for it considering its source. I am not debating Tyler the individual, but Tyler the defense counsel for the ILGWU.

Roy Wilkins, Executive Secretary of the NAACP, responding to a Jewish Labor Committee attack on the Association, stated in a letter dated October 31, 1962, to Emanual Muravchik as follows:

...We assert with the greatest emphasis that nothing, absolutely nothing, in Mr. Hill's recent or more remote statements can be construed as anti-Semitic. This is a grave charge to make. It requires more substantiation than your flip reference in a part of a sentence. The charge is not only against Mr. Hill, but against the NAACP itself. We do not deign to defend ourselves against such a baseless allegation. Its inclusion in the resolution, as well as in the statements to the press by Mr. Zimmerman is unworthy of an organization like the Jewish Labor Committee which, in the very nature of things, must be conversant with the seriousness of such a charge and with the evidence required to give it substance. No such evidence has been submitted in this case beyond the citation of the use by Mr. Hill of one word, "ethnic," out of a total of 4,500 words in his testimony before the House subcommittee. The relevance of his comparison of the ethnic composition of the membership and the leadership of the ILGWU can hardly be questioned in this context. [Wilkins also said:] We reject the proposition that any segment of the labor movement is sacrosanct in the matter of practices and/or policies which restrict employment opportunities on racial or religious or nationality grounds. We reject the contention that bringing such charges constitutes a move to destroy 'unity' among civil rights groups unless it be admitted that this unity is a precarious thing, perched upon unilateral definition of discrimination by each member group. In such a situation, the 'unity' is of no basic value and its destruction may be regarded as not a calamity, but a blessed clearing of the air.

In this connection, it is well to reiterate a facet of this discussion which appears to have escaped the attention of the various reviewers and resolution writers. It is that Herbert Hill, our Labor Secretary, has but one duty and that is to serve the interests of the Negro worker through the NAACP. Other groups, including trade unions, have powerful machinery to protect their principal interests. Mr. Hill is employed to maintain anti-discrimination work in the employment field as his top and only priority. He is not for trade unions first and Negro workers second. He has no divided loyalties.

In the years to come the effective work of the NAACP in fighting for a decent, socially conscious labor movement that is sensitive to the needs of the Negro worker will be appreciated. If trade unions in the United States are to be more than just another "business enterprise," more than just organizations that negotiate terms under which labor is bought and sold, then the struggle today for an immediate end to anti-Negro practices within the unions will provide the social basis for defending the labor movement tomorrow.

March 1963

1. Tyler "The Truth About the ILGWU," *New Politics* Vol. 2, No. 1, pp. 6-18.

2. *The New Leader* (January 21, 1963).

3. Incidentally, what is interesting about Tyler's answer is that it is almost exactly what I predicted he would say. I wrote in my previous article that "Dubinsky's spokesmen will answer that this is done to prevent Communists from taking over the union." Tyler performed as expected. Naturally, he did not quote my rebuttal about this anticipated canned reply which was that "one can only compare" such an answer "to the argument that we should suspend the U.S. Constitution and the Bill of Rights because they endanger the country in fighting subversion."

4. *Let's Be Human,* October, 1962, Newsletter of the National Labor Service.

5. That many of these tens of thousands are "relative newcomers," as he puts it, helps naught, since tens of thousands of the more than 120,000 have been in the industry for many years and are "newcomers" only "relative" to those who have been there for decades.

The UFT Strike: A Blow Against Teacher Unionism

STEVE ZELUCK

Seven years ago the United Federation of Teachers (UFT) won a collective bargaining victory that made its parent organization, the American Federation of Teachers (AFT), a significant force on the American educational scene. Today, the policies of this same United Federation of Teachers have precipitated a crisis in the AFT of such proportions that the existence of the organization is threatened. The current [1968] UFT strike over the issue of community control and last year's UFT strike, largely over the issue of the "disruptive child," have led to a confrontation between the union and the entire black community which both sides now see as a struggle for survival.

How have such issues as these become the key to the survival of a trade union? To understand this, one must be aware of several unique aspects of teacher unionism.

The American Federation of Teachers is unquestionably the dominant voice of the teachers of urban America. Its chief competitor, the National Education Association (NEA), has become more militant (mostly in response to the militance of the AFT), but each collective bargaining election finds the NEA increasingly reduced to a rural and suburban base, and even that base is being hotly contested. Its numbers still exceed those of the AFT but the difference is qualitative: in losing the cities, the NEA has lost the center of social weight and power in modern society. Today the AFT, and not the NEA, is the key to the schools.

But at the same time that the AFT has been winning urban teachers, the cities themselves have been changing. In particular, the black urban population has grown enormously and the black movement has emerged as an aggressive force determined to win a measure of the power so long denied it. In this way, the growth of the AFT has won it new power but it has also placed the union at the vortex of the crisis of the American society. Every decision of the union has effects far beyond its membership or the "industry" in which its members are employed.

Given this situation, the union must choose between two alternative strategies. It can enter into genuine and close cooperation with the insurgent forces of the ghetto around a wide range of issues, forging an alliance against the establishment. whose interest in educational improvement or the welfare of the ghetto is minimal. Or it can form an unacknowledged bloc with the status quo and the educational bureaucracy against the ghetto community (and ultimately against the students). It may be said that the second alternative is reactionary and unthinkable, that it could lead ultimately to the destruction of the union. Reactionary and destructive, yes, but in the absence of a carefully elaborated alternative, hardly unthinkable. There are powerful forces in the AFT now, many of them quite unaware of the implications of their position, who by both action and inaction are driving the union in precisely this direction. The unity and survival of the AFT will be decided in the immediate future by the clarity and decisiveness with which it chooses between the two courses open to it.

If a bold and comprehensive alliance with the civil rights movement is essential to the survival of the AFT, it is equally the only road to significant educational change in the United States. Public education, especially of ghetto and working class children, has historically been starved for funds and there is no reason to believe that this is about to change in any meaningful way. In fact, there are "good" reasons for this social indifference. The American establishment sees education mainly as providing the skilled personnel necessary to maintain the economy; that is, the American educational system is an indirect subsidy to business. Inasmuch as the economy still needs pools of unskilled, menial labor, it is considered wasteful, if not actually dangerous, to try to educate everyone. In addition, the deep reservoir of racism in our society leads to the belief that such an attempt would be not only wasteful but futile.

The civil rights movement, by its own efforts, has already stimulated some very significant changes in education. But for all their significance, these changes have been at best token, paralleling the "success" of anti-poverty programs. A coalition of civil rights forces, teachers and the trade union movement is needed if the demand for educational change is to be taken seriously.

Such a coalition is also needed by teachers in their daily work. Students, after all, are not commodities. Few people would think of blaming an auto worker for the wasteful or unsafe design of a car. But teachers are held responsible for their "product." The first person blamed for the obvious failure of our schools is the individual teacher. It is not hard to point out that teachers' responsibility is at best derivative and subordinate, that the failure lies with those who hold the reins of power, that teachers are only their front men, the instrument of their indifference, and that attacks on teachers, individually or collectively, even when justifiable, are scarcely able to effect any substantial change in the situation.

However, the teacher is so visible and so vulnerable, and the daily pressures are so intolerable, that such attacks are becoming the central concern of teachers in urban schools. Once again, the only way out is to redirect the resentment of the community toward the real culprits. This means that the union must not only face the facts of the monstrous conditions in the schools, but must take the lead in exposing them and placing responsibility for them where it belongs, with the real decision-makers and wielders of power—those who determine the allocation of resources in our society. It also means that the union must commit itself fully to the struggle for equality and not be content with tokenism—convention resolutions, trips to the South and conferences on Negro History. (It should not be forgotten that the AFT did make one real act of commitment when it expelled many of its locals for refusing to integrate immediately after 1954.) Only such policies can be effective and successful in defending teachers against abuse and unwarranted attacks by a frustrated and resentful community.

Another important gain from such a coalition would be the realization of the demand for teacher power. The historically legitimate demand that teachers, and not the educational bureaucracy, control the schools (by means of election and recall of principals, the determination of curriculum, and so forth) has never, given the unquestionable failure of the schools, been more pertinent than it is today. At the same time, it is today totally unrealizable, especially in the cities, without the consent and cooperation of the black community.

If effective education and practical democracy require that authority be wrested from the establishment-dominated city boards of education, the aim of "teacher control of the schools," it must be obvious that the means to this end have to be modified to fit the new context of an erupting ghetto mobilizing to gain control over the institutions that dominate their lives. The movement for community control in the ghetto is aimed at taking power away from the boards of education, paralleling the aim of the teachers' movement. The two efforts are inseparable; neither can be won alone or at the expense of the other.

Abstractly, of course, community control of schools does not necessarily lead to educational progress. There are thousands of middle-class schools with de facto community control without any positive educational consequences. Less abstractly, the extension of community control to urban schools entails obvious dangers. If the teachers' movement remains isolated from this development, it will be all too easy to focus on teachers as the core of the failure of the schools. Further, if the movement for community control fails to produce significant changes (as is likely in the absence of the vast sums needed for schools and urban reconstruction), the most probable result will be demoralization, desperation and cynicism.

But in action these dangers can be averted. Community control that is the product of mass activity and involvement, especially if it is won in cooperation with the teachers' movement, is quite different from the sort of control that is handed down (and strictly limited) by a beneficent bureaucracy. Such control contains the potential for the self-mobilization of teachers, students and community to bring about serious, constructive changes in the educational system.

Today, in the cities, to counterpose teacher power to community control is to sabotage both and to surrender a great opportunity to shift the center of power in the schools in the direction that the teachers' movement has long sought.

To all these urgent reasons for an alliance between the teachers union and the ghetto and working class community must be added the fact that recent years have seen a great increase in the number of black teachers in northern urban schools—one-third of the staff in Detroit and Chicago, three-quarters in the District of Columbia (New York City's 8 percent is anomolous)—and that this trend is continuing. These figures, large as they are, understate the actual weight of black teachers in the AFT. The union is still, in most cities, actively opposed by the NEA and any significant defection of black teachers could easily destroy the union outside New York City.

For all these reasons, the AFT has been forced by historical circumstances to face the question of its relationship to the black movement, not as an abstract moral issue but as a matter of the life or death of the union. Given these pressures and needs, transcending those facing any other union in the country today, it is hardly surprising that the AFT is the first union to have developed a significant opposition on a national scale, one which has proposed union recognition of the ghetto's right to self-determination with all that implies for the schools and the union and which won 25 percent of the vote for its presidential candidate. The existence and growth of this caucus gives hope that the proposed course toward the community that has been discussed here will be adopted. If so, the teachers union could begin to have the same healthy vanguard influence in society and in the labor movement that is shared by the teachers unions of France and Japan.

If there are forces pressing the union to move in a more progressive, more democratic direction, there are also, unfortunately, powerful counter forces. The first of these is the current social and political climate. Teachers, even union teachers, are not immune to the current demand for "order über alles" or to the unacknowledged racism endemic in our society. Nowhere does this problem, and the dangers implicit in it, appear more clearly than in the recent history of the single most important unit of the AFT, the 50,000-member United Federation of Teachers.

For many years the UFT was thought of as the "left wing" of the AFT. The origins of its leadership in the Socialist and Liberal parties and its relatively democratic structure and operation gave it an air of progressiveness, personified by its former president, Charles Cogan. Even after the UFT failed to support the school boycotts of 1964 (a failure not due to any criticism of the boycott as a tactic or softened by the offering of any alternative), the black and liberal movements continued to see the UFT as fundamentally "on our side."

In the last 15 months, this attitude has been completely shattered. The UFT's totally punitive approach to the "disruptive child" in the strike of September 1967 and its adamant opposition to any meaningful community participation in the schools (hiding behind its legitimate demands for "due process") have embittered relations between the union and those who should be, and once were, its closest allies. The breach has reached the point where both black and white teachers are ready to engage in strikebreaking on a scale that threatens the future of the union.

This crucial development in the UFT can be traced to two factors: the objective work conditions for teachers in ghetto schools and the subjective needs of the leadership of the UFT. The objective factor is all too well known. The complete lack of meaningful and relevant education for the poor of all races, combined with the increasing consciousness of blacks, have produced an explosive mixture that makes teaching, especially conventional teaching, a frustrating, demoralizing and at times even hazardous occupation. The role of leadership in such a foreboding situation can be all-important. It can organize and direct the frustration and indignation of the teachers at those who are responsible for the crisis of the schools. But to do so, the leadership must be prepared to offer an alternative to the status quo, one which poses the need for drastic educational changes, recognizes the necessity for a vast mobilization of forces to effect these changes and commits the teachers union to take the lead in beginning such a mobilization.

Without such an alternative, teachers will increasingly fall prey to reactionary notions. The destructive tendencies within the union will grow, pressing the union leadership and the schools further to the right and leading to a debacle. This is what has occurred within the UFT. Unwilling to fight for new alternatives, the leadership capitulated to the growing destructive climate and by striking in September, set into motion a chain of events of which it is no longer the master.

The first overt step in the capitulation of the leadership was taken in the spring of 1967 when the UFT demanded the right of classroom teachers to expel the "disruptive child." No measure other than this was proposed by the union to deal with these children. Once the UFT adopted this demand, the fissures between the union and the community widened into a chasm. The demand was later dropped but the damage had been done. The remaining ties between the union and local civil rights organization were all but severed. (For ceremonial purposes, the UFT retains the services of Bayard Rustin.)

This was predictable and presumably was considered and weighed by the UFT leadership before adopting the demand. But to the surprise of the leadership, the black community went further, for the first time making aggressive efforts to break the strike and gaining the support of a number of black and white teachers. Still more ominous, a sizable number of black teachers, in New York and across the country, quit the union.

Unfortunately the leadership disregarded this warning signal. Instead of reconsidering its posture and strategy[1] the union plunged six months later into an even more direct confrontation with the black movement. Local black communities, dissatisfied with the Board of Education's performance, sought to assume some of the Board's authority (a transfer of authority that had been promised to the three experimental community governing boards by the Board of Education but never actually granted). None of these demands involved any diminution of union rights.

Instead of encouraging and associating itself with this democratic movement and thus being in a position to influence it and prevent its possible transformation into an anti-union movement, the UFT launched a bitter campaign in league with the Board of Education to block any effort at community control of schools. With this decision, the union's divorce from the civil rights movement was complete. The union was headed for a confrontation that could only end in the present strike.

The current strike, reams of speeches to the contrary notwithstanding, is not over the issue of due process or teachers' rights. Here is some of the evidence:

1. After six years, the UFT's contract still contains no provision whatever controlling the involuntary transfer of teachers, a provision that is common in other school contracts. In New York City, involuntary transfers are governed solely by Board of Education rules. The UFT has always lived by these rules and permitted

involuntary transfers on a mass scale without objection, much less active opposition. Even worse, the UFT has remained totally passive in the face of transfers and firings of hundreds of teachers for opposition to the war, support of community control, or attempts to teach in the manner proposed by Paul Goodman, Jonathan Kozol, Herbert Kohl and others.

2. The attempts of the local governing boards to transfer involuntarily were an issue solely between the Board of Education, which had been doing so all along, and the local boards, which had been promised that right. At no point did the actions of the local boards violate the union contract.

3. Since under the existing Board of Education rules, teachers may be transferred without charges being filed, with the consent of the Superintendent, the local board was acting in accord with existing rules in not filing charges originally.[2]

Unquestionably the Board of Education rules cited are a gross and indefensible violation of due process and must be fought. But for six years the UFT leadership has accepted these rules with remarkable equanimity. Their sudden concern with due process (a concern that does not extend to the many teachers involuntarily transferred by the Board of Education) is, under the circumstances, less than convincing. In view of the bitter campaign the UFT leaders have waged against community control, it becomes clear that the due process issue is merely a dodge.

Those who still had doubts about the UFT's goals in the strike should have been convinced by an event just prior to the third resumption of the strike on October 11, 1968. Several labor leaders brought Shanker a proposed basis for settlement which had the tentative approval of the Board of Education and the local governing board. The main points were: 1) recognition of agency shop for the UFT; 2) restoration of the disputed 83 teachers to their *teaching* positions in the district; 3) written guarantees of due process; 4) the UFT to publicly recognize and support community control and decentralization; 5) the UFT to join the governing board in demanding funds from the Board of Education to assure the effectiveness of the experimental districts as well as for general educational purposes and 6) the details of the previous points to be negotiated between the UFT and the local governing boards. The UFT rejected this proposal.

The UFT is on record as favoring decentralization. That record is purely ceremonial. Its actions have included deliberate sabotage of the experimental districts, an unparalleled lobbying effort, deals with anti-labor forces and ultimately the strike.

From the inception of the community control program the UFT has collaborated with the Board of Education to undermine and sabotage the program. The UFT made no protest when the Board of Education refused to grant the local boards any real rights or powers. The UFT was silent when the experimental districts were short-changed in supplies and staff. The UFT participated in the Board of Education-inspired attacks on the experimental districts on the grounds of "chaos" and "racism" at I.S. 201. The UFT tried to negotiate a special agreement last Spring which would have encouraged experienced teachers to leave the experimental districts. One result of this campaign, by the way, is that by the spring of 1968, despite public appeals by David Spencer, the chairman of the local governing board, for teachers to stay in the UFT, less than one-fourth of the staff at I.S. 201 were union members.

Politics has its own logic of development. As the union moved constantly to the right, it was thrown into closer and closer collaboration with forces it had always opposed in the past. The UFT joined the citywide supervisors association, the spokesman of the educational bureaucracy, in a court action to bar the introduction of more black and Puerto Rican principals in the schools (five out of 900 principals in New York City are black). A few weeks later, the union, looking for support in its efforts to prevent passage of any significant decentralization bill, found it among the same state legislators who were responsible for the anti-strike, anti-labor Taylor Law. The UFT not only formed a bloc with them and won the first round in its fight to prevent community control, it paid its debt by officially extending electoral support to them.

None of these efforts gained a definitive victory over community control. The confrontation really began when the Ocean Hill-Brownsville governing board tried to transfer the disputed teachers (despite persistent stories in the *New York Times*, no one was fired), and it began on this issue of "due process." It is tragic that the local board should have used the question of teacher transfer as the focus of its struggle with the Board of Education. But given the UFT's position on community control, even prior to the strike, it is not surprising that the weakest aspect of community control—the notion that the ills of education can be attacked through "teacher inadequacy"—should have come to the fore. An implacably hostile UFT was hardly in a position to help correct the sometimes erratic course the ill-defined movement for black self-determination has traveled. In this way an historic opportunity to pose to the black movement a set of demands which could unite all those seriously interested in better schools and a better society was destroyed by the parochial, intellectually provincial and politically bankrupt leadership of the UFT. (Of course the UFT is not the sole example of this provincialism; witness the decision of the United Auto Workers leadership to cease its efforts to register white auto workers for fear they would vote for Wallace.)

At this writing, with the third strike still on, it remains to be seen if the UFT can compel the abandonment of the community control program, its real—and at last, publicly admitted—goal in striking. Given the political climate and the relative disorganization of the black movement, the union may well win, possibly with the eager help of those same anti-labor, reactionary legislators whose aid they have had before. But in winning, the union will take on itself the blame for the death of community control. In winning, the union will be blamed for the inevitable increase in racism and decrease in education in the schools. In winning, the union will have contributed heavily to the black-white polarization that is taking place in this country, with all that portends.

The UFT has also placed a powerful weapon in the hands of its enemies. Many leaders of the establishment have favored decentralization for their own reasons, as a pacifier to an aroused black community (a concession which may have gotten "out of hand" once the black people seized hold of it) and secondarily as a way of weakening the union, a tactic which the union could outflank only by a bloc with the community. If decentralization is killed, the establishment can put the blame on the union. If, on the other hand, some significant decentralization is achieved, the union will be faced with hostile, and now anti-union, local boards as well as the still-powerful Board of Education.

The situation in New York is not unique. The same issues are bound to arise in other cities. However, the large numbers of black teachers in urban locals outside New York will provide considerable resistance to any efforts to adopt the UFT approach. In the District of Columbia the union has actively supported community control and even sees the movement as an aid to teacher defense and authority.

The near state-of-war between the UFT and the black community even before the strike had its effect on the August convention of the AFT. Community control became the single most prominent issue of the convention. But though the delegates were unhappy, they were also uncertain and hesitant. As a result, a compromise resolution was passed which is not likely to settle anything.

Now the issue must be faced squarely. If the AFT is to move forward or even maintain its current strength, it must act clearly to recognize and welcome community control as a blow at establishment control of the schools and a step toward better schools and a greater teacher voice in the schools. The union must affirm its natural alliance with the civil rights movement and commit itself to consultations on all issues of vital concern to both movements. In particular, the AFT should adopt a policy of consultation with the community in drawing up contract demands and in planning joint campaigns and united actions. In line with this new commitment, the AFT should stop temporizing with the AFL-CIO and demand that the federation launch a real campaign against racism within and without its ranks.

This is a choice point for the teachers union. One path leads toward a new alliance and a unique role in American education and the American labor movement. The other, the path of conventional wisdom, and "unionism-as-usual," leads only to bitter defensive struggle, fragmentation and the dissipation of the store of ideals joined to power that is implicit in the union of teachers.

December 1968

---

1. It is always difficult, but necessary, to consider the role of individual and subjective forces in social processes. Such considerations are important, especially in explaining the UFT's drift to the right during the past year. In the spring of 1967 it became clear that the UFT would have to strike for a contract. At the same time, the leaders had serious doubts about the membership's response to a strike call. It was in this context that the explosive (and rallying) issue of the "disruptive child" was raised. The issue was dropped before the strike was settled but there was open dissatisfaction

in the ranks over the terms of the new contract; in fact, both secondary-school vice-presidents urged a "no" vote on sound grounds.

The widespread discontent continued to pose a grave problem for the leadership in the spring 1968 election and this undoubtedly contributed to the decision to take a further step to the right. Seizing on tactical errors by some community leaders, the union launched a massive campaign against community control of the schools, in the name of "due process" and the defense of teachers' rights.

2. Documented details of points 2 and 3 can be found in the brochure, "The Burden of Blame," issued by the New York Civil Liberties Union.

Three Months After the UFT Strike

STEVE ZELUCK

What has been happening in the New York City schools and the United Federation of Teachers (UFT) since the end of the strike? Several points may be of interest: the UFT's hysterical and bureaucratic response to my critical article on the UFT strike[1]; the UFT's intensified campaign against community control; and the state of the teachers and the union three months later.

The UFT, in response to my article, requested that the Executive Council of the Empire State Federation of Teachers (ESFT) present a resolution to the Federation's convention, censuring me for "anti-union activities." These "anti-union activities" consisted, in addition to the article itself, of the fact that the New Rochelle local of the American Federation of Teachers (AFT), of which I am President, had held a meeting to discuss the strike at which representatives of Ocean Hill and *official representatives* of the UFT presented their views. (Among the UFT representatives were Vice President John O'Neill, several of the teachers involuntarily transferred and their chapter chairman, Fred Nauman, who participated as a resource person.)

The following censure resolution was passed by the Empire State convention by a vote of 56 to 38:

"Whereas, it is a basic principle of trade unionism that when one

local is on strike, other locals of the same international assist the sister local and

Whereas, it is the responsibility of the leadership of the other locals to inform themselves of the issues in the strike from the president of the striking union and

Whereas, the UFT was on strike in a struggle that was unique since it was not a strike for monetary gain but one to protect our members from harassment and intimidation and

Whereas, we firmly support the right of dissent and freedom of expression between the constituted bodies of the Federation and its constituent bodies and

Whereas, Steve Zeluck, the president of the New Rochelle local did prepare an article highly critical of the UFT for publication in the November issue of *New Politics* and

Whereas, Mr. Zeluck arranged a meeting in New Rochelle to give a platform to a dissident UFT vice-president and a member of the Ocean Hill-Brownsville Governing Board for members of his union

Therefore, be it resolved that this convention express its disapproval of these actions by censuring Mr. Zeluck for his anti-union activities.''

The ritual nod to the "right of dissent and freedom of discussion" is exposed as meaningless, given the fact that the resolution was adopted without debate about what was written in the article or said at the meeting. Even more disgraceful, the UFT succeeded in preventing any discussion whatever of the strike at the state convention. The censure is being appealed to the AFT's Public Review Board.*

Editor's note: On May 28, 1971, the AFT's Public Review Board declared the censure resolution invalid; it ordered the ESFT to expunge the resolution from its 1968 convention record and directed that the substance of the decision be submitted to the AFT's newspaper, the *American Teacher,* for publication. In reaching that decision, the Review Board ruled that the procedures by which the censure resolution had been prepared, introduced and passed "fell far short of the requirements of due process." As the Board noted, the resolution was prepared by the UFT's executive officers and delivered, as a "late-filed" resolution, to the ESFT convention at its opening session Friday evening (without notice to Zeluck) by the UFT's Legislative Representative. It was approved that evening before Zeluck's arrival by the Resolutions Committee, of which both Zeluck and the UFT's Legislative Representative were members. On Saturday it was approved by the ESFT convention which, as the Review Board's opinion remarks, "was composed of

Far more important for the future of the UFT are its post-strike attitudes toward the black and Puerto Rican communities. All during the strike, the UFT insisted that the strike was not aimed at the community's role in education but solely to protect teacher security by assuring due process. Without repeating the pros and cons of the strike, it is instructive to ask—Now that the strike is over and the teachers have due process, is the UFT at this time encouraging that community involvement in education which it said it supported?

An indication of the answer is that the UFT continues its guerrilla warfare against the community. It rejects the idea that its best strategy would be to work with the community against the Board of Education and the power structure which obstruct better education. Through its unfortunate influence on some of the Jewish organizations, the UFT has succeeded in heightening tension around the issue of resurgent anti-Semitism. The union is busily engaged in intensifying the campaign it began during the strike in an effort to consolidate its support among teachers and in the Jewish community.

On inspection, evidence for the charge boils down to statements by two teachers and scattered individual comments. Not one responsible leader of the black movement or any member of the three *local* boards of education has been implicated in any way. For obvious reasons, the UFT continues to inject the virus of racist appeal into the situation.

Clearly, the UFT is determined to complete the job by killing all elements of community control by a legislative fight. To assure victory, it is attempting to rally the support of Jewish organizations and politicians, as well as politically sensitive politicians, generally. To further its narrow organizational ends, the UFT is perfectly

---

delegates representing some 40,000 members of the UFT, the local union which had taken umbrage at the activities of Mr. Zeluck, while the other delegates represented locals with a total membership numbering only about 5,000 teachers."

Zeluck's appeal was filed with the Review Board in January 1969. The attorneys for the UFT and ESFT objected to a hearing, however, and delayed decision on the appeal for almost two and one-half years. As the Review Board's opinion comments, "The impartial observer perusing the file of letters would be led to conclude that the ESFT or its counsel were very reluctant to have the matter submitted to the scrutiny of the Board."

willing to exploit the legitimate fears of Jews, mindless of the fact
that its distortions and exaggerations help to arouse the racism of all
kinds that the union claims to fight.

The UFT's sins cannot, however, excuse the behavior of two
teachers, Al Vann and Les Campbell, whose statements, at the very
least, are susceptible to racist interpretation. These black "leaders"
are typical of those who, having rejected the possibility of the unity
of black and white workers in common struggle and, lacking an
alternative policy, are driven in desperation to reactionary alternatives such as racism, black capitalism (in cooperation with the Ford
Foundation) or relying on that part of the establishment which is
quite satisfied to see black and white or black and Jewish workers at
each others' throats. By the use of such methods, these "leaders" are
obviously playing into the hands of the conservative leadership of
the UFT and are, in fact, preparing the groundwork for a disastrous
defeat for all workers, black and white.

The UFT's refusal to move toward a rapprochement with the
community even after the strike is further illustrated by the kind of
parent participation in contract deliberations it is considering.
Instead of using this opportunity to involve some representative of
the black and Puerto Rican community, the UFT currently plans to
invite only a representative of the conservative, middle-class United
Parents Association.

The Union's role in the PS 39 dispute points in the same
direction. In this case, the *central* Board of Education instructed
nine teachers to report to the *local* district headquarters (IS 201) if
they wished to work on a day when the schools in the district were
officially closed with the approval of the Board of Education. The
teachers and the UFT refused this order because to have obeyed it
would have constituted, they feared, at least backhanded recognition
of the rights of local school boards. This, the UFT refuses to do on
any level or any issue, no matter how petty.

That demoralization and a sense of futility in the schools are on
the rapid rise will be denied by few. (One suburban community—and
not a wealthy lily-white one—reports having received 600 applications for September jobs from New York City teachers.) The
unpardonable and irresponsible manipulation of the anti-Semitism
issue is revealed by the readiness of so many teachers to accept the
charge. It is just one more indication of the mounting sense of
insecurity that has gripped them, even with "due process."

To this climate, the UFT has added another ingredient—its refusal to defend teachers who are being harassed, involuntarily transferred and even fired for their refusal to support the strike or their insistence on working with the community today. (The American Civil Liberties Union and the Emergency Civil Liberties Committee have dossiers on these cases.)

It remains only to add that the strike may have weakened the union seriously, even in a short-run, pragmatic sense. No one knows the exact figures of union membership today. But it is an open secret that thousands of teachers, black and white, are refusing to pay dues. Can there be any doubt that this will have a negative effect on the UFT's bargaining position in the current negotiations (unless Mayor Lindsay capitulates, as he shows every sign of doing in his desperate effort to be re-elected)?

Three months after the strike the union continues to be guided by a policy which is splitting the membership, in part on race lines. It continues to antagonize those forces, black and Puerto Rican, which are most concerned with the schools and could be the union's best allies. It continues policies which can only exacerbate racism in the schools and in the community.

If the worth of a strategy is measurable to any degree by the consequences following implementation, there can be little doubt today that the strike produced a disastrous pyrrhic victory.

March 1969

---

1. Steve Zeluck, "The UFT Strike: A Blow Against Teacher Unionism," *New Politics*, Vol. VII, No. 1.

Black Protest,
Union Democracy
and the UFT

ALBERT SHANKER / HERBERT HILL

Editor's note: The correspondence that follows between Albert Shanker, President of the United Federation of Teachers (UFT) and Herbert Hill, National Labor Director of the National Association for the Advancement of Colored People (NAACP), originally appeared in *Issues in Industrial Society,* published by the New York State School of Industrial and Labor Relations at Cornell University. The correspondence resulted from an article by Herbert Hill ("Black Protest and the Struggle for Union Democracy") in that journal's first issue.

Hill's article included a brief section on the American Federation of Teachers (AFL-CIO) and its New York affiliate, the UFT, in which he said that there were "charges, especially from the AFT's nationwide black caucus, the African-American Teachers Association, of growing conservatism on the part of the union leadership and of its insensitivity to Negro demands and community interests." He went on to discuss the emergence of profound differences between blacks and organized labor on basic community issues as a result of the UFT's 1968 strike, reflected in the alliance between the UFT and other labor unions, especially the "discriminatory building trades craft unions who feared that black-controlled school boards would insist upon awarding lucrative school construction and maintenance contracts to Negro-owned contractors who employ the majority of black skilled workers still excluded from the major AFL craft unions." The section also mentioned the $50,000 donation made to the UFT by the New York AFL-CIO Central Labor Council, a sit-in demonstration at the office of Harry Van Arsdale, head of the Council, by a group of Negro and Puerto Rican unionists to protest the Council's action in support of the strike and a public statement by "an influential group of Negro and Puerto Rican labor leaders" criticizing the UFT, endorsing the Ocean Hill-Brownsville governing board and attacking the Central Labor Council and its affiliated unions for its position. There was a quote from the American Civil Liberties Union report which concluded that "the UFT had used 'due process' as a smokescreen to obscure its real goal . . . to discredit decentralization and sabotage community control."

I: ALBERT SHANKER'S LETTER

If the rest of Herbert Hill's article, "Black Protest and the Struggle for Union Democracy" contains inaccuracies and misstatements in the same volume and magnitude as his few paragraphs on the American Federation of Teachers (AFT), it is no wonder that he has no credibility as an honest defender of union democracy. His "analysis" comes off simply as anti-unionism. Of course he's entitled to his point of view, but not to misstatements of fact and not to distortions:

1. Hill identifies the AFT's black caucus as the African-American Teachers Association (AATA) led by Edward Simpkins. First of all, the AATA is a New York based non-union organization, separate and apart from AFT, although some people may belong to both. AATA began as the Negro Teachers Association formed primarily by black union members for the purpose of bringing Negro teachers together on common concerns. That association steadily lost membership, according to our knowledge of it, as it began to move towards a separatist-nationalist point of view; and finally, under the leadership of Albert Vann and Leslie Campbell, it published viciously anti-Semitic material in its journal and lost the sympathies of many more black teachers, the majority of whom remain in the

union. The policies of the AFT's black caucus, whose membership, not surprisingly, is pro-union and integrationist, bear little resemblance to those of the African-American Teachers Association.

2. Edward Simpkins does not lead the AFT's black caucus. He has been out of the Detroit system for about two years now and did not, therefore, attend the last AFT convention as a delegate. He was, to correct Hill again, not a leader of a black caucus, but a leader of the New Caucus in the AFT, an integrated caucus (as all caucuses in AFT are integrated) which disagreed with the administration on a number of different issues. Incidentally, Mr. Simpkins, a very able educator, worked with the rest of the Detroit Federation of Teachers leadership on a decentralization plan for Detroit schools which was undoubtedly good for Detroit but which came to be nowhere near as far-reaching a decentralization plan as that supported by its sister local, the UFT of New York City. The New Caucus, under his leadership, supported AFT Resolution 114, which advocates community participation and involvement in the schools, which was supported also by the Progressive (administration) Caucus, and which passed with a near unanimous vote at the 1968 convention. I do not wish to seem to be saying that difficulties and differences over the issue of community control did not or do not exist within the AFT. They do. But there have been sincere and successful attempts to work out compromises on that and other controversial issues for the sake of union solidarity with AFT; Hill ignores this and instead exaggerates and even falsifies the differences.

3. Hill refers to the "bitter opposition of the United Federation of Teachers . . . to a decentralized school system operated by neighborhood school boards." Why does he neglect to mention that the New York City school system is now beginning to operate under a decentralization law negotiated between and agreed upon by the UFT and a majority of black and Puerto Rican legislators? It is true that there had been great conflict over this issue; that it is common knowledge. An honest reporter, it seems to me, should certainly point out efforts on both sides to rebuild strained relationships particularly where they have had demonstrable success.

4. The organization which accused UFT of using due process as a "smokescreen" was not the American Civil Liberties Union (ACLU) but a New York affiliate, the NYCLU, which has earned a reputation for using civil liberties as a "smokescreen" for a political point of

view and which engendered considerable opposition to its policies on the school issue within its own ranks.

It is true that many unions and the Central Labor Council in New York (as well as the AFL-CIO nationally) supported the UFT strike; it should surprise no one that they would support a basic trade union struggle for the preservation of hard-won rights like job security and fair hearings. Yet, according to the *New York Times,* as Hill points out, a group of black and Puerto Rican trade unions opposed it; but a larger group of black trade unionists, including members and officials of unions with large black memberships, supported UFT and signed a full page ad which appeared in the *New York Times.* Hill reads his *Times* very selectively, it seems.

The Ocean Hill-Brownsville crisis and the decentralization controversy were extremely difficult, even agonizing situations for black as well as white teachers, who showed great courage throughout that struggle and maintained their conviction that rights for one group cannot be won by trampling on newly won rights of another. Had the dismissed teachers been black and the local board involved white, the union's action would have been exactly the same. For Hill to deal with what became a terribly complicated and sensitive social issue with a simple black *vs.* white racial analysis is most unfortunate.

It is especially unfortunate in view of the UFT's and AFT's record and activity as active participants in the battles for human rights. AFT was among the first international unions to expel Jim Crow locals. Teacher unionists have long been active participants in the struggles of the civil rights and labor movements for equality and dignity for workers and the poor. AFT locals, including UFT, are thoroughly integrated in their ranks and among elected officials and staffs. If UFT is, as Hill implies, a "racist" union with no meaningful internal voice for blacks, why is it that thousands of black and Puerto Rican paraprofessionals do not seem to agree? These community workers have chosen the UFT as their collective bargaining agent and at this writing UFT is on the verge of a strike in an effort to win decent salaries and working conditions for this section of its membership. How is it that Hill, in his close examination of race relations within unions, failed to notice this situation in the UFT?

It is unfortunate that in his discussion of so important an issue as the effects of growing organization among minority groups within unions, Hill treats the labor movement, which is, with all its problems and shortcomings, one of the best integrated and most democratic institutions in our society—and one of the most effective forces for the enactment of progressive social legislation—simplistically as part of "the white power structure." Any constructive contribution he might be able to make to the furtherance of democratic rights is thus vitiated.

It is especially disappointing that the Cornell School of Industrial and Labor Relations would choose to print a piece so highly opinionated against unions without an accompanying piece presenting the labor point of view. Those of us who have supported their work are very disturbed.

II: HERBERT HILL REPLIES

If Albert Shanker did not hold a position of power, his gross distortions and his pathetic attempts to score debater's points would hardly merit a reply. However, because Shanker, as President of the United Federation of Teachers, unfortunately exercises great control over the education of more than a million public school children, his letter underscores the tragedy of the American labor movement and requires a detailed response.

Shanker attacks my article as "anti-union" because he can neither understand nor acknowledge the racism which pervades much of organized labor in general and the UFT in particular. Exposure of racist practices in labor unions is frequently countered by those whose power is vested in maintaining the racial status quo, by cries of "anti-unionism," "anti-Semitism" and "anti-Americanism." This response is, of course, a significant measure of the moral and intellectual bankruptcy of all the Al Shankers in organized labor.

Before dealing with Shanker's allegations point by point, I feel it is necessary to comment on a revealing aspect of his letter. Shanker obviously operates on the presumption that any disagreement with him constitutes an attack upon his union and to attack his union is to attack all unions. He equates himself and his power with that of all organized labor. This is simply the Shanker version of the cult of personality. As for my " . . . credibility as an honest defender of union democracy," I am proud that my "credibility" is with the black rank and file membership of many unions across the country, including the UFT, who are struggling for genuine internal democracy and for an end to demagoguery and racism within labor organizations. And now to Shanker's arguments.

The African-American Teachers Association, as Shanker acknowledges, was formed by black union members. Shanker, however, carefully avoids giving the real reason for the formation of the association. The African-American Teachers Association was originally formed as the organization of black teachers who were, justifiably, angered over UFT's adamant refusal to support the 1964 boycott for integrated schools in New York City. Does Mr. Shanker recall that boycott, and the fact that it was organized by his good friend and colleague, Bayard Rustin?

Does Mr. Shanker's acute "historical sense" recall that, although the international union, the American Federation of Teachers filed an *amicus curiae* brief in one of the school segregation cases in the 1950s, local union leadership in major cities across the country placed serious obstacles in the struggle for planned integration of pupils and faculty?

Furthermore, Shanker and his fellow union leaders use a double standard regarding strikes. When unions strike and crush the legitimate aspirations of the black community, parents and teachers who cross picket lines are castigated as "scabs." But when union members, encouraged by their leaders, cross the picket lines established by black people fighting for school integration or community control they are not "scabs," but heroes.

Shanker, who is so proud of his union's "integrationist" stand, has a very short memory. Every effort at racial integration supported by the civil rights movement was fought by the UFT leadership. Those of us active in the movement were repeatedly accused of "forcing integration." Teacher rights and union rights, like states rights, are always dragged out as the principle for which the union will fight to the death.

When Shanker denies that the New Caucus was a black caucus he is simply not telling the truth. The New Caucus was formed by black teachers in the struggle for community control of the public school system and did, of course, receive some support from white school teachers in opposition to Shanker's ruinous policies.

I am fully aware that Edward Simpkins is now on leave from the

Detroit public school system, but he was most active during the period I wrote about in my article. Shanker is again violating the truth when he implies that Simpkins was not an important figure in opposing Shanker and his policies. The fact that Edward Simpkins is not presently teaching in the Detroit public school system or that he did not attend the last AFT convention as a delegate is irrelevant. Simpkins was a leader of the black caucus at the 1968 AFT convention and unsuccessfully opposed David Selden for the presidency of the AFT. Although Shanker has a very selective memory, I assume that he can recall that the resolution at the 1968 convention advocating "community participation and involvement" in the schools, even with the amendment offered by Simpkins, did not satisfy many of the black delegates at the convention.

Shanker dismisses the African-American Teachers Association as an organization which allegedly lost the sympathies of many black teachers. But AATA and similar organizations have been formed in Philadelphia, Detroit, Chicago and other cities because of the deep frustration black teachers experience within the union. In several cities, as a result of conflict over racial issues, some of these organizations called upon black teachers to drop their union membership. In Philadelphia, for instance, more than 100 black teachers left the union. Because AFT locals are in control as collective bargaining agents, however, independent black organizations find it difficult to compete. Until there are viable independent alternatives or, as in Washington, D.C., predominantly black locals with black leadership, the majority of black teachers will probably remain members of the union. However, a sense of disgust with and rejection of the union leadership has led to the creation of black caucuses both inside and outside the union. Of course both are dangerous to Mr. Shanker and his counterparts in other locals for they represent organized opposition to those now in power.

Shanker writes utter nonsense when he refers to " . . . sincere and successful attempts to work out compromises . . . ." regarding the issue of community control and school decentralization. He is certainly aware of the split in the Progressive Caucus, which AFT President David Selden quit in the course of his dispute with Shanker. As every member of the UFT knows, Shanker is the major spokesman for the hardline opposition to community control within the union and is currently conducting a purge of all union members who differ with him.

Does Shanker recall that the UFT was silent during the Urban League's fight to get more black and Puerto Rican teachers into the New York City school system? The UFT never joined in the effort to eliminate the insidious licensing examination that effectively prevents large numbers of nonwhite teachers from entering the school system. It could be, of course, that the UFT is more than satisfied with the examination system precisely for this reason and because the union exercises some measure of control over it. The percentage of black teachers in New York City is 8 percent, although well over 50 percent of the pupils are black and Puerto Rican. The percentage of black teachers in Washington, D.C., is over 90 percent and in Philadelphia it is over 30 percent. The Washington local of the American Federation of Teachers vigorously supported the Ocean Hill-Brownsville school board and its struggle for community control, as did other AFT locals with large black memberships. Most AFT locals are in cities with large black school-age populations and with growing black membership concentrations within the union. This is, of course, precisely what Mr. Shanker fears most.

Shanker writes that " . . . the New York City School system is now beginning to operate under a decentralization law negotiated between and agreed upon by the UFT and a majority of black and Puerto Rican legislators." This is sheer fabrication; it flies in the face of all the facts. The UFT under Shanker's leadership absolutely opposed all plans for genuine school decentralization with community control. Under the personal leadership of Shanker, the UFT opposed the original Allen plan supported by many civil rights organizations to integrate New York City schools, an action which split the union's executive board with Shanker securing a narrow margin of support. The original Board of Regents Bill was about to be enacted by the state legislature until Shanker led over 2,000 UFT members into the state capitol and succeeded in killing the bill by threatening wholesale political reprisals. The incontrovertible fact is that the UFT has consistently opposed every meaningful school decentralization proposal except the one finally acceptable to Shanker.

The presently operational New York City decentralization plan, supported by the UFT, provides only for minimal administrative decentralization without meaningful community control. Such administrative decentralization merely means that the controlling power is shifted from the central staff of the Board of Education to the board's field staff with no change in the flow and distribution of power to the black community. A basic distinction must be made between genuine decentralization with community control, that is, without a re-apportionment of power. Shanker's every action was to make certain that real power remained with the old school bureaucracy. Unless power and control are shifted to local school boards, decentralization is meaningless. It is merely an administrative device and the power remains where it always was.

The truth is that all black and Puerto Rican members of the 1969 New York state legislature together with a small number of white legislators supported the original decentralization bill, which Shanker describes as "radical and extreme." The second bill was a greatly watered-down compromise version and was substantially different from the original bill supported by black and Puerto Rican members of the legislature but opposed by Mr. Shanker and the UFT. Shanker's assertion that the law finally enacted by the legislature was " . . . negotiated between and agreed upon by the UFT and the majority of black and Puerto Rican legislators," is the grossest distortion of the truth. The final bill was authored by the Republican leadership in the state legislature, not " . . . negotiated . . . by the UFT and the majority of black and Puerto Rican legislators." There was negotiation on an earlier Democratic-sponsored bill that collapsed, not on the bill which finally passed. And the bill that did pass, the one supported by the UFT, might be described quite properly as a recentralization bill, not a decentralization bill.

Basil Patterson, the leading black exponent of community control in the state legislature, voted against the bill and he stated, as quoted in the *New York Times* of May 1, 1969, that "it's decentralization but not community control. The community boards are subject to the central board." Samuel D. Wright, a black assemblyman from Brooklyn and a member of the Ocean Hill-Brownsville School Board, also voted against the final bill. Inquiries to members of the state legislature clearly indicate that the vote on the school bill occurred during a long and bitter impasse, with the choice between the compromise bill and the disastrous Marchi proposal, and that as a result of Shanker's actions in the state legislature there was little alternative to voting for the compromise measure as the legislative session ended.

Let us examine the so-called decentralization law of which Mr. Shanker is so proud. Before Mr. Shanker's bill was adopted all high schools in each local school district operated under the jurisdiction of the district superintendent and the central board. Mr. Shanker's bill removed the high schools entirely from the jurisdiction of the District Superintendent. The principals of high schools are now directly responsible to the central board. As a result, the entire high school system has been recentralized.

As for the rest of the school system, the crucial controls over fiscal power, curricula power, hiring power, capital construction power and other powers are left substantially in the hands of the central board of education. This is Shanker's idea of decentralization. The only change of any significance is in the hiring of district superintendents, which is now done by local school boards instead of the central board. This is true, however, only below the high school level.

Maurice R. Berube of the Institute for Community Studies of Queens College and a close observer of these developments aptly sums the matter up as follows:

The UFT is 'for decentralization' in much the same fashion as the backlash Parents and Taxpayers said they were for integration a few years back. The union has ardently campaigned against strong decentralization plans, while 'for decentralization' just as PAT opposed busing, school pairings, and education parks, while 'for integration.' Only recently have school activists discarded the ambiguous term. They now speak of community control to signify the Bundy idea of public power over budget, curriculum, and personnel. And make no mistake about it, the UFT is dead set against community control.

Berube quotes Jimmy Breslin's comment that Shanker is but "an accent away from George Wallace." [1]

The "demonstrable success" that Shanker claims in rebuilding "strained relationships" means that he got a law enacted by frightening whites, provoking an anti-Semitic hysteria, and defaming leadership in the black community. As a result of Shanker's efforts, the "strained relationships" he refers to most certainly remain strained. Is Shanker so unaware of how he is regarded by black people in New York City and that the *Amsterdam News,* the newspaper with the largest circulation in New York's black community coined a new phrase to describe white backlash and fakery—Shankerism?

David Livingston of District 65 of the National Council of Distributive Workers, a predominantly black and Puerto Rican union, was undoubtedly correct when he stated that Albert Shanker set back the cause of labor unionism in the black community at least 100 years. Mr. Shanker thinks that "a simple black *vs.* white racial analysis" is a misrepresentation, but in reality this is his problem, not mine, and one that is certain to remain with him for a long time.

In his fourth point Shanker states that it was " . . . not the American Civil Liberties Union but a New York affiliate, the NYCLU . . . which criticized the United Federation of Teachers during the Ocean Hill-Brownsville School controversery " What arrant nonsense. There is no other way for the American Civil Liberties Union to express itself on a New York City matter except through its one and only New York affiliate. There is no other New York City affiliate. Contrary to Shanker's suggestion, the NYCLU *is* the voice of the ACLU in New York City. What Shanker carefully fails to mention is that it is a matter of public record that the ACLU officially endorsed the position of its New York affiliate, that the ACLU policy statement is identical with that of the NYCLU. Page six of the October-November 1969 issue of *Civil Liberties in New York* (official publication of the NYCLU) contains the statement under the heading, "ACLU Supports Community Control Throughout Country." It is also interesting to note that the ACLU affirmed its support of the NYCLU without a dissenting vote by the national board.

Of greater significance is that fact that the Committee on African-American History of the United Federation of Teachers unanimously adopted a resolution endorsing the study of the New York Civil Liberties Union entitled, "The Burden of Blame." The Committee stated that the report was " . . . a bona-fide contribution to African-American History . . . said study presents in perspective certain facts of great importance that have been misunderstood and misrepresented." The Committee also " . . . commends the New York Civil Liberties Union for the publication of said study . . . ." This was the report that documented the campaign of distortion and hysteria by the UFT and charged that the union was using the issue of due process as a "smokescreen" to prevent community control of public schools. Shanker, as a punitive measure, dissolved the Committee on African-American History Human Relations Committee.

As to Shanker's charge that the NYCLU has "... earned a reputation for using civil liberties as a 'smokescreen' for its political point of view," which "engendered considerable opposition to its policies on the school issue in its own ranks," the question must be asked, among whom? And where does this so-called "considerable opposition" come from? Only among those people organized by Shanker himself through Herman Benson and Stephen Vladeck. Benson, whose wife Revella Benson is a staff member of the UFT, was co-leader of the Shanker-manipulated caucus inside the NYCLU together with Stephen Vladeck who is the attorney for the Council of Supervisory Associations, the organization of principals, assistant principals and district superintendents in the New York City school system which is now closely allied with the UFT. Vladeck was the attorney for the Council of Supervisory Associations in the well-known case, *Schwartz* v. *Shanker,* in which the New York Civil Liberties Union represented the plaintiff, Jeffrey Schwartz, a student who was suspended from school for six months and denied his regents scholarship by the principal of Jamaica High School for possession of an underground newspaper. The NYCLU won the case over Vladeck's opposition. It is of course a matter of public record that the Shanker-supported Benson-Vladeck slate was defeated for executive board positions in the NYCLU election of June 1969.

Shanker is correct in pointing out that the Central Labor Council in New York together with the AFL-CIO nationally supported his position. That should surprise no one. What would be surprising indeed would be the opposition of the AFL-CIO and that of the New York Central Labor Council to racism. Have they ever spoken out or taken any action in opposition to the discriminatory practices of the building trades unions and other labor organizations? Have these same union officials who supported Shanker denounced the vile brutality of white construction workers who beat up students and peace demonstrators in the streets of New York City? The *New York Times* of May 13, 1970 reports that leaders of more than a dozen New York City labor unions condemned the construction workers' attack on war protesters. Conspicuously absent is the name of Albert Shanker. Of course, one would expect Harry Van Arsdale, president of the New York City Central Labor Council, Raymond R.

Corbett, president of the State AFL (who also represents the discriminatory Iron Workers Union) as well as Peter J. Brennan, president of the New York AFL-CIO Building Trades Council, to support Shanker and the UFT in their efforts to destroy black community control of local school boards. Many millions of dollars each year are spent for construction, maintenance, repair and other services by the Board of Education which has in violation of the law permitted the building trades unions to control job opportunities and thereby exclude black workers and black contractors. The building trades unions were among the first to support Mr. Shanker in his attempt to destroy the Ocean Hill-Brownsville experiment in community control because black control of local school boards would for the first time give black communities control over the awarding of lucrative construction and repair contracts for work now controlled by the all-white craft unions. Real community control would result in enforcement of the legal prohibitions against racial discrimination in public construction, which are continually violated by the building trades unions in New York City.

Shanker's Orwellian logic notwithstanding, the overwhelming majority of black union members in New York City opposed his actions and that of the UFT during the school strikes I described in my article. On November 25, 1968, a statement was adopted by 200 black and Spanish-speaking labor leaders at a conference sponsored by the Negro American Labor Council which condemned Shanker and the union's position in the strongest possible terms. Under the auspices of the Negro-American Labor Council, a large group of black and Puerto Rican union leaders responsive to the will of their membership, participated in an all-day sit-in demonstration at the AFL-CIO Central Trades and Labor Council to protest the Council's support for the UFT strike which was opposed by the nonwhite membership of local unions. This was in striking contrast to the few black union leaders who under great pressure from the Central Trades and Labor Council signed the *New York Times* ad Shanker referred to in his letter. The *New York Times* of November 14, 1968 reports the confrontation between black and Puerto Rican union leaders with Harry Van Arsdale under the headline "Shanker is Called 'Racist' by Labor Leaders Here" and the *Times* for the same day carried a page one headline reading, "Puerto Rican and Negro Unionists Threaten a City Labor Revolt."

I would also call Shanker's attention to the statement released on September 14, 1968 by the Black Caucus-UFT:

We state our unequivocal support of Rhody McCoy and advise Al Shanker that we oppose his irresponsible actions in calling a strike against the community. . . .

Richard Parrish, a national vice-president of the AFT and assistant treasurer of the UFT since 1962 and one of the original organizers of the union, voiced the authentic sentiments of the black union members throughout the city of New York when he stated in the course of a television interview on September 15, 1968 that the UFT was engaged in "a strike against the black community" and that the UFT school action was "not a strike of workers against employers, but a collusive action of supervisors, teachers, and custodians against black parents and students." This of course explains why Shanker is now conducting a campaign against Parrish and other black leaders who opposed his policies within the UFT.

Shanker's double-talk and double-think in relation to the para-professionals in the New York City school system are additional examples of his distortions. Everyone acquainted with the labor movement in New York City knows that Shanker belatedly started to organize the paraprofessionals in an effort to prevent another union from securing an organizational base among these workers who had become a potent force in the classrooms and in the school system. What really motivated Shanker in relation to the para-professionals is his fear that the black paraprofessionals, who are rooted in their communities, represent a potential danger to the UFT in future disputes.

The UFT won an election to represent the paraprofessionals by exactly 11 votes. The contending union was District Council 37 of the American Federation of State, County and Municipal Employees (AFSCME), a union with an honorable record in relation to the black community. Victor Gotbaum, head of District Council 37, has described to me the "thoroughly dishonest UFT campaign," and has protested Shanker's tactics to the AFL-CIO. David Cole, the impartial umpire under the internal disputes plan of the AFL-CIO ruled that the acts of the UFT were in direct violation of Section 5, Article 20 of the AFL-CIO constitution. The AFL-CIO's impartial umpire noted that Shanker and the UFT had engaged in libelous accusations against District Council 37 of the AFSCME.

Shanker's much publicized commitment to "due process" is again revealed in his firing of two black UFT organizers, Marvin Rogers and Jim Howard, who were hired to organize paraprofessionals. Marvin Rogers, who was fired exactly one day before he was to receive tenure on the union staff, filed a complaint on March 25, 1970 with the National Labor Relations Board charging the UFT with violating section 8A (3) for discrimination because of racial prejudice and Teacher's Representatives Union (TRU) activities. Marvin Rogers who had been active in the union of the UFT's staff employees, the TRU, filed a second charge with the NLRB under section 8A (1) (2) (5) charging Shanker with refusing to bargain with the TRU, the organization of UFT employees. Those charges of unfair labor practices against the UFT are currently pending with the National Labor Relations Board.

Jim Howard, who was also hired to organize paraprofessionals was dismissed immediately after the UFT won the election. He too has protested Mr. Shanker's high-handed and dictatorial methods.

Marvin Rogers was given special, second-class treatment on the UFT staff. It was unilaterally decided in violation of the UFT agreement with the Teacher's Representatives Union to pay Rogers on a per diem basis without any union benefits. Instead of receiving the regular salary of a UFT organizer, Rogers was to get $25.00 a day with no pay for holidays, no health benefits, no pension rights and no expense allowance. Mr. Shanker had in fact created a new category of cheap labor within the UFT.

The Teacher's Representatives Union immediately went to arbitration on behalf of Marvin Rogers. The arbitrator ruled that Rogers was a full-time employee and a bona-fide member of TRU, subject to all the benefits of its agreement with the UFT and he recommended further negotiations to arrive at an agreement. But the new negotiations soon reached an impasse and TRU returned to the arbitrator for a determination. At this point Shanker fired Marvin Rogers the day before he was to receive staff tenure. The UFT owes Rogers approximately $5,000 in back pay which Shanker refuses to acknowledge, and he still refuses to return to arbitration. The fact that both Jim Howard and Marvin Rogers are black again confirms Shanker's racial bigotry. His efforts to destroy the Teacher's Representatives Union also reveal him as a union buster, and it is my intention to tell this interesting and important story in greater detail after the NLRB has acted on the pending charges against the UFT.

Shanker's practices in regard to due process and freedom of expression are further indicated in the internal union conflict related to the public release of the *Lesson Plans in African-American History*. Here I will let the teachers speak for themselves:

The recently issued "Lesson Plans in African-American History," published by the UFT with much fanfare, has some interesting facts behind it which are unknown to the general public. Every contributor to and co-editor of the book including Zippy Bauman and Paul Becker of the Teachers Action Committee opposes UFT policy on the very issue which determines true commitment to the Black community, community control.

Not only was the book delayed for over two years, but the UFT subsequently refused to list the names of the people who were responsible for it. The book was originally printed with the names of the members of the committee listed on the back but the UFT went to additional expense to have the cover reprinted to exclude the names. The only exceptions it allowed were Joyce Haynes and Richard Parrish, the co-chairmen of the Committee on African-American History. Mrs. Haynes has protested directly to the American Federation of Teachers [the national union] demanding that the credit for the "Lesson Plans" go to "the seven Black and seven white teachers who wrote them and to no one else."[2]

I have carefully examined both the original and the altered version of the UFT book, *Lesson Plans in African-American History*. The cover of the original version says that it is "edited by Margot Webb." Her name is removed from the edition released to the public, as are the names of the 14 writers who contributed essays. Shanker also deleted and in other ways altered material in the book. Former members of the dissolved African-American history committee have explained to me that when the 50 lessons were completed, Shanker turned the manuscript over to an unidentified person for revisions. Committee members said they were never permitted to meet with the editor nor were they ever told of his qualifications regarding African-American history. According to the committee, Shanker's editor deleted and added material in the book without any consultation whatsoever with the authors.

The nature of the changes is most interesting. The three chapters on Malcolm X were reduced to one and in place of the other two lessons a chapter on Booker T. Washington was substituted. Also deleted from the book was the conclusion of the Report of the National Advisory Commission on Civil Disorders (Kerner Commission) that "our nation is moving toward two societies, one black, one white—separate and unequal."

Significantly a quotation from a famous speech made by Frederick Douglass 112 years ago was also removed. The passage which was omitted reads:

Those who profess to favor freedom yet deprecate agitation, are men who want crops without plowing up the ground; they want rain without thunder and lightning. They want the ocean without the awful roar of its many waters.

Power concedes nothing without demand. It never did and it never will. Find out just what any people will quietly submit to and you have found out the exact measure of injustice and wrong which will be imposed upon them, and these will continue 'til they are resisted with either words or blows or with both. The limits of tyrants are prescribed by the endurance of those whom they oppress.

Shanker forced other changes including material on the life of W.E.B. DuBois and ordered destroyed 10,000 printed covers of the book because they contained the names of the committee members. Mr. Shanker explained to the outraged authors that the list included persons who did not support the UFT school strikes.

In the edition released to the public the back cover which originally contained the names of the committee members has been removed and an advertisement for the publications of the A. Philip Randolph Institute has been substituted. (Richard Parrish who is Assistant Treasurer of the UFT states that "the A. Philip Randolph Institute receives $500 a month from the UFT for services rendered.")

Those of us acquainted with the rise of totalitarianism will recognize the full implications of Shanker's efforts to rewrite history. It is clear that the totalitarians of both the right and the left were not the only ones who tried to do this, but history and the conscience of civilization has its own way of settling accounts with those who violate the truth and the rights of oppressed people.

January 1971

1. Maurice R. Berube and Marilyn S. Gittell, *Confrontation at Ocean Hill-Brownsville* (Frederick A. Praeger, New York, 1969), pp. 136-162. See also the important exchange between Dwight Macdonald and Michael Harrington, pp. 222-246.

2. The December 1969 issue of the newsletter of the Teachers Action Committee, formerly Teachers for Community Control.

III: UNIONS AND POLITICS

The Ambiguities
of Anti-Communism

JAMES R. PRICKETT

As an attempt to build support for the current National Maritime Union (NMU) insurgency Henry Spira's chapter "Rebel Voices in the NMU" (pp. 47-56) deserves our admiration. But as history (and it is history only tangentially) it is reprehensible. Spira paints the anti-Communist campaign as a kind of golden era marked by a new birth of freedom and the total absence of red-baiting. Joseph Curran's campaign, then, created no need for radical soul-searching for there were no negative or disturbing aspects about it (until it was successful). Yet my own research reveals that Curran's campaign, like Walter Reuther's in the United Auto Workers (UAW),[1] displayed both a radical and reactionary side. However Jeffersonian Curran's rhetoric may have been on occasion (and it was not always Jeffersonian), it should have been clear to all that Curran was attempting to outlaw the political participation in the union of the dominant group of radicals. His moves against the Communists involved key questions about union democracy, the right to criticize union officials and the freedom to hold unpopular views, but his radical allies generally ignored those issues. What is striking about the NMU is not that Curran betrayed his radical supporters (opportunist politicians have been known to do that to radicals before) but that anti-Communism appears to have a reactionary dynamic, quite apart from the politics of its practitioners. A full-scale history of the NMU is important, but I will concentrate here on the period described by Spira—the postwar anti-Communist drive.

The NMU split probably began with the crisis in the Communist Party following the Duclos article. Party members demanded to know why William Z. Foster's views, now deemed correct, had been withheld from the membership. More important, they saw the opportunism of the war years and the undemocratic structure of the Communist Party as two sides of the same coin.[2] It was not enough simply to change the line. As one communist put it, "No political inventory would be complete . . . which did not deal with the mechanics of our policy-making."[3] But the mechanics of policy-making was the last thing that the leadership wanted discussed. They were willing to confess their sins and reconstitute the Communist Party free of Browder and Browderism but they also wanted to see an end to the widespread questioning and ferment within the party. The questioning continued and further expulsions were necessary. In addition to the "Browderites," a group of "left-wing sectarians" were expelled for advancing the "petty-bourgeois slogan of 'freedom of criticism' to facilitate their propagation of views hostile to the party."[4] By 1945, the purges reached the waterfront: NMU leaders Jack Lawrenson, Hedley Stone, Charles Keith, Thomas Ray and Harry Alexander were all expelled from the Communist Party.

Still, at the 1945 convention, the discord was not obvious. The no-strike pledge, a major issue in the UAW, had only four detractors and Harry Alexander and Jack Lawrenson both spoke in favor of what was finally a unanimous resolution upholding the pledge. There was a clue that all was not well. Curran proposed an amendment that would limit NMU office-holding to those seamen who had their first citizenship papers and Lawrenson and Ray spoke for the amendment. In Curran's own speech, he expressed a new-found, weary conservatism:

> At the outset let me remind you that we are governed by a certain system. We may not like its laws, but we have to live under them. . . .
> We have got to be real about these things. We haven't got a revolution on the horizon.[5]

But Curran and Lawrenson needed better issues to separate them from the Communists: the limitation of the political rights of aliens was not a particularly popular cause in the NMU. And they could hardly focus on the NMU's wartime collaboration policies for they were, in large measure, the architects of those policies. Whether by accident or by careful planning, the Curran campaign focused around two issues: the Committee for Maritime Unity and the ouster of vice-president Joseph Stack.

The Committee for Maritime Unity (CMU) was a federation of offshore and dockside CIO unions with Harry Bridges and Curran as co-chairmen. In his report to the NMU National Council shortly before his resignation, Curran had nothing but praise for CMU:

> The establishment of this organization was so successful that the AFL actually set up the AFL Maritime Trades Department . . . we have actually accomplished, for the first time in our industry, unity of action of all seamen, longshoremen and officers. . . . These gains [of June 15] were all the more spectacular because we had not had the time to formulate, through CMU, united proposals. . . . We were able, however, to co-ordinate them in such a way that the greatest gains were made through this unity.

Speaking of the September strike, which "Stone later claimed . . . was prolonged because of Communist politics,"[6] Curran said that "we were able to achieve the greatest gain in the industry, and to prove, once and for all, that the shipowners were not going to get away with their policy of pitting one union against the other."[7]

At the next CMU board meeting, Curran announced that he wanted to resign but the other members convinced him that he should wait until the NMU board meeting. Curran agreed, but then announced his resignation before the board meeting. He made two basic arguments: the NMU was "in an intolerable situation . . . being governed by the actions of three small craft unions, 3,000 miles away, and representing one-fifth of our membership." He also noted that the *Daily Worker* favored the CMU, and that by so doing, "it was giving orders from the Communist Party to its members in our union, particularly the leading ones, such as McKenzie and Stack, who as I said before have officially spoken for the party."[8] Treasurer Stone noted that the NMU had been ready to settle on September 17, but the CMU forced them to stay out until September 20.[9]

The resignation touched off a furious controversy within the union. In the first issue where the resignation was discussed by the membership, there were 23 letters supporting the resignation, and 22 letters opposing it. Yet the letters attacking the move generally were signed by ports or entire ships, while those supporting the president most often came from individuals. Curran's supporters also saw the move as the beginning of an internal attack on the Communists. Communist influence will soon be gone, gloated one member, adding that "if the Commies think otherwise, what a stiff jolt they are in for." Another member told Curran "you have my support in your fight to keep the NMU American."[10] Despite what seemed to be strong initial support, the Communists did not take the issue to the membership. Instead the CMU dissolved.

Curran's second line of attack was aimed at the most vocal opponent of his CMU resignation, and the newest, and therefore the most vulnerable, addition to the executive board. When vice-president Blackie Myers decided not to run for re-election, Joseph Stack, agent of the Port of New York, was elected instead. Immediately, President Curran preferred charges against Stack. A five-man trial committee was appointed to hear the charges and they voted three to two in favor of Stack but at a disorderly, and possibly illegal, meeting, the minority report was upheld. The issue was not resolved until the 1947 convention when Curran announced that he would not work with Stack and narrowly ousted Stack by a vote of 353 to 351 with four ballots voided.[11]

The major charge was that Stack had been "making false, vicious and irresponsible statements aimed at discrediting the president before the membership and the labor movement." In addition, there was a bizarre bill of particulars accusing Stack with a number of miscellaneous crimes including opposition to Republican Spain, opportunism in the 1938 elections, incitement of racial conflict and "membership in the Communist Party for opportunistic purposes."[12] But this grab-bag was just for the record; it soon narrowed down to the major charge. James Drury, a member of the trial committee who had voted to remove Stack, noted that it was the "slanderous, irresponsible statements made against the President of the Union" that were at the heart of the anti-Stack case. To allow Stack to stay in office would mean, Curran argued in a revealing statement, that "the president of your organization . . . will be looked at by the shipowners as a man who has no control over any of his staff officers."[13] Apparently, Curran considered the elective post of NMU vice-president as just another one of "his staff officers."

What were those "slanderous, irresponsible statements" that the president found so disturbing? Nothing more than the vigorous expression of the argument that the demise of the CMU was detrimental to the NMU membership and beneficial to the ship-owners. According to the anti-Stack faction of the trial committee, Stack issued a statement saying that "the actions and manner in which the president of our Union resigned as co-chairman on the committee for Maritime Unity and his statement to the press and the *Pilot* amount to treason against the membership of the National Maritime Union. . . ." When questioned about another controversial statement, Stack told the trial committee that "the manner in which the president resigned and handled the whole affair in CMU, I say yes, it was a Christmas present—the greatest shipowners ever got and probably will get for a long time."[14] Stack's rhetoric is certainly extravagant, but it is hard to argue with the report of the 1947 convention's appeals committee:

> The Committee . . . feels compelled to call to the delegates' attention that a Union official, elected by secret ballot, by members of this Union, cannot be gagged and prevented from freely expressing his views. He has a right to freely express his views as an official and as a member of this Union. To decide otherwise, is to set a precedent where an official or member of the Union who may say something that some other official does not like, may find himself in danger of either being removed from office or thrown out of the Union. The right of each official and each member to speak his mind must be protected.[15]

But Curran's radical allies disagreed and Keith, Lawrenson, Stone et al. called for the removal of Joe Stack because he dared to criticize Curran forcefully.

In a sense, it is misleading to say that the two main issues were the Stack ouster and the CMU resignation, because it obscures the fact that there was a conscious effort to make the campaign almost issue-less. Moreover, the real issue, whether there should be a wave of repression against the Communists, was never openly discussed by those favoring that repression. Curran took special care to put a radical face before the membership and to obscure his real plans. He was willing to attack President Truman's "reactionary foreign policy which uses relief as a political weapon to bolster crumbling, unrepresentative governments abroad, and gives military aid to be employed against the peoples striving for democracy."[16] Along with other anti-Communists, he voted for a boycott of ships bound for Greece and a resolution on Indonesia which complained that "imperialist Dutch interests backed by giant American corporations and an interventionist foreign policy, are waging murderous warfare against 70 million Indonesian people."[17] As late as 1949, Curran was still playing this game. A look at the resolutions of the April, 1949, National Council reveals that Communist Party membership:

> Shall be sufficient to disqualify a candidate from membership.
> The Greek government in seeking the destruction of the Greek trade union movement has instituted a wave of mass terror. . . . The Marshall Plan aid going to Greece is being used by the Greek government for these infamous ends.
> We unhesitatingly support the struggle of the Indonesian people.
> [The NMU condemns] Spanish fascist tyranny.[18]

At the same time, Curran was arguing that it was necessary to scrap some of the democratic machinery of the NMU to successfully destroy the evil power of Communists. In August 1947 Curran proposed an investigating committee (to be called the Committee on Un-NMU Activities perhaps?) to fight communism. In his argument, he made a crucial, ominous admission:

> . . . this proposition will require some drastic changes in the trial procedure of our union constitution. At the same time it will go a long way towards making it extremely difficult for members of the Communist Party or any other members or officers of our Union to continue activities contrary to the principles upon which the Union was founded.[19]

Curran defended this proposal by arguing that the Communists were so skilled at manipulating the present procedures of the Union that they were able to frustrate the democratic expression of the majority. In one of his extensive weekly diatribes, Curran complained that Communists

come to the meeting well organized, having met before the meeting.

... They are trained and disciplined and above all are prepared to stay all night at a meeting in order to tire out the non-Communist members ... they do everything possible to disrupt the meeting, raising points of order ... and whenever votes are finally taken they ... make a short count on the vote if it is against them. ... Communists make it their business to see to it that they are on every important committee and if you will notice in our union, the same faces, the same ones are on almost every committee.[20]

At the 1947 convention, Curran and Keith tried to gain the delegates' endorsement of a Communist purge. Keith proposed an amendment to the NMU constitution which read:

No religious, political or any other organization shall be officially permitted to interfere in the affairs of the NMU. The membership shall determine by secret ballot when such an organization is interfering in the affairs of the NMU to the detriment of the best interests of the Union and in violation of the fundamental principles, objectives and democratic procedures laid down in the constitution.

There was considerable debate followed by a roll call vote, and the amendment was defeated by 372 to 314.[21] On the only substantive issue that the Curran forces had raised, whether being a Communist disqualified a man from being a good union official, the Communists were clearly victorious.

But that battle turned out to be a minor skirmish at the convention. The Curran forces wisely concentrated their efforts on organizational matters. There was a series of tests of strength at the convention: the Stack trial, the battle over the seating of Josh Lawrence and the charges brought against Alexander. The Curran forces won those battles, and it was those victories that convinced the delegates that the Communists were through and that Curran was in. There are in every union a number of opportunists, men who shift their position in order to retain their jobs. In the NMU there was more at stake in retaining an office than in most unions. Generally, a defeated official must return to a less interesting job in the shop with a cut in pay. But he can still live in the same house with his family. In the NMU, he would have to go to sea. Guessing wrong in an NMU faction fight could mean exile from your wife and kids. These opportunists ignored the votes over principled issues and simply looked at the organizational issues. Curran's organizational victories at the convention led to his sweep of the offices in the 1948 NMU elections. Immediately, he began to expel his Communist opponents, then his non-Communist radical opponents and finally his conservative opponents.

Spira's summary of the degeneration of the NMU after Curran's victory is excellent; there is no need for me to add atrocity stories of my own. His account of the struggle between Curran and the Independent Caucus is an important corrective to the slanted study of Philip Taft.[22] Still, some major issues are ignored. Should the radicals have argued that an elected vice-president should be removed simply because he criticized the president? Should the radicals have supported the creation of a Committee on Un-NMU Activities? Should the radicals have supported drastic changes in the trial procedures? Should the radicals have said that the united strike action, which forced the NMU to stay out for three days to help their brothers in other unions, was undesirable and nothing more than a communist plot? Indeed, the major issue is never discussed: should the radicals have joined with Curran in Curran's attempt to destroy the largest and best-organized group of radicals in the NMU? The question probably never occurred to Spira but I think that the answer to that question is clearly no.

There are two considerations that Spira never mentions. First, the anti-Communist campaign was conducted during a period when the Communists supported militant strike action and independent politics. Naturally, this made them many enemies both in and out of the labor movement. To some extent it was, then, the Communists' radicalism, rather than their earlier wartime collaboration, that made it possible for radical anti-Communists to be successful. Second, intrinsic in the attack on the Communists was a defense of Curran. Even the Socialist Workers Party, a longtime foe of lesser evils, fell into this trap. In their pamphlet on the NMU, they took Curran at face value:

> The disruptive activities of CMU became so scandalous that its national co-chairman, Joseph Curran, felt impelled to resign and denounce the CMU.

> Finally, the NMU members got a first hand revelation [about the Communists] from NMU President Joseph Curran at the February 18, 1946 New York membership meeting.[23]

The net result of the campaign could easily have been predicted in advance: the credibility of Curran over that of his radical opponents was enhanced. It is ironic that those who did their best to create that credibility were later destroyed by it.

December 1968

1. James R. Prickett, "Communism and Factionalism in the UAW, 1939-1947," *Science & Society* XXXII (Summer, 1968).

2. The following is an incomplete list, including only the letters published in June, of contributions to the CPA discussion page in the *Daily Worker* which reflected this position: Jon Peters (June 21); Benjamin Cheskis (June 23); E. Van Haagen (June 27); Ruth Dombrowski, Tanya M. (June 28); Abe Straus (June 30); B.C. (June 11); C. Soloman (June 11); Samuel Greenberg (June 11); Al Lowe (June 16); Lester Moss (June 17); E. Selden (June 20).

3. "An Association Member," CPA Discussion Page, *Daily Worker*, June 13, 1945.

4. Irving Howe and Lewis Coser, *The American Communist Party: A Critical History* (New York: Frederick A. Praeger, 1962), p. 449. Howe does not footnote that phrase and he may have made it up.

5. *Proceedings of the Fifth National Convention of the National Maritime Union of America* (1945), pp. 81, 75-76, 331, 332, 327-28.

6. Max M. Kampelman, *The Communist Party vs. the CIO: A Study in Power Politics* (New York: Frederick A. Praeger, 1957), p. 80. In a masterpiece of understatement, Kampelman notes that "the strikes were finally settled" but neglects to say that the settlement came three days later.

7. Quoted in Robert Eugene Randolphe, "History of the International Longshoremen's and Warehousemen's Union, 1945-1951," (Unpublished MA Thesis, University of California at Berkeley, probably 1952), pp. 45-46.

8. NMU *Pilot* January 3, 1947.

9. Philip Taft, *The Structure and Government of Labor Unions* (Cambridge: Harvard University Press, 1954), p. 201; Kampelman, *CP vs CIO*, p. 80.

10. "Voice of the Membership," NMU *Pilot*, January 3, 1947.

11. NMU *Pilot* April 4 and April 11, 1947; *Pilot*, October 17, 1947.

12. "Stack Trial—Minority Report," NMU *Pilot* April 4, 1947. The complete text of both majority and minority reports are in this issue.

13. *Proceedings of the Sixth National Convention of the National Maritime Union of America* (1947), pp. 973, 982.

14. "Stack Trial—Minority Report," NMU *Pilot* April 4, 1947.

15. *Sixth Convention Proceedings* p. 969.

16. NMU *Pilot*, March 21, 1947.

17. Kampelman, *CP vs. CIO*, p. 87; Grange Bowen McKinney, "Communism in the National Maritime Union, 1937-1948," (Unpublished MA Thesis, UCLA, 1963), pp. 49-50. Both Kampelman and McKinney appear to have picked this resolution as a horrible example; I rather agree with its sentiments.

18. NMU *Pilot*, April 15, 1949.

19. *Ibid.*, August 1, 1947.

20. *Ibid.*, March 28, 1947.

The Unambiguity
of Labor History

HENRY SPIRA

James R. Prickett's crucial error is that he has fallen for the myth that the Communist Party always represents "the Left." If Prickett follows the press, he must perforce be aware that it was the French Communist Party, embracing the French establishment, which defended law and order against leftist revolutionaries during the recent general strike of ten million French workers—an action inspired by radical students which brought the French economy to a standstill. The Communist Party assisted de Gaulle and is willing to settle for a few government posts as a reward for being hangman and betrayer of the French Revolution.

Reporting during the French upsurge, Henry Tanner concluded (*New York Times* May 19, 1968):

> If the Communist party has managed to take over the movement, then, ironically, the institutions are safe and the political contest is likely to move back into the National Assembly, with votes of confidence and votes of censure and traditional speeches—and sooner or later a new election.

This was a repeat performance of the Party's role in the mid-forties when it preferred sharing power with de Gaulle to taking over the reins, at a time when the Party controlled the majority of the French Resistance movement—a people in arms.

The seamen's struggle is not a family quarrel between radical brothers but part of the fight against Establishment manipulators. The Communist Party has no confidence, no faith in the self-assertion of workers or students. Their faith resides in the sanctity of the power structure: the Soviet Union, the Party apparatus, wheeling and dealing with men in power, parliamentary eyewash. The Communist Party, like the capitalist elite, is deathly afraid of, and intent on destroying, spontaneous, independent workers' power.

Currently the Party's counter-revolutionary activity centers around crushing the Czech people's drive for self determination; yesterday, it was Hungary and East Germany. The Communists' leftist rhetoric is irrelevant and obscene. While the Party praises and distorts a martyred Che Guevara, it withheld support from Guevara's fighting guerillas because it was unable to control the movement and shunt it into parliamentary gabbery.

For the Communist Party it is a question of who stifles and subdues workers, peasants and intellectuals attempting to guide their own destiny. The Party would like to see the Kremlin do it, but it would be perfectly content if Moscow could come to an agreement with Washington, and divide the job between them.

The authoritarianism of the Party in imposing its line without regard to the people's needs, is also reflected in its relation to its own membership. The Communist Party is a closed corporation; its ranks have as much say over determining the Party's line as your neighbor has in setting the Democratic Party's line. Communist Party membership is not based on loyalty to the underdog, the class struggle or the revolution—such allegiance may well be inconsistent with Communist Party adherence.

Although Prickett is gifted with the touch of a talmudist, he has a very genius for befuddlement. When the juggling of 23 sources, taken out of context, clashes with reality, it is the footnotes which have to give way. The foundation of his errors is apparent in his opening paragraph, where he describes the Communist Party machine within the NMU as a "group of radicals." His myopia is maintained throughout, winding up with his ironic peroration. He concludes: "It is ironic that those who did their best to create that credibility [of Curran] were later destroyed by it." Prickett should be aware that Curran was a creature of the Communist Party, and that it is the Party which must answer for taking a finky bos'n off a ship and transforming him into a tin god. It was this Pygmalion, this infallible Stalin Jr., who turned against his creators.

Prickett, with a certainty acquired through insulation from the living movement, asserts that moves against the Communists involved questions of democracy. Prickett has a Newspeak problem. Communist Party democracy gave everyone the right to agree with them. Dissenters were smeared, slandered, hounded out of office, deprived of their livelihood and beaten up by Party goon squads. The Party, unable to defend its stewardship of the NMU in open debate, discredited the very ideals of trade unionism through its dictatorial machine control. Fighting to smash the Party machine was fighting to defend the membership's right to control its own union.

During the Hitler-Stalin Pact days, the Communist Party echoed Molotov's dictum, "Fascism is a matter of taste!" With the Nazi invasion of Russia, on June 22, 1971 the imperialist war turned into a struggle for national liberation. Now explain to working seamen that "The Yanks are not coming" becomes transformed into "Keep 'em Sailing!" overnight. From leftist phraseology the Party turned to super patriotism, the only group within the labor movement to support a National Service Act to conscript labor, advocate a permanent no-strike pledge after the war, demand that John L. Lewis be jailed for treason because the miners were forced to strike.

In maritime, the Communist Party faction endorsed Coast Guard hearing units to whom they pledged their aid in "weeding out undesirable elements," thus setting the stage for the screening of all militants by the Coast Guard. The Party acted as fingermen for the draft boards in turning over seamen who "overstay their time on the beach." They welcomed shipowners into the NMU hiring hall and taught classes in "Readin', Writin' and No Strikin'." No effort was made to enforce the union contract. Sellout agreements were hailed as victories. The Communist Party policy was unconditional surrender to government agencies and the shipowners. *Business Week* (March 18, 1944) noted that Communist dominated unions have "moved to the extreme right wing position in the American labor movement."

The opposition developed not because of the Party's radicalism, but because of its betrayals, because the Party was running the NMU through a brutal machine necessitated by its inability to muster the seamen's voluntary support for a policy of scabbing and selling out the needs of the men they were presumably representing.

Today's Joseph Curran and a Communist union functionary could still readily change places. Neither would have to change his operational procedures; they'd feel at home in each other's shoes. On the opposing side of the battle lines, radical activists operate on the principle of participatory democracy: they base themselves on the free expression of people in motion; they are the megaphones of masses expressing their own hopes, aspirations and frustrations. They try to inspire people with the radical concept that they can change their own existence, that they have a basic right to take control away from forces that are manipulating them.

For Prickett, the way it really was is irrelevant. He strains, pushes and distorts to justify the Party's role within the NMU. Prickett, like Hubert H. Humphrey, echoes the theme that every day and in every way, things were getting better and better. Unity was euphoric, conditions even more enchanting, seamen were happy and content under the democratic radical Party leadership. This hallucinatory dream turned into a nightmare after perverse radical anticommunists started feuding.

Our perspicacious historian develops a convenient case of amnesia while discussing the Committee for Maritime Unity (CMU). The NMU at that time had about 90,000 members, the four other CMU seamen's unions had a combined membership of 25,000; under CMU arrangements all unions had one vote. Thus the Stalinists saw the CMU as a vehicle for maintaining control over the NMU. The irony is that the CMU was so successful that the AFL set up its own Maritime Trades Department. That's some unity: a federation of CIO maritime unions confronting the AFL-MTD in hostile array, waiting for a spark to explode into waterfront jurisdictional warfare. The NMU's *Pilot* while labeling AFL maritime officials "finks" asked the ranks to join the unity move.

The fake Stalinist "unity" reached its low point when the San Francisco CMU Port Committee on November 22, 1946 (CMU Bay Area Bulletin No. 38) gave the striking Masters, Mates and Pilots union, a 24-hour ultimatum to pull their picket lines off the docks, or have them smashed. The Party offered Curran the opportunity to pose as a militant. Curran told the NMU membership on December 30, 1946: "My name was attached to that ultimatum, and I did not approve of it, and the NMU does not approve of strikebreaking or smashing picket lines."

Another aspect of Communist Party "unity" is that they broke the maritime unions' common contract expiration date of September 30. With CMU, CIO maritime contracts terminated on June 15. In the name of unity, the Party created a chaotic situation lending itself to disunity, the impossibility of united action in struggle with shipowners, an invitation to jurisdictional warfare and scabbing.

In quoting the June 15 gains, Prickett, with some research, might have added that the NMU membership denounced the original recommendation made by Curran and all the Communist Party officials on May 29, 1946, while the September strike involved a "me too" action, attempting to get what the West Coast AFL maritime unions had already won. In discussing Stack, Prickett could have offered a more balanced picture by mentioning Stack's flagrant incitement to racial battles in the NMU by his printing of an allegedly anonymous letter in the *Pilot* (January 24, 1947), not to mention the fiasco of the Stack-directed Great Lakes Strike in August 1946.

Our imaginative researcher speaks of CMU's "strong initial support." Did the seamen really support a policy to unite CIO seamen in order to clobber other waterfront trade unionists? NMU seamen weren't given a chance to express themselves. The membership was refused a referendum on this vital issue. Thus Curran, in a statement on January 17, 1947, charged the (Party) majority on the National Council with denying the membership voice and vote: "The real issue is no longer CMU. The real issue now is—Do you, the membership in a rank and file union have the right to pass judgment in a secret referendum vote on major issues in your union? They say no. I say yes."

Prickett wants to know whether radicals should have joined with Curran to oust the Party. Anti-Communist radicals weren't supporting Curran, they were supporting the rights of working seamen to rid themselves of a bureaucratic weight which had been dragging them down for years. On a question such as the membership's right to a secret referendum on major issues after they had been fully discussed, how could a genuine radical not offer his support?

For a brief period, Curran was able to rest on the discontent within the NMU—he attacked the Party from the left and gave militants an opportunity to breathe. After the Party stranglehold was broken, Curran returned to Communist organizational methods and reconstituted a dictatorial machine. At that time, as always, radicals supported the democratic rights of Party members within the NMU.

Curran is an opportunist. The Party took this puppet off the ships and set him up on a lordly pinnacle. Because it never based itself upon support of the ranks, the Party was extremely vulnerable; not as a radical organization, but as a group whose interests were contrary to the needs of the seamen. It is instructive that while Curran could defeat the Party through the democratic process, he needed the New York Police Department to oust the non-Communist radicals. As the Cold War was heated up, Curran turned once again into the flag waving patriot in 1941-1945 Communist Party fashion.

The current NMU opposition, grouped around James Morrissey's *The Call*, is different from all previous oppositions. It is unique in that it is not based on a split within the officialdom of the National Maritime Union. It is composed of seamen who are fed up with being pushed around; seamen who are asserting themselves after being freed from the decade long Communist Party brainwashing which equated J. Curran with J. Christ; seamen who are determined to make the decisions affecting their lives.

December 1968

Labor Insurgency
and the Legal Trap

BURTON HALL

"A trade union," the attorney for the Canadian Labor Congress (CLC) told an Industrial Inquiry Commission in March 1963, "is a free association of workers who come together to improve their conditions of work and for other social purposes." Workers may be required to join it, he argued, but the basic principle still remains: "if an institution continues to function as a trade union, it must be a free association of workers."

Maurice Wright, the CLC's counsel, posed that definition for the purpose of demonstrating that the Canadian district of the Seafarers' International Union of North America (SIU) was no union at all—not by Canadian standards, anyway. He summed up the SIU this way:

It is a captive legion of dragooned and helpless individuals. It is a racket; it is not a union. Like the constitution of the USSR, the constitution of the Seafarers International Union of Canada makes profuse reference to the principles of democracy and contains elaborate provisions designed to put the principles into effect. In both cases, behind the facade of the documents, there is the reality of totalitarian rule.

Wright went on to document his charges: he described the "Do Not Ship" list by which Hal Banks, ex-convict and boss of the SIU of Canada, had blacklisted 4,000 Canadian seamen; he outlined the SIU pattern of violence, itemizing 75 acts of violence and intimidation perpetrated by Banks' "hoodlum empire" from 1956 to 1962; he demonstrated the practice of election fraud and rigged conventions, by which the SIU is and was run from the top down; he gave examples of the officials' use of the union's journal and membership meetings as instruments for brainwashing the membership; and he showed the lavish misappropriation by the SIU officials of the union's money for the officials' private benefit. In short, he demonstrated (although this was not his purpose) that the SIU of Canada, which had been set up in 1948 by the parent SIU of North America ostensibly to save Canadian seamen from the pro-communist Canadian Seamen's Union, was a characteristic example of the North American bureaucratic union establishment. Wright argued, and the Commission headed by Justice T.G. Norris agreed, that the SIU should be eliminated from Canada as fundamentally (though neither one used the word) "unCanadian." Wright argued:

We have stated that the SIU is not a part of the Canadian labor movement—it is a growth upon it. Equally, we submit, that the SIU is not a part of Canadian society—it is a growth upon it. We submit that your Lordship should be prepared to recommend whatever social surgery is necessary to relieve both the trade union movement and society from this growth. There is no place in our social structure for a hoodlum empire which works hand-in-glove with certain shipping companies to the advantage of both and to the disadvantage of the workers and the general public.

Wright's point was well-proven, and the criminal charges against SIU boss Hal Banks amply emphasize its social urgency. In 1964 Banks was found guilty both of perjury before the Norris Commission, for which he received a 30-day sentence, and also of having hired thugs to beat and cripple for life, Frank Walsh, an officer of the Merchant Service Guild, for which Banks was sentenced to five years. He is also charged (he has not yet been tried for it) with having hired goons to beat Richard Greaves, president of the (Canadian) National Association of Marine Engineers. But the question remains: why should Canadians be so self-righteously shocked by revelations concerning a totalitarian "hoodlum empire" which, if not typical of the North American (Canadian as well as United States) union establishment, is at least characteristic of it?

In any country the character of labor unions, as well as of other organizations, is shaped largely by the legal climate in which they exist. In Britain, as in several of the British dominions, Wright's phrase about "free associations" is virtually an accurate statement of a union's legal status. A union continues to exist in Britain only because the workers support it. A British worker, for example, may freely quit his union and join another, thereby cancelling the power of the first union to bind him in future collective bargaining and empowering the new union to do so instead. As a result, the union is compelled actively to seek the workers' support in order to stay in existence.

Not so in the United States—or in Canada. In both countries, the law is such that unions existing there are much more accurately described as state, or at least quasi-state, institutions than as free associations of workers.

Not entirely state institutions. Union officials in the United States and Canada are not directly appointed by the top officials of the state (as in the Soviet Union), nor does the national government have power to "intervent" unions (as in Argentina) and appoint new officials to replace the existing ones. But the legal spider's web that surrounds labor relations in the United States maintains incumbent union officials in power over the workers, and it insulates the power and status of those officials against possible rejection by the workers over whom they rule. And it is that legal apparatus, that legal spider's web, that establishes the statist or quasi-statist character of American unions.

In the ordinary law of agency, it is elementary that the agent's power exists only so long as the person he represents authorizes him to act as agent. But not in the area of American labor relations. A union certified by the labor relations board, or (without certification) merely recognized by the employer, is established by that fact as the exclusive representative of all the workers in the appropriate bargaining unit. At the initiation of this process the workers may (or may not) have something, collectively, to say about whether that particular union should be their representative. But once a union has become certified or recognized, that particular union remains the workers' exclusive bargaining representative and the legal spider's web makes it extremely difficult for the workers "represented" to get rid of the existing union or to replace it by another.

Dissatisfied workers can, of course, petition for a representation election in which all the workers in the "appropriate" bargaining unit will be able to vote for or against "decertification" of the existing union, or for or against "certification" of a new union. That right is guaranteed by statute; but like so many statutory and constitutional rights it is grievously restricted in practice.

First of all, workers seeking to decertify their established union, or to certify a new one, cannot petition at any time for an election; they must do so during a particular 30-day period that comes around only once every three years: it is the period less than 90 days but more than 60 days before the expiration of the existing collective bargaining agreement. At all other times they are barred from petitioning.

Barred by what? Not by any provision in any law, regulation or rule. They are barred by a "policy" of the National Labor Relations Board (NLRB) which dates back to 1942, which was adopted with the unanimous support of union officials and employer representatives. But that policy is ironclad; it has grown from a two-year bar to a three-year one, by consensus of the unions and the employers, and forms a fundamental (though unwritten) cornerstone of our labor relations law.

Very well, suppose the workers, dissatisfied with their present union, nevertheless wait one year, two years, perhaps three years, until the 30-day period comes around. Now they can petition. And in a few industries, where collective bargaining is still on a small scale, they may even succeed. But in most industries the "appropriate" bargaining unit is not what it was when unions were first established. In those barely-remembered days the workers at a particular factory, or in a particular division of a factory, comprised an "appropriate" unit, and the union became certified by being chosen in an election of that unit. But, again with the general approval of employers and officials of established unions, the rules have been changed: the "appropriate" unit is now whatever unit is actually bargained for. In the steel or auto industry such a unit would extend from coast-to-coast; in most industries with established labor relations patterns it is at least multi-employer, involving tens of thousands of workers. Those workers who have decided to petition for an election must produce the signatures of 30 percent of the workers in the unit—in most instances a simple impossibility. So much, after 34 years, for the Wagner Act's guarantee to all workers of the rights of "self-organization" and "to bargain collectively through representatives of their own choosing." As a practical matter, most workers are stuck with whatever union is already established as their representative; they have no practical possibility of replacing it with a union of their own choosing.

In its 1952 statement calling for democracy in labor unions, the American Civil Liberties Union argued, "unions should be democratic because [among other reasons] the power which they hold over the individual worker is largely derived from government." Discussing the existing pattern of labor relations statutes, the ACLU noted that "these statutes provide that government shall certify [particular] unions . . . as the exclusive bargaining representatives of all workers within the bargaining units;" in exercising these powers derived from government, said the ACLU, labor unions "should maintain the same democratic standards required of government itself."

But, unfortunately, democracy in state institutions can be guaranteed only by the state, and one hand of the government, in washing the other, has a tendency to entrench further the power of the government bureaucracy as a whole. When Congress, prodded by a public sentiment hostile to certain union bureaucracies, produced the Kennedy-Ervin bill for the purpose of "reforming" those bureaucracies, the method of reform that it came up with was one which placed *discretionary* power to act or not to act in the hands of the Secretary of Labor, a politically-appointed official who, traditionally, represents the union establishment within the federal administration. And it was that method of reform which Congress enacted into law when it adopted the Kennedy-Ervin bill, renaming it, at the last moment, the Landrum-Griffin Act.

Under the "reform" act, union members are barred from asserting their democratic electoral rights directly; instead, they must take their appeals to the Secretary of Labor—which means that they must appeal to the political ally of their union bureaucrats to defend them against those union bureaucrats.

As a practical matter, the Labor Department official who passes on their appeals may be even more than the *political* ally of union bureaucrats. For example: After the officers of Building Service Employees' Local 32-E were convicted in federal court in 1966 for receiving bribes from employers to sell out the working membership, the parent International Union placed a trusteeship over the local— not to clean things up but simply to suppress the membership's unrest. Six months later, in an election conducted by the International's trustee, a slate headed by one of the convicted officials was elected to office, without opposition and with the active support of the International's trustee. That operation was master-minded by the International President's executive assistant, a certain Thomas Donahue. A few months later, early in 1967, the same Thomas Donahue was appointed Assistant Secretary of Labor in charge of union democracy matters; that is to say, he became the man who ultimately passed upon the appeals of rank and file union members for protection of the membership's rights to fair and democratic union elections. Donahue held that position until the Johnson administration left office in January 1969; when he left, the Building Service Employees International Union rehired him, in substantially the same job as before but at a higher salary and with a fancier title. That is what is known as the "labor-liberal alliance."

The result of such alliances is that unions whose officials are on friendly political terms with whatever administration controls the White House are virtually exempt from any action within the Labor Secretary's "discretion" having to do with union democracy. One set of union officials on friendly terms at least with the administrations of recent years has been the bureaucracy that controls the Brotherhood of Painters—and which controlled the racket-ridden Painters' District Council No. 9, in New York City, until 1967. From 1961 to mid-1967, ordinary members of the District Council filed a wealth of complaints with the Secretaries Goldberg and Wirtz—but every one of them was denied in the "discretion" of the Secretary. Sometimes a reason for denial was given, sometimes no answer at all was made to the complaint, sometimes the Secretary admitted that serious electoral violations had occurred; in *all* instances, however, Secretaries Goldberg and Wirtz refused to take action on behalf of the complaining members. When the Brotherhood placed a trusteeship over the District Council as an excuse to do away with elections altogether and thereby keep Martin Rarback, the boss of the Painters' District Council, in power, Secretary Wirtz—in his "discretion"—still refused to take action on a complaint filed by rank-and-file members. Fortunately for the members, however, the law permits them (in a trusteeship case only) to bring suit themselves, and they did so. Although Secretary Wirtz intervened in their suit on the side of the Brotherhood—i.e., *against* the complaining members—the federal court rejected Wirtz's arguments, voided the trusteeship and directed an election under judicial supervision, with the result that Rarback was voted out of office and one of the complaining members was elected in his place.

In ordinary election cases union members are not so lucky. They cannot go to court, themselves, to enforce federal statutory standards of electoral democracy. Thus, when the incumbent officials of Cutters' Local 10 of the International Ladies' Garment Workers ran the local's 1968 election in the usual ILGWU manner, by arbitrarily ruling several opposition candidates off the ballot, by denying an opposition group the right to have a slate designation on the ballot, by using the union's facilities to distribute their own campaign literature but denying it to oppositionists, and by a host of other violations of law, the opposition candidates had no recourse but to wait until after the election and appeal to the Secretary of Labor. The election was in February; as required by law they exhausted appeals within the union (for four months) before appealing to the Secretary in June 1968. In October 1968, conceding that there was merit to the members' complaint, the Secretary's representative advised them that their charges were (for reasons never explained) "not suitable" for litigation. They wrote back asking,

Why are they "not suitable," Mr. Kleiler? What further violations can be committed by Union leadership before the government takes action? Especially in view of the fact that our Manager saw fit to admit the expenditure of $10,000.00 to prove their innocence.

We will greatly appreciate it if you will promptly advise us how we should explain to our fellow-union-members that the United States Government does not find it "suitable" to protect the rights guaranteed us by the LMRDA.

In answer, by a letter dated mid-November, Frank Kleiler, director of the office to which appeals are initially directed, conceded that the Labor Department's investigation had indeed revealed almost a dozen specific (and serious) violations of the union electoral provisions of federal law; but, referring to "certain procedural weaknesses" (never specified), he went on to say that "it was determined . . . that rather than chance an adverse decision on procedural grounds, this case was not suitable for litigation." More protests were made by the members but Kleiler insisted, "I see no need to amplify my letter." Finally, in January 1969, Kleiler cut off further discussion, writing that "no purpose would be served by further correspondence."

On those occasions when, for some reason or other, the Secretary does take action, the result is often no better—not only because relief is long-delayed but, often of equal importance, the Secretary's supervision turns out to favor the incumbents. Thus, in the 1969 rerun of the National Maritime Union's 1966 election, insurgent members—who had forced the rerun by successful appeal to the Secretary—were faced with such electoral rulings by the Secretary as one which denied ordinary members the right to campaign inside the union hall (while union officials exercised that right freely) and another which permitted union officials to distribute campaign material aboard ships but denied that right to oppositionists. The result of such rulings (one of which permitted National Maritime Union (NMU) officials to include in the list of eligible voters thousands of non-members of NMU, non-maritime workers who were not even eligible under the NMU constitution to become members of NMU) was, of course, the handy re-election of the incumbent officials.

And when, in 1968, the United States Supreme Court ruled that members of the huge (26,000-member) Hotel, Motel and Club Employees' Local 6 were entitled, because of recent election abuses, to an election supervised by the Secretary, the rules that Secretary Wirtz set up for the new election so favored the incumbent officials, and so hamstrung all opposition candidates, that the opposition "Membership Party" in Local 6 declined to run at all, leaving the new election uncontested.

Substantially, the record of action and inaction on the Secretary's part reflects a basic law of politics: it indicates what reliance upon a non-judicial arm of the state to reform a quasi-state institution comes to as a practical matter. To the extent that the reform act, especially by its "Bill of Rights of Members of Labor Organizations," permits union members to go directly to the courts, it has accomplished a genuine democratic reform. But the rights directly enforceable by judicial means do not extend (except incidentally, in the case of a trusteeship) to electoral democracy. In the latter area the Secretary's "discretion" remains supreme. And the exercise by the Secretary of Labor of that "discretion" turns even the pressure for democracy into a device for further solidifying the alliance between union bureaucracies and the government bureaucracy.

Just how solid that alliance is already may be illustrated by the sequel to the Norris Commission's investigation of the SIU of Canada.

Banks, deposed as President of the SIU of Canada, remained Vice-President of its parent International, the SIU of North America, in which capacity he continues to draw a salary of $20,000 per year. (He is also Vice-President of the AFL-CIO Maritime Trades Department.) In 1964 he fled to the United States, jumping $1,000 bail on his contempt of court conviction, for perjury before the Norris Commission, as well as $25,000 bail on his conviction for conspiracy in the assault on Walsh. Paul Hall, president of the SIU of North America, not only kept him on his $20,000 salary but (according to the SIU's financial reports) extended some $50,000 to him, in 1964 and 1965, as "advance payments" on "organizational expenses" as well as loans of some $25,000 for "personal necessity." But that was only a beginning of the benefits that awaited Banks.

In 1967, the government of Canada demanded Banks' extradition to Canada to serve his conviction for perjury, a crime among those specified in the United States-Canadian extradition treaty. United States Commissioner Salvatore Abruzzo upheld Canada's claim and ordered that Banks be turned over to Canada. But then attorneys for the AFL-CIO approached Secretary of Labor Wirtz, asking him to intercede with Secretary of State Dean Rusk on behalf of Banks. And although the State Department's legal department agreed with Commissioner Abruzzo that Banks should be extradited, Rusk, late in March 1968, intervened and saved Banks from Canadian justice. When reporters asked Rusk what authority he relied upon in overruling both Abruzzo and the State Department's legal adviser, Rusk replied that he relied solely upon "my own sense of old-fashioned justice."

Maybe the AFL-CIO's request, by itself, had turned the tables. Or maybe Rusk's sense of "old-fashioned justice" was related to the fact that on April 3, 1968 only a few days after he had intervened to save Banks from extradition to Canada, the SIU of North America donated $50,000 to the presidential campaign of Hubert Humphrey and another $50,000 to committees that had been organized to support the re-election candidacy of Lyndon Johnson. It is upon such considerations, at any rate, that the "liberal-labor alliance" operates.

At virtually every step, workers in rebellion against their union's officials are confronted by that "alliance"—as a hostile force. But even if they were not, the odds would still be tipped against them within the legal and administrative spider's web that envelops the field of labor relations. Not that there are no instances in which union rebels have been successful within the spider's web; the point is simply that for any particular group of rank and file workers the chances of success by the administrative route are minimal—so extremely minimal as to argue strongly against their reliance solely upon that route.

That is not to say that rank and file workers should make no use of the administrative procedures open to them. So long as the system of government-backed bureaucracy is imposed upon them by force of law, the rebels' first recourse must be to make use of whatever procedures are available to them within that system. But to rely upon those procedures, to rest their hopes for success upon administrative or legal victories, would for most groups of union rank-and-filers be self-defeating.

What, then, should they do—*other* than hope to fight their way out of the legal/administrative spider's web by the procedures available to them within it? Should they merely bide their time, holding opposition meetings and distributing leaflets? Or should they take some manner of action aimed more directly against the system in which they find themselves trapped?

One obvious avenue is that of attempting, by some form of direct as opposed to administrative action, to push the established union officialdom aside by demanding that the employer bargain directly with the rank-and-filers' own organization. Unfortunately, that avenue was obvious to Congress, also—so obvious that Congress (by amendments adding sections 8(b)(4)(C) and 8(b)(7)(A) to the National Labor Relations Act) has declared it to be an "unfair labor practice" for workers to strike or even merely to picket so long as one of their demands is that the employer recognize or bargain with an organization other than the already-recognized union. The result is that workers who take that avenue will, most likely, be faced with a cease-and-desist order, which may ripen into a federal court injunction, and with the likelihood, in the case of a rank and file strike, of an employer's suit for damages.

As a practical matter, therefore, that avenue would seem to be effectively barred. But it is interesting to observe that the barrier applies only in the event that the rebellious workers demand that the employer recognize or bargain with their own, separate organization. If no such demand is made, if they merely protest against specific conditions, they may be faced with other forms of legal attack but not quite the same, and (most likely) not quite as effective an attack as would occur if they did make the demand. All of which suggests the form of direct action toward which the system of state-administered labor relations compels rebellious rank and file trade unionists.

There are, of course, a multitude of instances in which that particular form of direct action has been employed successfully, perhaps the classic instance being the series of post-World War II wildcat strikes in the East Coast longshore industry. What gave that revolt its peculiarly effective character was the fact that the rebelling longshoremen, rather than demanding that employers bargain with their rank and file organization, demanded instead that their corrupt union leadership renegotiate with the employers the terms of the collective bargaining agreements. It would seem that direct action of that kind, addressing its demands to union leadership and the employers jointly, is the approach which—when coupled with the parallel exercise of whatever legal and administrative procedures are available to the rebellious workers—comprises the rank and file strategy best suited to cope with the facts of bureaucratic labor relations.

An obvious virtue of such a strategy is that it confronts the entire power structure—not only employers but government-backed establishment unions as well—as its enemy. Another is that a fight over shop issues, over down-to-earth working conditions, has a much more infectious quality than a mere quarrel between rival unions, if only because the issues are more easily and clearly understood by workers in other shops and other industries. All of which points toward the hope that a movement based upon such a strategy might become general enough to embrace a major segment of the entire work force.

It cannot be said with any certainty what effect that strategy, if carried out more widely, might have on the system of administered labor relations. Nor can it be said with any certainty whether the new era of labor revolt, which would seem to be rendered ultimately inevitable by the increasing bureaucratization of that system, will ever occur. But it is at least possible that a more general and widespread reliance upon rank and file direct action, coupled with the use of whatever legal procedures are available, could shake that entire administrative system.

After all, the overall objective of the labor relations statutes is to minimize industrial disturbances by encouraging orderly collective bargaining. But if backstairs contracts, arranged between the employers and the officials of government-supported establishment unions, cannot keep disturbances to a near minimum, then the system fails. As a result, rank and file protests against bad conditions, and against sellout of collective bargaining agreements, become protests—and possibly effective protests—against the entire system of government backing of certain established unions and against state administration of union-management relations.

June 1969

Meanwhile, Back at the Labor Department

BURTON HALL

The 1969 election dispute in the United Mine Workers of America (UMWA) is by now a familiar story. It and its grim aftermath—the murder of Joseph Yablonski, his wife and his daughter by a gang that included at least one officer of the Mine Workers' union—have been widely publicized, as they should be, and have focused, as no other dispute has in the past ten years, attention on the internal affairs of one of the major "respectable" International unions. In doing so, they have brought into question an up-till-then rarely questioned article of the modern liberal faith; namely the insistence that, deep down inside, all is basically well with the major trade unions and that, since they are pillars of the modern Establishment, their internal affairs should not be looked into too closely. It is an article of faith that extends from the mysterious[1] *American Labor Magazine* and the self-consciously "liberal" *New America* (the latter being the official journal of the ultra-respectable but intensely sectarian "Socialist Party") to the union bureaucrats themselves and to a lengthening succession of Secretaries of Labor. The assumption on which it is based, insofar as it is something other than bureaucratic self-interest, is that the incumbent officials of the major unions represent "Labor," even though ordinary workers have, as a rule, little to do with choosing them and nothing to do with selecting those particular unions to be their collective bargaining representatives. From such an assumption it follows, of course, that the rank and file workers who, either independently of or in opposition to the incumbent officers of whatever union is by law placed in power over them, might fight for better wages and better working conditions are a divisive and subversive "anti-Labor" force—a force which all friends of the Labor Movement must conspire to repress, lest it otherwise subvert or embarrass the established representatives of "Labor."

The fact that every United States Secretary of Labor since 1959—two of them Republicans and two of them Democrats—has acted in accordance with that article of faith should occasion no surprise. Nor would it matter much, were it not for the fact that the Secretary of Labor is the public officer charged by law, in particular by the Labor-Management Reporting and Disclosure Act (LMRDA) of 1959, with protecting the democratic rights of union members.

Perhaps the best way of showing how it is that the successive Secretaries of Labor have looked upon their duties is to discuss the performance of their duties in regard to trusteeships. A trusteeship, in the labor world, is a device by which an International union removes some or all of the officers of a local union or district or other subordinate body and appoints new officers to run its affairs without being answerable to the membership. For example, the United Mine Workers has trusteeships over 19 of its districts within the United States—and since the UMWA has, in all, only 23 districts within the United States, that means that the greater part of the union is run from the top down. In fact, the UMWA has been in large measure run that way since the beginning of the Lewis era, half a century ago. And although the UMWA relies upon the trusteeship method of rule a little more strongly than other unions, its use of that technique for quelling local opposition and destroying local democracy is not at all uncommon.

The LMRDA [Labor Reform Act] charges the Secretary of Labor with the principal duty of challenging improper trusteeships by suit in court, but alternatively allows union members themselves to sue if the Secretary, in his wisdom, refuses to do so. And the LMRDA further provides that, in any suit—whether by the Secretary or an individual member—any trusteeship that has been in force for more than 18 months shall prima facie be presumed to be improper. Ever since the LMRDA was enacted in 1959, rank and file members of the UMWA, and of other unions, have been coming to the Department of Labor and asking the Secretary's representatives to do as the law directs the Secretary to do: to go into court to challenge the trusteeships improperly and unlawfully maintained over their local unions or local districts. And the Secretary—or rather the three Secretaries (one Republican and two Democratic) who headed the Department of Labor from 1959 to 1964—have been turning a deaf ear.

In 1964, after UMWA members, in particular, had been badgering him for five years (and after some of these members had begun to talk of bringing suit themselves), the Secretary instituted the one and only legal action that has ever been instituted by him challenging trusteeships: he brought suit in court against some (not all) of the UMWAs. Oddly enough, however, the suit did not proceed very far. In fact, today, some six years after suit was filed, the case is still awaiting trial. And we are still waiting for the Secretary of Labor—any Secretary of Labor—to bring the second such suit.

Obviously, it would be uncharitable to criticize the Secretary's poor handling of the UMWA trusteeship case, in view of his (or their) failure to bring any other trusteeship case in all these 11 years. Nor would it be fair to say that he has been inactive. In every other instance in which union members have complained to the Department of Labor concerning a trusteeship they have received from the Department a polite request to withdraw their complaint and, if they ignored the request, a formal letter telling them that under the peculiar circumstances of the case (which, for some reason, never seem to be spelled out in the Secretary's letter) litigation is "unwarranted" or would be "unwise." And if the union member, himself, goes to court? Even then the Secretary will not remain inactive. In all likelihood he will go to court too—but in *opposition* to the union members, i.e., in support of the union officials who maintain the trusteeship. (Thus when rank and file members of the New York Painters' District Council No. 9 went to court attacking a fraudulent trusteeship imposed over their District Council, the Secretary appeared as *amicus curiae* on behalf of the International, i.e., in support of the trusteeship. When after hearing the evidence (and despite the Secretary's arguments), the Court was persuaded that the trusteeship had been imposed in bad faith and for unlawful reasons,[2] the Secretary was asked how he had handled other trusteeship matters. The Secretary's representative replied that, oh yes!, the Secretary was active in the matter of trusteeships; he was even then "vigorously" pursuing a case against the UMWA trusteeships! That was three years ago and the "vigorously" pursued UMWA trusteeship case has yet to come to trial).

Meanwhile, in a long list of cases, members who, having gone to the Secretary for action against fraudulent or otherwise improper trusteeships, and been told by him that litigation in their cases was unwarranted or unwise, have gone to court themselves and have been successful in having those trusteeships declared illegal and thereby put out of existence. The lawbooks are now teeming with decisions supporting members' suits against such trusteeships. There has yet to be handed down, however, the first judicial decision in a trusteeship case that the Secretary has considered "warranted" or "wise."

The Secretary's performance of his duties in regard to elections has not been very different from this. Hosts of union members have complained to him about the rigging and stealing of their elections. The law directs him to bring suit whenever he finds, as a result of his investigation, that a violation of the LMRDA has been committed and has not been "remedied," providing further that, if a court finds that the violation "may have affected" the election's outcome, it shall set the election result aside and order a new election under the Secretary's supervision. And on relatively rare occasions—especially in those circumstances where it is not politically disadvantageous for him to do so—he has actually instituted such an action. It is far more common, however, for complaining union members either to receive no reply to their complaint; or to receive a reply admitting that violations occurred but contending (without any reason given) that they couldn't have affected the election's outcome; or to receive a reply admitting that violations occurred that may have affected (and probably, in fact, did affect) the outcome, but that for some unexplained reason litigation is unwarranted or unwise.

What can the union member do then? Not much, for the law does not allow him to bring suit himself; it provides that the method of complaint to the Secretary is the *exclusive* remedy for stolen union elections. The LMRDA even goes so far as to eliminate those rights that union members formerly possessed at common law to challenge stolen elections. In this area—in contrast with the trusteeship area—Congress has, as the United States Supreme Court observed some six years ago, turned protection of union members' rights over to "the special knowledge and discretion of the Secretary of Labor"[3] —a "special knowledge and discretion" that has proved of singularly little worth in the record of trusteeship litigation.

To show just how the process of election appeal works—and how the Secretary's "special knowledge and discretion" are exercised in fact—an example might be helpful. An interesting one concerns the election of International officers of the Retail Clerks International Association (RCIA), AFL-CIO, in June 1968. The RCIA is one of our larger "respectable" unions, with a membership of some 540,000. According to the official count, some 190,000 ballots were cast in the June 1968 election, with the administration slate winning by margins running from 31,014 to 43,716. Partly because the election meant a changing of the guard (the incumbent president, James A. Suffridge, was retiring and had selected his former administrative aide, James T. Housewright, to replace him), there was a substantial group in opposition.

Calling itself the "Reformation, Revitalization, Reconstruction" (or RRR) slate, the opposition group nominated a former Vice President, John T. Haletsky, to head an almost-full slate of candidates. Like all opposition groups, however, it lacked funds and other material resources; as a result it had observers in less than half of the 247 RCIA locals in which the election took place.

But in some locals it was able to do a competent job of checking; and in 21 locals in particular, which had turned in some 40,108 votes by the official tally, it was able to prove myriad violations of law; illegalities that included ballot box stuffing, unlawful use of union funds to aid the administration-slate campaign, intimidation of RRR campaign supporters by officials allied with the administration slate, polling places which the administration-allied officials refused to open at all, polling places which the administration slate's local allies closed two hours before the announced closing time and a gamut of more garden-variety electoral violations. Since those 21 local unions had, according to the official count, voted about six-to-one for the Administration slate (Housewright getting 33,410 to Haletsky's 5,741), those violations may obviously have gone a long way toward affecting the election result.

And just as obviously, these were not the only violations committed in the course of the election. In the Montreal local, for example (and it was not one of the 21), ballot-box stuffing was so open and notorious that even the RCIA's International Executive Board agreed that its vote should be disregarded. (The official tally from that local showed 3,682 votes for Housewright to Haletsky's 849.)

In fact, even the violations committed in the 21 locals themselves plainly affected the vote in others. For example, the Clifton, New Jersey local (one of the 21) printed, at union expense, between 3,000 and 5,000 pieces of administration-slate campaign literature and distributed them to members of a Newark local that was not among the 21; similarly, the Buffalo local (one of the 21) paid for the printing and distribution of engraved invitations to support the administration slate and sent them to officers of other local unions.

But even more revealing is the involvement of the International's officers directly in election rigging. For example, on the night before the election, a group of administration-slate supporters under the direction of Jack Loveall, the RCIA's Acting Organizing Director for the Metropolitan New York Division and Housewright's successor as Administrative Assistant to Suffridge, made telephone calls to each of the election judges of New York City Local 888, falsely notifying them that the election had been postponed. Their purpose is, of course, obvious: Local 888 was strongly pro-RRR (its members ultimately voted 8,146 to 628 for Haletsky over Housewright). Loveall himself made most of the telephone calls and all but a few were made from his motel room; but in addition to him the group making the calls included the RCIA's Director of Collective Bargaining, its Assistant Director of Organizing for the Eastern Division, and several other top-level or nearly top-level officers. The bill for the telephone calls was paid for out of the treasury of a local union then under International trusteeship.

Or for another example: two months before the election, the RCIA's Organizing Director for the Northwestern Division (and himself a candidate for International Vice President on the administration slate) sent a letter on official RCIA stationery to each of the local unions in his Division (and to some other locals for good measure), in which he warned the local officers against certain RRR supporters (one of whom he mentioned by name) who were, according to the letter, "going into Local Unions on the West Coast . . . to contact the members directly." His letter described this as a "Hollywood-New York conspiracy" and warned that it would "create turmoil among the members of your local union and undermine your leadership as well as lose votes for the officers that your Local Union nominated." His letter—an official communication from an RCIA Organizing Director to local unions—offered the following suggestion:

Our strong recommendation is that if these people show up in your jurisdiction, that they be shown the way back to California by whatever means is necessary.
In the meantime, it would be wise to alert a large group of key members in your Local to be on the lookout for them so you can be alerted promptly.

This was one example among many. Among others were the letters that Suffridge, the retiring International President, wrote on official RCIA stationery, addressed "to the International Executive Board, the Officers and Members of all RCIA Local Unions and Councils, and all International Representatives," in which he announced his retirement, declared his support for the administration slate, and branded the RRR's campaign as "scurrilous." And there was the matter of threats, for—as reported by several RRR candidates and as a federal court, in a related case, had found as a fact—RRR candidates had been threatened by Suffridge himself, by Loveall, by two International Vice Presidents and by an Assistant Organizing Director. Without specifying any particular example, the Secretary of Labor later conceded in a memorandum of law that, "In the course of this election, the International officers and their supporters violated the Act and the RCIA Constitution in numerous ways."

In March of 1969, the Labor Department replied to the complaining RCIA members by saying that "it was determined" that "there is not probable cause to believe that the violations found may have affected the election outcome"; thus, although the letter then proceeded to describe in general terms such violations as open (nonsecret) voting, the denial to opposition candidates of their right to have observers at the polls and the tally, campaigning by election judges and other election officials, ballot tampering and ballot box stuffing, interference with campaigning, use of union monies to campaign, false notices that the election would not be held, etc., it concluded by saying that the violations "have been brought to the attention of the RCIA officials."

It is the view of most federal courts that, once the Secretary has turned down an election complaint, the union members can do nothing about it.[4] But the question has never been decided by an appellate federal court, so it remains open. The complaining RCIA members therefore took it to the federal court in the District of Columbia and the Court agreed [*DeVito* v. *Schultz,* 300 F. Supp. 381 (D.D.C. 1969)] that they deserved a fuller explanation of the Secretary's failure to bring suit. The Court ordered the Secretary to produce a statement within 30 days. The Secretary did, and it is truly a fascinating document.[5]

The statement casually remarks that it was "not practicable" to investigate any local unions other than the 21 locals in which the complaining members had assembled their evidence. This despite the fact that the vote from the other 225 locals (excluding Montreal) was obviously affected by violations of various kinds—including the failure of the RCIA's International Canvassing Board to examine the validity of all ballots as required by RCIA's constitution. (A sample check conducted by the Department showed that 2.85 percent of the unchallenged ballots, not checked by the Canvassing Board, were cast by persons whose names do not appear on the list of eligible voters—but the Department refused to make use of this discovery outside the 21 locals.) And also despite the complaining members' specific request that an investigation be made of the 130 locals in which they had no observers at all.

Confining its attention to the 21 locals, the Department concluded that violations "may have affected" 20,737 of the votes reported from those locals. The Department's usual practice, upon such a finding, is to deduct the possibly affected votes from the winner's total and add them to the loser's; in this instance, however, it merely deducted them from the administration-slate's margin. No explanation was given for this departure from usual practice but it is obvious that, had the Department followed its usual practice, it would have *eliminated* the administration-slate's International-wide margin of victory in regard to nine of the 11 contested offices (including the International Presidency), and thus compelled the Secretary to bring suit for a new election.

Deducting those 20,737 votes, along with the 3,682 votes cast for

Housewright by the official tally of the Montreal local, brings Housewright's total vote for International President down to 87,366. If those "possibly affected" votes were added to Haletsky's total, the latter would come to 93,495, thus topping Housewright International-wide. But the Department chose not to add them to Haletsky's total; thus Housewright's "corrected" vote topped Haletsky's uncorrected total of 69,076. As a result, when the Labor Department's statement was submitted to the Court, the latter concluded that there was *some* rational justification for the Secretary's failure to act. The Court ruled that it "may not substitute its judgment for the judgment of the Secretary, nor may it usurp matters which Congress has delegated to the special knowledge and discretion of the Secretary"; for that reason, "unless the Secretary's action is plainly beyond the bounds of the Act, clearly defiant of the Act, or patently arbitrary and capricious, the Court, having taken a peek at the merits and being satisfied that it doesn't fall in those extremes, at that point is directed to withdraw its exercise of jurisdiction in favor of the agency" *(DeVito* v. *Shultz,* 72 LRRM 2682).

One of the more significant, but overlooked features of the Yablonski-Boyle dispute in the United Mine Workers of America (UMWA) leading up to the election of December 9, 1969 and to the murder of the three Yablonskis, consists of the repeated appeals to the Secretary of Labor made by Yablonski's attorney and campaign manager, Joseph Rauh, beginning as early as July 9, 1969 and continuing into the post-election period, for an investigation into the denial of electoral rights of the opposition candidates and their supporters. The legal basis for these appeals was and is section 601 of the LMRDA, which empowers the Secretary of Labor "when he believes it necessary in order to determine whether any person has violated or is about to violate any provision of [the] Act" to make an investigation, that power carrying with it the power to inspect such documents, to enter such places, and to question such persons "as he may deem necessary."

In his July 9 letter, Rauh asked Secretary Shultz to exercise his investigatory powers, in the light not only of the stalled trusteeship case, the fiscal scandal involved in the nonrepayable loans made by the International to the trusteed districts, the sudden increase in the nomination requirements for International office (from five locals to

50), but also a wealth of strong-arm and other illegal acts that had been committed within the preceding two weeks. These involved a physical attack on Yablonski (he was knocked unconscious by a blow from behind), the violent disruption of a pro-Yablonski rally by salaried officials of the UMWA and certain persons hired by them; the discriminatory disbanding or de-chartering of pro-Yablonski locals; threats and bribes made to Yablonski supporters, the ruling "out of order" of Yablonski nominations, while Boyle nominations were pushed through at various locals; the use of union monies and the union's journal to support Boyle's re-election campaign; denial to Yablonski of the right to have literature mailed at his own expense to members and a variety of other clear violations of the LMRDA. The July 9 letter was followed by letters of July 18, July 25, July 30 and August 13, describing a long series of similar violations, including a threat by a salaried employee of one of the trusteed districts to kill a pro-Yablonski local union president. Copies of the letters were sent to the UMWA but not one of approximately 100 alleged violations was either denied or explained by it. All this effort elicited a threat by the Department to investigate, but nothing more.

Meanwhile, Yablonski brought a succession of suits to protect himself against reprisal, to obtain use of the union's mailing lists for his campaign literature, to stop the officials from using the union's journal as a campaign instrument for Boyle and to obtain supervision of the election; the first three were successful, the fourth to only a limited degree because, as U.S. District Judge George Hart orally observed, "The trouble is, as I see it, so far as this Court is concerned, when you start talking about a fair election you are not talking about anything much that I can do anything about." Judge Hart's observation was an entirely correct statement of the law; so was his later comment:

The Secretary of Labor will attend to this election business ex post facto and . . . the Courts can't get involved therein. If you want to say that is a funny way to do things, I couldn't agree with you more.

In the course of this fourth suit it was revealed that the UMWA didn't have a membership list at its headquarters and its officials didn't know how many local unions they had; Secretary-Treasurer Owens testified, at various times, that it had 1,338, 1,350 and 1,297;

the membership figure was given, variously, as 225,000, 200,000 and 193,550. Owens could give no explanation for having printed 275,000 ballots or for having mailed out 224,000 to local unions and having kept 51,000 of them himself, except that he had sent 10 percent over the regular amount to each local (which would account for only 212,905). As Judge Hart observed, "There seems to be a lot of things going on here and, particularly, the way these ballots are, apparently, handled, kind of willy-nilly."

Rauh gave the Secretary a detailed round-up of these events in a letter of December 1, 1969 and reported as well a handful of new incidents of threats and ballot-box stuffing; in the letter he requested an investigation and the stationing of government representatives at the polls. Rauh's letter to the Secretary was backed up by a telegram from Congressman Ken Hechler of West Virginia. But in his testimony to a Senate subcommittee months later (in May 1970) Schultz said that he didn't know of any reason for an investigation, and that he would still refuse to act if he had it to do over again because any action on his part might have assisted the Yablonski group.

Secretary Shultz's refusals persisted after the election. While Yablonski was pursuing his intra-union appeals, prior to making an election complaint to the Secretary, Rauh again requested an investigation and the impounding of election records, and while doing so compiled a list of 86 specific election day violations committed at various local unions, involving the unexplained possession of ballots by members before they even came to the polling places, the casting of ballots for members by officials (one local president cast 25 ballots himself), the refusal of officers in locals where Yablonski had won a majority to send the election tallies in, "assistance" and "coaching" given voters by officials, threats made to Yablonski observers, and so on. The list, sworn to by Yablonski's son as having been drafted by him from informants believed by him to be reliable, was supplied to Secretary Shultz and, subsequently, printed in the *Congressional Record* (thanks to the assistance of Congressman Ken Hechler[6]). But still the Secretary could think of no reason to investigate or to take any other action.

After the murder of Yablonski was discovered in January 1970, along with that of Yablonski's wife and daughter, Rauh again tried to contact Secretary Shultz—but unsuccessfully. On January 13,

Rauh wrote still another letter to Shultz, asking him to use his investigatory powers and detailing some of the already-demonstrated evils, all of which were and are within the Secretary's investigatory jurisdiction. But Secretary Shultz remained uninterested until a formal election complaint was filed later in January, the complaining member (Trbovich) having first exhausted his remedies within the UMWA itself. By then the matter had received sustained, nationwide publicity. But even so, Shultz's interest remained passive, for the investigation that followed limited itself to an inquiry into the violations specifically alleged by Rauh. In March, with much fanfare, Shultz announced that his investigation—which he credited with having performed some monumental accomplishment (even though it had not looked into anything other than the specifically complained-of violations)—had sustained the election complaint, and he instituted suit to set the election result aside. As late as May 1970, however, Shultz still maintained—in testimony before Senator Harrison Williams' subcommittee—that he knew of no connection between the election and the Yablonski murders, even though by then two grand juries had indicted five people for the murders, one of them the president of a UMWA local closely linked with the Boyle regime, and even though information had developed indicating that the man who had attacked Yablonski from behind (with a karate chop) at an early election rally had received $1,500 from the UMWA.

Shultz's professed lack of knowledge of anything to do with wrongdoing on the part of the UMWA's officialdom is, oddly enough, repeated by a variety of others—liberal academics included. Thus in a book published this year (April 14, 1970), a UCLA professor of industrial relations who proclaims himself expert on these things, announces sagely that the United Mine Workers of America is one of those fine, respectable unions that "notably" has remained "virtually free of fiscal scandal"[7]; it is thus to be distinguished from the unrespectable ones about which he gives juicy, though somewhat outdated, details in his book. Surely, coming in April 1970, that must be ranked among the preeminent bloopers of our age. But that it is something more than a blooper is suggested by the fact that the author goes on to whitewash the Boyle dictatorship inside UMWA by calling it "strong rule" and by adding that John L. Lewis "dominated" the UMWA for 40 years "without a murmur of financial scandal about him"[8] —a statement that in itself makes one wonder whom the author listens to for his "murmurs."

In the UMWA, "fiscal scandal" has long been linked to bureaucratic dictatorship. Some of the highlights of that "fiscal scandal" were made public last year, before Hutchinson's book could have gone to press: among them the payment by UMWA of $190,000 to Boyle's daughter for doing nothing, the appropriation by the International officials of several million dollars from the Pension Fund by the method of non-interest-bearing deposits in the UMWA-owned bank, the use of $1.5 million of the UMWA's money to finance a secret and unreported pension fund for the top International officers only, enabling them to retire on full salary (the fund was so secret that, in addition to their failure to report it as required by law, UMWA officials actually denied its existence), the unexplained and often unreported payment of large sums of money for no apparent purpose, the massive "loans" to various districts (loans to two districts alone amounting to $5.5 million in the years since Boyle became International President), and so on and on.

Just how these "fiscal scandals" relate to the more serious evils of union bureaucratism can be suggested by two minor examples, both of them pointed out by Yablonski himself in a letter last November to the UMWA's traveling auditor. One concerns UMWA local 7086 in Beckley, West Virginia, which in the 1968 UMWA convention was allowed more delegates (24 in all) than any other UMWA local. (All 24 delegates turned out to be officials of the International or of District 29.) The local's reports indicate that it is far from being UMWA's largest local: it has 2,850 members, of whom 2,400 are pensioners; the 450 working members work in some 40 small mines scattered throughout the district. Its office and mailing address are the same as District 29's yet in 1968 it reported as "administrative and office expenses" some $31,540, or more than the entire district's administrative and office expenses. Back in 1959, when unions were first required to file reports with the federal government, the local reported an outstanding "loan" from District 29 of $83,621.51, and, in the years since then, has reported "payments" to the District totaling $71,200—but the District's reports have never acknowledged the existence either of the loan or of the payments. Needless to say, the local's reports also show unusually high expenditures for professional and other fees, as well as a $6,000 pension paid to the father of a District representative.

Similarly, UMWA Local 5997 in Welch, West Virginia, which has never had an election of officers (its officers, all of them district officials, were appointed ten years ago by International Vice President George Titler, at a time when he was District President), has a "loan" and "payment" relationship with District 29 that is unacknowledged by the District, the loan totaling $45,882 in 1951 and the payments from 1959 to 1963 coming to $21,737.44; after 1963 the loan ceased to be mentioned in any reports at all. Although, as Yablonski commented in his letter, "I am unaware of any significant organizing activity in the Welch area, and, to my knowledge, no local union has ever borne the expense of such efforts," the local had listed as "organizing expenses" for the period 1959 through 1967 some $32,222.12. (Yablonski, having served several years on the UMWA's Organizing Committee, may be presumed to have been knowledgeable in that area, among others.)

It need only be remarked that one of the duties of the Secretary of Labor is to enforce the financial reporting requirements of the LMRDA, to press criminal action for failure to file proper or honest reports, and to investigate any suspected violations. What, if anything, any Secretary of Labor did in this area in regard to the UMWA until 1969 is not apparent. At this writing he has even failed to take action regarding the failure of the UMWA to submit financial reports for the year 1969—and when questioned about it by Senator Williams' subcommittee in May 1970 was unable to give coherent reply.

The Secretary's attitude need occasion no surprise. He is, after all, an appointed official and his administration's liaison (whatever administration it may be) to "Labor." It is his political duty to woo "Labor," just as it is the duty of the Secretary of Agriculture to woo the major farm organizations; his usefulness to his administration depends upon his ability to deliver "Labor's" support for the administration and its policies. That means for one thing that the officials of the "respectable" unions—and the definition of "respectable" is broad enough to include not only the Retail Clerk's Association and the Mine Workers, but the Operating Engineers and the Ladies Garment Workers as well—have a claim on his affections, or at least his complicity, whether the administration he serves is Republican or Democratic.

Then there is the danger that someone inside the unions might, on some occasion, make trouble for employers. This is something that neither Boyle nor, in his later years, even Lewis has been inclined to do; instead, the Boyle regime has devoted much of its energy to denouncing and otherwise assaulting anyone who sought to get better safety conditions for miners. The UMWA's hostility toward any kind of safety measures and its failure to demand these of the employers is what led not only Congressman Hechler but Joe Yablonski himself into battle with the Boyle regime; the first and greater part of the "platform" that Yablonski announced on May 29, 1969 as the basis for his candidacy consisted of a detailed program for mine health and safety. Needless to say, a rank and file movement that raises such issues is not likely to gain the sympathy of any administration appointee.

It is of interest that, testifying before Senator Williams' subcommittee in 1970, Secretary Shultz gave as his reason for not investigating Yablonski's charges the fear that such an investigation might assist Yablonski and his supporters. But he needn't have bothered to say it. His unresponsiveness to the rank and file movement—to *any* rank and file movement—is politically so inevitable that it seems almost harmless, until we remember that this is the official whom working people are required by law to look to for protection against bureaucratic oppression.

The attitude of the Secretary—whoever he might be in the future—cannot easily be changed; it is part of the enduring political reality. What can and should be changed is the legal arrangement that requires union members to look to the Secretary, to the political ally of their union's bureaucracy, for protection against that bureaucracy. But neither the union bureaucracy, nor a "liberalism" that looks upon that bureaucracy as the authentic voice of "Labor" is likely to look with any favor upon such a change, for union bureaucrats are quite happy to have "their" Secretary stand between "their" members and the courts. On issues concerned with the internal affairs of unions, the union bureaucrats remain politically active, and ever-ready to carry their "liberal" and "socialist" admirers with them.

Plainly, modern liberals should either change the nature of their "liberalism" or else give up their claim to be friends of the common working man. Hopefully, they will change the nature of their liberalism—but the change that is needed is no minor one. Any defense of the interests of the slaves of the modern industrial Establishment means a break with traditional alliances of some importance. Just possibly, modern liberalism might not survive the rupture.

June 1970

1. Mysterious because, so far as this writer can determine, no one ever pays for a copy of it or for a subscription to it and because its backers can only be deduced from the political "line" it expresses. I, among others, have received it free-of-charge and without request ever since it was begun more than two years ago; its allegiances, quite obviously, are with the union bureaucracies—but only with one faction among them, which might be identified as the pro-CIA crowd. Its response to the murder of the Yablonskis was to publish a long diatribe entitled "Equal Time for Tony Boyle," which denounced Yablonski, accusing him and all who supported him (his lawyer, Joseph Rauh, his sons, and such supporters as Mike Trbovich) of evil and corrupt motives. *New America's* response to the murders was less flamboyant: it darkly hinted that anyone who pressed for a closer look at the Boyle regime in the UMWA was in some way a patsy for "reactionary enemies of organized labor."

2. *Schonfeld* v. *Raffery,* F. Supp. 128 (S.D.N.Y. 1967), *affirmed,* 381 F. 2nd 446 (2nd Cir. 1967). For an evaluation of the argument presented by Secretary Wirtz in the *Schonfeld* case, see footnote 1 to the district court's opinion, 271 F. Supp. at 131: ". . . the weakest area of the Secretary's brief . . . is in its thin treatment of the facts, largely and uncritically rested upon the testimony of the Trustee."

3. *Calhoon* v. *Harvey,* 379 U.S. 134 (1964); see also, "Law, Democracy and the Unions," this volume, pp. 109 to 120.

4. For a rare exception to this view, see *Schonfeld* v. *Wirtz,* 258 F. Supp. 705 (S.D.N.Y. 1966).

5. I am indebted to the Haletsky group's attorney, Mozart G. Ratner of Washington, D.C., for a copy, as well as for the other information.

6. Hechler's interest in the United Mine Workers seems to have stemmed at least in part from puzzlement over the UMWA's angry opposition toward any legislation in behalf of mine safety (*cf. Congressional Record* for March 6, 1969, H1505; for April 28, 1969, H3133; and especially the exchange of letters in the same for July 15, 1969, H5952-5954). A list of 23 insertions in the *Congressional Record* by Hechler relevant to the UMWA, 9 of which were prior to Yablonski's announcement of his candidacy, is given in the *Record* for January 19, 1970, H37.

7. John Hutchinson *The Imperfect Union: A History of Corruption in American Trade Unions* (New York, E. P. Dutton, 1970), p. 371.

8. *op. cit.,* p. 372.

The ILGWU
and the Labor Department

BURTON HALL

In 1960, shortly after Benjamin B. Naumoff had been appointed to the post that is currently titled New York Regional Administrator of the Department of Labor's Labor-Management Services Administration (LMSA), his friends did him the generous ceremony of holding a dinner in his honor. His friends, on this and on other occasions, were the top officers of the International Ladies' Garment Workers' Union and certain employers allied with the ILGWU. Invitations for the dinner, under ILGWU letterhead and signed by the union's General Counsel, were sent out to union officials and employers and were posted on the New York Region's bulletin boards, asking all friends of Ben Naumoff in the labor movement and elsewhere to purchase tickets for the dinner at $10 a seat and/or $100 per table, and/or to otherwise contribute. At the dinner, as a climax to the ceremony, the sponsors awarded to their honored guest, Benjamin Naumoff, a color television set. He accepted it.

This happy occasion was only one instance among many in the long, close and continuing friendship between Benjamin Naumoff and the top officials of ILGWU. Since then there has been a host of other benefits—whether or not all of them have been non-monetary it is hard to say—to attest to the warm affection with which Benjamin Naumoff is regarded by all within the official ambit of the ILGWU.

But what has Naumoff done in return, to merit such affection?

Naumoff's agency, or what is now known as the LMSA, is the one set up within the Labor Department to carry out the duties of the Secretary of Labor under the Labor-Management Reporting and Disclosure Act (or Labor Reform Act) of 1959. Those duties include such matters as enforcing the Act's guarantees to union members of protection against fraudulent, undemocratic or otherwise unfair conduct of their unions' elections. The Act requires that union members, after appealing for three months within their unions, bring their complaints of electoral violations to the Secretary of Labor—which, in the New York Region, means to Mr. Naumoff—and he, *in his discretion*, will decide whether any action should be taken to protect the union members' rights. If he decides that *no* action should be taken, the union members are barred by the Act from going to court or anywhere else for relief. Under the Act, the LMSA has other duties including enforcement of the Act's various criminal provisions.

Ever since his appointment in 1960, Mr. Naumoff, under a succession of various titles, has been in charge of enforcing the Labor Reform Act in the New York Region—a Region that currently embraces New York, New Jersey, New England, Puerto Rico and the Virgin Islands and which, until recently, included Pennsylvania, West Virginia, Maryland, Delaware and the District of Columbia as well—thus having geographical jurisdiction over almost the entire array of local unions, joint councils, joint boards and so on, within the organizational structure of the ILGWU, as well as over that International itself. And in his official capacity Naumoff has been extraordinarily indulgent toward the ILGWU. One may search the records and find hardly a single action taken by or within the New York Region to challenge or set aside any election conducted by any of the several hundred ILGWU locals within that area. This, despite the fact that the ILGWU's absurdly restrictive electoral and elegibility requirements, blatantly violative of the law, set forth in the ILGWU constitution itself and thus made applicable to every ILGWU local union, would seem to make ILGWU elections an obvious target of the Labor Reform Act. Time after time, members of ILGWU local unions have complained to Naumoff's agency that their electoral rights have been infringed by serious violations of the Labor Reform Act—and, time after time, Naumoff's agency has ignored them or has simply refused, on technical grounds, to do anything about it. More about this later.

The "selective" way in which Naumoff's agency enforces the Labor Reform Act can most simply be demonstrated with regard to certain other provisions of the Act. For example, the Act contains a number of criminal provisions and gives the responsibility for the initial steps in the enforcement of those criminal provisions to the Secretary; that is, to the LMSA. The fact that those provisions are in fact enforced as regards some unions but not as to others is not, in itself, terribly shocking—but it reveals the attitude with which Naumoff's New York Region regards its functions. And that makes it worthy of attention.

One such criminal provision is Section 503 of the Act, which makes it a federal crime punishable by a year in jail or $5,000 in fines or both, for a labor organization to make any loan or loans to any of its officers or employees which result in a total indebtedness to the labor organization on the part of such officer or employee in excess of $2,000. It happens that the ILGWU is and for some time has been violating that criminal provision. It has made and still makes loans of two kinds to its officers and employees: "mortgage" loans, at the bargain rate of 4 percent interest, and "personal" loans, unsecured and interest-free. As a result, many ILGWU officers and employees are currently indebted to ILGWU for sums far in excess of $2,000. There is no reason to suppose that the loans were made or are being made for any scandalous purpose; moreover, since the larger "mortgage" loans seem to be reasonably secured, there is no apparent danger of any officer or employee absconding. What makes these loans noteworthy is the fact that, although they appear to violate a criminal provision of the Act, the ILGWU and its officers seem to enjoy an immunity from prosecution that demonstrates the peculiarly favorable status it enjoys in the New York Region of LMSA.

Officers of *other* unions have received jail sentences for having caused, or participated in, the making of such loans by their unions. As recently as December 1970, on a prosecution initiated by Naumoff's New York Region, two officers of a local union that is *not* part of ILGWU were sentenced in federal court in New York City to six months each in jail for having caused their union to make a loan totaling only $3,000 to a fellow officer of that union. Nor was there anything particularly scandalous about that loan. But while officers of *non*-ILGWU unions go to jail for such relatively minor violations of Section 503, the officers of ILGWU remain unchallenged. Thanks to an indulgent New York Regional Administrator, hardly a breath of criticism is voiced by LMSA concerning ILGWU—and those few criticisms that have been uttered within the agency by Naumoff's subordinates have been quickly stifled by intradepartmental disciplinary punishment of the critics.

According to the financial reports filed by ILGWU with the Labor Department (and available for public inspection in the offices of the New York Region), the ILGWU's "mortgage" loans to officers and employees have, since the Labor Reform Act went into effect in September 1959, totaled as follows:

Year	New Mortgages Given	Old Mortgages Returned	Balance Due at End of Year
1960	–	–	$565,014.97
1961	$ 94,900.00	$42,953.35	616,961.62
1962	144,600.00	57,008.41	704,553.21
1963	166,455.46	88,101.67	782,907.00
1964	126,867.53	151,517.94	758,256.17
1965	97,600.00	118,557.94	737,298.23
1966	86,600.00	70,156.59	753,741.64
1967	79,100.00	58,226.16	774,615.48
1968	(data not available from report on file)		
1969	–	108,077.82	624,260.28

Obviously, in the years 1960-1967, some $796,122.99 in *new* mortgage loans were given. Assuming that at least some of these were in sums greater than $2,000, it seems apparent on the face of things that criminal violations of Section 503 were committed, even without reference to the fact that, in addition to these new mortgage loans, the ILGWU also made and continues to make personal loans to officers and employees some of whom are already indebted to ILGWU on mortgage loans.

Yet despite the appearance of serious violations of law and, presumably, despite suggestions made with the usual frequency that at least a routine audit be conducted in regard to ILGWU's finances generally, nothing appears to have been done by the New York Region for some eight years after passage of the Act. It is not until we come to the ILGWU's report for 1968 that we see an indication of action on its part. The ILGWU's report for that year provides for the first time an itemized list of the mortgage loans outstanding. It lists some 62 officers and employees of ILGWU—including the ILGWU's salaried General Counsel, five International Vice Presidents and the Assistant President—who were, as of the end of 1968, indebted to the ILGWU on mortgage loans. Typed at the top of the list is this revealing statement:

Heretofore, we have recorded and reported these mortgage loans as investments in Schedule 3 as "Other Assets", but are now reporting them in Schedule 1 upon the insistence of the Department of Labor.

It is not clear from the report whether the mortgage loans specified in the list were made before or after the date, September 14, 1959, on which the Labor Reform Act became effective, but it is apparent that at least *some* such loans were made *after* that date. And the statement at the top of the list indicates that, at least at the time the report was filed, the ILGWU was aware of the fact that such loans, made after the effective date and resulting in debts greater than $2,000, constituted criminal violations of Section 503. The same awareness is indicated also by the fact that the ILGWU's 1968 report, unlike previous ones, buries the total figures for new mortgages given to such an extent as to make those figures indeterminable on the basis solely of what is reported for that year.

That awareness—or, rather, the ILGWU's admission of it—implies an additional awareness that any subsequent loan increasing the indebtedness of any officer or employee already indebted on a mortgage loan of $2,000 or more constitutes a crime in and of itself, even if the mortgage loan itself was made before September 1959. Indeed, the ILGWU (along with everybody else) was put on notice to that effect long ago when the LMSA published an interpretation of Section 503. The published interpretation states that an indebtedness created before the Act's effective date (and hence legal at the time of its creation) is not rendered retroactively illegal by Section 503; it also states:

However, if the total indebtedness was $2000 or more on the effective date of the Act, section 503 (a) would make illegal any loans after that date which would increase the total indebtedness by any amount. Further loans would be prohibited until the total indebtedness had been reduced to the point where an additional loan would result in a total debt to the union of $2000 or less.

It is somewhat surprising, therefore, to turn a few pages back in the ILGWU's 1968 financial report and find that during this same year the ILGWU made (as it had in previous years) additional loans to various of its officers and employees who were already indebted to it on mortgage loans for sums greater than $2,000. Thus, the ILGWU reports that in the year 1968 it made a $2,000 interest-free personal loan to Gus Tyler, the Assistant President, increasing Tyler's total indebtedness at that time—personal loan plus existing mortgage debt—to approximately $14,000. And Tyler was just one of some 14 ILGWU officers and employees who, although already indebted to ILGWU on mortgage loans for sums greater than $2,000, were given additional personal loans during the year 1968—all in apparent criminal violation of Section 503.

And the pattern has continued. The ILGWU's financial report for the year 1969 indicates that, in that year, some 17 officers and employees who were already indebted to ILGWU on mortgage loans for sums exceeding $2,000 were given additional "personal" loans substantially increasing their total indebtedness. One of these was an International Vice President who, though already indebted to ILGWU for close to $3,000 on a mortgage loan, borrowed an additional $2,000 from it in 1969.

What is more, there seems to have been an increase in 1969 on one or more of the mortgage loans. Thus a business agent on the International's payroll whose mortgage debt had been reported as $13,836.18 at the end of 1968 is reported, as of the end of 1969, to be indebted to ILGWU on that same mortgage loan in the sum of $18,719.39, an increase of almost $5,000. A check of the total figures indicates that this is no mere typographical error; apparently a substantial new mortgage loan was made in 1969 despite official ILGWU disclaimers. This same business agent received, in addition to the increase in his mortgage loan, a personal loan in the sum of $1,000. All this is openly stated on the financial reports submitted to the New York Region, yet it is apparent that everyone concerned had reason to know nothing would be done about it.

Aside from the ILGWU's seemingly bland assurance that it was immune from prosecution under Section 503, these figures illustrate an interesting feature of modern unionism: the union's disproportional generosity toward its officers. It contrasts sharply with the fact that ordinary members of ILGWU, the ones who pay the dues that in turn pay not only for the officers' salaries but also for the officers' 4 percent-interest "mortgage" loans and interest-free "personal" loans, are given no loans at all by ILGWU. Many of these ordinary members of ILGWU draw wages of less than $75 per week under ILGWU-negotiated contracts[1]; upon retiring they receive pensions of only $75 per month. Yet it is not to them that the "progressive" and "socially-enlightened" ILGWU extends such generosity as it can afford but, instead, that generosity is extended only to the ILGWU's officers and salaried employees.

As of this writing, the ILGWU has not got around to filing its financial report for the year 1970, so we still await information as to its most recent dealings.* But there seems no reason to doubt that it continues to make loans with little regard for the law—just as there seems no reason to doubt that Benjamin Naumoff and his New York Region will continue to turn a blind eye.

It would appear, that most of the ILGWU's loans are being bit-by-bit repaid. The fact that they violate federal criminal law, therefore, may seem curious. But it is a fact that they do—and the fact is obviously known both to ILGWU's top officers and to the New York Region of LMSA. The crime itself, therefore, is nowhere near as important as the fact that it has been committed openly by

---

Editor's Note: The ILGWU's 1970 report reveals that during the year the ILGWU made loans in varying amounts to at least 17 officers and employees who were already indebted to the ILGWU on mortgage loans for sums greater than $2,000 each. For example, Clifford Depin, the ILGWU's non-Spanish-speaking "manager" for Puerto Rico, had a mortgage indebtedness to ILGWU of $24,476.45 at the beginning of 1970, reduced to $24,388.36 by the end of the year; additionally, however, he received a personal loan in the sum of $2,000 during the year. This, of course, was in addition to his salary, allowances, etc., for the year of $17,880.30. International Vice President Sam Janis, whose mortgage indebtedness was down to $10,924.36 at the end of 1970 (from $11,524.98 at the beginning of the year), also took a $2,000 personal loan. At the low end of the scale was International Vice President Angela Bambace, who borrowed $350 during 1970 and whose mortgage indebtedness was $6,384.21 as of the end of the year. (Their salaries, allowances, etc. for 1970 were $24,295.99 for Janis and $22,799.67 for Bambace.) Since each of these 17 personal loans further increases a total indebtedness to the labor organization that was already in excess of $2,000, each constitutes a separate crime. But the chance of any prosecution on the part of Naumoff's office appears to be nil.

As for the mortgage loans themselves, Jack Anderson's syndicated column of May 18, 1971 reports that the government and the ILGWU agreed, early in 1971, to reduce them to "legal levels" by October. Just how that will be accomplished remains—as of this writing—to be seen.

the ILGWU with what would appear to be assurance on its part that there would be no unpleasant repercussions. And most important of all—indeed, the sole reason for discussing the matter here—is the fact that the New York Region, while plainly knowing all about these repeated violations of Section 503, allows them to go unpunished, again and again, while at the same time zealously prosecuting similar violations of Section 503 when committed by other, non-favored unions. The existence of these loans, in other words, is a statistical demonstration of what is euphemistically referred to as "selective" enforcement of the Labor Reform Act by the New York Region—or, in plainer language, of the degree to which the ILGWU and its top officers are given immunity from enforcement of the various provisions of the Act—and not only of those relating to financial matters.

Covering up Section 503 violations is only one of the many—and one of the least valuable—services that a friendly Regional Administrator of LMSA can perform for his good friends in a union bureaucracy. A much more valuable service (one much more harmful to union members) is non-performance of his duties under Section 402 of the Act. That section mandates the Secretary of Labor, upon the filing of a complaint by a union member alleging violations of electoral rights within the union, to investigate and, upon finding a violation of law, to bring suit to set aside the election and conduct a new one. The law makes this remedy the exclusive one; a union member is barred from challenging a union election in any way *other* than by complaint to the Secretary (that is, to LMSA) under Section 402. Therefore, when an LMSA Regional Administrator or other official "friendly" to a particular union decides not to enforce the section in regard to that union, the officials of that union are given virtual immunity from any effective challenge to the way they run their elections.

This service has been and still is particularly valuable to the ILGWU officials, since ILGWU election procedures are probably *more* violative of the law's requirements than those of any other union. That was especially so up to mid-1968, when the ILGWU's constitution—binding upon all locals, joint boards, joint councils, etc.—barred from candidacy for any full-time office any member who had not already held such an office or graduated from a special "training course" controlled by the officialdom, and also barred from candidacy for any office any person whom a committee appointed by the incumbents deemed, "in its opinion," not qualified "because of lack of knowledge or of ability." Until 1968, these restrictions applied to the elections conducted by every ILGWU local union—yet they were never challenged by the LMSA. In May 1968, those particular provisions were quietly dropped by ILGWU because of a Supreme Court ruling in a suit brought by the Labor Department against a *non*-ILGWU local union, but a host of outrageously unlawful restrictions remain in force. For example, the ILGWU constitution still requires that a member elected to any full-time office, prior to his installation and as a condition to holding the office, submit to the International an undated but executed resignation from the office to which he has been elected. Moreover, it permits the officials of a local union to bar from nomination any member who fails to get the hand votes of 5 percent of the persons attending the nomination meeting, and it permits the committee appointed by the incumbents to remove from candidacy any person whom *it* considers (without trial) "guilty of violating" the ILGWU constitution or the local's bylaws. That these restrictions violate the law's requirements needs no careful pointing out; the wonder remains that they have *never* been challenged by LMSA.

One of the most notable features of ILGWU elections, however, is not contained explicitly in its constitution: that is the use by ILGWU officials of hired thugs to intimidate the membership. This extra-constitutional feature takes, however, a variety of forms. For example, when the 8,000-member Cutters' Local 10 held its election of officers in February 1968 and the newly-formed Independent Cutters' Club opposed the incumbents, one of the Independents attempted to distribute leaflets outside the election place. Abe Dolgen, then Assistant Manager of the local (he has since become Manager) walked up accompanied by a well-known gangland figure and said to the member, "If you distribute those leaflets here, I'll have you beaten up." The member looked at Dolgen, then at the gangster, and stopped distributing leaflets. A few minutes later the threat was extended by William Weiss, then a business agent and now Assistant Manager: as the price of "peace," Weiss demanded that the member turn over *all* his leaflets. The member surrendered those that were in his possession; then Weiss called over two young thugs who had been stationed nearby and had them accompany the member to the room used by the Independents as their campaign headquarters, where the two thugs forcibly confiscated all the campaign material.

In Local 10's 1971 election, the practice was continued. Thugs were brought into union meetings to intimidate oppositionists—most notably at the nomination meeting and at the installation meeting immediately following the election—and, with Local 10 Business Agent Bernard Zionsky directing them, were stationed in seats next to and directly behind the leading oppositionists. Their purpose was not only to intimidate but also to harass physically the oppositionist members. Thus, at the installation meeting, when oppositionist Eugene Libow stood up to speak, the thug stationed next to him wrapped his legs around Libow's and actually held on while Libow struggled toward the speakers' platform. Meanwhile, an oppositionist member speaking on the speakers' platform was physically assaulted by Local 10's sergeant-at-arms. The thug who had wrapped his legs about Libow's later explained his reasons: "I do," he said, "what I'm paid for."

Similar techniques were used in the 15,000-member Knitgood Workers' Local 155 in New York, where an opposition rank and file group was formed just before the February 1971 election. (In the 1968 election several of its members had run for office as individuals.) At the nomination meeting, the group's leader, Edward Tucker, was physically attacked by two business agents; threats of various kinds were made to rank-and-filers who had announced as candidates and to members distributing leaflets in favor of the rank and file group; during the actual voting process, a business agent who had been asked to stop campaigning in the voting area loudly threatened Tucker with physical violence. These and similar methods of intimidation caused two women workers who had announced their candidacies for union office on the rank and file slate to withdraw from candidacy at the nomination meeting. And the remaining rank and file candidates were denied even the right to nominate each other: all nominations, including those of oppositionist rank-and-filers, were made by the incumbent officials, ordinary members being denied the right to the floor except for purposes of declining nomination.

The only legal recourse of union members whose electoral rights in their unions have been infringed is to complain to the Department of Labor—which for members of unions located within the New York Region means a complaint to Regional Administrator Benjamin Naumoff. In 1968, members of Cutter's Local 10 and of Knitgoods Local 155 complained—and, predictably, Regional Administrator Naumoff denied their complaints. Since the violations complained of were too obvious to ignore (in Local 10, members were not even allowed to have their names go on the ballot until they had submitted undated, signed resignations), Naumoff relied on procedural technicalities: he said that the members had not appealed within the union soon enough after the election to meet the requirements of the ILGWU's constitution and hence their subsequent complaints to the Labor Department could not be acted upon. (The ILGWU constitution sets a 10-day time limit.) That objection wore a little thin in regard to Local 10, where one member had appealed within the union less than ten days after the election, and where other members filed further appeals within the union before that appeal had been disposed of, before complaining to the Labor Department. Since in other litigation, the Labor Department has consistently maintained and still maintains the position that *any* timely appeal within the union is sufficient to meet the law's requirements, it has never been able to explain why it adopted a different position in regard to ILGWU members. The complaining members took the Secretary of Labor to court, demanding that he (or the LMSA) apply the same rules to ILGWU elections that he applies to the elections of other unions; the court, however, ruled that the Secretary's exercise of his "discretion" in regard to election complaints was outside its jurisdiction, and therefore dismissed the members' suit.

Meanwhile, the same process of appeal within the union and ultimate complaint to the Secretary is being repeated—with regard at least, to ILGWU Locals 10 and 155. (The law requires that members appeal for three months within the union before complaining to the Secretary.) But the end result is virtually certain. The friendship between Regional Administrator Naumoff and the ILGWU officialdom is an enduring and reliable one; it can be counted on. Not only are Naumoff and the ILGWU officials on a first-name basis; not only are they cognizant of their common interests as bureaucrats, governmental or private, engaged in the "union business"; not only do they sponsor and/or attend each other's testimonial dinners (in

January 1971, for example, they all attended the "Debs Day" dinner at which their host, the Socialist Party, presented its annual "Morris Hillquit Award" to ILGWU International Vice President Charles S. Zimmerman); not only do numerous intangible and not-so-intangible favors flow back and forth among them. The friendship of these bureaucrats runs deeper than any such mundane considerations would suggest. It is truly a perfect one, founded upon political nostalgia and Social-Democratic rhetoric. It would even be a beautiful one if its purpose were not (in addition to the covering-up of financial hanky-panky) to aid in the oppression of rank and file workers.

May 1971

1. The collective bargaining agreement currently in force between Knitgood Workers' Local 155, and the employers in New York City, New Jersey and Long Island calls for weekly wages of $71.75 for inspectors, hand sewers, finishers, crocheters and floor girls, accounting for more than half the workers in the industry. Take-home pay is much lower, between $57 and $59 for a full week. Sweatshops have not disappeared; they are hiding behind an ILGWU union label.

The Colonization of the International Trade Union Movement

DAVID LANGLEY

The conflicts shaking the large international trade union organizations today pose a basic question: does a worker's internationalism still exist or has it been obliterated during the last decades by coalitions of national interests and by the dominating spirit of the great powers? The weakening of the influence of the Internationals sometimes gives that impression. It is worthwhile, then, to review this question, at least as we see it from Washington.

Internationally, the working class has been frustrated in two of its major goals: its effort to prevent the First World War through a general strike; and its attempt to rekindle from the ashes of the Second World War the trade union solidarity existing prior to 1914. Neither attempt was able to withstand the pressure of external forces. Even today the movement remains affected by this.

Born in Paris in 1945, in the wake of the enthusiasm engendered by the Liberation, the World Federation of Trade Unions (WFTU) was not able to survive two major political decisions: Stalin's decision to impose a totalitarian regime on the area occupied by the Red Army, and the defensive reaction of the West as manifested by the Marshall Plan and followed later by the Atlantic Pact. As a result of the intransigent opposition of the leaders of the WFTU to the plan for the economic reconstruction of Europe, the Western trade unions left the WFTU and formed the International Confederation of Free Trade Unions (ICFTU). The most intense phase of the Cold War began at that time and the great powers—the United States no less than the USSR—considered the trade union Internationals nothing more than tools for combatting the enemy. The enslavement of the WFTU after the departure of the democratic member organizations was soon complete. It is still true, although the conflict between the USSR and China, as well as the slow acceptance of "polycentrism" in the Communist movement, may open some prospects of change in the long run.

The structure of the ICFTU, composed of large independent organizations with a real working-class tradition, offered varying degrees of resistance to attempts to control it. From 1949 on, backed by almost one-third of the total paying membership, American influence was significant. It was immediately reflected in the programs of the ICFTU, which is very practical in economic matters. It promoted full employment instead of concentrating on reforms in the structure of capitalist systems. In effect, its first years of existence were almost entirely devoted to the anti-colonial struggle, often with success, particularly in North Africa.

It was during the honeymoon between American and non-American members of the ICFTU that the American Federation of Labor subtly started the activities of its "Committee for Free Trade Unionism," of which the head and principal instigator was the former general secretary of the American Communist Party and current director of the International Department of the AFL-CIO, Jay Lovestone. The effect of this very curious individual on the international orientation of American trade unions since 1943 has been so significant that it is essential to recall certain facts.

We must first point out that however influential it may be, Lovestone's attitude is certainly not representative of all American trade unions, and particularly not of the organizations formerly affiliated with the CIO, which maintain contact today through the Industrial Union Department of the AFL-CIO, chaired by Walter Reuther. These labor leaders have always fought Jay Lovestone's tactics and personality. They continue to do so as far as possible. However, the president of the AFL-CIO, who has limited opportunity for intervening in trade union affairs at the industrial level, has almost unlimited powers on the international level due to the Federation's constitution. It is George Meany who, in the last

analysis, decides fundamental questions. Jay Lovestone has depend-
ed on George Meany, personally, for 20 years in order to put his
international politics into effect and vice versa. We will analyze only
this policy, which is the official line of the AFL-CIO, referring to it
as "American" But any generalization would be unjust. We should
not take the major section of the American labor movement to task
since it is definitely in the mainstream of free trade unionism.

The AFL Committee for Free Trade Unionism was created during
the war to come to the assistance of trade unionists in the countries
freed by the Allies and to counter Communist influence in every
possible way. Its role was also to resist the WFTU where trade
unions of the Allied countries, both Communist and non-
Communist, including the AFL's rival, the CIO, were beginning to
cooperate. The AFL had refused to affiliate with the WFTU and
welcomed the split in the international trade union movement as
justification of its position. The return of German trade unionism to
the international family definitely deprived Lovestone's committee
of one of its two reasons for existence. The second remained:
systematic anti-Communism. In order to succeed in his crusade,
Lovestone used a network of personal friends, almost all of whom
were part of his former Communist machine, stationed in various
parts of the world with considerable, untraceable funds at their
disposal. According to a series of articles published in 1965 by the
Washington Post and *The Nation,* the largest part of these funds
comes from government sources, including special services such as
the Central Intelligence Agency. This is confirmed by another series
of articles describing the activities of the CIA, published at the end
of April 1966, by the *New York Times,* which said that "the CIA
gives technical assistance to the majority of Latin-American countries to help them form anti-Communist police forces. The CIA is
the promoter of front organizations of students, workers, liberal
professionals and business men, farmers and political parties. . . . It
organizes the contacts between these groups and trade union
organizations, American institutions and foundations. It has spent
money on electoral campaigns, supporting moderate candidates
against leaders of the left such as Cheddi Jagan in British
Guiana. . . ."

The absence of trade union content in Lovestone's politics finally
aroused a number of trade unionists. At the same time, the general

decline of colonialism took the wind out of the ICFTU's sails. The diversity of regimes in the developing countries couldn't help but complicate its task.

Very often the intoxication of independence had no use for an ally in the political battle against the colonial power which, by its systematic anti-Communism, seemed to threaten the "non-alignment" of certain countries; and economically underdeveloped systems could not profit from trade union remedies born of the experience of highly industrialized countries. This meant the decline of ICFTU influence among the underdeveloped countries and disaffiliation en masse, particularly of African organizations. From Washington's point of view, the Confederation, in spite of the numerous promises of its new General Secretary, Omer Becu, ceased to exist as a useful instrument for fighting Communism in the developing countries.

The general agreement of the United States government and George Meany (who is not above castigating the ICFTU Secretariat as a nest of homosexuals and inefficient bureaucrats) could only end in a change in the direction of influential American funds on the international scene. They have established their own institutions and have chosen obedient organizations which accept, and depend on, external financial assistance.

The AFL-CIO first of all set up the American Institute for Free Labor Development in Latin America (AIFLD). Presided over by George Meany, the AIFLD Executive Committee is a bipartite one, made up of "enlightened" management and utilizing government and business funds, for the most part. Its personnel consists predominantly of trade union elements from the various sectors and areas of operation. Its avowed purpose is to insure greater welfare to workers within the framework of capitalism in places where American private enterprise plays a determining role in the economic and political life of the respective countries. Here is the language used by George Meany to the Businessmen's Committee for Latin America (headed by Rockefeller financial interests—"liberal Republicans") in New York on April 2, 1966: "We believe in the capitalist system and we are members of the capitalist society. We are dedicated to the preservation of this system, which rewards the workers, which is one in which management also has such a great stake. The investors of risk capital also must be rewarded. . . . We are not satisfied, no, but we are not about to trade in our system for any other." The administrator of the AIFLD, former trade unionist William C. Doherty, Jr., added recently during a speech to the same assembly of businessmen: " . . . that when the government steps in to run an industry, that the private individual relationship between a private and free trade union and private and free industry goes out the window."

To date there has been no serious opposition from non-Communist trade union circles to the activities of the Institute, whose cost represents several million dollars per year, in part because the ICFTU's Inter-American Regional Office for Latin America (ORIT) is already dominated by the United States. The Institute has also given its sanction, with impunity, to the coups d'etat in Brazil and Bolivia, for example, as well as military intervention in the Dominican Republic.

Encouraged by this experience, the AFL-CIO began to expand to other continents. In New York it created the Afro-American Labor Center, whose administrator is Irving Brown, director of the ICFTU liaison office to the United Nations, closely associated with Jay Lovestone, former representative of the AFL in Europe, and intimate friend of Lafond and LeBourre in the French anti-Communist labor organization, Force Ouvriére. The Center, unlike the Institute, does not have any apparent management participation (after all, there are fewer American private enterprises in Africa than in Latin America). But its income comes from the same sources.

In Asia, they are still in the preparatory stages, with a research bureau in Rome which has "sub-research offices" in Singapore, Tokyo and elsewhere. Supervision, however, is from Washington, under the direction of another former and active associate of Lovestone, Harry Goldberg, member of the International Department of the AFL-CIO.

The Committee for Free Trade Unionism of World War II vintage has disappeared only on paper. Lovestone has rebuilt it in his own fashion.

The ICFTU Congress held in July 1965, in Amsterdam, almost completed the rupture in the free trade union front because of the American unions' threat of withdrawal, brandished by Meany, angry at the attitude of the Tunisians, Canadians and even of certain Americans. The atmosphere has not improved since then. Recently,

Meany told the Executive Committee of the AFL-CIO that the ICFTU was useless and that one day the question of disaffiliation would be posed. Five years before this, the former assistant Secretary of Labor, George Cabot Lodge, "liberal Republican," son of the former U.S. Ambassador to Vietnam, expressed a similar opinion in his book on free trade unions in emerging nations. He advised the use of bi-partite institutions (such as the present AIFLD) and the International Trade Secretariats associated with the ICFTU rather than the ICFTU itself which, according to him, had been "discredited." His ideas were quickly put into practice under the Democratic administration, hesitantly under Kennedy, with vigor under Johnson.

American money was asking to be used. The first guinea pig chosen was the PTTI, the communications workers' international and the first region chosen was Latin America. It was this experience which gave birth to the Institute (AIFLD). But other trade secretariats were likewise subjugated. Of the 17 ITS (International Trade Secretariats), two are in the lead of the "subjugated": the PTTI, whose general secretary, a Swiss citizen, was dismissed when he dared to ask how much money his organization was spending in Latin America. He was replaced by a Polish exile, S. Nedzynski whose attitude left no room for doubt. Even today the PTTI spends more of its budget in Latin America than in the rest of the world and is a transmission belt for the operations of the Institute, the Centers and research offices of Lovestone.

The International Federation of Commercial, Clerical and Technical Employees (IFCCTE) has had the same fate. Directed by a German, E. Kissel, from a rival union to the big confederation, DGB, the IFCCTE elected an American, James T. Suffridge, president of the retail clerks union (RCIA), as president of the International in 1964. He is one of the rare "liberal Republicans" in the AFL-CIO and is considered by George Meany as his protégé. The patron and protégé were so successful in their efforts, that Adolphe Eidro of Force Ouvrière, at that time vice-president of the IFCCTE, considered the formation of an autonomous European regional organization. He realized that almost all the representatives of the IFCCTE in the various parts of the world (Latin America, Lagos, East Africa, Malaya, Tokyo) were in effect employees of Suffridge's RCIA. The general secretariats of the PTTI and of the IFCCTE are staffed with "personal assistants," appointed and paid by the respective American affiliates.

The International Federation of Petroleum Workers (IFPCW) has always been a strictly American affair. The President, the General Secretary, the headquarters, almost all the personnel, are American. Its declared membership is 850,000 and its income from dues is $80,000 per year. Nevertheless, it maintains two dozen employees, with salaries at an American level (around $10,000 per year on the average) and offices dispersed all over the world. Where does this money come from?

The English language edition of ORIT's *Bulletin,* published in Washington, contains other interesting information about the use of the ITS on the Latin American "front." A "political fever chart" is published in the *Bulletin* each month indicating the degree of danger of subversion in the various countries and the medicine provided by the AFL-CIO, the ORIT and the ITS to cure the sickness. Shock treatment is insured by the Lovestone-Doherty Institute, the PTTI, the IFCCTE and the IFPCW. According to Robert Goss, assistant general secretary of ORIT, it is on these three ITS that "we have always counted and which have always cooperated with one another." In the same statement made recently in Washington, he expressed regret that other ITS, active during a certain period in Latin America, have ceased to cooperate effectively.

The first was the Public Services International (PSI), when the new president of its American affiliate (American Federation of State, County and Municipal Employees), New Yorker Jerry Wurf, realized that his predecessor, A. Zander, spent more than $100,000 per year on permanent Latin-American operations, without a trace showing up in the union's accounts, and that considerably greater sums were spent by its representative, Howard McCabe, who took part in the commando tactics of the AFL-CIO as representative of the PSI, particularly in British Guiana.

The powerful International Transport Workers' Federation (ITF) was not able to escape contamination during the five-year reign of its former general secretary, P. de Vries, who left office in 1965. It was intimately involved in Brazilian and Dominican affairs, since it had been working in Latin America for some 40 years and was long considered an authentic expression of the Latin American workers' wishes.

The experience of the International Union of Food, Drink and Tobacco Workers did not seem any better, because at the beginning of this year it withdrew its support of the international representatives in Latin America and reorganized its structure on that continent, basing its activities on the authentic organizations of workers in Mexico and Venezuela.

Only two ITS seemed able to conduct activities independent of the AFL-CIO: the Miners' International Federation and the International Metalworkers' Federation, the latter having vast resources and a great probability of success.

Seen from afar, the last ITS active south of the Rio Grande, the International Federation of Plantation, Agricultural and Allied Workers, which lives almost exclusively on subsidies from the ICFTU, seems especially concerned with the defense of British interests east of the Suez.

"The CIA Leads the Dance," someone wrote recently in a syndicalist journal, in discussing internal trade union opposition in Spain. Perhaps he was thinking of Lovestone. But Lovestone's attempts to interfere are not limited to that country, as we have tried to show by a few examples. He is everywhere that he can utilize a right wing splinter group, whether it be the Triantafilakis and Theodorou in Greece, the former general secretary of the UGT in Tunisia, Tlili, or in the trade union organization Domei in Japan.

At present, when the press is publishing material on the CIA's infiltration of American institutions, including foundations and such universities as Michigan State University and the Massachusetts Institute of Technology (which has just terminated the ties of its Center for International Studies with the CIA), this seems the right moment to throw light on the imbroglio of foundations, institutes and centers through which Jay Lovestone and his associates have been trying to subjugate the international trade union movement for the past 20 years. American trade unionism has nothing to lose and everything to gain from such an exposure.

POSTSCRIPT: THE CIA AND LABOR

Recent disclosures on CIA subventions to labor organizations have shed light on some of the more unsavory background of what we called the attempted colonization of the international labor movement.

A provisional balance sheet so far shows the following picture:

International Federation of Petroleum and Chemical Workers' Unions (IFPCW). In an interview to the *Denver Post* of February 26, Loyd Haskins, general secretary, denied that his organization had ever "knowingly accepted CIA funds either directly or indirectly." He also said that the only private foundations for which the federation had received funds were the League for International Social and Cooperative Development of Denver, and the Midland International Foundation in Indianapolis. The *Washington Post* reported that there is no record of any "Midland Foundation" in Indianapolis in the foundations list of the Internal Revenue Service. The "League for Economic and Social Development," as it is called in the *Washington Post* story, was founded recently by several people, including O.A. Knight, the former president of the IFPCW and of the Oil, Chemical and Atomic Workers' Union. In an official statement, Haskins later confirmed that it was the policy of the IFPCW to accept foundation funds.

Haskins did not comment on reports that the IFPCW, according to its own financial report to its 1963 world congress in Athens, Greece, had received in 1960 and 1961, $40,000 from the Andrew Hamilton Fund of Philadelphia, which has been identified as a CIA "dummy" foundation.

In this statement to the *Denver Post,* Haskins said: "It is inconceivable to us that any funds we have received from any sources could in any way be connected with the CIA. Our activities in opposition to the U.S. oil companies operating around the world are obviously not in accord with U.S. foreign policy positions." He neglected to add that the IFPCW is probably the only international trade union organization which has publicly and in principle taken a position against nationalization including, of course, nationalization of the oil industry.

He also said that the reports on CIA subventions to his organization came from the International Chemical Workers' Federation, a trade union International based in Geneva, Switzerland, which has been involved in a jurisdictional dispute with the IFPCW. It is not clear in what way this makes CIA subventions to the IFPCW more legitimate. Three European member unions of the IFPCW have disaffiliated from the organization since the disclosures.

International Federation of Clerical, Commercial and Technical Employees (IFCCTE). The main U.S. affiliate of this organization is the Retail Clerks' International Association (RCIA), which is reported to have received $38,000 in 1965 from the Granary Fund, another CIA front. James A. Suffridge, president of the RCIA, told the *New York Times* in an interview that he had never heard of the Granary Fund, and denied that the RCIA had ever received money from the CIA.

The report on activities of the IFCCTE for the period from 1961 to 1964 shows that during that period the RCIA contributed about $198,000 to the IFCCTE, which represents a large amount even for a rich union. Furthermore, the *Christian Science Monitor* of February 27, 1967 writes that "records suggest that the retail-clerk-supported IFCCTE located in Geneva might have got foundation funds directly."

Public Services International (PSI). Arnold Zander, former president of the American Federation of State, County and Municipal Employees (AFSCME), said in a statement to the *Washington Post* of February 23 that, through Gotham Foundation grants to the AFSCME, the CIA had channelled funds to the PSI for six years (1958 to 1964). The amounts involved rose from $7,500 in 1958 to $60,000 in 1964.

Zander said he was unaware at the time that the money came from the CIA, that he had never inquired about the source of the funds, and that he still sees nothing improper in the arrangement. He said he learned that Gotham was a CIA front only in the last few days as a result of newspaper stories.

Most of this money seems to have been used in South America. According to a *New York Times* report of February 23, the international activities of the AFSCME were run by two CIA agents who helped organize strikes in British Guiana in 1962 and 1963 against former Prime Minister Cheddi Jagan.

The *New York Times* story says: "At first the union leadership was unaware that the funds were actually CIA money but when the real source of the money was learned shortly afterward, the union leadership decided to maintain the relationship because funds were not available elsewhere."

When Zander retired in 1964 as president of the AFSCME, his

successor, Jerry Wurf, disapproved of the subsidy and cancelled it.

International Federation of Journalists. According to the *New York Times*, the American Newspaper Guild received nearly one million dollars in foundation grants since 1960 to finance its "South American and other overseas activities." The money came from two foundations which have been identified as CIA fronts (Andrew Hamilton and Granary) and three foundations which refused to disclose their sources of income and other contributions.

The bulk of the money is believed to have gone to finance Guild activities in Latin America, conducted through the Inter-American Federation of Working Newspapermen's Organizations. According to a former senior Guild official, the federation "spends a great deal of its effort combating the Communist newspaper unions and associations in South America." The federation, he said, was organized for this purpose in 1960, the first year it received a contribution from the Granary Fund. (*New York Times*, February 18, 1967.)

"Another fund that has been linked to the CIA is the Asia Foundation, which helped finance a three-month journalism seminar for South Vietnamese journalists last year in Saigon. The seminar was arranged through the International Federation of Journalists (*New York Times*, February 19.)

According to the latest reports, the Newspaper Guild has cut all ties to foundations reported to be CIA fronts.

International Union of Food and Allied Workers' Associations (IUFAWA). The general secretary of the organization, Juul Poulsen, said in an interview to the *New York Times* that persons in Latin America had been passed off as representatives of the Union although they were unknown at its headquarters in Geneva. He said they were taking their orders from Andrew C. McLellan, an American who had become AFL-CIO representative in Latin America after serving the IUFAWA in the same capacity for a year. "Poulsen said that once his union had learned about Mr. McLellan, it acted at the end of 1965 to reorganize its Latin-American activities." (*New York Times*, February 23.)

Postal, Telephone and Telegraph International (PTTI). According to the *Washington Post* (February 24), the organization has been one of the chief recipients of CIA subsidies to labor. The main U.S. affiliate of the PTTI is the Communication Workers of America of which Joseph A. Beirne is president. Beirne, who is also secretary-treasurer of the American Institute for Free Labor Development, denied that the AIFLD had received funds from foundations subsidized by the CIA. He also said that he doubted that "the exposés were a service to the country." (*New York Times*, February 21.)

American Institute for Free Labor Development. In the *Washington Post* of February 24, Drew Pearson and Jack Anderson described the financing of the AIFLD as follows:

"Biggest spender of CIA money is AIFLD, composed not only of the Meany-Lovestone faction in the AFL-CIO, but Peter Grace of the Grace Steamship Line, Juan Trippe of Pan American Airways, and Charles Brinckerhoff of Anaconda Copper. To this partnership, labor is supposed to put up $200,000 and business $280,000. However, since labor's share is raised on a collection basis, some unions don't come across. Central Intelligence not only makes up the difference, but adds several million dollars besides—all through dummy foundations."

According to Pearson and Anderson, the same applies to the African-American Labor Center, of which Irving Brown is the director. Irving Brown has denied any knowledge of CIA financing.

International Confederation of Free Trade Unions (ICFTU). On February 19, the *New York Times* reported that the ICFTU had received subsidies from the Foundation for Youth and Student Affairs, a "conduit" for the CIA. On February 20, the ICFTU denied that it ever received directly or indirectly funds from the CIA or from the Foundation. Pearson and Anderson, writing in the *Washington Post*, may have provided the key to the contradiction by their report that ORIT, the regional organization of the ICFTU for the Western hemisphere, is the recipient of CIA funds. They write that "its parent, the International Confederation of Free Trade Unions, is too liberal for Lovestone, but ORIT takes direction from Lovestone and with it takes CIA money." Writing in the *Saturday Evening Post*, May 13, 1967, Thomas Braden, a former CIA agent, said that he had given CIA funds to Irving Brown, as well as to Victor Reuther.

Lovestone. "Jay Lovestone, sometimes called Meany's minister of foreign affairs . . . takes orders from Cord Meyer of the CIA. No CIA money for labor is spent without Lovestone's approval, and few labor attachés are appointed to American embassies abroad without his OK." (Pearson and Anderson, *Washington Post*, February 24.)

All stories come back to Lovestone, who is revealed as the chief architect of the subjugation of AFL-CIO foreign policy to the CIA and to the attempted colonization by the CIA of the international free trade union movement. His efforts in recent years, aided by the remnants of his former Communist machine, of which Irving Brown and Harry Goldberg are among the most prominent today, have gone toward turning the free trade union movement into an instrument of the most reactionary trends in American foreign policy.

In the above essay, we contended that for several years a large-scale attempt to subvert the international free trade union movement, backed by virtually unlimited United States government funds, had been under way and that it had resulted in the partial or total takeover of several international labor organizations. This contention has been amply confirmed and substantiated by the investigations of the press.

Several spokesmen for some of the organizations mentioned in the press have called these press reports "irresponsible." This raises an interesting question. Responsible to whom and irresponsible by what standards? What seems to us irresponsible is the acceptance on the part of trade unions, of CIA subsidies, not their disclosure in public. Or is it assumed that there should be honor among thieves? Fortunately, not all international trade union leaders are thieves, and traditional trade union standards of honor still prevail in some quarters.

The picture, sad though it may seem, is actually encouraging. It shows that there has not only been colonization but also resistance to corruption. This is proof that the methods which Lovestone learned to use in the Communist Party will not work in the free trade union movement, at least not in the long run.

Out of the 17 International Trade Secretariats (international trade union federations), only a few have been affected by this political corruption, and all but three or four have withdrawn from it by themselves. The fight which Reuther and the UAW have begun against the policies of Meany-Lovestone will no doubt contribute to rolling back the infiltration of the CIA-Lovestone machine until it is no longer important in international labor. The time may not be far away when we can write of the decolonization of the international trade union movement.

June 1967

Labor Lieutenants
and the Cold War

SIDNEY LENS

The fact that George Meany's AFL-CIO has withdrawn from the International Confederation of Free Trade Unions (ICFTU) does not mean that it has lost interest in what is euphemistically called "international affairs," or that it has modified its role as aide-de-camp to the Central Intelligence Agency and the State Department. Back in 1951 the righteous Mr. Meany insisted that "we are totally independent of any government control or influence," but it wasn't true then, it isn't now, and it isn't likely to be in the near future. On the contrary Meany and his organization are so closely linked to the foreign policy purposes of the American government, and so interlinked with its actual machinery, that it is difficult to tell where one lets off and the other begins. The AFL-CIO international affairs department, headed by Jay Lovestone, has what amounts to veto power over the choice of most labor attachés and most labor officials for the Agency for International Development (AID). The AFL-CIO has its own designate, George P. (Phil) Delaney, on the State Department roster to act as liaison, and it does regular business from all the rumors one hears in Washington with a specific high official of the CIA. Unlike the Soviet labor unions which are totally under the thumb of Party and State, the American labor federation is more of a partner who occasionally has differences on this or that point.

In this ex-officio role the Meany clan has been involved on behalf of the United States government in many unappetizing projects, as follows:

1. As part of its delirious anti-communism it promoted splits in the French and Italian labor movements.

2. It helped moderates to short circuit militant and radical elements for control of the German unions.

3. It has subsidized outright spying and intelligence activities by foreign labor groups.

4. It actively espoused and paid for strikebreaking at Marseilles and other European ports where workers refused to unload American arms shipments.

5. It financed a general strike aimed at overthrowing the government of Cheddi Jagan in British Guiana.

6. It—and its allies—worked with Brazilian militarists to impose a dictatorship on the Brazilian people.

7. It and its client union in the Dominican Republic helped in the coup against Juan Bosch and later endorsed American intervention to prevent his return to power.

8. It helped to power reactionary union leaders in Greece.

9. It infiltrated American Embassies with labor attachés who share its views and put them into practice.

10. It has been a prime supporter of American armament and American intervention in Cuba, Vietnam, Congo and elsewhere.

11. It has educated tens of thousands of foreign unionists in its own brand of anti-communism and set them loose, with money and encouragement, to wreak havoc with left-of-center labor leaders.

Above all it has done for the United States government what the government could not do for itself—namely, created a "labor" base in many countries to further the policies of the cold war. Without the Meany clique American imperialism would have been much more isolated, and the political map of the world much less conservative. The unions of Europe might have emerged more radical and their governments a few notches to the left. The various military alliances such as NATO would have had much tougher sledding in the face of sharper labor opposition.

I do not wish to imply that the Meany group—Jay Lovestone, Irving Brown, Andrew McLellan, William Doherty, Jr. and others—has always and on every point been in agreement with the policy of the United States government. These men were actually cold warriors *before* official policy turned in that direction in 1947, and have remained more hawkish than Washington even in recent years both under Johnson and Nixon. On the other hand, they have denounced fascist Spain, apartheidist South Africa and the military dictatorships of Paraguay and Haiti when the U.S. government was willing to sleep in the same bed with these forces. Irving Brown gave considerable aid to unionists in North Africa fighting French imperialism, and was on good terms with Ben Bella in Algeria. But their anti-colonialism and their anti-fascism have been subordinate to their anti-communism. An AFL-CIO Executive Council statement in 1959 proclaimed that "the longer colonialism lasts, the greater is the danger of communist penetration." It is significant that these men have never condemned American colonialism in Latin America and they defend it arduously in Vietnam.

The seeming contradiction stems from the political origins of the Meany coterie—in particular Lovestone and Brown. In an interview a few years ago Brown told me he would prefer to fight communism by building genuine mass movements overseas—unions, student groups, women's councils, peasant organizations. But the Lovestoneites began with the assumption that the Soviet Union and communism were the *main* enemies of progress and they concluded that if their primary strategy failed—of building mass movements—they had a duty to help suppress communism by whatever means were at hand, including American militarism. Whatever their former antipathy to Western imperialism they saw it as very much a lesser evil to communism, and in the course of time stopped mentioning it; it disappeared from the compendium of evils. Under the hard-nosed Lovestone-Brown doctrine the conflict with communism is a *permanent* war in which only one side can survive and the other be destroyed. Consequently, as in hot war, you do not speak of the good points of the enemy or your own bad points, and you permit no charity to neutrals. When the U.S. Chamber of Commerce proposed more trade with the Soviet Union, Lovestone and company denounced it on the grounds that it would "only finance and facilitate further Soviet aggression against the democracies."

Like the Stalinists of the early 1930s who called social-democracy the "twin" of fascism, the Lovestone-Brown anti-communists of the post World War II period called neutralism a "twin" of communism, to be shunned and destroyed with the same vigor. And since neutralists and nationalists in the Third World usually accepted communist support in their struggles against imperialism, the Lovestone-Brown-Meany strategy evolved into one of total war not only against communism but against nationalism, neutralism and of course revolution.

The turn of labor's leadership toward an active part in America's cold war began during World War II with two AFL leaders of divergent purpose: David Dubinsky, President of the Ladies' Garment Workers' Union, and the late Matthew Woll of the Photoengravers'. Prior to this period AFL interest in international affairs was minimal. The Federation did join the International Secretariat of Trade Union Centers (ISTUC) in 1910, dedicated to "closer association between the trade unions in all countries," to collecting "uniform trade statistics" and to mutual help in "industrial disputes." These purposes were modest enough so that Samuel Gompers could feel comfortable in ISTUC ranks. But when a successor organization, the International Federation of Trade Unions (IFTU)—the so-called "Amsterdam International"—denounced capitalism after World War I and called for the "socialization of the means of production," the AFL refused to join it. For almost two decades it confined its activities to lobbying for higher tariffs to protect some of its constituent unions and against foreign immigration. Then in 1937 the menace of fascism in Europe and the competition with the CIO at home, drove it temporarily into IFTU ranks. On the whole, however, the AFL's participation in international affairs was remote and of minor importance.

World War II, however, changed all this. The United States was on the verge of becoming the single dominant capitalist power in the world and the labor leadership was called on to play a new game. Dubinsky and Woll were strange allies in initiating the project. The peppery head of the garment union, a colorful dress cutter who had once been a Socialist, hated the Communists in part as a matter of principle and in part because of internecine war in his own union. Woll, an arch conservative who had once acted as president of the National Civic Federation, an organization of employers and right wing unionists formed by industrialist Mark Hanna and supplied with money by the Morgans and August Belmont, hated Communists and radicals because of his intense dedication to capitalism.

Even before the United States entered the war it was obvious to these two men that something had to be done to help old unionists in Nazi and Fascist clutches. The Labor League for Human Rights which they established in 1940 "for war relief purposes and for support of labor causes everywhere," did provide humanitarian aid for European unionists still in or coming out of the underground. Dubinsky's New York locals raised $300,000 to help rescue many and keep them in food and shelter thereafter. But this was only half the objective, for the other eye was cocked on the communist bogeyman, and as the war drew to a close Dubinsky and Woll, now aided by Meany and William Green, then president of the AFL, got down to the more serious business at hand. In 1944 they set up the Free Trade Union Committee (FTUC) to revive unions in Europe and Japan and "to help such unions . . . to resist the new drives of totalitarian (i.e. communist) forces." For executive secretary they chose, ironically, the former head of the Communist Party, Jay Lovestone.

Lovestone was an ideal selection. He spoke the lingo of European Marxists and he had scores of good friends in the leftist movement and the underground across the ocean. He also had a small band of associates—Brown, Harry Goldberg, Henry Rutz—equally conversant with left wing rhetoric and equally anxious to save European labor from the "Communist menace." This was an invaluable windfall both for Dubinsky, Woll, Meany and company, as well as an American government which had virtually no one who knew the difference between "surplus value" and surplus food.

Lovestone was then in his mid-forties, an active man with a flair for conspiracy. Edwin Lahey of the Knight press once called him "part cloak and dagger, part cloak and suit." He had been one of the founders of the Communist Party and its General Secretary in 1929 when Moscow ordered him expelled for right-wing "deviationism." In the three-way fight between Stalin, Trotsky and Bukharin he had picked the wrong horse—Bukharin—and had suffered the consequence of separation, but for the next decade he continued to espouse the Soviet cause. After forming the Communist Party (Opposition) he tried to gain readmittance to the Communist International, he defended the Soviet Union as a "genuine workers state," and he differed with the official Party only over domestic affairs. When Homer Martin of the auto union was embroiled in a fight with the Communists he became Martin's mentor and placed one of his followers as Martin's assistant. It was only in 1941 that he gave up the ghost, dissolved his small group, and went to work for Dubinsky, a man with a penchant for picking up discarded leftists who "mend their ways." Subsequently he also left his mark on George Meany, whose star was then beginning to rise, and who as a good American and good Irishman felt viscerally the pangs of anti-communism and anti-colonialism that Lovestone could put into erudite and sophisticated verbiage.

Before long the planet was covered with old and new Lovestone-ites, some on the Free Trade Union Committee's payroll, some on that of the AFL, all eager, bright-eyed figures. Henry Rutz was assigned to Germany; Richard Deverall, former executive secretary of the Association of Catholic Trade Unionists, to Japan; Harry Goldberg to Indonesia (later Italy); and Irving Brown, son of an active teamster and a remarkably capable young man, everywhere. (According to a laudatory biographer in 1952, Brown had "his fingers in more than 100 individual projects." According to a less laudatory labor associate "Irving was everywhere, but he . . . had a negative appraoch. All he wanted to do was to short circuit the communists.") The team also included Mrs. Page Morris, an Arab-Moslem expert once an assistant to OSS's Bill Donovan; Maida Springer; Elly Borochowitz; Carmel Offi and many labor attachés who were "cleared with Jay" before being assigned their posts. Serafino Romualdi, a former Italian socialist who had been picked up by Dubinsky long before Lovestone, joined the force independently and carved out a niche as Latin American delegate. In later years the anti-Communist crew was augmented by Andrew McLellan, William Doherty, Jr., Ernest Lee (Meany's son-in-law) and others.

The magic weapon of this labor-CIA, apart from strident polemic, has been and still is money—secret dollars from the U.S. government's treasure chest. Though Brown claims he has doled out only $100,000 over two decades, a top labor figure in the Marshall Plan and AID programs who was stationed in Europe during all this period puts the figure at "many millions." The late Westbrook Pegler put the figure at "millions," and Robert Lewin of the Chicago Daily News said $5 million as of 1950. A CIA agent named William Braden published an article in 1967 which claimed he had turned over large

sums to Brown for his work in Europe and that subsidies to the
Italian and French unions fostered by Brown alone cost the United
States government about $2 million a year. Back in 1952, I
met a German union leader who claimed Brown had given him
$100,000 in a single transaction.

At any rate, the first item on the agenda was to prevent the
Communists from gaining a foothold in the German union movement. Europe was then digging out from war and hunger. A labor
leader who could feed himself and lay his hands on a few
typewriters, mimeo paper and mimeograph machine was miles ahead
of anyone striking up independently. The German Communists, of
course, were getting this sort of aid from the Soviet Union; Brown
copied the technique, ostensibly on behalf of the AFL, but actually
for and with the connivance of the United States government. In
"Operation Food" the AFL sent 5,000 food packages to German
unionists of their choice, 15,000 to France, 2,000 to Austria and
5,000 to Greece. By such methods Brown built up a cadre of
simon-pure anti-Communists in the German labor movement and the
American military government put restrictions on union activity so
that a moderate, old-line leadership could re-emerge and take over.
Dubinsky was probably right when he wrote in January 1949 that
"had it not been for the extensive educational activities"—read:
dollars—"of the Free Trade Union Committee of the AFL . . . the
communists . . . might by now have seized control of the reviving
German trade unions."

In France and Italy, where central labor federations were
controlled by Communists, Brown's work consisted of artificially
splitting the movement. A wave of strikes in May 1947 offered the
excuse in France for some of Brown's friends—business unionists and
mild socialists—to withdraw from the General Confederation of
Labor (CGT) on the ground that the walkouts were politically inspired. Aging Leon Jouhaux, leader of French labor for decades,
opposed the split, insisting it would be better to work within the
CGT to win a larger constituency, but he was overruled and carried
along. The resulting Force Ouvrière was a cipher at birth, its main
base in a few white collar unions, and remains so today. The only
thing it did not lack was cash, generously supplied by Brown from
an inexhaustible stockpile.

The Italian split took a different turn, for here Brown and Harry

Goldberg made common cause with the Catholics whom they prodded out of the General Confederation of Labor, and supplied with the general wherewithal for operations. The Nenni Socialists refused to accept Brown's blandishments and won his unswerving hostility for remaining with the Communists. It should be noted that this was a time when the followers of Stalin were moderate to an extreme, participating in "bourgeois governments," cooling the colonial revolution, working avidly to increase capitalist production, yet Lovestone, Brown and Co. were already adopting the hard line soon to become legion with the cold war. They were, indeed, among the first cold warriors and undoubtedly influenced its future course. Moreover, their activities were evidently broader than simple conspiracy, for there is considerable evidence they helped gather intelligence as well. Among the organizations subsidized by Brown, for instance, was the Free Trade Union Center in Exile, head-quartered in the Force Ouvrière offices. According to the *New York Times* of October 5, 1957 this interesting organization with few, if any, members "appears to have at its disposal a working intelligence division." The German railroad union, under Hans Jahn, also seems to have operated a "working intelligence division." According to Donald Robinson, a former AFL-staffer who wrote a highly friendly article about Brown in *Reader's Digest*, Jahn "told me about an undercover organization he has set up. . . . Irving Brown helped us."

Everywhere the story was the same. Where there was a Communist-dominated union the idea was to disrupt it; where there wasn't, the idea was to immunize against it by supporting "safe" anti-Communists. Particularly shameful was Brown's endorsement of Fotis Makris in Greece, a rightist adventurer who became union chief after the communists were purged and who is now a supporter of the Papadopoulos military dictatorship. And even more distressing was Brown's underwriting of a strikebreaking operation. Around 1949, Communist unionists at Marseilles and other ports were refusing to unload military shipments from New York. Brown thereupon picked up a character named Pierre Ferri Pisani who formed the Mediterranean Committee for the purpose of getting the weapons unloaded. His thugs beat up, hospitalized, tossed into the river, even killed dock workers and Communists until they cleared the waterfront. Their actions were so disgraceful the Socialist mayor of Marseilles, Gaston Defferre, appealed to the head of his party to help stop them. But the depredations continued, all quietly subsidized by Irving Brown's special funds.

By the early 1950s the names Irving Brown and Jay Lovestone had become anathema to most union officials in Europe, including those in England, Scandinavia, and other countries, with a socialist bent. "Brown's maniac anti-communist attitude," the Swedish Federation of Labor said in 1955, "is a valuable asset to communism." Within the inner circles of the ICFTU this maniac anti-communism caused ceaseless rifts, with Meany insisting that ICFTU's leaders were "ineffective in organizing workers against communism," and the others arguing that the way to deal with the problem was to relax tensions and orient on positive measures. The result was that periodically Meany threatened to withdraw from ICFTU or demanded the ouster of a General Secretary, and above all that he and Lovestone maintained an apparatus throughout the world independent of the ICFTU, and usually at variance with its policies.

When the AFL and CIO merged in December 1955, there was some hope that Walter Reuther would be able to drive Lovestone from the scene. It is now known that on one occasion, around 1951, Walters's brother Vic accepted $50,000 from the CIA agent Braden for transmission to certain German unionists, but generally the Reuthers eschewed clandestine operations and had the same general criticisms of Lovestone as most European movements, namely that his anti-communism was of the "maniac" variety. With merger, then, it was believed that Reuther could force Meany to dispense with Lovestone's services and jettison the whole Lovestone operation. This hope proved vain, first because Reuther was preoccupied with too many other differences with Meany to make this a public fight, and second because Meany was not amenable to bargaining on this point. Actually Lovestone's position, far from being weakened became more entrenched, so much so that Meany took him out of the wings where he had been functioning for years as seemingly nothing more than the secretary of the Free Trade Union Committee and made him the official head of the international affairs department of the AFL-CIO.

Collaboration with the United States government, instead of tapering off, became more open. Late in 1959 Joseph Beirne, President of the Communication Workers', conducted a school for

16 Latin American unionists at Fort Royal, Virginia. Instead of financing it with union funds he conceived of the intriguing idea of getting the money from the International Cooperation Administration, predecessor of AID. This gave Beirne greater latitude, for he was able not only to pay education costs but the salaries of the Latin unionists for a period of nine months. After this experience Beirne suggested to Meany that the pattern be widened, and out of this suggestion was born in 1960-61 the American Institute for Free Labor Development (AIFLD). I knew two of the men who were offered the directorship of this institution at the time—both said they turned it down because of whispers of CIA financing. The money for the project, they were told, was to come partly from a certain Michigan Fund, a highly suspicious organization which, under investigation, turned out to have an address but no telephone, and was later shown to be a CIA conduit. The man who did get the job, Serafino Romualdi, denied there was CIA money in AIFLD, but the rumors have been persistent. Moreover, the CIA interlaced with all significant activity of this kind, if only because it sat in at interdepartmental meetings of the government where international labor matters were discussed. Another disturbing feature of AIFLD was its link to management. Meany was president, but chairman of the board was J. Peter Grace of W. R. Grace & Co., which owns shipping firms, sugar haciendas, distilleries, box factories, textile mills and what have you in Latin America. Vice-chairman was Berent Friele, a Nelson Rockefeller man, and among the trustees were also such sterling friends of labor as the presidents of Anaconda Copper and Pan American Airways. In theory, business, labor and management were to put up one-third each for the educational programs of AIFLD, but in fact the government has paid 80 percent of the $2 million a year for this purpose, and has paid 100 percent for the social projects department which spends much larger sums building housing units, etc. for safe, anti-Communist unions south of the Rio Grande.

That the tens of thousands of unionists who have taken AIFLD courses are used for negative anti-Communist work (and some recruited to the CIA) is evidenced from AIFLD's own reports—such as these samples: "Former AIFLD Students Help Oust Reds from Uruguay Port Union." "Two Institute Graduates Challenge Communist Control of Honduran Union." A Colombian, Hugo Solon

Acero, eliminated "the last vestiges of communist influence in the regional federation of Cundinamarca." When Brazil was seized by military golpists in 1964 William Doherty, Jr., present AIFLD head, boasted that AIFLD graduates "were so active that they became intimately involved in some of the clandestine operations of the revolution before it took place.... Many of the trade union leaders—some of whom were actually trained in our institute—were involved . . . in the overthrow of the Goulart regime." They were also placed in charge of hundreds of unions taken over by the Castelo Branco dictatorship because the unions were considered radical.

Perhaps the most disgraceful chapter in the international activity of AIFLD and the AFL-CIO was their sponsorship of the British Guiana strike of 1963 aimed at overthrowing Cheddi Jagan. According to columnist Drew Pearson the strike was "inspired by a combination of U.S. Central Intelligence money and British Intelligence." It began when Jagan introduced a bill similar to the American Wagner Act which would have given the workers of the Man Power Citizens Association (MPCA)—and others—the right to vote as to who would represent them. Had the law passed Jagan undoubtedly would have gained control of the largest union in the country, since it was made up mostly of East Indian supporters of his regime. To bypass the plan the Guianese labor federation, prodded by American labor and native AIFLD graduates, went out in a general strike. Both before and after there was a suspicious shuttling of many American labor officials to this tiny country of 600,000 people—Doherty, Andrew McLellan, Ernest Lee, Gene Meakins of the Newspaper Guild, Gerard P. O'Keefe of the Retail Clerks, Pat Terril of the Steel Workers, Ben Segal of the Electrical Union, William McCabe, a special AFL-CIO representative, and four or five others. There is no question but that these men—with the exception perhaps of Segal—plowed the ground for the strike, and that the money to keep it going came from United States government sources. McLellan told me he didn't know exactly how much AFL-CIO money was raised for strike benefits in Georgetown but estimated it at $50,000. On the other hand a local official in British Guiana named Pollidor informed me that the strikers were getting three dollars a week in food benefits for the length of the strike, 11 and one-half weeks. Since there were 20,000 to 25,000 out, that comes to between $700,000 and $850,000. Jagan charges that AFL-CIO acted as a conduit for $1.2 million to those who were trying to overthrow him. Either way there is no question that these monies came from covert sources of the CIA. Jagan didn't fall at the time but his regime was sufficiently undermined so that CIA could put the coup de grace to it soon thereafter.

Another interesting bit of counter-revolutionary activity engaged in by AIFLD and the AFL-CIO was in the Dominican Republic. The AFL-CIO group there is an organization called CONATRAL. (When I visited its office in 1963 they brought in the U.S. labor attaché, Fred A. Somerford, to brief me and act as interpreter.) CON-ATRAL, in line with the anti-neutralist policy of Lovestone and company, had opposed Juan Bosch, the only democratically elected president of that country in four decades, from the outset. A few weeks before Bosch was overthrown by the militarists, CONATRAL ran an ad in the newspapers calling on working people to put their faith in the "armed forces" to defend them against communism. And though United States Ambassador John Bartlow Martin supported Bosch, Somerford, CONATRAL and the American military attachés opposed him. It is an open secret in Washington—especially among the labor specialists in the State Department and Department of Labor—that CONATRAL, Somerford and the U.S. military attachés were involved with the Dominican generals in overthrowing Bosch. And when a revolution broke out to return Bosch to power two years later, CONATRAL and the AFL-CIO were on the side of American intervention. I happened to be in Romualdi's office at the time the intervention was taking place, and he could see nothing wrong with it. It was necessary to "defeat communism" because whenever you have dissident officers and a militia, he told me, it opens the door to the Muscovites—as in Cuba.

This is typical of the Meany-Lovestone record in foreign affairs throughout postwar history. For Africa they have fashioned another institution called the African-American Labor Center (under Brown's guidance), which does not have employer participation, but is also dependent on the United States government for its money; and for Asia more recently the Asian-American Free Labor Institute. Each receives about a million dollars a year for educational work and other sums for social projects.

In 1967, when the press accused the AFL-CIO of receiving CIA money Meany vehemently denied it. "I suppose," he said, "it's just my natural ingrained opposition to spy activities." It must also have been the natural ingrained opposition of conspirators and cold warriors to revealing their connections with an intelligence agency, for it is now indisputable that CIA conduits were supplying funds to leaders of the State, County and Municipal Workers,' to the Oil Workers,' to the Newspaper Guild and to others. The Oil Workers', for instance, received sums from such CIA-foundations as the Andrew Hamilton Fund of Philadelphia. Arnold Zander, former president of State-County concedes that he accepted similar monies from other foundations. So did Gene Meakins of the Newspaper Guild. Nowadays the labor factotums claim they get money from AID—not the CIA—but it is noteworthy that they are not quick to publicize their relations with this agency either, perhaps because as Richard Dudman of the St. Louis *Post-Dispatch* notes, AID is now "picking up in part the old Central Intelligence Agency secret subsidies that were uncovered and suspended two years ago." A letter of May 15, 1968 by Ernest Lee of AFL-CIO to Rutherford M. Poats, deputy administrator of AID was made public in April 1969 by the auto union. It asks AID to provide an additional $1.3 million—$300,000 for the Retail Clerks, $300,000 for the oil union, $300,000 for the Communication Workers and the rest for four other organizations.

Back in 1951, in a brash speech, George Meany listed AFL accomplishments on the international arena such as the following: "primarily due to our effort there has been established the Force Ouvrière." In Germany it "was the AFL which broke the communist stranglehold on the trade unions." "Our European representative, Irving Brown, participated in cleaning the port of Marseilles of communist control." "We have established numerous contacts with resistance movements in the Soviet bloc." "On the China mainland, we are aiding the underground democratic forces."

If the Meany-Lovestone coterie are not official members of the CIA they are cheating it out of dues. The rank and file of the AFL-CIO have nothing to say about these activites. AFL-CIO conventions are made up almost exclusively of porkchoppers appointed by the International presidents, rather than elected by the membership of the national unions. There is never a discussion by the rank and file of AFL-CIO foreign policy. Meany runs the show on his own, with the blessings of labor leaders who are either pliant or who are equally rabid in their anti-communism. For all practical purposes then the AFL-CIO under Meany has become another agency of the United States government insofar as international affairs are concerned, and just as counter-revolutionary in its outlook.

June 1969

Coalitionism:
From Protest to Politicking

JULIUS JACOBSON

In the past two years there has been a sharp decline in the civil rights movement. Most disheartening is that the more militant, non-traditional wings of the Negro struggle, those primarily responsible for elevating the Movement to a Revolution, have suffered most: CORE exists largely on paper, SNCC is but a shadow of its former self, the Southern voter registration drive which once boasted 1,000 activists has collapsed, the school desegregation campaign is limping badly, North and South, Martin Luther King's campaign in Chicago suffered a defeat. Paralleling the weakened condition of the civil rights movement, and to an extent because of it, is the appalling fact that after more than a decade of struggle, the Negro people are hardly any better off today than they were before the Supreme Court's historic desegregation decision of 1954. In many respects they are worse off. For the Negro, the Great Society has become an even greater ghetto.

The overwhelming resistance of white America to the Negro cry for social justice is, of course, the major reason for the defeats suffered by the Movement. It is now clear that most American institutions, whatever their origins or pretensions, to one extent or another, have racial barriers. And behind these institutions, upholding the barriers, are the American people whose racism is pervasive and deeply rooted—far more so than we thought 15 years ago.

Given this resistance, even if the civil rights movement operated unifiedly and flawlessly, it could not have shattered America's racist wall. Nevertheless, the extent of the reverses cannot be attributed solely to insurmountable external circumstances. The Movement could have loosened more of the mortar in the wall had it not also been sapped of vitality by its own internal evolution as many civil rights activists, with freedom of choice, moved into one of two warring camps: Black Power versus Coalition Politics.

While I identify with the more militant wing of the civil rights movement, it would be disingenuous to hide my view that the content given to Black Power by its most prominent advocates is politically indefensible and has had disastrous organizational consequences.

Nevertheless, the cry of Black Power is an understandable reaction to the violence of white racists, the frivolousness of white liberals, the savagery of Johnson's massacre of nonwhites in Vietnam in a war that places a special, fatal burden on American Negro youth. It is also an understandable reaction to the conservative tendency in the Negro movement—coalition politics.

It is the coalition view that the Negro cannot go it alone to win his rights. He must, in the white world, find allies who are prepared to march shoulder to shoulder with him out of moral conviction and self-interest. These allies, according to the theory, include the trade union movement, liberals, idealistic churchmen, organizations of the poor. To further their common interests in democracy and social justice they find within the Democratic Party a political arena of operation. In a sense, such a coalition was operative in the thirties and forties when a tacit alliance was created in New Deal days between the major Negro organizations, the CIO, liberal groups and the Roosevelt Administration. In recent years, however, coalition politics has emerged as a rounded, political dogma with full-time theorists. It is an important new development.

Roy Wilkins, head of the NAACP, is an advocate of coalition politics. He has said so and, on the whole, behaves accordingly. Thus, he orients toward liberal, labor and Democratic Party "friends of the Negro people." But Wilkins is also the head of a mass organization of Negroes. As a result, in the event of conflict between his mass Negro base and one of the presumed allies of the Negro people, the allies in the White House or in the AFL-CIO cannot take

Wilkins for granted. For example, in the disputes between Negroes and unions which have flared into the open in recent years, Wilkins has spoken sharply about the racial practices of some unions, saying things that one ally does not customarily say about another.

On the other hand, the full-time theorists—Bayard Rustin, Tom Kahn of the League for Industrial Democracy (L.I.D.), Michael Harrington and others—have no mass base to which they are responsible. They certainly do not have to answer to a Negro membership. They are beholden only to their ideology of coalition politics. Therefore, if one wants to know what coalitionist theory means and implies, it is not by studying the uneven record of Roy Wilkins, but by examining the more internally consistent writings and actions of the theorists of coalition.

Let it be said at the outset that at the core of coalitionism raised to a dogma lies the politics of accommodation: accommodation to the Johnson Administration, to the war in Vietnam, to the trade union bureaucracy. Coalitionism, too, is an elitist philosophy. "From Protest to Politics," says Bayard Rustin. What this turns out to mean is "from protest to manipulation," maneuvering and bargaining among union bureaucrats, government spokesmen and coalitionist architects in a proper, civilized manner. For example, A. Philip Randolph who, sadly enough, has made his peace with George Meany largely on the latter's terms, doesn't believe that "all" demonstrations must be eliminated immediately but, he writes in the November 1966 issue of *The Federationist*, an official publication of the AFL-CIO, "I believe that the time has come when the street marches and demonstrations have about run their course. I believe that the strategy now in order is to shift from the street to the conference room for the purpose of discussion of the problems in the interests of an answer."

Bayard Rustin summed up the theory in a well-publicized article:

The future of the Negro struggle depends on whether the contradictions of this society can be resolved by a coalition of progressive forces which becomes the *effective* political majority in the United States. I speak of the coalition which staged the March on Washington, passed the Civil Rights Act, and laid the basis for the Johnson landslide—Negroes, trade unionists, liberals, and religious groups.[1]

Of these groups, the coalitionists find the trade union movement the Negro's most natural ally. "The labor movement, *despite its obvious faults*," according to Rustin, "has been the largest single organized force in this country pushing for progressive social legislation." Tom Kahn expresses the same thought in his pamphlet, *The Economics of Equality*. In his chapter on the Negro-Labor Alliance, he writes. "Even when its program is *inadequate*—and many criticisms can be leveled at the AFL-CIO—it is the single most powerful bulwark against conservative and reactionary interests." Gus Tyler, Assistant President of the ILGWU, believes that "the massive impress of the labor movement in a great liberal coalition is changing the face of the nation."[2]

The idea of a Negro-Labor alliance is an appealing one. The trouble is that it is an *idea*: that is, since the abstract needs and interests of trade unionism and the Negro people converge at so many points, the two should be natural allies. However, so many of the unions have been taken over by aged, bureaucratic cliques that today there is no solid alliance, certainly none from below, of the Negro masses and the trade union movement.

What is important to note is that the coalitionists who preach the vital necessity of a Negro-Labor alliance today and are guided in their actions by coalitionist concepts, never give an idea of what the Labor half of this partnership-to-be looks like! It is an extraordinary omission, especially since most of them will admit (see the lines we have italicized in the above quotations), that there are "obvious faults" and "inadequacies" afflicting the labor movement. Exactly what and how extensive are these failings? What is its vision? What are the internal practices of labor organizations? What is their record in action? Are they democratic organizations? And so forth. These are questions assiduously avoided by most coalitionist theorists, for good reason. They head organizations financed by trade union treasuries (according to Drew Pearson, the L.I.D. received CIA funds, as well) and act as publicists for the trade union bureaucracy in the civil rights movement. To reveal the trade union establishment as it actually is would not only embarrass their patrons but expose the central fallacy of coalitionism.

Given the special social-economic roots of the trade union movement it is unquestionably a potential force for democracy and, of necessity, among the first institutions to be thwarted and suppressed by authoritarian regimes. Thus, trade unions are not permitted in Russia, China, Cuba, Spain, etc. (Government or party-sponsored herding of workers in order to supervise them and meet production goals has nothing to do with unionism.) But it does not follow that because unions can only exist in countries with at least minimal democratic rights that the unions themselves are therefore democratic organizations. They are only a relative and *potential* force for democracy.

In the United States, the trade union movement is a paradox because its existence is contingent on a broader democratic social context while the bulk of American unions, in their internal methods, resemble authoritarian, even totalitarian, societies. In totalitarian societies, power resides in the hands of an elite or party which cannot survive the emergence of democratic institutions and denies the exercise of fundamental democratic rights of individuals and organized dissent. Those who violate the totalitarian order run the risk of economic deprivation, imprisonment, physical abuse, etc. Of course, the analogy finds one of its limits in that the absence of democracy is natural to totalitarianism but not to unionism. Our point, however, is that it is the bureaucratic aberration that prevails and is growing in the labor movement which begins to resemble, in its internal practices, political dictatorship.

The picture we present of the AFL-CIO is not to be taken as a sweeping condemnation of all its affiliates. The Packinghouse Workers cannot be coupled with the Carpenters; the United Automobile Workers is worlds apart from the Operating Engineers. Even within Internationals dominated by reactionary, corrupt leaderships, there are locals with a healthy, democratic atmosphere. And there are trade unionists from many Internationals who are playing a positive role in the peace movement in contrast to the pro-war attitudes of the AFL-CIO top leadership.

Nor is it our intention to urge radicals and civil right activists to turn their backs on a Negro-Labor alliance which could, indeed, change the face of the nation. On the contrary, it is our opinion that instead of scorning the labor movement, young radicals should become a part of it since so many of them are teachers, professionals and white collar workers. By their participation as active trade unionists they could do a great deal to change the face of the labor movement by struggling from within the AFL-CIO to crack the thick layers of bureaucratic crust and to make a meaningful reality of the slogan for a Negro-Labor alliance.

The coalition apologists for the union officials may be aghast at the irreverent suggestion that there are similarities between union structures and habits and totalitarian societies. However, can any of them recite a list of unions where a member can announce at a union meeting that he has formed an opposition, that he wants space in union publications to present his group's point of view, time at meetings to speak, etc.—in other words that he expects all the rights associated with political democracy?

What happens when rank and file members of the Painters Union, the National Maritime Union, the International Association of Machinists, the Seafarers International Union, not to mention such unions as the Operating Engineers, voice their dissent or have the courage and stamina to organize an opposition? We know from experiences past and recent, that the union dictatorships respond with all weapons at their command—from job discrimination, to expulsion, to skull cracking (and sometimes murder). This is true not only in the unions mentioned above but in most of the Internationals; and not only in the old line conservative craft unions but in many that boast of being progressive and far-sighted.

Take the International Ladies' Garment Workers' Union whose socialist ancestry is invariably invoked by the leadership to cover up some particular violation of democracy and to help it project a liberal image. How much liberalism is there within the ILGWU for a dissident? Suppose a group of workers feels that there is no justification for a union with the standing, prestige and resources of the ILGWU to negotiate a contract, as it just did in the eight-state area around New York, which provides that *by 1969* cleaners and others will get $65 a week, $67-$72 for shipping clerks, $68 for examiners (this is less than the poverty line of $4,000 a year for a New York family of five) and not very much more for the more skilled "better paying" jobs.

And let us suppose that these workers, primarily Negroes and Puerto Ricans since they are the ones confined to the lowest paying jobs, are joined by other ILGWU workers who are moved by a sense of outrage that their union (along with the Amalgamated Clothing Workers) is sabotaging the anti-poverty program where it involves training the young (mainly Negroes and Puerto Ricans) in needle-craft skills. (If one's reading is limited to the works of Rustin, Kahn, Harrington, Tyler, or the editors of *Dissent*, one will never learn that it was the ILGWU and the Amalgamated which, in 1963, knifed all efforts at government subsidization of workers' training in garment skills. Nor can it be learned that, as this is being written, the U.S. Department of Labor, at the instigation of the ILGWU, is trying to shut down a seamstress training program for girls in a Neighborhood Youth Corps anti-poverty project.)

Suppose these workers decide that the best way to improve their conditions is to organize in their own interests as they can presumably do in a democracy. They announce to the ILGWU leadership and membership that they have organized an opposition—a faction—one of whose objectives is to oust Stulberg [past president of ILGWU] and Gus Tyler from their positions in the ILGWU. Moreover, this opposition demands its normal democratic rights: to distribute literature freely, speak at meetings, get a column or two in the union paper to present its program, etc. What would happen? How would the ILGWU leadership respond? The questions are rhetorical. We know what would happen and so do the theorists of coalitionism. These insurgents would risk expulsion and the loss of their jobs.

The reality is that the ILGWU is governed by a self-perpetuating bureaucracy which has so devised the union constitution that it is virtually impossible for an opposition to overturn the leadership, or even to exist.

Because the coalitionists tend to support labor officials, they undermine attempts by rank and file unionists to reform their unions. It is these union insurgents who can be the real allies of the Negro people.

Along with bureaucracy in the unions there is corruption, not only of spirit, but in its crassest form: pay-offs, bribes, collusion with employers, fantastic salaries and expense accounts for union leaders.

There is Martin Rarback, Secretary-Treasurer of Painters District Council 9, recently indicted for taking $840,000 from employers. His reward—a new union job given to him by the Special Trustee appointed by the President of the International. Or take the example of Joseph Curran, President of the National Maritime Union, who squeezes out of his 30,000 seamen an income ranging from $80,000 to $100,000 a year, plus a chauffeur-driven limousine. Meany, a Spartan, draws $70,000.

These are not exceptional cases, nor is corruption limited to nationally known figures. Take the case of Charles Johnson, first vice-president of the Brotherhood of Carpenters and Joiners. A man of many jobs—and many salaries—Mr. Johnson receives $37,700 for his vice-presidential post, $31,200 as President of the Carpenters District Council of New York City and $23,962 as President of Local 1456. That's a cool $92,862. He does hold other posts, however, and no doubt there are other fairly spectacular salaries.

One of the most daring confrontations we have seen with the problem of union corruption by a prominent coalitionist is Gus Tyler's description of its dangers:

Beyond the acceptance and solicitation of bribes and the misappropriation of treasury funds is corruption of the spirit: disregard of democratic procedures and individual rights, insensitivity to the real problems of the membership, dedication to self rather than the cause—in short, the whole gamut of rot that comes to characterize any case-hardened bureaucracy ruling without inner compulsion or compassion. Unless unions find means and men to meet this inevitable challenge, the great power of labor can itself become an ultimate peril to the humane and democratic values of our civilization.

One has the right to expect at least a chapter to follow, investigating the extent to which "the whole gamut of rot" has infected the union movement today. Not a word. Instead, we are treated to such homilies as "The truth of the matter is that labor leaders are, after all, only people, subject to the same weaknesses of flesh and spirit as the rest of mankind. They are neither subhuman nor superhuman, merely human."

The truth of the matter is that Tyler's reflection on the poverty of human nature is neither interesting nor pertinent. Tyler knows that what he warns against—"disregard of democratic procedures," "insensitivity to the real problems of the membership," "the whole gamut of rot"—actually permeates the union movement today. He knows it because he lives in it.

Apologists for the trade union bureaucracy will, on occasion, point to the AFL-CIO Ethical Practices Committee as evidence that the leadership is not indifferent to the dangers of corruption among its affiliates. But this Committee, itself, its history (or lack of one) and composition is evidence of the immorality of the trade union leadership. The Committee was formed after the merger of the AFL and the CIO in response to government pressure and not out of any deeply felt compassion for rank and file rights, in order to prepare the expulsion of the Teamsters Union and several others, although the Teamsters Union was no more corrupt than many of those which sat in judgment on it. Having satisfied the government, the Ethical Practices Committee soon became a dead letter. Today it is even difficult to find out its membership. (I spent days contacting people active in and knowledgeable about labor affairs before I learned the names of the members of this Committee guarding the moral virtue of American unionism. Nobody knew.) It turns out that this Ethical Practices Committee consists of five union leaders and is chaired by George Harrison, whose ethical credentials include his leadership of one of the most racist unions in the AFL-CIO, the Brotherhood of Railway Clerks.

The AFL-CIO's level of commitment to ethics was revealed by Walter Reuther when he informed the UAW, at its special April convention, that the rules of the so-called ethical practices code were "adopted . . . in the Roulette Room of the Monte Carlo Hotel in Miami Beach." The occasion was an Executive Council meeting of the AFL-CIO in Florida.

New York Times correspondent, Damon Stetson, commented recently on another Executive Council meeting in Florida: "The winter meetings here of the American Federation of Labor and Congress of Industrial Organizations have become almost as much of a focal point for bankers, Government officials, labor consultants and hangers on as for union leaders."

At this 1967 Council meeting there were representatives from Rothschild and Co. to promote pension fund investment in common stock. John Roosevelt, Vice President of Bache and Co., was fraternizing with Executive Council members, while Earl Fillilove, Chairman of the Building Trades Employers' Association of New York City, made Bal Harbour his home for two weeks to discuss mutual problems with union leaders in the construction trades. Three representatives of the First National City Bank threw a party attended by union dignitaries, including George Meany. Stetson sums up the life-style of American labor leaders: "the conferences in front of a cabana by the pool, the informal exchange in the lobby of the Americana Hotel, the discussion over stone crabs or steaks at some of Miami Beach's best restaurants are almost as much a part of labor's business today as are the formal meetings of the AFL-CIO Executive Council." Why do we never hear the details of union corruption from the theorists of coalitionism?

Perhaps the most acute symptom of the labor movement's decay is its inability to attract the idealistic and socially committed segment of the younger generation. The apathy and hostility of the young toward the union movement is a bitter pill for the theorists of coalition politics. Tyler laments that "labor's repute is at a nadir among progressive intellectuals and militant youth." That should not be so difficult to understand. For the radical young have good reason to feel that Big Labor is as venal as most other institutions of the American Establishment; particularly when one considers the AFL-CIO record in those areas of greatest concern to them— American foreign policy and civil rights.

In the modern world, labor is obliged to take a stand on almost all of the burning social and political issues. And because of the stands it takes, the union leadership well deserves the contumely of radical youth and progressive intellectuals. Above all, the AFL-CIO deserves condemnation for its subservience to the Democratic Party, for its actual record on civil rights and for its unrelieved reactionary stand on questions of war and peace.

The same AFL foreign policy experts who collaborated with the CIA in 1954 to overthrow the Arbenz regime in Guatemala determine the foreign policy and activities of the AFL-CIO today. A comparable achievement recently was its collaboration with the CIA to overthrow the Jagan regime in British Guiana.

In every world crisis of this decade threatening peace the AFL-CIO has distinguished itself as a fierce hawk. It cheered Kennedy at the Bay of Pigs. It cheered Kennedy as he went to the brink in the missile crisis a year later. (Meany took it on himself—he knows his subordinates well—to wire the President "the support of the entire labor movement.")

It cheered Johnson when he ordered the Marines to invade the Dominican Republic. (Jay Lovestone, Meany's foreign policy brain-truster, did have a demurrer: he thought it would have been wiser to send regular Army men instead of Marines who have a bad reputation in Latin America.) It cheers Johnson's every intensification and escalation of America's filthy war in Vietnam.

At its Bal Harbour meeting in March, the AFL-CIO Executive Council warned against bombing pauses in Vietnam and declared that limiting air strikes in North Vietnam to military targets means that the United States "has paid dearly in the loss of planes and pilots." Mainly out of "consideration . . . of simple patriotism" and to help the United States that is "engaged in a painful war in defense of freedom," the Executive Council went on record giving its "unqualified support" to the Treasury Department's savings bond payroll deduction plan.

It comes as no surprise that at the huge April 1967 peace demonstration in New York, organized labor was virtually unrepresented, while at the right wing counter-march a month later some of the largest contingents were supplied by the trade unions.

It is significant that in the whole of Tyler's book there is not a paragraph dealing with these—or any—foreign affair positions and activities of the AFL-CIO. This reticence is not unique to Tyler. In the articles and pamphlets by the theorists of coalitionism promoting their version of a Negro-Labor alliance, their discussion of labor's stand on decisive questions of war and peace would barely fill an index card. They avoid the subject for two reasons: first, labor's record on foreign policy can be catalogued somewhere to the right of moderate Republicans, which is damaging to the image they want to project of a "socially progressive" union movement; and second, a number of the more prominent theorists of coalitionism have themselves regressed into mild critics of, sometimes shamefaced apologists for, American imperialism, which obviously limits their capacity for indignation over AFL-CIO policy.

The executive director of the League for Industrial Democracy, Tom Kahn, does not deny that he supports the bombing of North Vietnam, while the coalitionists' most prominent spokesman, Bayard Rustin, until recently a pacifist, is noticeably absent among the signers of anti-war petitions. In a recent column for the *Amsterdam News* criticizing civil rights activists "who now devote nearly all their energies to opposing the war and want to know why I don't do likewise," it becomes clear that one of the reasons he doesn't engage in peace work (he needn't "devote" himself but the truth is that he doesn't even lend his name), is that he is not that much opposed to the war. Not only is he opposed to the demand for immediate withdrawal of American troops, he is apparently opposed to the

American cessation of bombing North Vietnam unless "both sides—not just the U.S." take peace initiatives.

More telling than that is Rustin's speech that touched on the peace movement at a conference of the "Democratic Left" which he assumed would be unreported and was therefore a less guarded and more accurate indication of his stand. Unhappily for him, his speech was reported in the May 8, 1967 issue of the *New York Times* which said:

Mr. Rustin, in warning against the influence of Communist groups in the peace movement, called upon the Committee for a Sane Nuclear Policy to expel Dr. Benjamin Spock, the pediatrician and national cochairman of SANE, for "political naivete" in working along with Maoists and Trotskyites to end the war in Vietnam.

and further, Rustin complained:

It's easier today to get a debate on whether the purpose of the Administration is to exterminate Negroes in Vietnam than to get Negroes out to discuss jobs.

While Rustin cannot possibly expel Spock from SANE, he and his colleagues have done some expelling of their own. At one time, they left a spot open for the "peace forces" when reciting the litany of coalitionist allies-to-be. But as the peace forces grew more militant and the architects of coalition more accomodating to the Establishment, the niche reserved for men of peace grew gradually smaller, until today it can be said that Rustin can at least have the compensatory satisfaction of having successfully phased out the peace movement as a candidate for the Grand Coalition-to-come.

It is easy to see why this premature expulsion was necessary. Writing about a meeting of civil rights leaders held recently to discuss a number of problems, the *New York Times* (June 15, 1967) reports:

Bayard Rustin, executive secretary of the A. Philip Randolph Institute, asserted that the civil rights movement could gain nothing without President Johnson's support, and that the President's support might be diluted if civil rights leaders took strong stands against the Administration's policy in Vietnam.[3]

Civil rights is the other area in which the union establishment has disgraced itself in the eyes of young radicals. On paper and in resolutions, the AFL-CIO is committed to racial equality in a most general way. One test of its sincerity is how it responds to various calls to action from the civil rights movement. Take the March on Washington of 1963, designed to further the cause of civil rights legislation. It won the support and sponsorship of an extraordinarily wide section of civil rights organizations, liberal groups, churches and individual unions. Notorious for its absence from the list of sponsors or supporters was the AFL-CIO. This was not an oversight. The AFL-CIO Executive Council discussed the March and refused to endorse it. More than that, it refused to recommend that affiliated unions give their endorsement, leaving it instead to "individual union determination."

The AFL-CIO bureaucracy's response to the anguished cry of Black Power is obtuse and reprehensible. According to Meany, who thinks Black Power is synonymous with black supremacy, "the advocates of black supremacy and white supremacy belong in the same camp and the American trade union movement opposes both equally." A more malicious rebuke to Black Power comes from Jack Rich, editor of the *Hat Worker,* the publication of another "progressive" union with a socialist background, the Millinery Workers. Rich refers to rioting Negro youths as "a bunch of hoodlums" and "just plain bums." He suggests that Stokely Carmichael "passed a course in surliness cum laude" and that "the Negro goons who go on racist rampages know exactly what Black Power means." For Rich, too, white supremacy and Black Power are equally evil.

How can union leaders equate the extremism of the oppressors with the extremism of the oppressed? As Bayard Rustin correctly pointed out last year, it is "both absurd and immoral to equate the despairing response of the victim with the contemptuous assertion of the oppressor." Is he prepared publicly to censure his allies in the labor leadership for their absurd and immoral equation?

One aspect of civil rights directly related to the labor movement is the question of "preferential treatment" for Negro workers, particularly the unemployed. The call for preferential treatment as a means of compensating weak, oppressed or disadvantaged minorities is a thoroughly democratic principle, and widely applied in the United States. Examples are legion; just one is the graduated income tax which is a form of preferential treatment for low income groups. With the exception of a few crackpots, no one denounces this principle of taxation because it discriminates against the rich in favor of the poor. What, then, is either unfair or extreme about the demand that Negroes who have been so long oppressed be partially compensated for society's crimes against them (including crimes by discriminatory unions which deprived them of a livelihood) by giving them preferential consideration in hiring practices? Yet, the response of the union leadership as a whole was summed up by George Meany in his testimony to the House Judiciary Committee in 1963 when he described preferential hiring as a "pitfall" that would "merely replace one kind of discrimination with another."

While Meany's objections, as usual, are clumsily stated, he can rely on more subtly expressed objections to preferential hiring from the theorists of coalition who usually sprinkle their conservative conclusions with radical phrases. Thus Tom Kahn warns us that "preferential treatment is the most militant demand of the 'black bourgeoisie.' " If true, the black bourgeoisie is far in advance of Tom Kahn.

Kahn's arguments against preferential practices unintentionally invoke the spirit of Daniel DeLeon and the battle-cry of his Socialist Labor Party, "Reform Is Chloroform," when he informs us (he considers it important enough to italicize) that *"so long as we have class unemployment and Negroes are disproportionately concentrated in the lower categories, only full employment can keep them engaged in the economy."* A variation on the same theme: " . . . there is the danger that the emphasis on preferential treatment sows the illusion that Negroes can make progress in a declining economy. . . ." And the revolutionary grand finale: " . . . preferential treatment, at least in the context of the present economic order, does not go to the root of the Negro's job problem." How DeLeon would beam if he could read these passages (without their conclusions).

Of course, preferential treatment does not go to the root of the Negro job problem! Neither will a ten cent an hour raise for any workingman provide him with all the comforts of the good life. Only socialism will do all that. But the ten cent an hour raise will help. That is one reason we support it, though it might "sow illusions," to use Kahn's hackneyed phrase. And that is why we support preferential hiring; not because it is the ultimate answer but it is at least a small democratic step in the direction of social justice.

Where DeLeon abjured reforms as part of his war against the "labor lieutenants of capitalism," and the capitalist class, Kahn uses the same language to serve the labor bureaucracy and as part of his struggle to elect Lyndon Johnson in 1968.

It is in the crucial area of the internal racial practices of the AFL-CIO, that coalitionism is most vulnerable and its theorists most embarrassed. For what happens to coalitionism if it is found out that its largest projected base is guilty of what the coalition is supposed to combat—racial discrimination? Or that the major obstacle to Negroes getting jobs in many instances is not created by the employer or the government but by the union? The theorists of coalitionism handle the problem in two ways:

1. Ignore, underplay or simply deny the evidence of racist practices in the AFL-CIO.

2. Through personal contacts in the labor movement and a training program for Negro applicants for apprenticeship training tests try to get Negroes placed in a few of the skilled trades. In itself, this is a worthy cause. But it is carried out in line with the higher principle that, no matter what happens, nothing is to be said or done to harm the union image.

Three years ago, Tom Kahn wrote: "The segregationist practices of the craft unions are well-known and among the ugliest chapters in labor history. They are now under fire from the AFL-CIO itself." But these ugly chapters are not merely part of history, they are still being written and they were not and are not "under fire" from the AFL-CIO. Indeed, at the time Kahn was minimizing union discrimination, thousands of Negroes were demonstrating against the discriminatory practices of the building trades unions.

Speaking before the California Negro Leadership Conference earlier this year, Rustin admitted "there is still discrimination in a minority segment of the American labor movement." This, he immediately qualified: "This is a scandal, however, that is being fought by every unionist, black and white, who is worthy of the name." (Judged by this standard there are few "worthy" unionists.) Rustin continued: "I myself am, in my own capacity, committed to end the *vestiges* of discrimination in the trade union movement, but I *absolutely refuse to conduct the battle along lines that will ultimately injure the labor movement.*" (Emphasis added.)

What Rustin is saying is that instead of protesting, Negroes should rely on him, and a few friends, to politick with labor functionaries inside the AFL-CIO. How this elitist quietism will be more helpful either to Negroes or the labor movement only Rustin knows.

He speaks of "vestiges" of discrimination in the union movement while others have come up with the figure of 155 locals out of 10,000 in the AFL-CIO which have exclusionist admission policies. But on March 31, 1967, the U.S. Department of Labor, despite its policy of justifying union officialdom, felt compelled to warn *500* trade union locals that they would be denied federal certification unless they dropped their discriminatory apprentice programs.

After conducting a series of hearings on allegations of racial discrimination in the building trades unions in 1963, the New York City Commission on Human Rights reported:

A pattern of exclusion exists in a substantial portion of the building construction industry, effectively barring non-whites from participation in this area of the city's economic life.

Responsibility for the exclusion rests directly on the shoulders of the unions which control the hiring procedures in the industry.

In March 1967, the Commission ended another series of hearings and its report noted that there were only "minimal" variations from the 1963 pattern, with only two major improvements—the electricians and carpenters unions.

Today, in nine union locals in the skilled crafts with 28,000 members, less than one out of 50 is nonwhite. In Sheet Metal Workers Local 28 there were no Negro journeymen in 1963 and none by March 1966, although the Local reported 12 "Spanish speaking" members. In the same period, two plumbers locals with 7,100 members had a total of 25 Negro journeymen in 1963 and 36 in 1966. While there has been an increase in the number of Negroes and Puerto Ricans accepted in the skilled unions' apprenticeship training programs, the figures reveal a continuing pattern of discrimination. Local 2 of the Plumbers Union admitted nine nonwhite apprentices in the 1963-1966 period but none at all during 1965-1966. (This is the local of which George Meany is still a member.)

One excuse offered by the union leaders for this deplorable situation is that the job shortage is to blame; that they cannot replace white union workers with Negroes for the sake of integration and that there are simply not enough jobs to go around. The ground is cut from under this argument by the fact that there are occasional labor shortages which the union meets by providing out-of-town union workers rather than bringing Negroes into the union-controlled labor pool.

Exclusionist practices are not restricted to New York. A study recently appeared on negro participation in apprenticeship programs with facts and figures which bear out the charges made by many civil rights leaders that discriminatory practices are widespread in the American labor movement. In Philadelphia, for example, no Negroes were admitted as apprentices or journeymen in three craft unions. In Cleveland, one of the worst offenders, there were a total of seven Negro apprentices in seven locals as of the Fall of 1966. The facts are more or less the same for most of the cities analyzed in the report. Nationally, the report reveals that in 1960, the number of Negro apprentices (in trades which are highly unionized) was 2.52 percent of the total (2,191 out of 89,966) which was only a modest improvement over the 1950 figures of 1.91 percent (or 2,190 out of 115,000).

In light of just the above small sampling of union racial practices what happens to Tom Kahn's assurance of three years ago that such practices are "now under fire from the AFL-CIO itself"?

The special instance of Sheet Metal Workers Local 28 not only yields further evidence of union discriminatory practices but provides a sharp insight into the mentality and role of coalitionism in action.

Sheet Metal Workers Local 28 admitted no nonwhites until 1966. It is a glaring example of the bitterness with which some craft unions resist democratic racial practices. The State Supreme Court ordered the union to give its first entrance examination in 1965. Before the court decision, the sheet metal workers apprenticeship training program worked on a father-son basis which, in effect, excluded Negroes.

The Workers Defense League and the A. Philip Randolph Educational Fund set up an Apprenticeship Training Program which recruited applicants and gave them an intensive course of study in preparation for such examinations.

When the 1966 test results were revealed, nine of the top ten scorers were Negroes; 26 out of the top 60 were Negroes. Local 28 was legally obliged to take them into the union as apprentice trainees. Embittered by the prospect of Negro apprentices, Local 28 went into court to try to invalidate the test results, arguing that the high scores of Negroes indicated irregularity. Those at the head of the WDL–A. Philip Randolph Apprenticeship Training Program would not go to court to defend the rights of the youngsters they had trained. To do so would have meant too sharp a confrontation with the union and might endanger their "coalition" with union bureaucrats. A press release issued by the WDL–A. Philip Randolph Institute on January 5, 1967, was a model of coalitionist politicking:

The Apprenticeship Training Program did not initiate the legal action because the history of our experience leads us to believe that where such matters can be settled amicably everybody benefits—the youngsters, the Union, and the training project itself. Therefore, our primary interest remains the placing of the youngsters on the job.

Legal action, however, was undertaken on behalf of the youths by the State Commission on Human Rights. So fearful were the coalitionists of disturbing the labor bureaucrats that they did not even come into the case *amicus curiae* in defense of their students. Instead, an *amicus* brief was entered by the NAACP. (This bears out our earlier point that although the NAACP may be coalitionist and conservative, it is nevertheless an independent mass Negro organization and therefore responsive to the needs of the Negro community, while the coalitionists, for all their radical rhetoric, are crippled by a primary allegiance to their dogma and their union patrons.)

In the courts, Local 28 lost in its attempt to invalidate the results of the test.

To our indictment of the American trade union officialdom and its coalitionist representatives, we add one more charge. The AFL-CIO is guilty of a disservice to the cause of trade unionism itself.

Since the 1955 merger, the AFL-CIO has not increased its membership and its proportionate strength among the working population has dropped from 22 percent to 17 percent. It has failed to make major gains in the South and has made only a dent among the millions of professional and white collar workers who are now more numerous than our industrial working class. While it would be difficult for even the best of union movements to organize the South and the white collar workers, these objectives cannot be met by a union movement that is steeped in bureaucracy and corruption. A precondition for success in these areas is a union movement that is alive, flexible, has a sense of mission and, above all, involves the rank and file in the life of the movement. In a word, it requires trade union democracy. Where it had made inroads in new areas, these successes have often been achieved in spite of the apathy or hostility of an aging union bureaucracy.[4]

Walter Reuther summed it up accurately at the UAW convention when he described the moral and organizational state of the unions as follows: "Unfortunately in the 11 years of the merger we believe that the AFL-CIO has become stagnant and is vegetating. I say, to put it simply and understandably, it has an acute case of hardening of the arteries."

If Reuther's diagnosis is correct, then the coalitionists' pretense that the labor movement is basically healthy is to do trade unionism the greatest disservice. Finally, the attitude of the labor bureaucracy forces civil rights militants to press for the decertification of discriminatory unions and obliges Negro workers to organize themselves into black unions.

The truth is that the coalition theorists are not primarily interested in a Negro-Labor alliance. They have their sights set on bigger game: the Democratic Party. The idea is for civil rights groups, unions and an assortment of liberal organizations to join forces and, in their united strength, gradually reshape the Democratic Party until it conforms to their image of a truly progressive people's party.

It is a utopian scheme. No such coalition is going to capture the Democratic Party. The Democratic Party has its own coalition, a network of hardened political machines which is not going to permit itelf to be taken over by Freedom Budget visionaries or permit the Party to be torn apart, with its consequent loss of political power, prestige, patronage and so on.

What has happened, instead—it was inevitable—is that the Democratic Party has captured the theorists of coalition. And without resistance! When Vice President Humphrey comes out of a conference with his arm around Georgia's Governor, Lester (ax-handle) Maddox, and announces to the world that Lester is "a good Democrat" he knows that he has nothing to fear from the theorists of coalition. They will still campaign for him in 1968.

After all, so much of their time is spent attempting to frustrate any manifestation of independence or radicalism. In 1966, arguing against independent Negro candidates in Alabama, Bayard Rustin wrote:

Now there might be a certain value in having two Negro congressmen from the South, but obviously they could do nothing by themselves to reconstruct the face of America. Eighty sheriffs, eighty tax assessors, and eighty school-board members might ease the tension for a while in their communities, but they alone could not create jobs and build low-cost housing; they alone could not supply quality integrated education.

The sectarian rhetoric—"reform is chloroform"—barely disguises the thoroughgoing accommodation to the Democratic Party. The truth is that two Negro congressmen from the South, plus 80 Negro sheriffs, 80 Negro tax assessors and 80 Negro school-board members would not overthrow capitalism but their election would have done more for the cause of the civil rights revolution than the election of dozens of liberal congressmen paying lip service to racial justice and supported by Rustin. What are they doing "to reconstruct the face of America"?

Reconstruction, however, is merely Rustin's ploy. He makes his message of accommodation completely clear—this time with Popular Front rhetoric—in the same article:

Southern Negroes, despite exhortations from SNCC to organize themselves into a Black Panther party, are going to stay in the Democratic party—to them it is the party of progress, the New Deal, the New Frontier, and the Great Society—and they are right to stay.

Gone is the radical pretense. Now he gets down to cases as he did in 1964, when he succeeded in persuading some but not all important civil rights leaders to declare a moratorium on demonstrations—"to observe a broad curtailment, if not total moratorium, on all mass marches, mass picketing, and mass demonstrations until after Election Day, November 3." The moratorium was signed by A. Philip Randolph among others. Yet Randolph was the man who organized the March on Washington movement, which Rustin supported, during World War II, without being shaken by those who accused them of disrupting the war against fascism. In 1964, however, they were ready to put the lid on the civil rights movement for the sake of the war against Goldwater. Rustin boasted that "demonstrations were down by 75 percent as compared to the same period in 1963." Domestication is Rustin's badge of personal honor. Today, he calls for the conference room instead of the picket line.

Martin Luther King also signed the 1964 moratorium. His evolution since then is a refreshing contrast to Rustin's: toward a reaffirmation of militancy. Writing in the *New York Times*, June 11, 1967, King said:

The many white political leaders and well-meaning friends who ask Negro leadership to leave the streets may not realize that they are asking us effectively to silence ourselves. More white people learned more about the shame of America, and finally faced some aspects of it, during the years of non-violent protest than during the century before. Non-violent direct action will continue to be a significant source of power until it is made irrelevant by the presence of justice.

The coalitionists reject the power of direct action in favor of maneuvering inside the Democratic Party. They say they want to drive the Dixiecrats out of the Party. Johnson has no such desire but he need not fear. The coalitionists cannot drive the Dixiecrats out of the Democratic Party and, moreover, when there was a critical division at the 1964 Atlantic City Convention over the seating of the Mississippi Freedom Democrats, the coalitionists were the allies of those who preferred the unity of the Party and the victory of Johnson to risking a split with the Dixiecrats.

Johnson has something to worry about on the Vietnam War. And from Democrats. Not from the leading coalition Democrats who have made their peace with the war in Vietnam but from Reform Democrats whose repugnance to the war has moved them far to the left of the Rustin strategists. Hundreds of Reform Democrats recently picketed their President when he spoke in New York. Can anyone imagine Rustin or Kahn picketing Johnson about anything today?

In 1964, the coalitionists rallied to Johnson under the banner of smashing Goldwater. Goldwater was smashed. There will be no Goldwater with whom to frighten liberals in 1968. More likely, there will be a moderate Republican with foreign and domestic policies not too different from Johnson's. No one really knows; not this writer nor the architects of coalition politics. *But the coalitionists no longer have to know the nature of the opposition.* They know the nature of their politics. They want a Democratic winner and Johnson seems their best bet.

Everything has its price in America. If you want an "alliance" with the trade union establishment as it is today, you can have it for a price. If you want to work for a coalition within the limits of the Democratic Party, you can do that—for a price. But the returns are slight and the price is high—the abandonment of political independence and socialist opposition.

December 1966

1. "From Protest to Politics" in the February 1965 issue of *Commentary*.

2. Gus Tyler, *The Labor Revolution,* (New York: Viking Press, 1967.)

3. There is evidence that Rustin's views on the war in Vietnam are alienating a number of coalition intellectuals.

4. F. Ray Marshall and Vernon Briggs, Jr. "Negro Participation in Apprenticeship Programs."

5. Gus Tyler, obviously sensitive to the decrepitude of the AFL-CIO Executive Council reassures us that: "As the old order changes, so does the old guard. A generation of top leaders exists with about one-third of the high command in the AFL-CIO Executive Council stepping out at one convention (1965); a younger generation steps in; and, in the wings, a generation still younger impatiently waits its cue." But if Tyler gave names and ages, we would know that the younger generation he refers to averaged 57 years of age—two less than the Council average of 59! We wonder who and how old is the "still younger" generation in the wings that Tyler is impatiently waiting to wheel into the AFL-CIO Executive Council.

Contributors

Fred Barnes is a journalist who worked as Jock Yablonski's press aide during the United Mine Workers' election campaign.

John Cole, a member of the Seafarers International Union since 1948, has been engaged in a struggle within the SIU for democratic unionism for more than ten years.

Charles Denby has worked in auto plants for 25 years and is the editor of *News & Letters.*

Clarice R. Feldman is an attorney who worked with Joseph Rauh for Jock Yablonski in 1969. After Yablonski's death, she and Yablonski's son, Joseph, joined in representing Miners for Democracy.

Fred Ferrara is president of Local 11 of the Hotel and Restaurant Workers Union.

Burton Hall is a New York attorney who has represented rank-and-file insurgents in several unions. (For more detail see the back cover.)

Herbert Hill is National Labor Chairman, NAACP and teaches at the New School for Social Research. He was Regents Lecturer, University of California, (Irvine), and was Distinguished Visiting Professor of American History, San Fernando Valley State College.

Julius Jacobson is the editor of *New Politics.* His collection of essays from that journal, *Soviet Communism & the Socialist Vision* has just been published by *trans*action *books.*

David Langley is the pseudonym of a long time specialist in international trade union affairs.

Sidney Lens, a former union official, has written a number of books on trade unionism and radicalism. He is an editor of *Liberation.*

James Morrissey has been an active seaman and National Maritime Union member for over 30 years. Chairman of the rank and file Committee for NMU Democracy since 1966, he has been active in the struggle against the Curran dictatorship.

James Prickett is a student of labor affairs at San Diego and has written for *Science & Society.*

Albert Shanker is president of the United Federation of Teachers.

Gus Tyler, who has written widely on trade union matters, is Assistant President of the International Ladies' Garments' Workers Union.

Henry Spira has been a seaman and a member of the National Maritime Union for over 20 years.

Stanley Weir, former merchant seaman, auto worker, teamster and activist in the International Longshoremen's and Warehousemen's Union is presently teaching courses for trade unionists at the University of Illinios.

James Youngdahl is an attorney who practices in Arkansas. He is the regional counsel for the UAW and the IWA. His articles have appeared in *The Progressive, The New Republic, The Nation* and various law reviews and union publications. He is a member of the National Committee of the Workers Defense League.

Steve Zeluck, a teacher, is an active member of the American Federation of Teachers and former President of its New Rochelle Local.